ETHNICITY, RACE AND INEQUALITY IN THE UK

State of the Nation

Edited by
Bridget Byrne, Claire Alexander, Omar Khan,
James Nazroo and William Shankley

T0317129

First published in Great Britain in 2020 by

Policy Press
University of Bristol
1-9 Old Park Hill
Bristol
BS2 8BB
UK
t: +44 (0)117 954 5940
pp-info@bristol.ac.uk
www.policypress.co.uk

North America office:
Policy Press
c/o The University of Chicago Press
1427 East 60th Street
Chicago, IL 60637, USA
t: +1 773 702 7700
f: +1 773-702-9756
sales@press.uchicago.edu
www.press.uchicago.edu

British Library Cataloguing in Publication Data
A catalogue record for this book is available from the British Library

Library of Congress Cataloging-in-Publication Data
A catalog record for this book has been requested

ISBN 978-1-4473-5125-2 (paperback)
ISBN 978-1-4473-5126-9 (OA pdf)
ISBN 978-1-4473-3632-7 (epub)

The right of Bridget Byrne, Claire Alexander, Omar Khan, James Nazroo and William
Shankley to be identified as editors of this work has been asserted by them in accordance with
the Copyright, Designs and Patents Act 1988.

The statements and opinions contained within this publication are solely those of the editors
and contributors and not of the University of Bristol or Policy Press. The University of
Bristol and Policy Press disclaim responsibility for any injury to persons or property resulting
from any material published in this publication.

Policy Press works to counter discrimination on grounds of gender, race,
disability, age and sexuality.

Cover design by Andrew Corbett

Contents

List of figures, tables and boxes   v
Notes on contributors   ix
Acknowledgements   xv

Introduction   1
Claire Alexander and Bridget Byrne

1   The demography of ethnic minorities in Britain   15
     William Shankley, Tina Hannemann and Ludi Simpson
2   Citizen rights and immigration   35
     William Shankley and Bridget Byrne
3   Minority ethnic groups, policing and the criminal justice   51
     system in Britain
     William Shankley and Patrick Williams
4   Health inequalities   73
     Karen Chouhan and James Nazroo
5   Ethnic inequalities in the state education system in England   93
     Claire Alexander and William Shankley
6   Ethnic minorities in the labour market in Britain   127
     Ken Clark and William Shankley
7   Ethnic minorities and housing in Britain   149
     William Shankley and Nissa Finney
8   Arts, media and ethnic inequalities   167
     Sarita Malik and William Shankley
9   Politics and representation   189
     Maria Sobolewska and William Shankley
10   Racisms in contemporary Britain   203
     William Shankley and James Rhodes

Conclusion   229
Omar Khan, Runnymede Trust

Recommendations   237
Omar Khan, Runnymede Trust
Bibliography   243
Index   289

The University of Manchester

Centre on Dynamics of Ethnicity

Economic
and Social
Research Council

List of figures, tables and boxes

Figures

1.1	Ethnic minority groups in England and Wales, 2011 Census	20
1.2	Ethnic minority groups in Scotland, 2011 Census	23
1.3	Ethnic minority groups in Northern Ireland, 2011 Census	24
1.4	Age profile of ethnic groups in England and Wales	26
1.5	Total fertility rate by migrant group, 1989–2008	27
1.6	Infant mortality rate by ethnicity in England and Wales for the birth cohort, 2014	28
2.1	Emigration, immigration, asylum and net migration in the UK, 1991–2017	39
2.2	Net migration by citizenship, 1991–2017	41
3.1	The ethnicity of police officers in the police force in England and Wales, 2017	55
3.2	Rates of stop-and-search per 1,000 members of the population by ethnic group, England and Wales, 2010/11 to 2017/18	57
3.3	Top Five areas for stop-and-search (per 1,000) by ethnic group	58
3.4	People aged 16 years and over who said they were victims of crime, by ethnic group over time	59
3.5	Percentage of people aged 16 years and over who said they were victims of crime, by ethnicity and gender	60
3.6	Percentage of arrests for terrorism-related offences between 2001 and 2017, by ethnic group	62
3.7	Percentage of youth cautions by ethnic group, England and Wales, 2005/06–2017/18	63
3.8	Percentage of children in custody by ethnicity, youth secure estate in England and Wales, year ends March 2008–2018	64

3.9	Percentage of adults in custody in England and Wales by their ethnicity over time, between 2009 and 2017	65
3.10	Conviction ratios of offenders in England and Wales by ethnicity, between 2009 and 2017	68
4.1	Age-adjusted odds ratio to report fair or bad health compared with White English people	77
4.2	Reported fair or bad health by ethnic group and age	77
4.3	Rating of the experience of respect and dignity while in hospital for patients with cancer, percentage of people answering 'good' or 'better'	84
4.4	Experience of overall care for patients with cancer, average score	84
4.5	Rating of GP care and concern: proportion reporting an overall positive experience	85
5.1	School population (England) and 2011 Census of population (England) by ethnicity	100
5.2	Percentage of pupils attaining English and maths grades (A*–C) by ethnicity, 2016/17	103
5.3	Percentage achieving attainment 8 scores by ethnic group and gender	104
5.4	Attainment 8 scores by eligibility for free school meals across ethnic groups	106
5.5	Percentage of students achieving at least three A grades at A level by ethnicity	108
5.6	Ethnic composition of state school exclusions in England	110
5.7	Destinations of school leavers Key Stage 5 (16–18) by ethnic group, 2017	114
5.8	Ethnic composition of apprenticeships from 2002/03 to 2017/18, England and Wales	115
5.9	Ethnic composition of UK-domiciled higher education student enrolment by university type (Russell Group versus New University) and ethnicity	118
5.10	Proportion of students from each ethnic group who obtained a 'good degree' split by Russell Group and New Universities (2016/17)	119
5.11	Ethnic composition of UK academic staff by gender, professorial category	122
6.1	Employment rates for men, 16–64, 2001–18	134
6.2	Employment rates for women, 16–64, 2001–18	134
7.1	Type of housing tenure (private renting, social renting, ownership) by ethnic group and variation between the 2001 and 2011 Censuses (England and Wales)	158

7.2   Percentage of households (HRP), by ethnic group, in   162
        under-occupied, required size and overcrowded
        accommodation, and change between 2001 and 2011
        Censuses (England and Wales)
8.1   The proportion of ethnic minority workers in sectors in   170
        the creative industries over time, 2011–15
8.2   Employees across the five main broadcasters in the   171
        UK by ethnic group
8.3   Ethnic diversity of leadership in arts organisations   174
        in England
8.4   Percentage of people aged 16 years and over who   177
        took part in arts in the past year, by ethnicity over time
        (two specified years)
8.5   Ethnic minority audience of the BBC, 2016–17   179
10.1   Trends in prejudice over time   208
10.2   Variations in reports of racist victimisation by ethnic/   210
        religious group (%)
10.3   Ethnic hierarchy of immigration preferences by leave/   220
        remain: percentage that would allow some/many
        migrants move to the UK

Tables

5.1   Ethnicity of the teaching workforce in state schools   112
        (primary and secondary) in England compared to each
        group's share of the working-age population, by gender,
        2016–17
5.2   UK-domiciled students by country of institution and   117
        ethnic group, 2016/17
5.3   Ethnic composition of UK/non-UK staff, percentage of total 121
6.1   Labour market characteristics of ethnic minority   132
        groups in the UK (men)
6.2   Labour market characteristics of ethnic minority   132
        groups in the UK (women)
7.1   Percentage of households privately renting their home   159
        by ethnicity (England, 2001–2011–2016)

Boxes

1   Case study   47
2   DIAMOND   183

Notes on contributors

Claire Alexander is Professor of Sociology in the School of Social Sciences at the University of Manchester. She has researched, written and published on issues of race, ethnicity, youth and migration in Britain for over twenty-five years. She is author of *The Art of Being Black* (1996), *The Asian Gang* (2000) and *The Bengal Diaspora: Rethinking Muslim Migration* (with Joya Chatterji and Annu Jalais, 2016). She has worked closely with the Runnymede Trust over the past decade on several projects aimed at diversifying the school history curriculum (see www.banglastories.org, www.makinghistories.org.uk, www.ourmigrationstory.org.uk) and on race equality in schools and higher education. She is Deputy Director of the Centre on the Dynamics of Ethnicity (CoDE) and is currently research director for the School of Social Sciences. She is currently working on two UK Research and Innovation (UKRI) funded projects – on race inequality and higher education, and on the Indian restaurant trade in Brick Lane.

Bridget Byrne is Professor of Sociology at the University of Manchester and Director of the Centre on Dynamics of Ethnicity (CoDE). She researches on questions of race, ethnicity, citizenship, gender and class. Alongside numerous academic articles, she is author of *White Lives: The Interplay of 'Race', Class and Gender in Everyday Life* (2006), *Making Citizens: Public Rituals and Private Journeys to Citizenship* (2014) and *All in the Mix: Race, Class and School Choice* (with Carla De Tona, 2019). She is currently researching the role of institutions in the cultural sector producing and mitigating ethnic inequalities.

Karen Chouhan is the National Education Union (NEU) Policy Specialist for Race Equality. She was previously a Senior Education Manager for the Workers' Educational Association (WEA), a national charity providing adult education including for the poorest and most disadvantaged people. She has lived in Leicester since 1975 and has worked in further education as an English and English for Speakers of Other Languages (ESOL) teacher, and in higher education for 12 years as the programme lead for the MA in Community Education and Youth Work at De Montfort Univeristy. She has also worked as CEO for a national race equality charity and has won several awards for her anti-racist work and for tackling Islamophobia. In 2005, she was named by the Joseph Rowntree Charitable Trust as a 'Visionary for a Just and Peaceful World'. They funded her work on 'Equanomics' (equality via economic justice) for five years.

Ken Clark is Senior Lecturer in Economics at the University of Manchester, a member of the Centre on the Dynamics of Ethnicity (CoDE) and a Research Fellow at IZA Institute of Labor Economics in Bonn. He has been researching the labour market outcomes of ethnic minority and migrant workers for nearly three decades and has published in a variety of academic journals in economics and related areas, as well as in policy reports. Using large survey data sets and econometric techniques, his work documents patterns of inequality between different ethnic and migrant groups and seeks to provide a rigorous evidence base for the development of labour market policy.

Nissa Finney is Reader in Human Geography at the University of St Andrews and Visiting Scholar at the Department of Urbanism at TU Delft (Delft University of Technology). She is a member of the Centre on the Dynamics of Ethnicity (CoDE) and of the Economic and Social Research Council (ESRC) Centre for Population Change, and Chair of the Royal Geographical Society (with Institute of British Geographers) Population Geography Research Group. Her work is concerned with how residential experience reflects and reproduces social inequalities. She has written widely on this topic and is author of *'Sleepwalking to Segregation'? Challenging Myths about Race and Migration* (with Ludi Simpson, 2009).

Tina Hannemann is Lecturer in Social Statistics at the Cathie Marsh Institute for Social Research, University of Manchester. She has studied demography in Germany, France and Sweden and in 2012 was awarded a doctoral degree with research on the impact of socio-economic differences on cardiovascular diseases across migration groups. Subsequently, she held a position as Research Associate at the University of Liverpool. In 2016, she took a research position at the University of Manchester with the Centre on the Dynamics of Ethnicity (CoDE) research group and later with the National Centre of Research Methods. Her research project investigated compensation methods for missing data in bio-marker surveys.

Omar Khan is Director of Runnymede Trust. For over a decade, he has published many articles and reports on ethnic and socio-economic inequalities, political theory and British political history for Runnymede and has spoken on topics including multiculturalism, integration, socio-economic disadvantage and positive action. These include giving evidence to the United Nations in Geneva, at the European Parliament in Strasbourg, on Capitol Hill in Washington, DC and at academic and policy conferences across the UK and Europe. He completed a DPhil in Political Theory from the University of Oxford, a Master's in Political Science from the University of Wisconsin–Madison and a Master's in South Asian Studies from the School of Oriental and African Studies.

Sarita Malik is Professor of Media, Culture and Communications at Brunel University London. Her research explores questions of social change, inequality, communities and cultural representation. She has written extensively on race, representation and the media, and on diversity and cultural policy. Her books include *Representing Black Britain* (2002), *Adjusting the Contrast: British Television and Constructs of Race* (2017) and *Community Filmmaking and Cultural Diversity: Practice, Innovation and Policy* (2017). Since 2014, she has led a large, international collaborative project titled Creative Interruptions, funded through the Arts and Humanities Research Council's Connected Communities programme. The project examines how the arts, media and creativity are used to challenge exclusion.

James Nazroo is Professor of Sociology at the University of Manchester, previously Director and now Deputy Director of the Economic and Social Research Council (ESRC) Centre on Dynamics of Ethnicity (CoDE), founder and now co-director of the Manchester Institute for Collaborative Research on Ageing (MICRA), and co-principal investigator of the English Longitudinal Study of Ageing and the Synergi Collaborative Centre (which works to understand and address ethnic inequality in severe mental illness). His research has focused on issues of inequality, social justice, underlying processes of stratification and their impact on health. For this he has made major contributions in relation to ethnicity, ageing and the interrelationships between these.

James Rhodes is Senior Lecturer in Sociology at the University of Manchester. His research interests focus on race and racism, urban sociology and deindustrialisation. His work has appeared in journals such as *Ethnic and Racial Studies*, *Sociology*, *Journal of Ethnic and Migration Studies* and *Urban Geography*. He is a member of CoDE.

William Shankley is currently a research associate at the Cathie Marsh Institute, University of Manchester. He is also a UK Data Service Impact Fellow and has previously worked as a research associate at the Centre on Dynamics of Ethnicity (CoDE), where he completed a PhD in Sociology examining the residential patterns and decision-making of Polish internal migrants in Britain. Before returning to academia, he worked in the international development sector on projects with refugees in India, Nepal and Sri Lanka. His research interests include whiteness, migration, citizenship and immigration policy.

Ludi Simpson is Honorary Professor at Manchester University and works with population, census and survey statistics, aiming to extend their use by communities and governments. He is the author of *'Sleepwalking to Segregation'? Challenging Myths about Race and Migration* (with Nissa Finney, 2009) and editor of *Ethnic Identity and Inequalities in Britain: The Dynamics of Diversity* (with Stephen Jivraj, 2015) and *Statistics in Society* (with Danny Dorling, 1999).

Maria Sobolewska is Professor of Political Science at the University of Manchester and works on the political integration and representation of ethnic minorities in Britain and in a comparative perspective; public perceptions of ethnicity, immigrants and integration; and the production and framing of public opinion of British Muslims. She is a member of Centre on Dynamics of Ethnicity (CoDE) and is currently conducting a study into how political representation of British ethnic minorities has changed in the last 30+ years since the historic election of 1987. She is lead investigator on an Economic and Social Research Council (ESRC) UK in a Changing Europe project: The 'Brexit Referendum' and Identity Politics in Britain (http://ukandeu.ac.uk/brexitresearch/the-brexit-referendum-and-identity-politics-in-britain/).

Patrick Williams is Senior Lecturer in Criminology at Manchester Metropolitan University and undertakes research and publishes in the area of 'race' and ethnicity, with a particular focus on racial disparity, disproportionality and differential treatment within the criminal justice system. Most recently, he authored *Being Matrixed: The (Over)Policing of Gang Suspects in London* (2018) on behalf of the Stopwatch charity, which foregrounds the narratives through storied recollections of young people's experiences of being registered and policed as a gang suspect. Having previously worked as a research and evaluation officer for the Greater Manchester Probation Trust (1997–2007), he continues to advise and support the development of interventions premised upon the principles of empowerment for a number of local and regional statutory and voluntary and community sector organisations.

Acknowledgements

CoDE (Centre on Dynamics of Ethnicity) at the University of Manchester has been working since 2013 to increase public and scholarly understanding of ethnic inequalities in the UK and to make the evidence of those inequalities more broadly available.[1] Data on racial and ethnic inequalities in a variety of arenas have been collected by the state and other institutions for the last 50 years. As a result, we know the inequalities and injustices exist, that your race and ethnicity have an impact on your education and job prospects, where you live and how and when you die. Yet we do not always fully understand either the complexities of these inequalities (how they are experienced differently by different groups) or the processes which produce them. This knowledge is critical if we are to challenge institutions to address the way in which they produce unequal or racist outcomes.

We are very pleased to join in partnership with the Runnymede Trust, which has 50 years of experience engaged in evidence-based interventions in social policy and practice to end racism. *Race and Ethnicity in the UK: State of the Nation*, written by experts in each field, sets out the patterning of ethnic inequalities in key arenas of social life, explores how they have changed over time and the impact of policy and practice.

We embarked on this journey with a Runnymede roundtable event at the end of December 2017 and we would like to thank all those who participated in that event. Thanks too to all the colleagues who collaborated on writing and/or commenting on chapters: Kalwant Bhopal, Karis Campion, Karen Chouhan, Ken Clark, Nissa Finney, David Gillborn, Tina Hanneman, Remi Joseph-Salisbury, Sarita Malik, James Rhodes, Ludi Simpson, Maria Sobolewska and Patrick Williams. Nick Asher was responsible for producing the visualisations of the data and we thank him for his patience in responding to our multiple requests for tweaks.

We would like to thank the School of Social Sciences at the University of Manchester for support for both CoDE and its partnership with the Runnymede Trust, with particular thanks to Chris Orme and Brian Heaphy. CoDE is funded by the Economic and Social Research Council (grant number: ES/R009341/1) which has also enabled this book to be Open Access (free to download).

Note

[1]   See www.ethnicity.ac.uk

Introduction

Claire Alexander and Bridget Byrne

> The question is not *who we are* but *who we can become.*
> Stuart Hall, 2017

Windrush 2018, racial landmarks and contested national (hi)stories

On 22 June 1948, the *Empire Windrush* arrived at Tilbury Docks, London from Jamaica, carrying 492 people, mainly young men and ex-servicemen, from across the Caribbean islands. The arrival of the ship, and its iconic scenes of be-suited and be-hatted young men disembarking along the gangplank, is often celebrated as a landmark moment in British history, heralding the start of large-scale postwar labour migration from the colonies and former colonies, and marking the birth of modern multicultural Britain. Seventy years on, and the '*Windrush* scandal' dominated the spring and summer of 2018, exposing the victimisation and deportation of members of the '*Windrush* generation', many of whom arrived between 1948 and 1971[1] as children with a legal right to remain in Britain, but without appropriate paperwork, and who had inadvertently fallen foul of the Home Office's much vaunted 2012 'hostile environment' initiative for illegal immigrants.

The political fallout from the '*Windrush* scandal' – underpinned by public and media outcry, which led to a belated public apology by the Prime Minister to Caribbean leaders in April 2018 (BBC Online, 2018a), followed by the reluctant resignation of Home Secretary Amber Rudd soon afterwards (*The Guardian*, 2018b) and the appointment of Britain's first minority ethnic Home Secretary Sajid Javid (BBC Online, 2018b) – has been most usually presented as an accidental pothole in the road to Britain's post-racial present. Subsequent months saw a rush to recognise and celebrate the 'valued' presence (BBC Online, 2018a) of the *Windrush* migrants, to be marked in an annual '*Windrush* Day' on 22 June 'to celebrate the contribution of the *Windrush* generation and their descendants' (Ministry of Housingm Communities and Local Government, 2018). The first of these events was celebrated in 2019, to a cautious welcome from anti-racist activists (Singh and Khan, 2019).

However, this neatly-bookended national (fairy)tale of arrival, exclusion, struggle and, finally, acceptance, erases both Britain's longer, broader and darker history of migration and racism, and the ongoing struggles for inclusion, recognition and equality in the present (Alexander, 2002, 2018). In particular, it highlights three key silences in the national (hi)story: first, around Britain's entanglement in a broader global history of European slavery, colonisation and empire, which paves the way for black migration and settlement. Second, the longer history of migration to Britain, which precedes the *Windrush* arrival by nearly two thousand years, and has erased the nation's inherently migrant roots in favour of an increasingly nativist discourse,[2] the consequences of which have been made dramatically apparent in the run-up to and aftermath of the Brexit referendum. And third, the 'flattening' of the histories of, particularly, black communities in Britain,[3] which have denied the place of black histories in the broader history of what David Cameron referred to as 'Our Island Story' (Alexander et al, 2012), its more demotic and contested formations, and its unequal racial present.

The story of the black presence in Britain must, then, be balanced with the recognition of hostility and exclusion. As David Olusoga evocatively comments, 'The Windrush story was not a rosy one even before the ship arrived' (Olusoga, 2018). Olusoga points to the attempts to deny the entry rights of black and brown British colonial subjects even as the Nationality Act 1948 – also marking its 70th anniversary – supposedly enshrined them, and the 'motherland' appealed for their labour to rebuild postwar Britain. Indeed, the 1948 act, ironically sharing its anniversary with the arrival of the Windrush, underscores the precarious place of black and brown citizens within the national imagination (Lidher, 2018), and which has marked the subsequent 70 years in which the limits of 'the nation' have become increasingly racially circumscribed.

Olusoga notes too that 2018 was 'overflowing with anniversaries' that capture this more fraught and entangled history. The year 1948 of course, and not accidentally, coincided with the 70th anniversary of the launch of the National Health Service (NHS), the iconic British institution, which is intricately enmeshed with the *Windrush* anniversary and the thousands of postwar Caribbean and South Asian migrants who made it possible, but whose contributions remain ignored or denied (Younge, 2018b). The year 2018 also marked the 50th anniversary of Powell's 'Rivers of Blood' speech, and the Commonwealth Immigrants Act, which denied full citizenship rights to East African Asian refugees, and the 50th anniversary of the Race Relations Act of 1968, which sought to tackle institutional racism in housing, employment and public services. We might add to these the 60th anniversary of the Nottingham and Notting Hill anti-black riots of 1958, and the murder of Kelso Cochrane the following May; or the 40th anniversary of the murder of Bangladeshi textile worker Altab Ali, or the 25th anniversary of the murder of black teenager Stephen Lawrence. We could point too to the centenary memorialisations of the First World War, with its hundreds of thousands of invisible colonial soldiers, supply workers and trench diggers. The shadow of 2017's 70th anniversary of Indian partition looms large, while more recent events, such as the first anniversary of the Grenfell Tower fire and the ongoing inquiry speak to the invisibility, denial and inequalities which still scar post-imperial Britain, and pose stark challenges to Britain's post-racial pretensions.

Of course, such landmark moments are not without their dangers. As the hasty government plans for a Stephen Lawrence Day and a *Windrush* Day clearly illustrate, acts of commemoration can substitute celebration for a more critical engagement with the past, and its traces in the present. Most often, what and who gets memorialised reflects the dominant national narrative and the interests of social, cultural and political elites, often in an over-celebratory and eulogising manner. This silences alternative voices and experiences – women; religious, sexual, ethnic and racial minorities; working-class, young, old and disabled people. At the same time, anniversaries bracket particular individuals, events, places and times from the broader, more banal, flow of 'everyday' encounters, exclusion, violence or solidarities, focusing on the spectacular rather than its context, or the 'moment' rather than its causes and consequences. And, of course, they form part of a range of practices of social and cultural classification and exclusion which draw the boundaries of who belongs to the 'nation', and who does not, who are the 'deserving/good' or 'undeserving/bad' immigrants (Shukla, 2016; Younge, 2018a) whose stories (or 'contributions') 'count', when, why and how they are made to 'count', and whose remain untold or uncounted.

The stories, people, places and objects of commemoration form the foundation of the way in which nations and nationhoods are narrated or imagined, most notably in times of transformation and tumult. They serve as an anchor for identity, as a weapon for those on the side of preservation and a target for those demanding change. Indeed, recent years have seen the explosion of high-profile campaigns around the globe – from the Rhodes Must Fall campaign in South Africa to the demolition of Confederate statues in the United States and #BlackLives Matter – which attempt to redress the balance; while nation-states and populist/nativist groups have, in their turn, attempted to reinscribe sanitised national (hi)stories, as in Poland or Turkey, the United States, Australia, Brazil and, of course, Britain (Hirsch, 2018b). In the British academy, culture wars have been re-ignited by student campaigns around decolonising the curriculum, and by furious claims and counterclaims of academic censorship and political correctness (McDougall and Wagner, 2018; Riley, 2018a). That such debates have traction beyond the ivory tower can be seen in the flush of challenging, popular and garlanded publications exploring the experience of race and racism in the national narrative (Akala, 2018; Shukla, 2016; Eddo-Lodge, 2017; Hirsch, 2018a). They remain constant too in the more conventional rose-tinted not-yet-post-imperial nostalgia of the imagination of mainstream Britishness: in the cinema and television (from *Darkest Hour* and *Downton Abbey* to *Beecham House*); in the neo-colonial, post-Brexit aspirations of politicians; in the resurgence of authoritarian populist political movements, and the embracing of their views at the heart of government; and, most worryingly, in schools and playgrounds, where the curriculum has long been a political battleground for competing views of national identity and cultural citizenship (Alexander et al, 2012; Alexander and Weekes-Bernard, 2017; Miah, 2017).

Anniversaries and memorialisations, then, offer not only a chance for celebration, but for reflection and re-evaluation. Rather than definitive and timeless landmarks, they provide staging posts in the national (hi)story, providing the opportunity to pause, to consider distance travelled, to examine where we are, and to (re)consider the road(s) ahead. They offer the chance to excavate hidden or forgotten stories, to revisit familiar stories, to rewrite (or rethink) the national story as we know it, and to imagine new and better ones.

Ethnic and racial inequality in Britain: continuity and change

The year 2018 also marked another significant anniversary in Britain's history of ethnic and racial inequality, and the struggle for equality: the 50th anniversary of the Runnymede Trust. Founded by Jim Rose and

Anthony Lester in 1968, the trust was founded as an independent think tank to provide evidence-based policy recommendations to 'nail the lie' of racism and promote race equality 'by providing timely, reliable and objective information' (Lester, 2003). In the introduction to *Colour and Citizenship*, published in 1969, Rose warned of the dangers of a country 'turning in on itself, if a loss of confidence was accompanied by increasing nationalism, and if apparent affluence were engendering selfishness, then the climate might be unhealthy for the growth of a multi-racial society' (Rose, 1969: 4). Fifty years on, nearly two decades into the 'War on Terror', in the midst of the migrant crisis enveloping Europe, the growth of extreme right and ultra-nationalist movements at home and abroad, and facing an uncertain post-Brexit future, Rose's warning still carries resonance.

Rose's study was significant not only in focusing attention on 'the facts' of racial inequality in Britain itself, nor on its comprehensive survey of key arenas of social life – employment, housing, education, income, policing and welfare – but in placing these facts in their historical and political context, and in relation to the policies and practices that engendered and addressed (or failed to address) them. He notes too that the experiences of 'coloured immigrants' in Britain cannot 'be satisfactorily explained in terms of class or the fact of strangeness' (Rose, 1969: 6) – that race or ethnicity (or what Rose glosses as 'colour') had an independent and enduring effect. Perhaps most importantly, it placed the onus for change not on 'coloured immigrants' themselves but on the post-liberal racial state, and on wider, white British society – on what he terms 'the social life of the nation' (Rose, 1969: 2)

Nevertheless, while Rose's message, nearly fifty years on, feels disturbingly contemporary, it is important to recognise the changes in Britain's racial landscape in the past five decades. The focus on the experience of 'the coloured man', while perhaps reflecting the demographies of immigration at the time, has been expanded and transformed through the presence and experience of women and families, the feminisation of migration and a recognition of the intersection of gendered and raced/ethnic experience. Similarly, the focus on 'immigrants' from the 'West Indies', India and Pakistan has been overtaken or undermined by the presence of successive generations of their British-born descendants, by the increasing diversity of Britain's immigrant communities in the last 30 years and the growth of mixed race British populations, and by new forms of local and global religious, ethnic and racial solidarities. The role of Britain's diverse black communities in challenging racial discrimination and inequality across a range of the social arenas Rose examines should also be acknowledged. We might, in contrast, note the relative lack of traction (or notable obstruction) from the machinery of the state in addressing those patterns of inequality, or indeed how it actively entrenches them.

Some of these shifts can be most easily traced at the level of terminology. Rose's label of 'coloured immigrants', while in keeping with the historical moment, also reflects the perception of black and Asian settlers as defined (and conflated) through phenotypical difference (as non-white) and as newcomers/outsiders to the (white) nation-state, as well as their shared position in the social and economic structures of the UK. This shared positioning, and the experience of exclusion and hostility which accompanied it, was to form the foundation for the political label 'Black', which was to dominate the struggle against racism in Britain through the 1970s and 1980s (Alexander, 2002, 2017; Virdee, 2014). The rise of ethnicity as a primary framework for identity from the mid-1980s onwards reflected not only the resurgence of 'culture' as the basis for political action, but also increasing divergence in the social and economic experiences between 'West Indian' (now labelled African Caribbean, or simply 'Black'), and 'Asian' groups (Brown, 1984). In turn, the category 'Asian' splintered around first national and then religious classifications, captioned initially as the split between Indian 'achievers' and Pakistani/Bangladeshi 'believers' and, later, in the wake of the *Satanic Verses* affair and the first Gulf War, through the emergence of 'the Muslim underclass' as a new folk devil. This division was clearly reflected in the fourth Policy Studies Institute survey, published in 1997, and tellingly subtitled *Diversity and Disadvantage* (Modood et al, 1997).

The focus on 'diversity' as a proxy for racial and ethnic identity can also be seen clearly in the proliferation of census categories, from the national origin labels of the 1991 Census (in which the variety of non-white national options were opposed to an undifferentiated 'White'), through the inclusion of religion and mixed race in 2001 (as well as the inclusion of 'White Irish' and 'White Other') and the insertion of White Gypsy/Traveller and Arab in the 2011 Census. The census has always trodden an uneasy line between reifying ethnic difference and reflecting changing identities ('mixed race'), and between illuminating patterns of inequality or pinpointing the new 'problem' categories (that is Muslims, Gypsy/Traveller, 'Other' Whites). As research by CoDE (Centre on Dynamics of Ethnicity) on ethnic diversity notes in passing, the framing of ethnicity questions in the census also marks a shift in understanding from a biologised notion of 'descent' in 1991, to 'cultural background' in 2001, to a simple 'ethnic group or background' personal identification in 2011 (CoDE, 2012). However, despite these shifts, the resulting categories frequently remain listed in colour-coded hierarchy which ranges from imagined white to darker skin-tones which is an inheritance from the earliest racial theories.

The rise of ethnicity and culture as a primary framework of identity – and the basis for political formation and activism – through the 1990s and into the millennium is apparent in the Runnymede Trust's report on *The Future of Multi-ethnic Britain* (Parekh, 2000). The landslide election of New Labour in 1997, and the run-up to the new millennium seemed to offer a brief period of optimism in the struggle for racial equality in Britain, with the publication in February 1999 of the long-awaited Macpherson report into the racist murder of Stephen Lawrence (Macpherson, 1999), the Race Relations Amendment Act in 2000 and the publication *The Future of Multi-ethnic Britain* (Parekh et al, 2000). Together, these reports and the act pointed at once to the entrenched and enduring nature of systemic racial and ethnic inequality in Britain, to a seeming government commitment to redressing these injustices, and to an alternative vision of multicultural Britain which chimed momentarily with the optimism of New Labour's post-imperial 'Cool Britannia' national rebrand.

The Future of Multi-Ethnic Britain (Parekh, 2000) – now 20 years old – illustrates both continuity and change with/from its predecessor. As with *Colour and Citizenship* (Rose, 1969), the report examines the ongoing issues of racial inequality across social arenas and institutions – employment, education, health, criminal justice – but also includes sections on arts, media and sport, and religion and belief, which reflects the growing emphasis on culture, identity and religion across the intervening 30 years. The optimism of the report can perhaps be seen in the long list of recommendations at the end (many of which have been taken up, if rather surreptitiously and slowly), but perhaps most notably (or notoriously) in its opening 'Vision for Britain', and its attempt to 'rethink the national story', which caused a media and political furore (Khan, 2015). It is here, in the 'vision', that the discursive shifts around race equality are most apparent – particularly in the hybrid liberal-pluralistic idea of the nation as 'a community of communities' as well as 'a community of citizens' (Parekh, 2000: 48). The public realm is one predicated on cultural diversity, recognition and respect within a framework of 'common values' (Parekh, 2000: 53) and 'human rights'. While this pluralist approach is balanced, uneasily, with the assertion of dialogue, interdependence and dynamism (Parekh, 2000: 'Identities in Transition' (chapter 3)), the dominant emphasis is on 'communities' of identity and culture, and on bounded ideas of difference – immigrants and their descendants are no longer 'coloured' but 'cultured'.

There is an inherent and unresolved tension in the report about what this means, and between two quite different theoretical understandings of key concepts – of the nation, community, culture and identity – which might be glossed as a Parekh-ian political theory versus a Hall-ian cultural studies approach. Nevertheless, in both framings, the focus has clearly shifted to cultural identity as the basis for recognition and for equality. Meanwhile 'the nation' is reimagined not as 'white', as in Rose's account, but as complex and multicultured. Importantly, the 'multi-' in multi-ethnic Britain refers as much to differences between (and within) minority ethnic communities as between them and the white majority.

At the heart of the report, as with *Colour and Citizenship* (Rose, 1969), stands a challenge to the nation, its leaders and citizens, to envision a more inclusive, more tolerant and more equal society for all. Echoing Rose's concerns three decades earlier, the report notes that Britain again stands at a 'turning point or crossroads', and asks:

> Will it try to turn the clock back, digging in, defending old values and ancient hierarchies, relying on a narrow English-dominated backward definition of the nation? Or will it seize the opportunity to create a more flexible, inclusive, cosmopolitan image of itself? (Parekh, 2000: 15)

The hope for a positive response to this challenge proved short-lived, however, when the urban unrest of 2001 and the attacks on New York in September that year ushered in a new, intense phase of the 'War on Terror', abroad and at home. This refocused attention away from ongoing racial and ethnic inequality and social injustice towards the seeming failures of multiculturalism and the apparent inability of Britain's ethnic minorities (now largely recast as 'Muslims') to 'integrate' into wider modern society (Meer and Nayak, 2015). While questions of race and racism largely fell off of the policy and political agenda, issues of religion, ethnicity and identity moved centre-stage, with evocations of 'parallel lives' and 'community cohesion' conjuring familiar and well-worn tropes of cultural difference and incompatibility that resonated strongly with the earlier 'race relations' framework (Alexander, 2004), but now with a sense of global urgency and threat (Kundnani, 2014) – both external and 'homegrown'.

The current context: post-millennial race and racism

Twenty years on from the Parekh report and facing a looming Brexit, the 'future of multi-ethnic Britain' seems even more uncertain and precarious. This period has seen the tightening of Britain's borders through the proliferation of increasingly draconian immigration legislation, both externally and in the intimate spaces of everyday life – at work, in hospitals, on buses, at home, on the streets (Back and Sinha, 2015; Jones et al, 2017). May's now-disavowed 'hostile environment' is the culmination of New Labour, Coalition and Tory administrations which have seen the growth of incarceration for asylum seekers and undocumented migrants (Bloch and Schuster, 2005; Bloch and McKay, 2016), the increased use of deportation and the stripping of citizenship (De Noronha, 2018b), and the expansion of the Prevent strategy into schools and universities in the name of 'freedom of expression' and the pursuit of 'British values' (Byrne, 2017; Miah, 2017). At the same time, there has been the increasing concern around everyday and institutional antisemitism and Islamophobia, the growth of Europhobic and nativist sentiment in the run-up to, and aftermath of, the Scottish independence and Brexit referenda, and the explosion of anti-immigrant and asylophobic violence against the backdrop of the so-called migrant crisis and the mainstreaming of far-right political parties across Fortress Europe and elsewhere. The relationship between political rhetoric, policy formation and public opinion is, of course, a complex one. Nevertheless, it might be argued that mainstream political fears around the rise of the UK Independence Party (UKIP), and the failures of successive governments, both Conservative and (New) Labour, to take a positive public stance around migration and racial equality in response – mediated through the interpretations of a hostile anti-immigrant and racist press (Sveinsson, 2008; Van Dijk, 2015) – and the eschewing of evidence-based policy in favour of high-profile dog-whistle gestures and punitive targets have contributed to this toxic atmosphere.

Despite this climate of hostility, Britain is now more ethnically, racially and religiously diverse than ever, and migration and multiculturalism form part of the mundane fabric of everyday life. The 2011 Census showed that just under 20% of the UK's population self-identified as other than White British, while the UK's Black and Minority Ethnic (BME) population doubled in size from 1991 to 8 million people (14%) in 2011. The census also illuminated important shifts in Britain's demographic profile, with not only the growth of long-settled Caribbean and South Asian communities, but also an increase in African groups (by 100%), Mixed (by more than 80%), 'Other Asian' (by 238%), 'Other Black' (by 186%) and 'Other' (by 46%) (CoDE, 2012). There were also 230,600 Arabs (CoDE, 2012) while the 'White Other' category increased by over 1 million people – the largest increase in any ethnic group category, and including 579,000 Polish migrants (ONS, 2015). Work by CoDE also shows that while Britain's BME communities are still largely concentrated in England's urban centres, there is increasing dispersal across its ex-urban and rural places (CoDE, 2012). And, despite the dominant political and public rhetoric around segregation, data show that all ethnic groups are increasingly mixing in terms of housing, cohabitation, marriage and the birth of children. These patterns are likely only to strengthen in the next census in 2021.

Nevertheless, and as the following chapters clearly show, racial and ethnic inequality, discrimination and racism remain entrenched features of 'the social life of the nation' (Rose, 1969) across all areas – from education to employment, housing to health, criminal justice and policing to politics, the arts, media and sport – and across all minority groups. The current moment, then, presents particular and unique challenges for tackling racial inequality in Britain. On the one hand, we have clear and consistent evidence of entrenched discrimination against ethnic minority communities and individuals, at a time of public and political hostility at levels not seen since the 1970s. On the other, we have an increasingly complex and fragmented tapestry of inequality within and between ethnic minority groups; a picture further fractured by intersectional considerations around class, gender, age, religion, region, sexuality, legal status and so on. This fragmentation is consolidated by the fracture of anti-racist activism and solidarity around the growth of increasingly narrow identitarian politics and political solipsism (Alexander, 2017, 2018).

However, complexity does not mean that racial, ethnic and religious inequality cease to matter, nor that they are irresolvable. Indeed, the current moment is also one of perhaps unprecedented recognition of the persistence of inequality at a state level: the government's Race Disparity Audit is one clear example (Cabinet Office, 2017),[4] while we might also point to the importance of the McGregor-Smith review on workplace inequalities, and the Lammy review of the criminal justice system, both published in 2017. We have also seen the proliferation of new policies and practices from, and at the heart of, key social institutions aimed at tackling entrenched disadvantage and discrimination, from the BBC and Arts Council, through higher education and the NHS, to politics and the trade unions. Of course, these policies sit alongside, and in tension with, the encroachment of the Prevent strategy and the implementation of increasingly draconian immigration legislation across those very same spheres. The complexities and contradictions pose very real and very urgent challenges to those working for greater social equality and justice in contemporary Britain, not only in understanding this shifting terrain, but finding ways to move forward, and together.

The state of the nation: a roadmap to change

Drawing its inspiration from Runnymede's landmark publications, *Colour and Citizenship* (Rose, 1969) and *The Future of Multi-ethnic Britain* report (Parekh, 2000), the current book offers a marker in the history of ethnic and racial equality in Britain. A partnership between Runnymede and the CoDE at the University of Manchester, the book provides an evidence-based account of contemporary patterns of ethnic and racial inequality, across a range of key policy arenas, which shape the lives of Britain's diverse black and minority ethnic communities. Working in collaboration with key experts in the field, the individual chapters trace the complex forms and dimensions of inequality in particular areas, and, importantly, how these have changed or entrenched over time, and in relation to particular policies and institutional practices.

Engaging with a variety of comprehensive and reputable sources, individual chapters trace what we know about ethnic inequalities in a range of fields in UK society and culture, including: citizenship and immigration, crime and policing, health, education, the labour market, housing, the cultural industries, politics, and racism. They situate this knowledge in an understanding of how things have changed over time in the last 50 years and the impact of major policies in the different areas. The next chapter provides an overview of the demography of the UK in terms of ethnicity, the age structure of different ethnic groups and their geographic locations. This is an increasingly complex picture and, as this chapter discusses, difficult to pin down because of the nature of data collection. As this introduction has briefly discussed, questions of terminology are complex, politically charged and shift historically. Racialised and ethnic identities are socially constructed and therefore mutable and changing. They are produced both through racist structures and discourses, as well as through processes of resistance and community-building. We start from the position that without naming these differences, we cannot address the inequalities they produce. We are addressing ethnic inequalities in this book and have largely used the term 'ethnic minority' to refer to groups or individuals when reporting on the statistical data. At the same time, we recognise that the categories used by the statistical agencies on which we rely do not often map neatly onto the ways in which individuals identify themselves.

The ways in which the data are reported can also have profound political effects. This is perhaps most marked in the current context by the growth of the 'White Other' category. As much of the data reported in this book has shown, the 'White Other' category has relatively good outcomes in a range of fields relative to the 'White British' category. So, if White Other are included in over-simplistic reporting of data, then this will have the effect of masking inequality and discrimination faced by other groups. We need to be wary of where the state, or other institutions, report at the level only of 'ethnic minority' outcomes. In addition, the majority of the 'White Other' category will not face racist discrimination, protected as they frequently are by white privilege. Yet at the same time, some groups within this category have faced overt and hostile discrimination: whether Jews experiencing antisemitism, a form of racism or, in the case of Eastern European migrants, rising anti-immigration hostility. Thus wherever possible, it is important to be aware of the complexities of the experiences of different groups within the term 'ethnic minority' and to be alive to the ways in which processes of racialisation impact on experience and outcomes.

As mentioned, the categories used for data collection have changed historically and they also vary according to the different data collection agencies for the countries of the UK. This can make comparison between the UK regions of England, Scotland, Wales and Northern Ireland difficult. For this reason, and for those of space, the discussion in the book tends to focus on England, where the vast majority of ethnic minority people in the UK live. However, where possible, data from the other regions of the UK are also discussed – as well as the different experiences of the increasing numbers of ethnic minority people living in suburban and rural areas. For similar reasons of data and space, we are not always able to draw out the complex interplay between ethnic inequalities and inequalities of gender, social class, disability and sexuality. In many cases, the data are not collected in ways which makes this possible. In addition, these intersections play out differently for different ethnic groups and limitations of space inhibit the proper discussion of this.

Nonetheless, and despite these limitations, collectively, the book provides a map of racial and ethnic inequality across all aspects of social and cultural life in Britain, while identifying points of intervention for policymakers. More than this, though, the book constitutes a snapshot of the current 'moment' in Britain, on the brink of Brexit and a precarious new, and unpredictable era for our multi-ethnic, multi-racial country. The *State of the Nation* offers an assessment of where we are as a nation and the concluding recommendations extend an invitation to imagine a different and better future.

Notes

[1] Between the British Nationality Act of 1948 which confirmed the rights of all British subjects in the colonies and dominions to enter and settle in Britain, and the 1971 Commonwealth Immigrants Act which effectively stripped the rights of Black Commonwealth immigrants to settle (Solomos, 2003).

[2] See www.ourmigrationstory.org.uk

[3] 'Black' here is used to refer to 'political blackness', including people of African, Caribbean and Asian descent (Alexander, 2017).

[4] See www.ethnicity-facts-figures.service.gov.uk

1

The demography of ethnic minorities in Britain

William Shankley, Tina Hannemann and Ludi Simpson

Key findings

- Britain's ethnic minority groups are primarily shaped by the country's past imperial history and colonialism of different parts of the world resulting in large immigration movements from the mid–20th century onwards.
- There has been an increase in the absolute size of each ethnic group between 2001 and 2011, except for the Irish group. And increasing diversity of groups, including mixed groups. The ethnic make-up of Wales, Scotland and Northern Ireland is different from England, with higher levels of people identifying as White and lower non-white diversity.
- Family and fertility differ across all ethnic minority groups with variations in age of mother at her first birth, number of children and choice of partnership type.
- Segregation levels across ethnic minority groups have decreased with neighbourhoods becoming more ethnically mixed.

Introduction

In order to assess the different social, economic, health and wellbeing outcomes across different ethnic minority groups living in Britain, we need to collect and analyse data based on measures of identity, which can expose unequal experiences and the effects of discrimination. As discussed in the introductory chapter, these identity categories are not straightforward and reflect political choices made in particular historical contexts. The categories used by the state on which these data are based have shifted over time, and people's identification with them will also change. This chapter will introduce the nature of ethnic diversity in the UK, giving an overview of the *size* and *location* of ethnic groups in the UK and how they have changed over time. It will consider the ways in which Britain's history as a global empire and related migration have shaped the categories we use today, which, in turn, determined the nature of ethnic diversity in the UK. The chapter will examine historic migration flows and current ethnic groups in the UK, the age structures of different ethnic groups, which reflect patterns and periods of migration as well as fertility and mortality patterns. Finally, it will consider the ways in which processes of migration have produced distinct residential patterns for different ethnic groups and how these are changing.

Immigration history and ethnicity in the UK

The demographic composition of Britain's ethnic minority populations continues to be significantly shaped by Britain's past imperial history and colonialism in different parts of the world, subsequent decolonisation, conflict and globalisation which have determined who, where and when immigrants settled in Britain. While there have been centuries of global contact, trade, migration and settlement in the UK (particularly in London and port cities such as Liverpool, Bristol and Cardiff), the groups that we tend to consider as the main ethnic minorities in contemporary Britain are historically connected to the migration of predominantly non-white migrants in the postwar period (Finney and Simpson, 2009). These migrants were generally taking up their rights as colonial subjects to move to Britain (a subject discussed in more depth in Chapter 2 on citizenship and immigration). While there continues to be a debate about the theorisation (or lack thereof) of the main ethnic categories used in Britain (see Nazroo, 1998 for a broader discussion on the problems with ethnic categorisation), in this section, we broadly trace the migration history of the main ethnic minority groups in the country.

As we discuss in Chapter 2, the control of movement into the UK as a phenomenon that began in Britain with the first restriction introduced in the Aliens Act 1905 and following the large-scale immigration of Jewish people from Eastern Europe and Russia (London, 2003). Over the last 60 years, since the British Nationality Act 1948, a series of immigration acts have further reduced the rights of colonial and post-colonial subjects to live and work in the UK. In the immediate aftermath of the Second World War, labour shortages and the need to rebuild Britain's infrastructure and the economy, as well as to support the growth of the newly formed NHS, meant that the UK government actively endorsed labour migration from across the Commonwealth. In the 1940s this included largely the migration of people from the Caribbean (migrants who provided the foundation of the Black Caribbean ethnic category for the census). These migrants began moving to the UK to settle in London and other major English cities. Unemployment across the Caribbean during this period and the prospect of employment opportunities in Britain facilitated the transatlantic migration aboard ships, for example, the SS *Empire Windrush*. The migration was possible, particularly because of the Caribbean migrants' British subject status, which, due to their citizenship, allowed them to move unencumbered to the UK.

Similarly, immigration from the Indian subcontinent has contributed significantly to ethnic diversity in Britain, with Indians, Pakistanis and Bangladeshis migrating in large numbers. Their migration has been facilitated by Britain's colonial connection with the region. Labour needs during the 1950s and 1960s also attracted many people from the region to fill labour vacancies, with many migrants (predominantly single men, with their wives migrating later) finding work in manual occupations such as manufacturing and the service sectors, and notably across the northern English towns. These can, in part, explain some of the residential settlement patterns of South Asian migrants across towns in the north of England (Peach, 2006; Finney and Simpson, 2009). Data from the 1971 Census showed Indian migrants (by this time the country had separated from Pakistan and Bangladesh) as the second largest migrant group in the UK (after the Irish) (ONS, 2013). Moreover, a second wave of South Asian migrants occurred in the 1960s and early 1970s and consisted of migrants who moved from East Africa where they were subjected to Africanisation policies. These policies favoured African citizens over Asians and expulsions made many of them refugees coming to Britain due to colonial connections (Robinson, 1986; Clarke et al, 1990). Many of the Asian expellees from East Africa had the right to settle in Britain as subjects.

Another group, the White Irish group, has a long history of migration to Britain, with early accounts stretching as far back as 1740, showing seasonal migration patterns across the Irish Sea (Collins, 1976). The potato famine in the 1840s was significant and motivated a large number of Irish people to move to escape the famine and settle in the UK, where they found work in mining, shipbuilding, engineering and linen production (MacRaild, 1999). The pattern of Irish migration to Britain has continued to the present day, with many Irish people moving to Britain for work, lifestyle and education reasons (Migration Observatory, 2017).

The ethnic Chinese group is largely comprised of migrants who originated in Hong Kong due to the area's historical connection with

Britain. The wider ethnic Chinese population in Britain comprises people of diverse origins and cultural backgrounds that were also associated with Britain and include people from Mainland China, Taiwan, Vietnam, Singapore and Malaysia (Chan and Chan, 1997). According to Au and P'ng (1997), Chinese migration to Britain has a long history that began in the 1880s. More recent migration from Mainland China has increased the size of the group, with many people moving to Britain for education and lifestyle reasons as well as along the asylum channel. More recently, Britain has experienced an increase in migration from Africa, hence the ethnic category 'Black African' has been introduced in the census and social surveys in the UK. Immigration from Africa to Britain gathered momentum from the 1990s when levels of immigration from African countries increased to approximately 20,000 people per year (Migration Observatory, 2017).

How we understand ethnic diversity (notably with the introduction of the 'White Other' ethnic category) substantially changed due to reconfigured immigration patterns, which were the product of the European Union (EU) expansion in 2004 (and subsequent expansions in 2007 and 2013). Before the EU enlargement, intra-EU migration between the EU15 countries was relatively stable (Moch, 2003; Burrell, 2009). This stable pattern (relatively equal immigration versus emigration) across the EU zone was the result of a similar level of economic development across the member countries. The EU enlargement admitted a total of 13 countries into the EU system from Central and Eastern Europe, with Cyprus, Czechia, Estonia, Hungary, Latvia, Lithuania, Malta, Poland, Slovakia, and Slovenia joining in 2004, followed by Bulgaria and Romania in 2007 and finally Croatia in 2013. For Britain, the expansion has resulted in a large and unexpected group of new arrivals, predominantly from the initial EU Accession 8[1] countries who migrated to take up employment in the labour market where there were labour supply gaps in sectors such as agriculture, construction and services (Burrell, 2009). Furthermore, the state has also implemented specific recruitment programmes to benefit from the later 2007 and 2013 EU accessions. This has steered migrants into the agricultural and farming sectors through the Seasonal Agricultural Workers Scheme (SAWS), which is restricted to migrants from Bulgarian, Romania and Croatia. A study by the Migration Observatory (2016) using Home Office Statistics found that between 2004 and 2011 approximately 540,000 accession migrants moved to the UK. As such, the number of accession migrants has resulted in a sharp increase in the number of people included within the 'Other White' ethnic category. Even though the economic recession in 2008/9 led to a slight decrease in the number of migrants moving from EU accession countries to Britain (Zaiceva and Zimmermann, 2016), they continue to contribute to an increase in the 'White Other' ethnic category. These new flows of migrants continue to challenge how we categorise ethnicity, particularly ethnic minority white groups in Britain, and our understanding of racisms, as discussed in Chapter 10.

Current ethnic minorities in the UK

In the last 30 years, notably since the 1991 Census, national governments in the UK have collected a variety of data referring to ethnicity (previously only the country of birth was collected). The ethnic categories used reflect a mixture of factors, including country of birth, nationality, language spoken at home, or racial category, national/geographic origin and religion. The statistical agencies of Northern Ireland, Scotland and England and Wales do not share a consistent format of categories, which makes a comparison between the UK regions rather difficult. In addition, census data collected have been fluid in terms of categories over the last three census rounds (1991, 2001, 2011), with additions such as 'Mixed' and 'Irish' in 2001, and 'Arab' in 2011 in the census for England, Wales and Scotland. Furthermore, for many individuals, these prescribed categories may not accurately describe their own (sometimes multiple) identities. As these are self-identified categories, even with consistent survey categories available, people may over time change their chosen ethnic group (Simpson et al, 2016). Nonetheless, despite these limitations and the inevitable loss of some complexity and diversity, without the collection of data in broad ethnicity categories, which can be taken as relatively high-quality approximations, it is a challenge to assess accurately the nature of ethnic inequalities in the UK and the dynamics of change over time and location within the UK.

Figure 1.1 shows the distribution of ethnic minorities in the last census, in 2011, in England and Wales. While we discuss data of the combined region of England and Wales, it is important to notice that there is much less ethnic diversity in Wales than in England. In 2011, Wales reported 93% of its inhabitants identify as White British (Welsh, English, Scottish or Northern Irish) while in England only 79% identify as White British.

The White British category covers four fifths of the total population in England and Wales in 2011, followed by the Other White group with about 4.4%. The largest categories among the non-white groups

Figure 1.1: Ethnic minority groups in England and Wales, 2011 Census

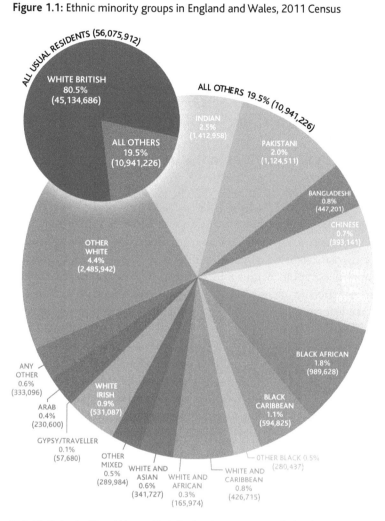

Note: All ethnic minorities which are collected in the relevant census are displayed.
Source: Census 2011, ONS.

are Indians (2.5%) and Pakistanis (2%) followed by Black Africans (1.8%), Other Ethnicities (1.5%) and Black Caribbeans (1.1%). The mixed categories, which were introduced in the 2001 Census, already amount to 0.8% for Mixed White and Caribbean, 0.6% for Mixed White and Asian and 0.3% for Mixed White and African. The new categories in the 2011 Census, Arabs and Gypsy/Traveller account for 0.4% and 0.1% respectively. Future censuses will show how these new groups develop and may also track the existence of other ethnic minority groups.

Comparing these data with the ethnic groups from the 2001 Census, several changes can be observed. The vast majority of the population in England and Wales identified as White British in both censuses, despite the decrease from 87.5% to 80.5%. Part of this decrease might be explained with the increasing share of mixed groups, as unions between White British and other ethnic minorities become more common and their offspring are more likely to identify as Mixed rather than White British only.

The second largest ethnic minority group, Other White, saw an increase of 60% from the 2001 Census as a result of the large-scale immigration from the EU Accession 8 countries which joined the EU in 2004 (Clark et al, 2018). This was again added to following the further expansion of the EU system in 2007 with the addition of Bulgarian and Romanian (EU Accession 2 countries) as members and, later, in 2013 of Croatia. Nevertheless, it is important to note that the Other White group also includes minorities and migrants who come from Old Commonwealth countries such as Australia and New Zealand, as well as migrants from the EU15 and their children, who can choose to self-identify as either White British or Other White.

All other ethnic groups experienced an increase between 2001 and 2011 with the exception of the White Irish group. The growth of certain ethnic categories could be the result of people choosing to switch ethnic categories as the specificity of the ethnic categories becomes more refined and better reflects their self-identification. The growth of the other categories corresponds to the groups' natural growth (fertility versus mortality) as well as further immigration. Jivraj and Simpson (2015) demonstrated that, among the Bangladeshi, Pakistani and Mixed ethnic groups, natural growth was the main driver for their growth. The numbers and multiple characteristics of migrants from South Asia will be reflected upon throughout this book, with their different characteristics resulting in various outcomes throughout different domains of British society, for example, in their attainment levels of the state education system (see Chapter 5). Meanwhile, for the White Other, Indian, Black African and Chinese groups, immigration was the main reason for population expansion. A noticeable increase across the mixed ethnic group categories could be a product of people switching to these categories as they are now available as well as an increase of inter-ethnic relationships.

Individuals identifying as Black African include those coming from a diverse range of countries and a considerable portion of asylum seekers and refugees. Some have moved as the result of famine, conflict and political unrest – particularly in Sub-Saharan Africa

(Migration Observatory, 2017; Clark et al, 2018) while others come for the prospect of higher education and economic opportunities. The Black African group differs considerably from the Black Caribbean group, whose migration history mainly relates to the *Windrush*-era immigration during the postwar period (Moch, 2003). Unlike many of the other ethnic minorities who are comprised mainly of recent migrants, the Caribbean group is largely made up of second- and third-generation British-born people. Furthermore, due to intermarriage and reduced migration from the Caribbean, the Black Caribbean group did not experience a large increase in recent years but the Mixed Caribbean group almost doubled in the same period (Simpson and Jivraj, 2015).

As mentioned earlier, the Irish group has one of the longest migration histories in the UK due to the contiguous position of Ireland to Britain and a long colonial history (Moch, 2003). Similar to other white minority groups, their size (0.9% in 2011) might be an under-representation of the actual population due to many British-born descendants of Irish migrants identifying as White British rather than White Irish.

The increasing Chinese ethnic group makes up 0.7% (2011) of the population (compared to 0.4% in 2001) and is comprised mainly of second- and third-generation British-born people as well as migrants from Mainland China and Hong Kong (Clark et al, 2018). The ethnic Chinese population in Britain is also composed of people from diverse cultural backgrounds and includes people with roots in Taiwan, Vietnam, Singapore and Malaysia (Chan and Chan, 1997). The Chinese group is well represented in professional occupations; however, many recent ethnic Chinese migrants find work in the ethnic food sector, particularly in the south-east and north-west regions of England (Clark et al, 2018).

The 2001 Census started to include mixed ethnic categories with White and Black Caribbean being the largest (0.5% in 2001 and 0.8% in 2011) followed by the White and Asian (0.6% in 2011). The mixed groups have emerged as a significant share of the population as a consequence of rising ethnic diversity and the birth of children of parents from different ethnic backgrounds (Bradford, 2006).

As mentioned, the comparison of ethnic minorities across the whole UK is very complex. Northern Ireland and Scotland used different ethnic minority categories in their census, more adapted to their population's diversity. In Figure 1.2 and Figure 1.3, we provide a brief overview of (aggregated) ethnic minorities in both regions according to data from the 2011 Census for Scotland and Northern Ireland.

Figure 1.2: Ethnic minority groups in Scotland, 2011 Census

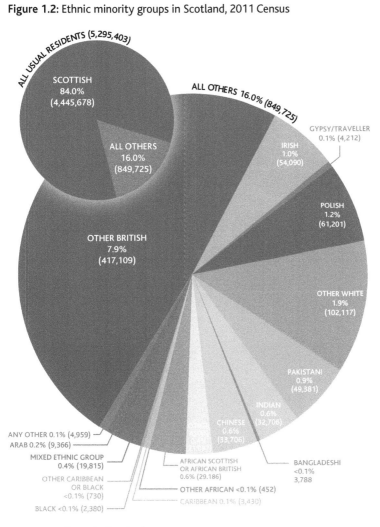

ALL USUAL RESIDENTS (5,295,403)

SCOTTISH
84.0%
(4,445,678)

ALL OTHERS 16.0% (849,725)

GYPSY/TRAVELLER
0.1% (4,212)

ALL OTHERS
16.0%
(849,725)

IRISH
1.0%
(54,090)

POLISH
1.2%
(61,201)

OTHER BRITISH
7.9%
(417,109)

OTHER WHITE
1.9%
(102,117)

PAKISTANI
0.9%
(49,381)

INDIAN
0.6%
(32,706)

CHINESE
0.6%
(33,706)

ANY OTHER 0.1% (4,959)
ARAB 0.2% (9,366)

MIXED ETHNIC GROUP
0.4% (19,815)

OTHER CARIBBEAN
OR BLACK
<0.1% (730)

BLACK <0.1% (2,380)

AFRICAN SCOTTISH
OR AFRICAN BRITISH
0.6% (29,186)

OTHER AFRICAN <0.1% (452)

CARIBBEAN 0.1% (3,430)

BANGLADESHI
<0.1%
3,788

Source: National Records of Scotland.

While in the Scottish census individuals have a wide range of 'white' categories to choose from, inhabitants in Northern Ireland can only identify as White or Irish Traveller in their census. In both regions, the combined White group accounts for 96% (Scotland) and 98.3% (Northern Ireland), which is much higher than in England (86%) but comparable with Wales (93%). The largest ethnic minority groups in Scotland, after Other British and Other White, are Polish (1.2%), Irish (1.0%) and Pakistani (0.9%). In Northern Ireland, the largest ethnic minority groups are Chinese, Indian and Other Asian, with each making up 0.3% of the population. As the ethnic minority

Figure 1.3: Ethnic minority groups in Northern Ireland, 2011 Census

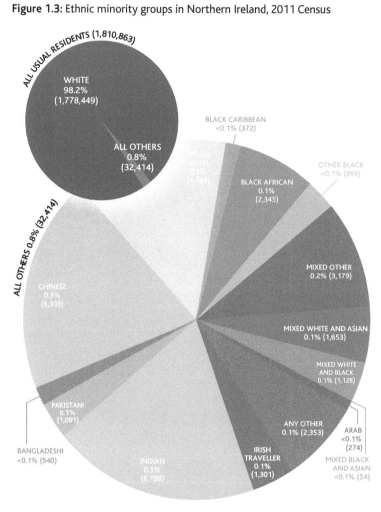

Note: More disaggregated groups are available for Irish Traveller, Other Asian, Black Other and Other Ethnic Group.

Source: National Records of Scotland and Northern Ireland Statistics and Research Agency.

categories differ substantially in definition and size between England and Wales, and Scotland and Northern Ireland, the rest of this chapter (and the other chapters) will concentrate on the data for England and Wales and present specific data for Scotland and Northern Ireland where appropriate.

Where possible throughout this chapter and the remainder of the book, data will be used to highlight the attainment and outcomes for these ethnic groups; however, often due to small group sample sizes and high diversity within the group, some groups cannot be analysed in depth. Specific discussions about the ethnic penalty and racism these groups face will be the topic of later chapters. For example, the Gypsy and Irish Travellers groups are discussed in more detail in the education chapter (Chapter 6), focusing on the high prevalence of education exclusion and low levels of educational attainment for this group. By comparison, the chapter on racism (Chapter 9) contains a more nuanced discussion of Islamophobia and the diversity of the Muslim population in Britain.

Age profile, fertility and family formation trends across ethnic minorities

As described earlier, each of the groups has their own specific history of immigration to Britain that shaped the current age profile of ethnic minorities in contemporary UK. Simpson and Jivraj (2015: 33) find that 'half the population born abroad and living in England and Wales arrived in the UK aged 15–29'. Age structure is a key characteristic for educational attendance and labour market participation, as well as family formation process, fertility and health patterns. It is not surprising that most ethnic minority groups have a younger age profile than the White British majority population group. This relates to classical theories such as the *healthy migrant hypothesis* that suggests, in general, younger and healthier individuals are more likely to migrate for educational and employment purposes. This is partly due to the selection effects based on the demands on the labour market and the physical and psychological strains of the migration process (Lu and Qin, 2014). Younger migrants are generally more economically productive and are unlikely to require or be eligible for state benefits.

Figure 1.4 shows the age profile of the 18 ethnic groups for England and Wales calculated by the age profiler of the 2011 Census (Simpson, 2015). There are three age groups with the middle group identifying the ages of economic productivity. The mixed groups have the youngest age profile, particularly the Mixed White and Black African group. These groups are composed of children whose parents come from different ethnic groups and represent some of the fastest-growing groups in Britain. For mixed groups 39% to 47% are under the age of 15; whereas only 4% are over 65. By comparison, the White Irish group has the oldest age profile with 31% of the group being over 65 years old and only 5% being under the age of 16. Their children and grandchildren may often identify as White British and thus mask the complete age profile of the Irish group.

Figure 1.4: Age profile of ethnic groups in England and Wales

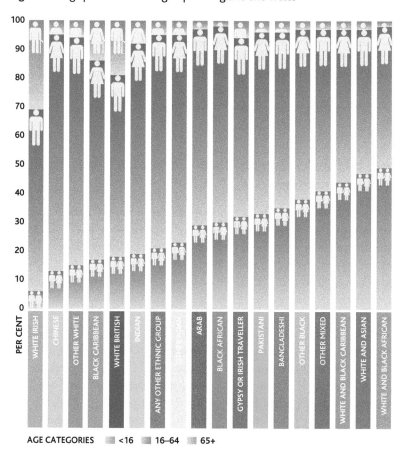

Source: 2011 Census England and Wales.

Figure 1.4 also shows that the Bangladeshi and Pakistani groups have relatively young age profiles, with large concentrations in the under 15 and the 16–64 age groups. Overall, for all groups the majority of people are in the age of 16–64.

As mentioned, the age profile of a specific ethnic minority group will have a profound impact on economic, but also demographic patterns, such as family formation and fertility trends. It must be noted that detailed ethnicity-specific fertility and mortality rates are not available from the ONS. Therefore, Kulu and Hannemann (2016) used data from Understanding Society – The UK Household Longitudinal Study[2] to examine the fertility of women from different ethnic groups in the UK (see Figure 1.5). Understanding Society is

Figure 1.5: Total fertility rate by migrant group, 1989–2008

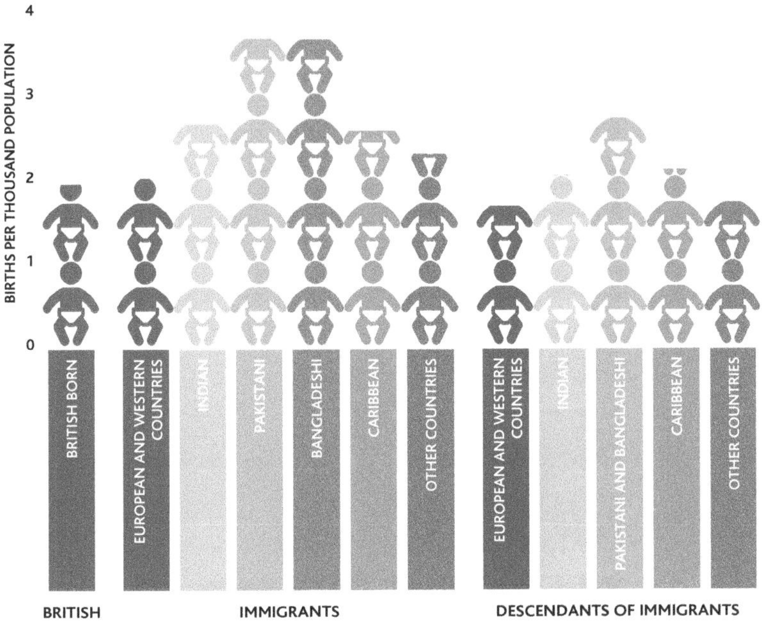

Source: Kulu and Hannemann (2016) based on data from Understanding Society.

a longitudinal study which replaced the British Household Panel. Data include a representative sample of UK residents as well as an Ethnic Minority Boost sample which enables researchers to study ethnic minorities in more detail without losing statistical power due to small case numbers.

First, Kulu and Hannemann (2016) found large fertility variations across ethnic minority groups. Fertility is measured as total fertility rate (the total expected number of children per women) and ethnic groups are constructed on the basis of country of birth rather than self-identified ethnic group. Immigrants from European and other Western countries showed very similar fertility to the British (defined here as individuals born in the UK, with both parents also born in the UK). They observed higher fertility for individuals born in India and the Caribbean and much larger fertility values for individuals born in Pakistan and Bangladesh. Especially the latter was found to be mostly due to higher propensities to have a third and a fourth child as well as experiencing an earlier start of family formation processes, and the more universal pattern of marriage and motherhood among women in those migrant groups (Hannemann and Kulu, 2015).

Figure 1.6: Infant mortality rate by ethnicity in England and Wales for the birth cohort, 2014

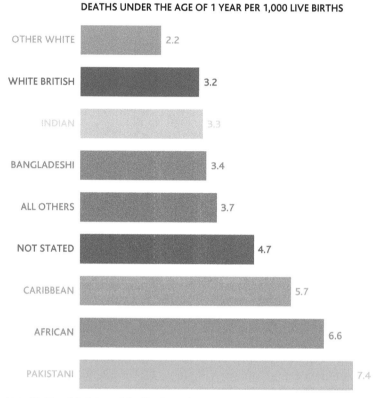

DEATHS UNDER THE AGE OF 1 YEAR PER 1,000 LIVE BIRTHS

OTHER WHITE — 2.2
WHITE BRITISH — 3.2
INDIAN — 3.3
BANGLADESHI — 3.4
ALL OTHERS — 3.7
NOT STATED — 4.7
CARIBBEAN — 5.7
AFRICAN — 6.6
PAKISTANI — 7.4

Note: Ethnicity of the baby as defined by the mother.
Source: ONS.

Second, the authors found that for ethnic minorities, who were born in the UK (descendants of immigrants, so-called second-generation immigrants), fertility levels are less different and fall between those of the British group and their parents' fertility values. Higher fertility among certain migrant groups has been attributed to differing economic and educational prospects as well as cultural differences in the definition of family and role of children. For instance, average household size is higher for Indian, African, Bangladeshi and Pakistani groups (Jivraj and Simpson, 2015) which can include multi-generational household members. These might have impact on fertility decisions as well as offer opportunities for child care provisions.

There is evidence that ethnicity plays a role in maternal morbidity and mortality differences (Kayem et al, 2011; Nair et al, 2014, 2016). The authors suggest that those differences are partly due to inadequate access to natal care and the presence of other morbidity conditions across the ethnic minority groups. Furthermore, Figure 1.6 shows the level of infant mortality rate for White British and various ethnic minorities in England and Wales in 2014. These show distinctive disparities, with the highest infant mortality rate values found among infants born into the Pakistani, African and Caribbean ethnic groups. While the Other White group demonstrates lower infant mortality rate than the White British group.

Over the life course, the social inequality encountered in the UK has meant that health risks increase with age for disadvantaged ethnic minorities (Jivraj and Simpson, 2015). For example, the high concentration of the Pakistani and Bangladeshi groups in the lower echelons of the labour market and low purchasing power contributes to their concentration in deprived neighbourhoods. These residential patterns have an impact on multiple measures of health (see Chapter 4), which can all increase their risk of health complications. In general, we would expect the mortality rates for ethnic minority groups to converge with the majority population, given a long enough adaptation period, where health behaviours slowly converge to those of the majority population. However, Lievesley (2010) emphasises that the underlying explanations are more complex and are often different across ethnic groups. A more detailed look at health difference across ethnic minorities is provided in Chapter 4.

Residential settlement and segregation

Residential settlement

As discussed, the data show that Britain continues to become a more ethnically diverse country – particularly in England where the majority of the ethnic minority groups reside. The census data paint a national picture of diversity but ethnic minority people are not spread evenly across the UK. This is a product of their migration history and the needs of the labour market at their time of arrival, the availability and affordability of housing as well as issues that relate to discrimination and racism (Peach, 1998; Finney and Simpson, 2009). Historically, ethnic minority groups have tended to settle in neighbourhoods in inner-city urban areas across cities in the UK. Over time they have, to an extent, suburbanised; however, ethnic minority people remain in smaller proportions, compared with White British people, in rural and suburban than in urban neighbourhoods. Newer migrants have subsequently moved to these ethnically diverse inner-city neighbourhoods for several reasons. First, their residential choice is shaped by social and kinship ties; second, the migrants are attracted to the diversity offered within these neighbourhoods; third, these diverse neighbourhoods offer migrants a reservoir of local knowledge about housing and labour market opportunities.

An interesting feature of migration from the new EU accession countries (13 countries located across central and Eastern Europe) has been their continued migration to neighbourhoods unaccustomed to large-scale immigration (Scott and Brindley, 2012). Many of these new migrants found employment in the agricultural and farming sectors in dire need of higher labour supply in regions such as the east of England, opening up these new geographies. Often, due to the scarcity of housing to accommodate the migrants, many of the businesses provided accommodation to support their workers. The changes to local labour market conditions explain how the association between ethnic minorities and place and the central focus on the urban setting has changed for migrants from EU Accession countries and shifted focus to suburban and rural places.

Ethnic segregation

The places where ethnic minority groups live have come under scrutiny as a product of moral panics after the terrorist attacks of both 9/11 in New York and 7/7 in London as well as the civil disturbances in a number of northern English towns (Bradford, Oldham and Burnley) in 2001 (reviewed in Finney and Simpson, 2009; Catney, 2015). There has been a fear that places associated with ethnic minority people are also associated with multiple social problems, which include crime, radicalisation and specific anti-British ideologies. These anxieties are often associated with specific groups. This segregation narrative tends to assume that residential clustering is necessarily a social ill. In these assumptions, the residential separation of groups is seen to indicate a lack of meaningful engagement between groups, low rates of English language learning and poor ethnic relations.

Yet there is increasing recognition that residential clustering has positive elements that are vital to the interpretation of ethnic minority groups' residential patterns. These include protective effects, where living in proximity to members of the same ethnic group can act as a resource for local knowledge, supporting language and culture maintenance. Residential proximity can be beneficial to the family, social and religious networks, as well as creating a buffer against intolerance and discrimination from the majority population (see Bécares et al, 2011). Furthermore, as Chapter 7 on housing will discuss in more detail, we need to question the assumption that residential clustering reveals a *desire* on the part of ethnic minority people to self-segregate. Research has shown the extent to which the residential decision making of many ethnic minority groups is constrained (Robinson, 1986; Peach, 1998; Phillips, 2006). In addition, residential clustering of ethnic groups also reflects choices made by white residents or potential residents.

Notions of ethnic ghettos and anxieties about acute residential segregation pervade the US narrative on racial minorities and have (to a lesser extent) featured in the debate on ethnic minorities in the UK. In order to discuss how acute residential segregation is in Britain, we have deployed a method to measure it. The most commonly used approach to measuring segregation is the index of dissimilarity (Catney, 2015: 112), This is a technique popularised by Massey and Denton (1988) that measures how evenly a group is spread across an area. 'The proportion of an ethnic group's total population in England and Wales living in a neighbourhood is subtracted from the proportion of the rest of the population that lies in the same neighbourhood' (Catney, 2015: 113). The absolute difference between proportions is then added across all areas. The result ranges between 0 and 100 with the highest level of segregation of a group indicated by 100 and an even spread of the ethnic minority group in a specific area indicated by a result of 0. The results thus provide a good measure of the residential segregation of different groups.

The 'index of dissimilarity', however, is not the only measure used to study residential segregation. More generally, we have to be cautious about the ways in which segregation is conceptualised and measured in order to reduce misinterpretation of the data. Problems raised regarding the use of various methods for studying segregation relate to, first, whether the areal unit the segregation analysis is built on is appropriate to assess a group's social interactions in a meaningful way and, second, whether segregation is the dominant mechanism that is occurring. An important issue with segregation work has been the question of whether the results are in fact masking the effects of deprivation. As already stated, the main ethnic minority groups we concentrate on are the product of different migrant waves who settled in the UK and their children and grandchildren. For example, the Pakistani group began migrating to the UK in large numbers in the 1970s to fill specific employment gaps in manufacturing and other industrial sectors. The subsequent class profile of the different ethnic minority groups steered many into living in specific houses in certain areas because of their affordability; this related to the housing options available to them and thus shaped their residential geographies. The same seems to be true with respect to the patterns of White Other settlement in rural locations where labour market practices have contributed to the concentration of migrants in particular areas. Therefore, ethnic segregation may, in fact, be partially a product of classed spatial inequalities and labour market mechanisms rather than solely the product of an ethnic minority group's ethnic identities.

Using the 'index of dissimilarity' to measure the residential segregation of different ethnic groups, Catney (2015) conducted a comparison of segregation across different groups using data from the 2001 and 2011 censuses. Catney (2015) found that residential segregation across all groups has decreased and, overall, neighbourhoods are becoming more ethnically mixed. The results also show that 'in over two thirds of districts, segregation decreased for Black Caribbean, Indian, Mixed and Black African ethnic groups, between 2001 and 2011' (Catney, 2015: 109). Focusing specifically on London, the results found that residential mixing increased in inner and outer London. In outer London, for example, segregation decreased by 12 percentage points for the Bangladeshi ethnic group and 11 percentage points for the Chinese ethnic group. Other large cities, such as Leicester, Birmingham, Manchester and Bradford, have also seen a decrease in segregation for most ethnic groups. In addition, there has also been an increase in residential mixing between the White British and minority ethnic groups. The findings that indicate a reduction in levels of segregation across all groups can be explained predominantly by two mechanisms, the first is the spreading out of people from more concentrated areas, and, second, the effect of natural change that is the result of the number of births versus deaths in ethnic minority groups (Catney, 2015). The difference in segregation levels between different groups can be predominantly explained by their varying migration histories to the UK, with more recent groups being affected by chain migration and migrants moving to live near friends and relatives; whereas more established group's may have formed families whose children subsequently move out of areas of concentration.

Conclusion

This chapter has shown how the demographic features of ethnic minorities in Britain are highly connected to immigration, fertility, mortality and residential segregation. The composition and size of ethnic groups in Britain reflects the history of immigration to the UK since 1945 and began with the arrival of migrants from the Caribbean, the Indian subcontinent, Ireland and countries in Africa. As these migration patterns change, so have the ethnic categories that are used to enumerate ethnic groups in specific areas (with differences between England and Wales and Scotland, for example). Moreover, over time new categories have been added to the census to capture this new diversity, including mixed groups and Arab and Gypsy and Irish Traveller categories in 2001 and 2011 respectively.

The younger age profile of many of the ethnic minority has effects for their labour force participation, as well as demographic patterns regarding fertility and mortality. The chapter has shown large differences in fertility across different ethnic minority groups with migrants from accession countries and Pakistanis, Bangladeshis and Indians tending to have higher fertility rates. However, the chapter showed that high fertility rates among immigrants are not continued by subsequent generations. Nonetheless, the average household size is still higher for Indian, African, Bangladeshi and Pakistani groups. Conversely, mortality is often lower for recent migrants due to a pre-migration selection effect in their country of origin (the healthy migrant hypothesis).

Finally, the specific residential pattern of ethnic minority groups – specifically non-white Muslims – continues to be the focus of integration and housing policy brought on by anxieties that have followed moral panics that residential clustering is a breeding ground for social ills such as terrorism. The data suggest that overall ethnic minority segregation is decreasing across the country. Moreover, the chapter has raised some significant questions about how we conceptualise segregation and understand processes that underlie segregation. For example, the exponential increase of the White Other population between 2001 and 2011 as a result of the EU accession has seen new housing practices bring issues of residential segregation into new geographies such as rural and suburban neighbourhoods. New questions emerge about the consequences of conceptualisations of segregation in these spaces and what the effects will be on the new white migrant groups living in these areas.

Notes

[1]   The term 'Accession 8' refers to the eight countries that joined the EU in 2004. These include Czechia, Estonia, Hungary Latvia, Lithuania, Poland, Slovenia and Slovakia.

[2] University of Essex. Institute for Social and Economic Research, NatCen Social Research (2015). Understanding Society: Waves 1-5, 2009-2014: Special Licence Access, Local Authority District. [data collection]. 6th Edition. UK Data Service. SN: 6666. doi:10.5255/UKDA-SN-6666-6.

2

Citizen rights and immigration

William Shankley and Bridget Byrne

Key findings

- Britain's long history of migration has been shaped by its empire and relationship to Europe.
- In the post-Second World War period, mass immigration from both Europe and the colonies was driven by labour shortages in the UK. Nonetheless, ethnic minority citizen-migrants were often met with hostility and racism.
- Immigration and citizenship policy since 1948 has been driven by a restriction of citizenship rights and rights of abode in ways which were often highly racialised.
- EU migration increased significantly to the UK after the accession of new countries to the EU after 2004, although there has been a decline since the EU referendum in 2016.
- Recent immigration policy and bordering practices have been driven by a desire to drive down and control net immigration.
- The creation of a 'hostile' or 'compliant' environment risks increasing the discrimination and harassment suffered by ethnic minority individuals and communities.
- The *Windrush* scandal sheds light on the abuses suffered by citizen-migrants under new immigration policies.

Introduction

Immigration policy emerges out of the state's attempt to control the movement of people across national borders. In Britain, immigration policy has developed over the last 100 years and has often been in response to the movements of racialised groups perceived as culturally different. Thus immigration policy is often used to define who are desirable and undesirable migrants and citizens in ways which are frequently racialised. This history has been fundamentally shaped by empire, and particularly the withdrawal of rights to UK citizenship and residence in the UK for many non-white subjects as the empire ended. It is also worth noting that Ireland has been a major source of immigrants to the UK in the last century but is not subject to modern migration controls.

In this chapter, we will initially provide a brief history of immigration to the UK over the 21st century and the policies the government has used to control migration and define British citizenship. This will include consideration of the impact that these policies have on ethnic minority British citizens, as well as migrants. We will then examine contemporary immigration patterns and policies, such as the Immigration Acts of 2014 and 2016 and bordering practices of detention, deportation and dispersal. The recent case of what has become known as the '*Windrush* generation' will be considered as a window into how contemporary state immigration practices have led to depriving citizen-migrants from mainly Commonwealth countries of basic rights. Finally, we discuss the implications of Britain leaving the EU on the country's future immigration policy.

Histories of migration

Britain has a long history of migration to the British Isles with a continual process of movement, trade and settlement between Britain and the wider world.[1] While the arrival of what would now be seen as ethnic minority people in Britain dates back to the first century AD, these processes intensified with enslavement, industrialisation and empire. The exploitation of world resources and the expansion of the British empire brought slaves, servants, sailors and workers as well as traders to Britain, alongside entrepreneurs and political and religious refugees who all helped to shape the culture and economy. Under empire, and prior to the introduction of the British Nationality Act 1948, under British common law everyone who was born in a dominion of the empire was classified as a British subject (Karatani, 2004). Formally at least, subjects of the empire had the right to move freely and settle in Britain. At the same time, colonised people in particular were often racialised and constructed as inferior and faced racist hostility to their settlement in the UK.

After the Second World War, migration to the UK intensified with the beginning of waves of mass immigration. Poland's role as part of the allied resistance led to approximately 200,000 soldiers settling in Scotland and London. After the conflict, many were unable to return home due to Poland's sovereign borders changing at the Conference of Yalta. With the Polish Resettlement Act 1947, Polish servicemen were allowed to be joined by their families (Stanchura, 2004).

Other European workers were also drawn into migrant recruitment programmes such as the European Volunteer Workers Scheme, which enlisted large numbers of Europeans displaced by the war to move to the UK and assist in the rebuilding effort. This European migration is frequently overlooked in the accounts of migration to Britain. Colonial migration to Britain also intensified in the post-war period, for example with recruitment drives in the Caribbean to attract workers to work particularly in the transport sector and the newly established NHS. Workers were also attracted from the Indian subcontinent, with many migrants moving to fill labour shortages in industries such as textiles in northern cities in England, cars and engineering factories in the West Midlands and light industries in the south. Migration from Ireland has also been a major source of workers for the UK over the last century.

Citizenship and immigration policy

The British Nationality Act 1948 provided the first definition of British citizenship and established the same rights for British-born and colonial-born people as a 'Citizen of the United Kingdom and Colonies' (CUKC or 'British citizen'). All CUKCs were also British subjects and they all had the same rights to enter, work and settle with their families anywhere within Britain's sovereign territory (Bloch and Schuster, 2005: 495). However, between 1948 and 1981, successive immigration laws and other policies restricted the rights of certain British and Commonwealth citizens to unrestricted entry and settlement in the UK. These were often based on racialised grounds so impacted on non-white citizens in particular. For instance, the Commonwealth Immigrants Act 1962 introduced a quota system to regulate the number of New Commonwealth migrants who migrated to Britain (Lukes et al, 2018). The Commonwealth Immigration Act 1968 introduced patriality, which required those seeking British citizenship to prove they had a parent or grandparent who already possessed British citizenship. This move saw the beginning of a shift in British citizenship from *jus soli* to *jus sanguine* or citizenship passed on by parental lines rather than place of birth and favoured white Old Commonwealth migrants (Byrne, 2014). The act was passed particularly to block the arrival of CUKC Kenyan Asians fleeing expulsion and Africanisation. Later amendments in the Immigration Act 1971 saw further restrictions to the movement of New Commonwealth subjects. The act introduced a system of permits that restricted the number of New Commonwealth migrants who could migrate to the UK to work, study and visit. Successive citizenship and immigration acts further closed the rights and pathways to move to the UK from former colonies. For example, the Nationality Act 1981 reclassified CUKCs into three categories that limited the right to abode in the UK only to those with close connections to the UK. These amendments were racialised as they privileged white migrants with Old Commonwealth connections above the rights of predominantly non-white people from countries with close ties to Britain.

Subsequent acts have continued practices of exclusion but tended to concentrate more on what has been defined as 'uncontrolled' migration, often focused on asylum seekers and those deemed to be illegal. The Refugee Council (2018) defines an asylum seeker as 'someone who has lodged an application for protection on the basis of the Refugee Convention or Article 3 of the ECHR [European Convention on Human Rights]'. As a signatory to the 1951 Refugee Convention, Britain has signed up to assist and protect anyone who has made a claim for protection in the country's territory. Multiple examples from the past thirty years show how asylum channels have provided a vital protection channel against conflict and famine across the globe. However, as these movements are sometimes characterised as 'uncontrolled' migration, the state has attempted to deter or restrict entry and service provision to asylum seekers and other migrants who are deemed unacceptable or problematic (Fekete, 2009). The Immigration Acts of 1993 and 1996, for instance, restricted appeal rights for some migrant groups and also sought to restrict the housing options to asylum seekers. This steered asylum seekers into substandard housing in specific areas (often white neighbourhoods) under the National Asylum Support Service (NASS) scheme, where they often experienced hostility. Later the Immigration Acts of 1999 and 2002 further constricted the rights of asylum seekers by removing their benefits and housing rights, and consolidated the appeals process, making it an offence to be an undocumented migrant in the country without a reasonable explanation. These were followed in the 2000s by more policies which aimed to make it harder for people to reach the UK to make a claim, and to make it more difficult for them while their claims were being considered, including the revocation of work rights and a system of dispersal (discussed later).

Figure 2.1 shows the figures for emigration, immigration, asylum and net migration in the UK in the years 1991–2017. It shows how the number of asylum seekers has fallen since the early 2000s and that they make up only a small portion of the overall immigration numbers to the country. Sturge (2019) found that asylum seekers only made up a total of 6% of the annual immigration numbers to Britain in 2016 (see Figure 2.1), although they often feature quite prominently in public discourse.

Figure 2.1: Emigration, immigration, asylum and net migration in the UK, 1991–2017

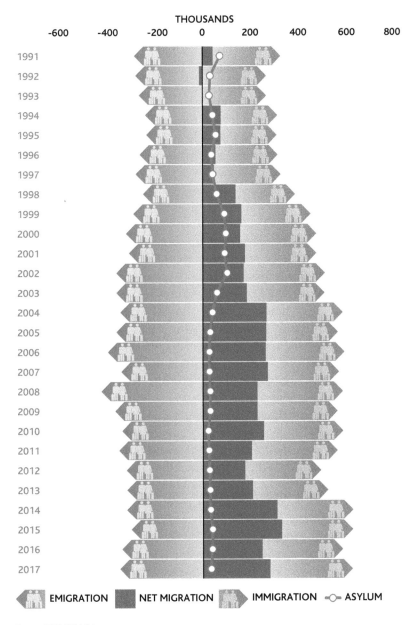

Source: ONS LTIM data.

EU accession

A significant change to the patterns of immigration to the UK has been a direct result of the expansion of the EU, initially in 2004 and then again in 2007 and 2013 respectively. Figure 2.2 shows that prior to 2004, the migration of EU15 citizens remained relatively constant at approximately 35,000 per year (Sumption and Vargas-Silvia, 2019). Nonetheless, after 2004, the EU admitted new countries from central and Eastern Europe, with Cyprus, Czechia, Estonia, Hungary, Latvia, Lithuanian, Malta, Poland, Slovakia and Slovenia joining in 2004; followed by Bulgaria and Romania in 2007, and finally Croatia in 2013. For Britain specifically, the initial 2004 expansion resulted in a large and unexpected patterns of migration from the 'Accession 8' countries, with migrants moving in large numbers to fill employment gaps in the labour market and sectors that included the agricultural, construction and services sectors.

Coinciding with this large-scale geopolitical change, Figure 2.2 shows an increase in EU migration to Britain occurred after 2004, with Home Office statistics (Burrell, 2016) estimating between 2004 and 2011 approximately 540,000 accession migrants moved to the UK. However, Figure 2.2 shows these high net migration levels fell around the same time as the financial crisis (2008 to 2012) to as low as 58,000 in 2009. Following this first large-scale migration, the government imposed a number of immigration policies to regulate the number of migrants from the 'Accession 2' (Bulgaria and Romania) cohort that were able to move to the UK, and later for Croatia. After the three accessions, Figure 2.2 shows that after 2013, a second wave of EU migration seemed to occur, peaking at 189,000 for the year ending June 2016. However, this number soon decreased after Britain's EU referendum result, with net migration falling to 101,000 in 2017 (Sumption and Vargas-Silva, 2019). The anti-immigrant sentiment expressed in the political campaigns around the referendum and uncertainty about future immigration status have had a profound impact on EU net migration levels (Becker and Fetzer, 2017; Hix et al, 2017) Small-scale studies across different EU migrant groups note an increase in experiences of hostility before and after Brexit (see, for example, Rzepnikowska, 2019). According to Sumption and Vargas-Silva (2019), the decline in EU net migration that followed the referendum result can be explained by a decrease in the net migration levels across all three EU groups, the EU15, Accession 8 and Accession 2 cohorts.

The following section considers how the British state has sought to control the numbers of migrants from different parts of the world

Figure 2.2: Net migration by citizenship, 1991–2017

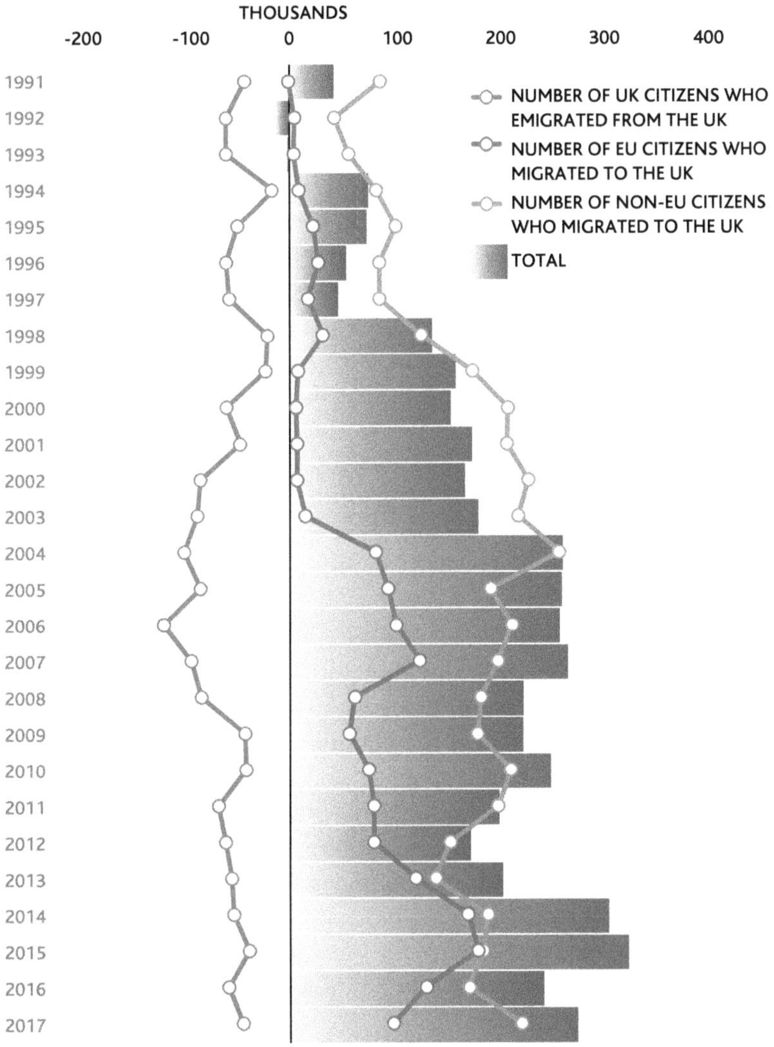

THOUSANDS

| -200 | -100 | 0 | 100 | 200 | 300 | 400 |

1991
1992
1993
1994
1995
1996
1997
1998
1999
2000
2001
2002
2003
2004
2005
2006
2007
2008
2009
2010
2011
2012
2013
2014
2015
2016
2017

NUMBER OF UK CITIZENS WHO EMIGRATED FROM THE UK

NUMBER OF EU CITIZENS WHO MIGRATED TO THE UK

NUMBER OF NON-EU CITIZENS WHO MIGRATED TO THE UK

TOTAL

Source: ONS LTIM table 2.00, reproduction of data from 'Net migration in the UK' report (Sumption and Vargas-Silva, 2019).

and the techniques it has also used to target those deemed to be uncontrolled migrants already in Britain.

Contemporary immigration policy and bordering practices (2010 onwards)

The state has sought to limit the number of migrants settling in the country and to restrict net immigration levels by using an array of the state's bordering arsenal to dissuade migrants from settling in the country and removing those are deemed to have settled illegally. This section will examine the following questions: what is bordering and what are the practices that the state uses to control and limit immigration, and how do these practices affect black and minority ethnic (BME) groups in Britain? Earlier we discussed how the state has revisited notions of citizenship to demarcate the rights various groups have and do not have to settlement and services in the country. In a similar way, the British state has also sought to regulate uncontrolled migration using practices such as detention, dispersal and deportation. Finally, the government has also redrawn its rights to remove citizenship from individuals as we shall discuss further later.

The most recent set of policies that the state has implemented to control immigration levels relates to the Immigration Acts of 2014 and 2016. These policies aim to reduce net migration levels but also have detrimental impacts on migrants and ethnic minority groups alike. The Immigration Acts of 2014 and 2016 have implications for controlled and uncontrolled migration to Britain and set out the following aims:

1) To restrict the number of migrants who can enter Britain by reducing the number of channels and visas available that migrants can use to apply to enter the country;
2) To change immigration policies and place the responsibility of checking a person's immigration status in-house within the housing sector, labour market and education system;
3) To make it easier for the government to remove people who violate immigration rules; and
4) To reduce the mechanisms that are available to people to contest and appeal against immigration violations. (Home Office, 2016)

The Immigration Acts of 2014 and 2016 have also imposed tighter regulations on migrants wishing to enter the UK, limiting visas for skilled workers and introducing stricter criteria for eligibility to stay permanently in the UK (Gower, 2015: 1). The Immigration Act 2016 tightened up the student visa system and limited the number of hours international students are eligible to work as well as ending the post-study work entitlement of international students.

The term 'hostile environment' was implemented in 2010, when Theresa May became Home Secretary, and the government's position towards immigration intensified, with its primary aim being to reduce net immigration – a core aim of the 2010 Conservative Party

Election Manifesto (Conservative Party, 2010: 21). The term 'hostile environment' has been replaced with 'compliant environment' after widespread critique and still represents an array of policies that include the in-house requirement for landlords to check the immigration status of tenants, eligibility checks within the NHS, and requirements for business and charities and other organisations to carry out ID checks to ensure their workers are eligible to be employed in the UK, as well as policies that permitted the removal of homeless EU migrants.

The introduction of the Immigration Acts of 2014 and 2016 and the 'hostile' or 'compliant' environment considerably impacts on ethnic minorities in the UK on a number of counts. The introduction of the acts has changed the language and vocabulary regarding how we talk about 'migration', 'citizenship' and 'belonging'. It has also taken practices designed to regulate borders and immigration into different institutions and parts of society. These acts place the responsibility for checking a migrant's immigration status in-house with landlords, businesses and the education system. Fines for employers who knowingly employ migrants without valid documents were increased to £10,000 in the Immigration Act 2014 and the Immigration Compliance and Enforcement team (ICE) activities were increased. These changes risk organisations and businesses incorrectly discriminating against ethnic minority people by being overly cautious in complying with the policies or using the policies to tacitly endorse discriminatory practices. For example, in the private rental sector of the housing market it has been found that landlords increasingly target ethnic minority tenants to demand their citizenship and immigration documents in an effort to comply with the Immigration Act 2014 (Craig et al, 2015). There is a paucity of research on the same restrictive practices being levelled against white tenants but it is likely that they are not scrutinised to the same degree. Flynn's (2016) work also found that immigration enforcement (ICE) workers regularly confront members of ethnic minority and migrant communities in West London as they enter tube stations, demanding to see documentation to prove immigration status. Aggressive and controversial bordering practices have included the 'go home' campaign vans sent out in 2014 by the Home Office, which were targeted in areas of high ethnic diversity.

Other examples of practices that have implications for ethnic minority groups can be seen in the implementation of a new minimum income requirement in July 2012. The minimum income requirement states that UK citizens and settled residents who wished to bring their spouses or partners from outside the EU into the UK have to earn a minimum of £18,600. This amount increases depending on the number of additional dependents (such as children) a citizen wants to join them in the UK (Sumption and Vargas-Silva, 2016: 2). Many ethnic minority families have transnational extended families and therefore the introduction of the new minimum income requirement restricts their rights for family reunification. An analysis by the Migration Observatory (2014, cited in Byrne, 2016: 8) found that 47% of British citizens in employment would not qualify to bring a family member, rising to 58% of people between 20–30 years old, or 61% of women of any age. This is likely to have a particular impact on certain ethnic minority groups, which, as we see in Chapter 6 have particularly low levels of income. The Pakistani and Bangladeshi groups, for example, are highly concentrated in routine and low-skilled work, and therefore are less likely to have the income to fulfil the minimum entry requirement. Furthermore, specific cultural practices within groups such as the Indian, Pakistani and Bangladeshi ethnic groups that include arranged marriages often do not match up with the 2014 and 2016 Immigration Acts' conceptions of relationships, making it harder for some members of ethnic minority groups to be able to bring their partners to the UK (Wray, 2016). As well as the change to the minimum income requirement threshold, 'since July 2012 the immigration rules for adult dependent relatives have been, in practice, almost impossible to meet. Applicants need to demonstrate that they require a level of long-term personal care that they are unable to get in their home country, either due to the cost or availability' (Yeo, 2017: 1). This change has made it near impossible for the adult dependents (parents or grandparents) of British citizens to join their family in the UK.

Detention, deportation and dispersal

At the same time as the Immigration Acts of 2014 and 2016 brought in changes to who was eligible to enter Britain, policies were implemented to make it easier for the government to remove people from the UK and also limited their scope for appeal and simplified the removal process. The changes on multiple fronts to *who* and *what* the government has deemed as 'good' or 'desirable' migration versus 'bad' or 'undesirable' migration has resulted in criticism from migrant rights groups and activists (Gower, 2015). According to Darling (2016: 231), broader changes to the structure and service provision of dispersal and resettlement programmes in Britain have resulted in asylum being 'an issue of public policy from which' profit is sought. For example, asylum accommodation provision has been transferred to private contractors.

According to Bloch and Schuster (2005: 497), detention 'differs from imprisonment in that the primary purpose of incarceration is not punishment for a crime committed' but a way of separating those the state believes have broken immigration law. Until the 1990s there were no Immigration Removal Centres (IRCs) in the UK and when large groups of asylum seekers entered the UK (for example, the Sri Lankans in 1987) they were housed in the prison estate (Bloch and Schuster, 2005). However, in the early 90s the government responded by building a permanent detention estate to house illegal immigrants, failed asylum seekers and later asylum seekers waiting their asylum outcomes (or on the fast-track asylum route) in order to prevent them being housed in prisons. Now the UK immigration estate is one of the largest in Europe and IRCs and holding centres are located across the UK, particularly near airports and seaports, to detain people arriving without documentation in the country and also to remove and deport people back to their country of origin (Silverman and Hajela, 2011). Out of seven IRCs, as of December 2018, six are outsourced by the government to private firms. Between 2009 and 2017, there have been between 2,500 and 3,500 individuals in immigration detention at any given time with numbers varying between 27,000 and 33,000 entering detention in each year (Silverman and Griffiths, 2019).

The largest category of immigration detainees is people who have sought asylum at some stage – accounting for about 47% of people entering detention in 2017. An increasing proportion of those detained are EU nationals (19 in 2017). The number of children detained has fallen considerably over the last 18 years, with 42 children detained in 2017. The parliamentary Joint Committee of Human Rights conducted an inquiry on immigration detention, which argued that decisions on detention should be made independent of the Home Office and by a judge. They also pointed out that the UK is the only country in Europe that does not impose time limits on immigration detention and suggested a limit of 28 days and that those detained should have access to legal advice. They also made recommendations on the care of vulnerable individuals and on the need to make the detention estate less prison-like (House of Commons, 2019).

Deportation is the state-enforced or enforceable departure of a non-citizen from a country and has grown as a practice the past three decades, with a slight decline since 2015 (although changes in government classification of departures over time makes this difficult to report). The Home Office (2017: 1) recorded that in 2017, 12,321 people were returned to their country of origin and this represented a decrease of 1% compared with 12,469 people in 2016. The top five countries of enforced removal or voluntary departure in 2017 were India (14% of the total) and Pakistan (9% of the total) and China, Romania and Albania (all at 6% of the total).

The state also uses dispersal (the movement of government-assisted asylum seekers to housing outside London and the south-east) as a method of bordering, with the Home Office, in 2000, creating a specific branch, the National Asylum Support Service (NASS), to deal exclusively with asylum seekers. The role of NASS was to process asylum applications and provide support with respect to housing and subsistence throughout the duration of their application (Robinson and Andersson, 2003). Frontline services that work directly with asylum seekers have found that dispersal and related bordering practices disadvantage ethnic minority groups disproportionately. Many asylum applicants who are dispersed across the UK have family members who are British citizens or settled residents and therefore dispersal undermines the supportive elements of social and family networks by moving applicants to places that are often far from these connections, thus taking a social and psychological toll. Problematically, the NASS and Home Office's arguments for dispersal are built on economic arguments put forth to lessen the demand and burden on housing and resources in London and the south-east. However, in reality, these do not take into account some of the challenges that asylum applicants face by being dispersed to places that are more deprived, less diverse (increasing the risk of hostility and racism) and unfamiliar with housing international migrants.

Resettlement has also been used by the British state, as part of its arsenal to regulate and control asylum seekers from a collection of Home Office programmes such as the Vulnerable Persons Resettlement Scheme (VPRS) that has been used to formulate Britain's response to Syrian refugee crisis across continental Europe. Compared to detention, resettlement exists as a relatively minor bordering practice, in terms of the number of asylum seekers/refugees it deals with. Britain has taken in a meagre number of Syrian asylum seekers compared to other EU countries (for example, Sweden and Germany). Britain's declared intention with the VPRS scheme was to take in 20,000 Syrian refugees in need of protection by 2020. By March 2017, 7,307 Syrian asylum seekers had been assisted with the scheme.

Box 1: Case study

Contested belonging: the case of the *Windrush* generation

Earlier in this chapter we described how the formerly expansive definition of British citizenship formalised in the British Nationality Act 1948 was gradually restricted. This process excluded many Commonwealth citizens from rights to enter and settle in the UK along primarily racialised lines, culminating in the establishment of 'patriality' in 1971 (mentioned earlier). The *Windrush* scandal of 2018 shed light on how Home Office practices and the aggressive 'compliant environment' linked to the Immigration Acts of 2014 and 2016 unsettled the status of some Commonwealth citizens who had settled in the UK prior to 1972.

Although these have been called the '*Windrush* generation' after the ship, the SS *Empire Windrush*, which brought the first mass migration from the Caribbean to Britain in 1948, the scandal has affected migrants from a range of Commonwealth (and other) countries. Although this generation were citizen-migrants, entering Britain with full rights, they have encountered problems under the new immigration policies in proving their status and rights. For example, some arrived as children travelling on their parents' passports and had never applied for travel or citizenship documents. Newly introduced immigration law, which requires people to have documentation to work, rent property and access benefits including health care, has meant that some migrants have lost jobs, been refused free access to NHS care and faced destitution. The Immigration Act 2014 also removed protection for Commonwealth citizens, who had up until then been exempt from deportation. As a result some citizen-migrants who had entered legally and had rights to reside in the UK have been detained or deported.

It is still unclear how many people have been directly affected by this scandal. The Windrush Taskforce has dealt with more than 6,000 individual possible cases by January 2019. It has issued documentation confirming status to more than 2,000 individuals and granted citizenship or indefinite leave to remain or no time limit to more than 4,000 individuals who arrived in the UK as minors (Javid, 2019). It is unclear how many people of the *Windrush* generation have been wrongfully deported, although it may be as many as 83, of whom 12 have subsequently died (Javid, 2019). The government has recently announced that it will pay up to £200 million in compensation to those whose lives have been damaged by the Home Office's misclassification of thousands of long-term residents as illegal migrants (Gentleman, 2019).

Deprivation of citizenship

Throughout the chapter we have talked about the different ways the state has implemented policy designed to deter migrants from staying in Britain for the long term, or creating obstacles that make it difficult for them to regularise their stay and proceed on a pathway to naturalisation and citizenship. However, since 1981 the state has also implemented powers of citizenship deprivation. Deprivation of citizenship is 'when an individual with British citizenship status – whether through birth, naturalisation or being a citizen of a British overseas territory or otherwise – has that citizenship removed by the British government' (CAGE, 2019). Ethnic minority people are more likely to have, or be deemed to have, the right to dual citizenship and are therefore more vulnerable to having citizenship removed. The Immigration Act 2014 amended the National Act 1981 by inserting three subsections to expand the powers by which and the circumstances when citizenship can be removed. For example, subsection 40(4a) grants the Home Secretary the power to deprive a person of British citizenship obtained through naturalization, even if it would render the person stateless. The increased powers came into force following the case of the Iraqi-born Hilal al Jedda and the British state's frustration over their failure to deprive him of his citizenship because the action would render him stateless (Ross and Rudgard, 2014).

The new powers permit the state to remove British people's citizenship if the state believes it is conducive to the public good, or if a person's citizenship has been obtained through means of fraud, false representation or concealment of material fact (Home Office, 2016). The measures have drawn attention following anxieties over the rise of the number of British citizens who have travelled to the conflict in Syria. Most recently, the state's powers have come under scrutiny as the result of the case of Shamima Begum, the British schoolgirl who had journeyed to Syria with two school friends to join ISIS (Islamic State of Iraq and Syria). However, the powers have been criticised for their targeting of ethnic minorities, particularly Muslim people (Dearden, 2019). The British state has suggested the new powers are reactive, as well as acting as a deterrent to citizens wishing to travel abroad to join groups deemed to be terrorist organisations (Dearden, 2019). Yet what is relatively unknown is the exact number of people against whom the British state has used these powers.

A freedom of information request showed that between 2006 and 2015, 35 decisions were taken to remove the citizenship of people on the basis of this being conducive to the public good, while 45 decisions were taken to deprive people of citizenship because their citizenship was obtained by means of fraud, false representation or concealment of material fact (McGuiness and Gower, 2017). More recently, data published by Dearden (2019) highlighted that there had been a large increase of citizenship deprivation cases relating to decisions that were deemed conducive to the public good. Dearden (2019) suggested that cases had increased from 14 in 2006 to 104 in 2017, and explained that the 600% increase related to cases such as that of Shamima Begum, where the state had used the powers to target those it viewed as having been involved in terrorist activity.

Conclusion

Britain has a long history of migration, which has been shaped particularly by its history of empire and its relationship with Europe. The question of immigration continues to be highly contentious and is framed in ways which can have a particular impact on ethnic minority communities, whether or not they are citizens or migrants. The 2016 EU referendum provided an example of the ways in which immigration and border control are particularly politically contentious, despite arguments about the economic contribution of migration (Vargas-Silva, 2015). Since 2010, policies that have rested on targets for net immigration and the creation of a 'compliant' or unwelcoming environment, particularly for those migrants deemed 'uncontrolled' or undesirable, have particularly affected ethnic minority communities. In-house ID checking in housing and education, while representing an attempt to reduce immigration numbers, has permitted acts of discrimination and racism against BME groups, LGBTQ migrants and asylum seekers. Many of these practices and policies have targeted BME groups specifically – both directly and indirectly – producing state-permitted forms of discrimination, including with reference to certain culturally embedded traditions such as arranged marriages.

Britain has recently entered uncharted territory as the result of the electorate's vote for Brexit. For Britain, the uncertainty regarding its relationship with Europe and the rest of the world as well as its position on trade and immigration has opened up the following as yet unresolved questions that are important for immigration:

- What type of immigration status will be offered to long-term EU residents living in Britain and will there be a minimum threshold imposed for EU migrants who can apply for this status?

- How will the government balance its need for migrant labour versus its self-imposed targets to decrease net migration?
- What changes to immigration policy will be introduced after the ending of free movement of EU nationals to and from the UK?

While these questions are still yet to be answered, Britain's moves to restrict immigration, and its definitions of desired and undesired migration and the ways in which this is racialised, become more complex.

Note

[1] Accounts of this history can be found at: www.ourmigrationstory.org.uk/

3

Minority ethnic groups, policing and the criminal justice system in Britain

William Shankley and Patrick Williams

Key findings

- The majority of employees in the criminal justice system in England and Wales (93.4% of police officers; 93.2% of court judges; 89.6% of tribunal judges and 94% of prison officers) come from an ethnically White background.
- While the rates of stop-and-search have declined steadily across all ethnic groups between 2010/11 and 2016/17, Black groups continue to face the highest rates of stop-and-search by police, with the rate being eight times that of white people in 2016/17.
- Ethnic minority groups are increasingly and disproportionately represented in the youth criminal justice system population.
- Ethnic minority people are increasingly and disproportionately incarcerated (rising from 26% in 2008 to 45% in 2018).
- Policy and politicians' focus on 'the gang' leads to criminal justice practices against racialised communities without an evidence base. Joint Enterprise powers have also been used disproportionately against ethnic minority defendants.
- Stop-and-search powers continue to be used disproportionately against ethnic minority people.
- Data analysed by Inquest shows a disproportionate number of ethnic minority people in custody compared to white people.

Introduction[1]

The criminal justice system (CJS) is a core public service, which is divided into three separate systems in the United Kingdom with different powers and institutions for England and Wales, Scotland and Northern Ireland (Gov.uk, 2018c).

In England and Wales the CJS is comprised of the police, Crown Prosecution Service, prisons and probation work. It is the combination of over 300 different organisations and institutions working together to deliver criminal justice. The purpose of the CJS as a whole is 'to deliver justice for all, by convicting and punishing the guilty and helping them to stop offending while protecting the innocent' (Gov. uk, 2018e: 1). The CJS is responsible for detecting crime and bringing perpetrators to justice by carrying out the orders of, for example, the courts, to collect fines, supervise community and custodial punishment (Clinks, 2018). In England and Wales, the Ministry of Justice oversees the Magistrates Courts, the Crown Courts, the Legal Services Commission and Her Majesty's Prison and Probation Service (HMPPS). In comparison, the Home Office oversees the police and finally, the Attorney General's Office oversees the Crown Prosecution Service, the Serious Fraud Office, and other government lawyers with the authority to prosecute cases.

Scotland and Northern Ireland, meanwhile, have devolved powers that extend to their CJS. Law in Scotland and Northern Ireland is divided into two main categories: civil and criminal law. In Scotland, the Scottish government has executive responsibility for the Scottish legal system, with functions exercised by the Cabinet Secretary for Justice (MyGov.scot, 2018a). The Cabinet Secretary for Justice has political responsibility for policing, law enforcement and the courts of Scotland, as well as the Scottish Prison Service. The key institutions involved in the Scottish CJS include the police, the courts, Crown Office and Procurator Fiscal Service, as well as correctional institutions (prisons, for example). By comparison, Northern Ireland has its own judicial system, headed by the Lord Chief Justice of Northern Ireland. The Department of Justice is responsible for administering the courts (Northern Ireland Courts and Tribunal Service) and has responsibility, as well, for policy and legislation about criminal law, legal aid policy, the police, prisons and probation (NIdirect, 2019). The justice system is made up of a number of agencies that include the Police Service of Northern Ireland, the Probation Board for Northern Ireland and the Criminal Justice Inspection Northern Ireland.

There have long been recognised inequalities in the CJS in the employment of and treatment of ethnic minorities. The systematic and institutional racism which was highlighted by the Macpherson report in 1999 persists in the UK with ethnic minority people disproportionately represented in the CJS at every level, from stop-and-search to arrests, conviction and imprisonment and deaths in custody. The Lammy review published in September 2017 explored the over-representation of ethnic minorities in the prison population in England and Wales and raised particular concerns around the disproportional representation of ethnic minorities in the youth justice system – with 41% of youth prisoners being ethnic minorities in 2016. Public confidence in the CJS is critical, particularly as it represents a coercive arm of the state. Police data (ONS, 2017) for England and Wales find that, over the years 2014–17, fewer Black Caribbean (71%) and Mixed (70%) people had confidence in the police compared to White British (78%) and Asian (79%) people.

This chapter will examine the statistical evidence of ethnic minority experience in respect to the institutions of the CJS. The first section concentrates on ethnic minorities and their relationship with the police, including questions of police discrimination and the employment of ethnic minorities in the police force and CJS. The second section considers the use of measures such as joint enterprise and how they have been used disproportionately against ethnic minority defendants. The chapter examines evidence of a process of racialisation in the interface between ethnic minority people and institutions associated with the CJS. This is where certain crimes, for example, gangs and terrorism, are racialised and associated with black and Asian people more than other ethnic groups, leading to higher rates of surveillance, arrest and prosecution.

Policing and discrimination

The police forces in the UK, as branches of the state, have a duty to serve and protect the British public by enforcing the law (Cashmore, 2001). These organisations are also obliged to follow those same laws while at work. However, as Bowling et al (in El-Enany and Bruce-Jones, 2015: 7) have noted, 'police powers were exempted from the first three Race Relations Acts of 1965, 1968 and 1976'. Thus anti-discrimination laws have historically had no influence over how policing processes were carried out, leaving the police able to act with impunity and without challenge to their inadequate provision of service (for example, in failing to respond to ethnic minority victims of racist violence) or discrimination in their actions. An example of the implications of the lack of coverage of the police by anti-discrimination laws was the criminalisation of black youth through disproportionate uses of the stop-and-search powers by the police in the early 1980s. This culminated in national uprisings across the country (Solomos, 1988). The consistent misuse of these powers has regularly been found to have done significant damage to ethnic minority communities' relations with, and trust in, the police forces in Britain (Bowling and

Phillips, 2007). The stop-and-search policies have been cited as one of the central issues in the complaints that ethnic minority groups make about the police (Delsol and Shiner, 2006). These discriminatory practices have been found to 'drain trust' in the police and subsequently, the CJS more generally (Lammy, 2017: 17).

The year 2000 potentially signalled a significant turning point in these processes. Following the Stephen Lawrence inquiry, the 1999 Macpherson report, which documented the findings of the public inquiry, made clear that the Metropolitan Police's handling of Lawrence's murder was marred by institutional racism (Garner, 2017; and see Miller 2010). The findings stated that the Metropolitan Police force was unable to provide a satisfactory service to people 'because of their colour, culture or ethnic origin' (Bowling et al in El-Enany and Bruce-Jones, 2015: 9). Following the recommendations of the 1999 Macpherson report, to ensure that 'all bodies were *fully* compliant' with the Race Relations Acts of 1976 – including the police – an amendment to the law was made (Moore, 2011: 4). The new Race Relations (Amendment) Act 2000 meant that the police could be held accountable for acts of racial discrimination. Nonetheless, the disproportionate targeting of ethnic minority people under stop-and-search laws continues to be a point of contention as will be discussed later in this chapter.

One of the recommendations from the 1999 Macpherson report was to examine the representation of ethnic minority people, particularly Black Britons, in the police force. Historically, the police force, alongside other institutions within the CJS, has been a racially white institution with an over-representation of white officers (Cashmore, 2001; Johnston, 2006). While the employment of a more diverse police force alone is unlikely to change the processes of institutional racism within the CJS, the under-representation of ethnic minority police remains a concern.

Figure 3.1 shows that, despite some increases in ethnic minority police, the majority of the police force in England and Wales remains composed of ethnically White British (93.4%) police officers. This figure exceeds the White British group's share of the total population (86.9%). Meanwhile, all ethnic minority groups (Asian, Black, Mixed, Other) remain under-represented in the police forces of England and Wales compared to their share of the population. Furthermore, in the CJS, data from 2018 show that 6.8% of court judges and 10.6% of tribunal judges were from an ethnic minority background, statistics far below their 14% share of the total population (Courts and Tribunal Judiciary, 2018). Examining

Figure 3.1: The ethnicity of police officers in the police force in England and Wales, 2017

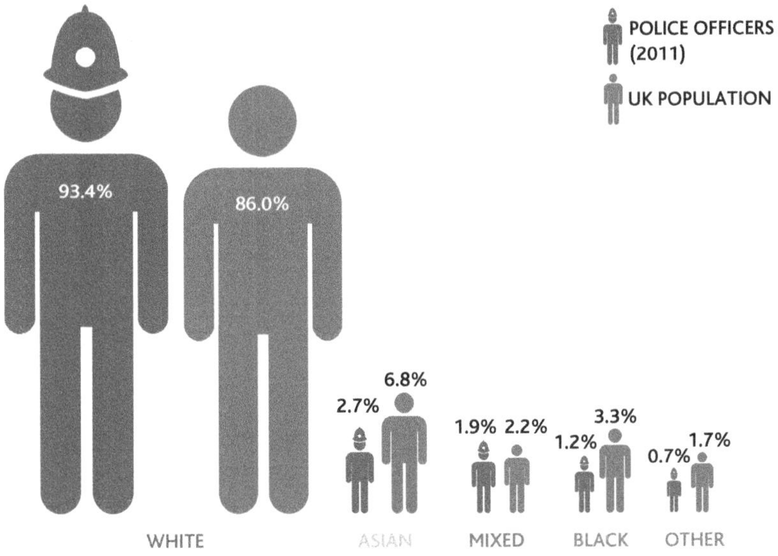

Source: Home Office (2018b).

the legal profession (where the ethnicity was known) white judges made up the highest percentage of both court and tribunal judges (93.2% and 89.4%). Meanwhile, judges from an Asian background made up the second highest percentage of court judges (3.1% of court and 4.8% of tribunal judges). Nevertheless, these statistics still represented an under-representation of their employment in these roles in the CJS compared to the pan-Asian group's share of the population (6.8%). Moreover, the data also show that 16.7% of non-legal tribunal members came from an ethnic minority background, which indicated an increase of approximately 0.4 percentage points since 2017 (Courts and Tribunal Judiciary, 2018).

Furthermore, among prison officers the 2018 data show that just over 94% of prison officers in England and Wales (where the ethnicity was known) came from an ethnic White background. Such statistics suggest an over-representation of the White group in relation to its share of the total population (86%). Comparing the demography of prison officers between 2015 and 2018, the percentage of prison officers from a Black ethnic background increased, from 2.3% to 2.7%. Equivalent data are not available to make a comparative analysis on the ethnic composition of the workforce across the police, court and tribunal judges, and prison officers in Scotland and Northern Ireland.

Stop-and-search

A further recommendation of the Stephen Lawrence inquiry addressed ethnic disparities in the police's utilisation of stop-and-search powers (Miller, 2010; Delsol and Shiner, 2006). The recommendations resulted in reforms to stop-and-search powers, some of which included: the requirement of the police to record the self-defined ethnicity of those they stopped, reasons for the search, outcomes of the encounter, and that a copy of these records that should be given to the person in question (Miller, 2010: 957). There are different stop-and-search powers available to the police to stop people, for example, section 60 of the Criminal Justice and Public Order Act 1994 gives police the right:

> to search people in a defined area during a specific time period when they believe, with good reason, that: serious violence will take place and it is necessary to use this power to prevent such violence; or that a person is carrying a dangerous object or offensive weapon; or that an incident involving serious violence has taken place and a dangerous instrument or offensive weapon used in the incident is being carried in the locality. (Metropolitan Police, 2017: 1)

S60 stop-and-search powers differ from the other powers because they can only be used if a decision is made by a senior police officer (Metropolitan Police Information, 2017).

Generally, the overall rates of 'stop-and-search' (those made under section 1 PACE [Police and Criminal Evidence Act 1984] and section 60 of the Criminal Justice and Public Order Act 1994) have declined at a steady rate across all ethnic groups, including (Figure 3.2), over the period 2010/11 to 2016/17. The fall in the rate of 'stop-and-search' has been most acute for Black ethnic groups. In 2010/11, there were 112 searches for every 1,000 black people; in 2016/17 that fell to 29 searches for every 1,000 black people. However despite these reductions, a disproportionality remains.

The most up-to-date data (2017/18) show that, despite the overall decline in the rates of stop-and-search for all ethnic groups, the rate for the Black ethnic minority groups, in particular, have remained higher than for other ethnic groups and the White majority ethnic groups. Shiner et al (2018: 13) noted that black people were stopped and searched 'more than eight times the rate of white people in 2016/17'. The RDA (Race Disparity Audit) (2018) added that in 2017/18,

Figure 3.2: Rates of stop-and-search per 1,000 members of the population by ethnic group, England and Wales, 2010/11 to 2017/18

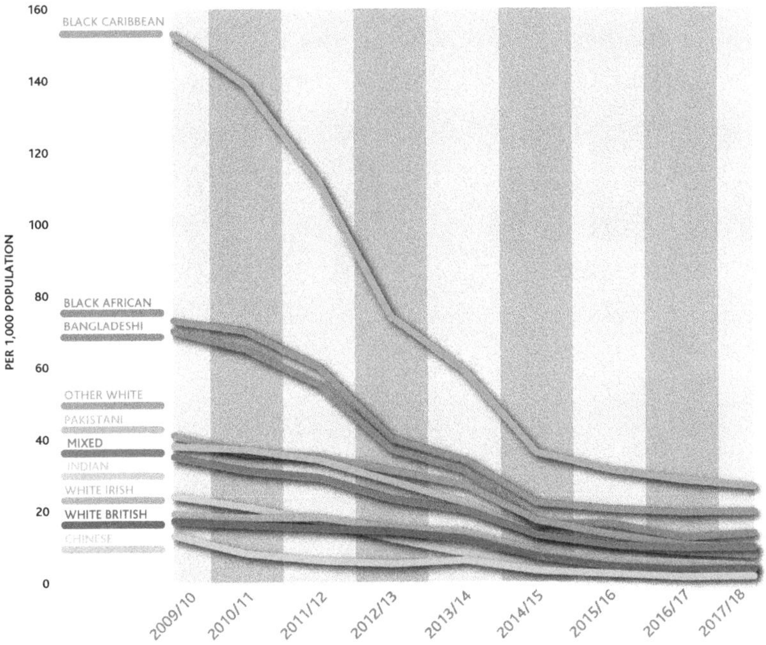

Notes: Includes searches under section 1 of PACE and section 60 of the Criminal Justice and Public Order Act 1994.
Source: Table SS_13 in 'Stop-and-search statistics data tables: police powers and procedures year ending 31 March 2017'. For access to data/tables see: www.gov.uk/government/statistics/police-powers-and-procedures-england-and-wales-year-ending-31-march-2017

for example, there were 3 stop-and-searches recorded for every 1,000 white people, compared with 29 stop-and-searches for every 1,000 black people (Figure 3.2). Thus ethnic disparities in stop-and-search continue, despite recommendations and amendments to the law. The 2017/18 data also show that there is a high stop-and-search rate among the White Other group. This high rate among the White Other groups relates to the criminalising of homelessness among central and Eastern European migrants in particular, a violation of the EU free movement rights (Pronczuk, 2018).

Area

While the disproportionality is clear in the national stop-and-search data, different patterns emerge when the data are analysed between different police forces. The data show high rates of stop-and-search among black people occurred across all police forces where data were

Figure 3.3: Top five areas for stop-and-search (per 1,000) by ethnic group

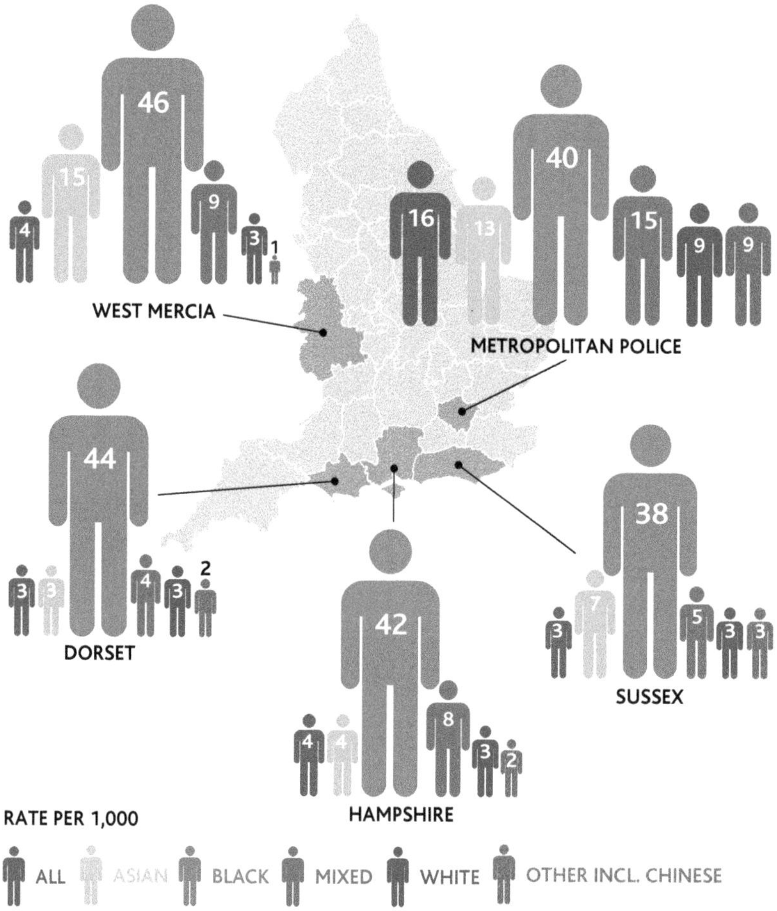

WEST MERCIA

METROPOLITAN POLICE

DORSET

SUSSEX

HAMPSHIRE

RATE PER 1,000

ALL ASIAN BLACK MIXED WHITE OTHER INCL. CHINESE

Source: Home Office (2018c).

available. In 2017/18, the biggest difference in stop–and–search rates between black and white people was in Dorset, where black people were 17 times more likely to be stopped and searched than white people (Shiner et al, 2018). The rate of black stop-and-searches was also high in the West Mercia area, where black people were 15 times more likely to be stopped and searched than white people. Finally, the Metropolitan Police force in London had the highest overall rate of stop-and-search, at 16 incidents for every 1,000 people (Home Office, 2018; Shiner et al, 2018). Similar data have not been collected across police forces in Scotland or Northern Ireland to reflect ethnic disparities within specific areas.

Figure 3.4: People aged 16 years and over who said they were victims of crime, by ethnic group over time

Source: Crime Survey for England and Wales, year ending March 2018 (ONS, 2018).

Victims of crime

There is a dearth of evidence on ethnic minorities as the victims of crime in the UK. Figure 3.4 suggests that people from the Mixed White/Asian and Mixed Other ethnic groups were the most likely to say they were the victims of crime (at 29% and 26% respectively). The percentage of White British groups who said they were victims of crime fell from 17% to 14% between 2013/14 and 2017/18 and is the lowest of all groups, apart from the White Irish. No other ethnic group experienced a significant change during the same period. No similar information has been collected for Scotland or Northern Ireland to undertake a similar analysis of ethnic minorities' experience of being the victim of crime.

Furthermore, Figure 3.5 shows that white men were more likely than white women to say they were victims of crime in the previous

Figure 3.5: Percentage of people aged 16 years and over who said they were victims of crime, by ethnicity and gender

MIXED — 27% / 24%

ASIAN — 17% / 18%

BLACK — 18% / 18%

WHITE — 16% / 15%

OTHER — 14% / 16%

Source: Crime Survey for England and Wales, year ending March 2018 (ONS, 2018).

12 months, with 16% and 15% respectively. While Figure 3.5 suggests some differences between men and women in the Mixed, Black, Asian and Other groups, unlike the White group, the sample for these groups is small and any generalisations based on the figures are unreliable.

Terrorism-related policing

The issue of domestic-related terrorism has had an increasingly high profile in media, politics and law in the last 25 years with the introduction of significant counter-terrorism policing methods and new laws. These have included the Terrorism Act 2000 (Choudhury and Fenwick, 2011; Anderson, 2012; Ip, 2013) used as a primary counterterrorism tool (Quinlan in El-Enany and Bruce-Jones, 2015: 16). The act has expanded police powers to stop, search, question, detain and arrest individuals suspected of engaging or planning to engage in terrorism-related activities (Quinlan in El-Enany and Bruce-Jones, 2015: 16). These expanded powers, particularly section 44 of the Terrorism Act 2000, have been particularly damaging to police–community relations. Section 44 gave the police the remit to stop and search people in order to look for 'articles' which might be used to carry out a terrorist attack. However, they were not required to satisfy the 'reasonable suspicion' provision to question potential suspects (Choudhury and Fenwick, 2011). Section 44, before its repeal, had a 'disproportionate impact on Asian ethnic minorities' (Parmar, 2011: 370). The stops made with this power were shown to produce low rates of terrorist arrests (Parmar, 2011), which was indicative of its ineffectiveness in actually preventing terrorist activity. For example, from the year 2000/01 to 2008/09, out of the 542,400 stops that were made under section 44, just 283 resulted in arrests for terrorism (0.05%) and none resulted in convictions (Choudhury and Fenwick, 2011: 31). Heavy criticism of section 44 and its misuse, including a ruling of the European Court of Human Rights declaring it to be a violation of human rights, eventually led to its repeal (Choudhury and Fenwick, 2011; Quinlan in El-Enany and Bruce-Jones, 2015).

The Metropolitan Police was observed to be the force which utilised section 44 most extensively before its repeal in 2011 (Choudhury and Fenwick, 2011: 32). In the year ending 2011, the Asian group made up 34% of all stop-and-searches. However, following policy changes and the increase of stop-and-searches under section 60 of the Criminal Justice and Public Order Act, the number of stops of Asian people gradually fell to 24% in 2014 (Figure 3.6). Figure 3.6 shows the stop-and-searches of persons made by the Metropolitan Police under section 43 of the Terrorism Act 2000 by self-defined ethnicity between 2011 and 2017. It is possible that this fall in the proportion of stops of people defining themselves as Asian may have been a temporary police reaction to the major concerns raised over the force's racial profiling tactics under section 44 of Asian ethnic minorities (Parmar, 2011; Choudhury and Fenwick, 2011), although this is not easy to decipher from the data.

Worryingly, the data show the percentage of arrests of the pan-Asian group since 11 September 2001 is far higher than for other ethnic groups. Related 2017 data show that 46% of the arrests made of the pan-Asian group resulted in a subsequent charge and a high percentage resulted in a conviction (50%). Yet, Figure 3.6 shows that other ethnic groups (White, Black, Other) have experienced low proportions of arrests and even fewer have resulted in convictions. As Choudhury and Fenwick (2011: 74) importantly note, the information required by the police to decide whether or not to make an arrest for terrorism-related offences is qualitatively different to the 'admissible evidence' needed in court that can lead to subsequent convictions. This perhaps helps to explain the

Figure 3.6: Percentage of arrests for terrorism-related offences between 2001 and 2017, by ethnic group

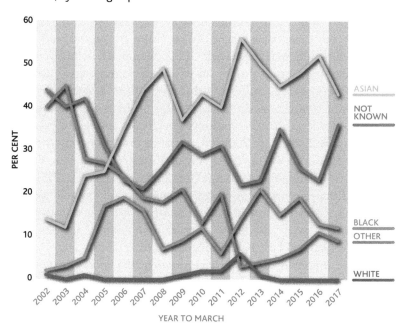

Source: Table A.11 – 'Statistics on the operation of police powers under the Terrorism Act in England and Wales 2000 and subsequent legislation'.

strikingly low number of convictions following arrest in the data since September 2001 (695 convictions out of 3,753 arrests, or 19%).

The link between these incidents and the data in Figure 3.6 is at best an extremely tentative one. Nevertheless, the wider point here is to shift the conversation away from the often-heard debate about 'Islamic extremism' in the post-September 2001 climate to prompt questions about the form and consistency of contemporary extremism(s) in Britain and how government, policing and the wider CJS might respond to it in future.

Young people in the youth justice system (under-18s)

The Lammy review (2017: 4) noted that its 'biggest concern is with the youth justice system', despite claims that it is 'regarded as one of the success stories of the criminal justice system' because of the overall reduced rates of offending, re-offending and custody. These positive representations do not translate directly to ethnic minority youth experiences in the youth justice system, as is seen later in this chapter. The current youth cohort also represents an important indicator of the future make-up of adult offender populations and the continued intergenerational damage that can be done to families who endure encounters with the police, the CJS and the youth justice system in Britain. Ethnic minorities in Youth Offender Institutions constitute 44% of the population who are incarcerated. As such, they present 'an ever-ready cohort to transition to the adult estate when they become 21 years of age' (Williams and Clarke, 2018).

Data show two patterns among young people who receive cautions in the youth justice system when their ethnicity is taken into consideration. First, the rate of cautions of white young people has declined from 89.7% of all cautions in 2005/06 to 82.8% in 2017/18 (Figure 3.7). Second, the proportion of cautions of ethnic minority youths has increased; for example, the percentage of black young people cautioned has increased from 5.9% of all young people cautioned in 2005/06 to 11.4% in 2017/18. Furthermore, the percentage of Asian young people cautioned has increased from 3.6% of all young people cautioned in 2005/06 to 4.9% in 2017/18. Finally, the percentage of Other ethnic group has increased from 0.8% of all young people cautioned in 2005/06 to 0.9% in 2017/18. Thus the current ethnic minority youth cohort is experienced a worsening situation over time.

Figure 3.7: Percentage of youth cautions by ethnic group, England and Wales, 2005/06–2017/18

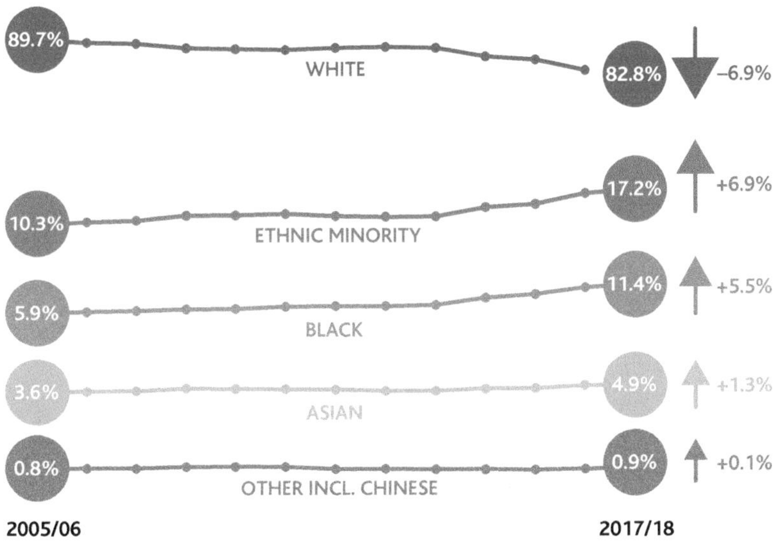

Source: Race Disparity Audit (Gov.uk, 2017).

The Youth Justice Board (2018) published a report on young people and children in the youth CJS and suggested the average custodial sentence length for indictable offences given to children has increased by five months over the last ten years, from 11.4 to 16.7 months (Youth Justice Board, 2018). Moreover, at any one time over the past year (2018) an average of just below 900 children were in custody and, even though overall the pattern indicates there has been an average fall of 70% over the last ten years, the pattern has slightly increased by 3% over the past year. The report also suggests that children in custody were largely incarcerated because of crimes categorised as violence against the person, and such crimes had increased (compared to other crimes) over the past year (Youth Justice Board, 2018).

As Williams and Clarke (2018) suggested, the ethnic make-up of the youth criminal justice population is indicative of the future ethnic demographics of the adult incarcerated population. This ethnic make-up is shifting, with fewer white children and more ethnic minority children in incarceration. As Figure 3.8 shows, the percentage of incarcerated white children fell from 74% in 2008 to 55% in 2018. By comparison, the rates of children in youth custody from a black background increased, from 15% in 2008 to 25% in 2018. Children from a black background now account for a quarter of the youth custody population in 2018

Figure 3.8: Percentage of children in custody by ethnicity, youth secure estate in England and Wales, year ends March 2008–2018

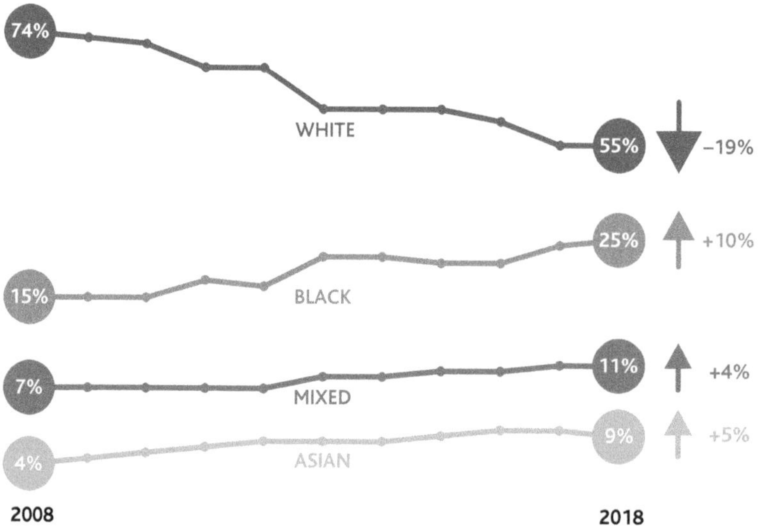

WHITE
74% ... 55% ▼ −19%

25% ▲ +10%
15% ... BLACK

11% ▲ +4%
7% ... MIXED

9% ▲ +5%
4% ... ASIAN

2008   2018

Source: Youth Justice Statistics: 2017 to 2018 (Home Office, 2018d).

(Youth Justice Board, 2018). The data also show an increase in the percentage of Asian and Other/Mixed groups in the youth CJS, although not as pronounced as for the Black ethnic group (Figure 3.8), whose school-age population (under-18) amounted to a 4.6% share of the total school-age population and indicated their large over-representation.

Ethnic minorities and custody

The data show that the percentage of people by ethnicity in custody in England and Wales has remained relatively constant between 2009 and 2017 across all groups (Figure 3.9). No similar data have been made available for ethnic minorities in custody in Scotland or Northern Ireland. Figure 3.9 suggests the percentage of people in custody across the White and Asian ethnic groups rose slightly between 2009 and 2016, with 78% in 2009 to 79% in 2017 for White groups; 6% in 2009 to 7% in 2017 for the Asian group. The results show the under-representation of the White group's share of the population (85.1%) compared to an under-representation of the Asian group's share of the population (0.8% Bangladeshi, 3% Indian, 2% Pakistani and 1.7% Asian Other). The percentage of people in custody for the Black and Mixed group remained constant between 2009 and 2017, with 3% in 2009

Figure 3.9: Percentage of adults in custody in England and Wales by their ethnicity over time, between 2009 and 2017

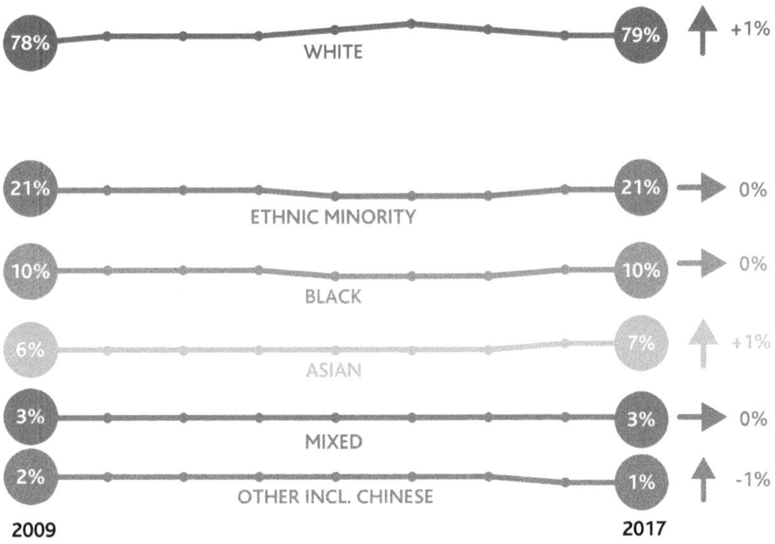

Source: Race Disparity Audit (Gov.uk, 2017b).

to 3% in 2017 for the Mixed group and 10% in 2009 to 10% in 2017 for the Black group; an over-representation of Black groups compared to their share of the population of England and Wales (3.6%). Finally, the Other including Chinese group decreased from 2% in 2009 to 1% in 2017, a finding slightly higher than their cumulative share of the population (Chinese as 0.9% and other 0.7%). While the ethnic make-up of people in custody has changed very little in the past ten years, there has been a lot of debate about the number of ethnic minorities compared to white people who have died in custody as is discussed in the next section.

Deaths in custody

In Britain, institutional racism and police violence has been a keenly debated topic in particular since the Macpherson report in 1999 (Bruce-Jones, 2015). According to statistics by Inquest (2018) a disproportionate number of people from an ethnic minority background have died as the result of constraint in police custody; since 1990, they number 151 out of 1,713 or 10%. Inquest's statistics, covering the period 2002–12, are even more striking: of 380 deaths in police custody in England and Wales (or as a result of contact with the police), 69 were from ethnic minority communities – 18%. Of the 509 cases of ethnic minority deaths in custody in suspicious circumstances that the Institute of Race Relations analysed from its database of cases between 1991 and 2014, the majority, 348, took place in prison, 137 in police custody and 24 in immigration detention (cited in El-Enany and Bruce-Jones, 2015: 4). Furthermore, one in three of the official classification of deaths was as a result of self-harm, and in 64 cases the person was known to have mental health problems. Medical neglect was a contributory factor in 49 cases, and in 48 the use of force appears to have contributed to a person's death (for a broader discussion on ethnic inequalities and health; see Chapter 4).

The racialisation and criminalisation of ethnic minority groups

One mechanism for the criminalisation of Black, Mixed, Asian and other minority ethnic communities is the notion and utilisation of the racialised term 'gang' (Williams and Clarke, 2018). The concept of the gang and its relationship to ethnic minority groups, particularly blackness, has an extensive history in Britain (Gilroy, 1987a; Keith, 1993). Williams and Clarke (2018) have argued that the more recent focus by policymakers and politicians on the gang has resurfaced after the social unrest in England in the summer of 2011. Labelling the social unrest as a product of an endemic gang problem in the country led to a flurry of anxieties where 'the media, politicians, think tanks and academics were quick to evoke the already established view of the gang problem' (p.7). While the government acknowledged there were some inherent problems with these racialised assumptions informing their approach to crime, this did not stop various policies and programmes being rolled out to target gangs as the site of serious criminality, for example, the Home Office's programme Ending Gangs and Youth Violence (EGYV). However, despite the dominance of the racialised gang narrative, in their analysis of policing in Manchester, Williams and Clarke (2016) found that white people overwhelmingly committed the largest proportion of police-defined incidents of serious youth violence (76% of the sample). Meanwhile ethnic minority 'people, and in particular young black men, were more likely to be identified as gang involved', with 89% of those registered as 'gang nominal'. Katz and Jackson-Jacobs (2004) add that in over a century of scholarly work there has yet to be any reliable evidence that links gangs with violent crime. Therefore, we have to ask the broader question: why has the government continued to pursue policies that target gang violence when it lacks any conclusive evidence to suggest the gang should continue to be a focus of their crime policy? A more recent example of the way the term 'gang' has been evoked in policy is how the notion has been attached to multiple crimes such as modern–day slavery, child sexual exploitation and crimes related to drugs and the county lines, and to knife crime. These are presented as racialised crimes and associated with gangs despite the lack of an evidence base to support this.

County lines, knife crime and racialisation

According to Quinn (2019), there has been a 152% increase in knife crimes in Kent between April 2010 and September 2018, with similar increases in knife crimes in Hertfordshire (89%), Staffordshire (88% increase) and Essex (44% increase). Reporting on the rise in knife crime in the Home Countries is regularly explained using the county lines framework that explains how violent crime travels in a similar way to drugs. This is supported by Assistant Chief Constable Nick Downing (head of the serious crime directorate for Kent and Essex police) suggesting 'we don't have a gang issue in Kent. What we do have is a drug issue from county lines coming in and we need to combat that' (Quinn, 2019: 1). However, this explanation serves to maintain the racialisation of this kind of crime, detaching the factors that contribute to violent crime from the Home Counties. Whittaker and Densley (2019) explain that poverty is the key reason why many young people in these areas participate in crime that stretches from the urban centres such as London. This has been amplified by the broader effects of austerity, which have reduced youth centres and the funding for youth activities.

Joint enterprise, racialisation and custodial sentences

The proportion of people of different ethnicities prosecuted and then convicted of a crime provides one measure of ethnic inequalities in convictions administered by the justice system. Figure 3.10 shows that between 2009 and 2017 there has been an increase in the

Figure 3.10: Conviction ratios of offenders in England and Wales by ethnicity, between 2009 and 2017

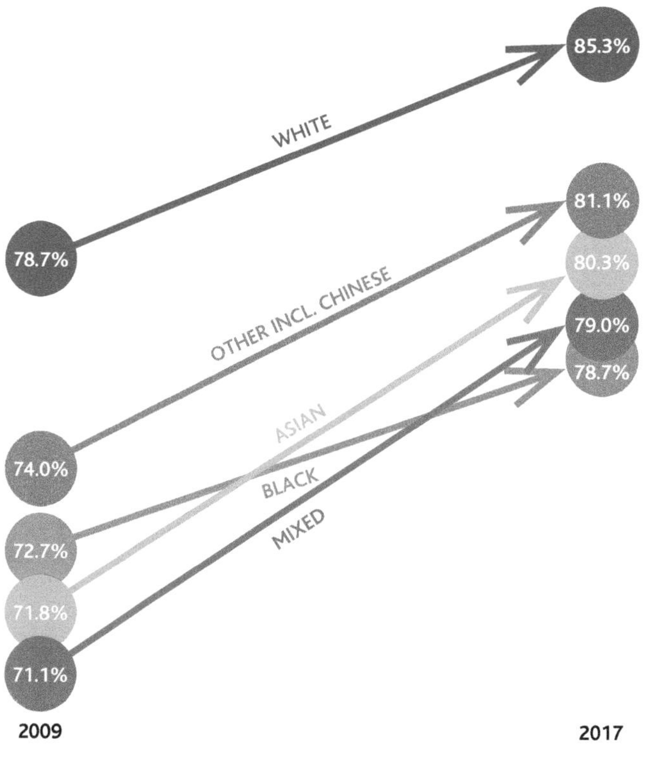

Source: Courts and Tribunal Judiciary (2018).

conviction ratio across all ethnic groups. In 2017, the data show that White offenders had the highest conviction ratio at 85.3%; whereas black offenders had the lowest conviction ratio at 78.7% in 2017. While there seems meagre ethnic disparity with respect to the conviction ratios across ethnic minority groups, practices undertaken by prosecutors in the judicial system highlight ethnic disparities in prosecution processes.

Joint enterprise (JE) 'is a doctrine in common law which has been developed by the courts in cases where more than one person is to be prosecuted for the same offence' (Williams and Clarke, 2018: 5). The doctrine is used as a 'collective punishment of groups where suspects may have played different roles, and in many cases, where a suspect was not in the proximity of the offence committed' (Williams and Clarke, 2018: 7). The reason JE has emerged as such a controversial apparatus used by the CJS is because its interpretation of the 'common purpose' provision, where this has been used to make a case for prosecution against all participants when a crime, for example, murder has been committed by only one member of the group. This is the case even if members of the group did not participate in or intend to commit that crime, depending on how the prosecution defines the group. Taken together with the racialisation of certain criminal labels such as the gang, the use of JE can go some way to explain why there is a disproportionality in the number of ethnic minority people serving custodial sentences compared to White people. The Cambridge Submission (cited in Williams and Clarke, 2018) found that the proportion of Black/Black British people serving custodial sentences on the basis of JE offences was 11 times higher than their share of the general population (37% compared to 3.3%). This suggests that JE powers are used disproportionately against black people.

Conclusion

The CJS is an expansive body of the state whose work seeks justice, from the initial stages of the police force and stop-and-search policies to various court processes that impose custodial sentences on those indicted and finally the probation service that attempts to support offenders back into the community and reduce re-offending (recidivism). However, this chapter has shown that ethnic minorities face multiple challenges at various stages of the CJS. The chapter finds that policies, such as stop-and-search, that have grown out of anxieties over terrorism and other forms of violent crime, are disproportionately used against ethnic minority communities rather than White British people. While such policies are historically situated, the contemporary racialisation of specific types of crime has led to stop-and-search being applied unevenly across ethnic groups and that, even though in many instances police action has been reviewed and found guilty of systemic and institutional racism and discrimination against ethnic minorities, there remains a disproportionate wielding of this power by the police force in Britain.

Inquiries such as that into the murder of Stephen Lawrence have shed light on the institutional racism inherent in the Metropolitan Police and their handling and dealing with ethnic minorities who are victims of crimes. That inquiry also draws attention to the lack of diversity within police forces up and down the country. This chapter shows that the police remain dominated by White British police officers and, while recruitment practices that stem from inquiries such as the one linked to the Stephen Lawrence case have increased the number of ethnic minority police officers, police data from 2016/17 show that ethnic minorities still constitute proportions of the police force that are less than their share of the total population (Gov.uk, 2018d).

While there has been an increase in terrorist-related attacks across the UK and mainland Europe, the chapter has found that police forces have excessively and disproportionately used the 'stop-and-search' powers particularly against non-White minorities. It is concerning that a high proportion of arrests using stop-and-search have resulted in relatively minor conviction rates for all groups apart from the pan-Asian group. This suggests that the racialisation, particularly of Asian minorities by the police, and their presumed links to terrorism, have led to policies such as stop-and-search amplifying racial undertones towards minority communities. The arena bombing in Manchester and attacks across London and mainland Europe have contributed to the escalation of anxieties about terrorism, with the public urging the government and police to do more. However, the problem is that these events have come during a heightened period of austerity cuts to the police force and other public institutions that have reduced the numbers of officers available for community policing. It seems that cuts in this environment could open up the risk of ethnic minorities becoming increasingly racially profiled with the heightened use of the stop-and-search policy. Another issue is there appears less anxiety regarding White terror or far-right ideology, which seems surprising, particularly given the murder of the MP for Batley and Spen, Jo Cox, in June 2016.

The chapter also found a worrying link between the narratives on gangs and the way that ethnic minorities, mainly black people, are treated in the CJS. A collection of high-profile cases has led to the prosecution being successful in convicting black defendants under the common law of joint enterprise. This approach has led to some ethnic minority people who have been accused of a crime being convicted because the legal cases have framed them using the gang label, and this has consequently led to custodial sentences. The problem is that the term 'gang' is regularly applied to ethnic minorities, more specifically black defendants than White British defendants, which shows the racialisation of the term 'gang' and how it has been encapsulated in the CJS and has led to extensive custodial sentences.

The chapter calls for more work to be done to uncover precisely what mechanisms contribute to ethnic minority people and households being more likely to be the victims of crime, as there is a tendency within the research in the UK to focus on policing, and ethnic minorities as the defendants and accused, rather than the victims of crime.

Note
[1]   With thanks to Karis Campion for initial research on this chapter.

4

Health inequalities

Karen Chouhan and James Nazroo

Key findings

- Ethnic inequalities in health outcomes, experiences of health care and employment in the NHS workforce are substantial and, in the main, have not changed over time.
- Ethnic minority people have an increased risk of poor health compared with white people, but there is considerable variation in this across groups and across particular health conditions.
- There is a substantial body of evidence demonstrating that the multidimensional social and economic inequalities experienced by ethnic minority people, including racism, make a substantial contribution to ethnic inequalities in health.
- Despite the evidence on these inequalities, the issue of ethnicity has taken a marginal position in policy work on inequalities in health, with some significant pieces of policy work almost completely neglecting ethnic inequalities in health, in part because they are often reified as reflecting biological and cultural difference. A reorientation of the public health focus to one that considers the social character of ethnicity, and the socially and economically determined nature of health, could help the development of meaningful policy in this area.
- Evidence suggests that the provision, through the NHS, of publicly funded primary care with universal access and standardised treatment protocols has resulted in equality of access and outcomes across ethnic groups.
- However, there are inequalities in access to secondary health care and dental care, and in satisfaction with care received.
- Ethnic minority people report less good experiences than White British people of almost every dimension of General Practice services. And ethnic minority people who had been diagnosed with a cancer saw their General Practitioner several more times than White British people before they were referred to a hospital.
- Stereotyping, discrimination, racism and cultural incompetence have been identified in the delivery of care across the health service.

This is illustrated in the chapter using evidence in relation to severe mental illness, interpreting services and sickle cell and thalassaemia disorders.

- Ethnic minority people are over-represented in the NHS workforce, but experience marked inequalities in type and grade of employment. This is reflected in pay bands, representation among senior staff and representation on NHS Trust boards.
- Only 7% of NHS Trust board members across England are from an ethnic minority group and more than two fifths of NHS Trusts have no ethnic minority board members.

Introduction

The relationship between ethnicity and health has received intermittent focus in work concerned with ethnic inequalities. However, a close examination of issues related to health is particularly useful for three reasons. First, it is here that we can see how broader social and economic inequalities translate into profound outcomes for ethnic minority people; and also how policy and practice typically translate the two deeply social phenomena of ethnicity and health into essentialised constructs that are typically reduced to biology. Second, by examining the ways in which health and social care are provided, and the outcomes of that care, we can explore how an institution that is central to our lives serves to address, or amplify, broader racialised social structures. Third, the provision of health and social care services continues to rely heavily on the labour of ethnic minority and migrant people, therefore an examination of the experiences and outcomes for ethnic minority employees in the NHS sheds light on the broader context of ethnic inequalities in the labour market. In this context, it is worth noting that a mix of racialised discourses have: framed 'migrants' as intruders and a drain on the NHS; located the prevalence of certain diseases in cultural norms; and positioned ethnic minority health care staff as 'fillers' and as less competent and desirable than White British workers.

Regrettably these discourses have had a surprising persistence and have been promoted in political and popular arenas. In 1948, those arriving on the *Windrush* to help rebuild after the Second World War and fill the gaps in health and transport were subject to explicit crude and violent racism and this hostility was not limited to personal prejudices.

> Migrants arriving in the first wave of mass migration endured verbal and physical abuse both within and outside the workplace. White trade unionists resisted the employment of migrants and imposed a quota system. Within the NHS, concern that importing overseas workers was likely to create tensions was recognised in a 1949 Home Office memo: 'It has been found that the susceptibilities of patients tended to set an upper limit on the proportion of coloured workers who could be employed either as nurses or domiciliaries.' (Jones and Snow, 2011)

This too colloquial approach to ethnic minority people – wanting them to work where 'natives' wouldn't or couldn't, and not wanting so many living and working in Britain – was perhaps best exemplified by Enoch Powell who, in 1963, as the Conservative Health Minister, launched a campaign to recruit trained doctors from overseas to fill the labour shortages in the NHS.

> 18,000 doctors were recruited from India and Pakistan. Powell praised these doctors, who he [Powell] said, 'provide a useful and substantial reinforcement of the staffing of our hospitals and who are an advertisement to the world of British medicine and British hospitals.' (Jones and Snow, 2011)

Five years later Powell gave his infamous 'rivers of blood' speech, in which he not only proposed stopping immigration but further proposed that there should be re-emigration. The content and tone of the speech was overtly racist, referring to wide-grinning piccaninnies and Negroes as offensive and noisy, and White people as being strangers in their own country who were unable to get access to hospital beds. In contemporary Britain, at the same time as the NHS is recruiting overseas and ruing the staff shortages caused by Brexit, we are once again being presented with hypocritical arguments about 'migrants' being a drain on the NHS. Importantly, as argued later in this chapter, this hostility and consequent social and economic disadvantage directly harms the health of ethnic minority people. In this context, it is valuable to consider how much things have changed since the 1960s and how legislative and policy frameworks have, or have not, addressed ethnic inequalities in relation to health.

Ethnic inequalities in health

Over the last few decades, following the 1997 Independent Inquiry into Inequalities in Health (chaired by Sir Donald Acheson), there have been numerous policy initiatives around inequalities in health, with the Department of Health's Strategic Review of Health Inequalities in England post-2010 (chaired by Sir Michael Marmot) being the most recent example. Given the range of these activities, it is perhaps surprising, to see that the issue of ethnicity has taken a marginal and somewhat contested position in this policy work, indeed the Marmot review (Marmot, 2010) almost completely neglected this issue. This marginalisation and neglect almost certainly reflects two contrasting viewpoints: that ethnicity somehow reflects exceptional genetic or cultural factors that drive differences in health experience; or that ethnic differences are simple reflections of class inequalities that are adequately captured by general discussions of socio-economic inequalities in health.

Nevertheless, differences in health across ethnic groups have been repeatedly documented in the UK (Marmot et al, 1984; Rudat, 1994; Nazroo, 2001a; Erens et al, 2001). In broad terms, a general measure of self-reported general health has shown ethnic minority groups to have an increased risk of poor health compared with the White groups, but considerable variation in this across groups. This is illustrated in Figure 4.1, which uses data from the 1999 Health Survey for England, and shows that Bangladeshi people have a more than three times higher risk of saying that their health is fair or bad rather than good, with a figure of more than two times higher for Pakistani people and almost two times higher for Indian and Black Caribbean people (Erens et al, 2001). Figure 4.2 disaggregates this comparison by age and shows that ethnic differences in health emerge from early adulthood and increase dramatically with increasing age. This means that the level of reporting fair or bad health, rather than good health, for White English people aged 61–70 is equivalent to that of Caribbean and Indian people aged 46–50, Pakistani people aged 36–40 and Bangladeshi people aged 26–30.

However, the extent of the difference in health varies across health conditions as well as across ethnic groups. In more detail, morbidity and mortality data have identified the following kinds of differences in health across ethnic groups (in comparison to White British groups):

- higher, but variable, rates of diabetes across all non-White groups;
- higher rates of heart disease among 'South Asian' people, but particularly among Bangladeshi and Pakistani people;

Figure 4.1: Age-adjusted odds ratio to report fair or bad health compared with White English people

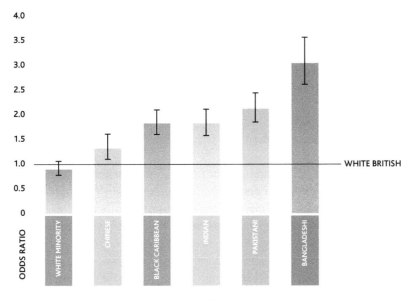

Source: 1999 Health Survey for England (Erens et al, 2001).

Figure 4.2: Reported fair or bad health by ethnic group and age

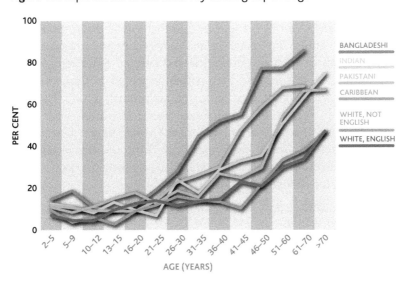

Source: 1999 Health Survey for England (Erens et al, 2001).

- higher rates of hypertension and stroke among Caribbean and African people;
- higher rates of admission to psychiatric hospitals with a diagnosis of psychotic illness for Black Caribbean and Black African people;
- higher rates of suicide among young women born in South Asia, or, more particularly, born in India;
- higher rates of sexually transmitted illnesses among Black Caribbean people; and
- higher rates of congenital abnormality and childhood disability among Muslim children.

Unfortunately, such findings and the analyses that underlie them do no more than provide a description of differences in health, but their complexity and specificity makes it tempting to read explanations from the ethnic categories used to characterise populations. For example, it is easy to speculate on what it is to be South Asian that might lead to a greater risk of heart disease (genetics, diet, and other health behaviours?) or what it might be about Caribbean families and cultures that lead to the high risk among young people of psychotic illness or sexually transmitted illness. Or how marriage patterns might lead to high rates of congenital disease in Muslim children. Given the ease with which explanations can be based on such stereotypes of racial difference/boundaries and cultural practices, it is not surprising that this is the direction that public health policy has moved in – ethnic differences in health are easily understood to be a consequence of supposed biological and cultural differences, which are reified, generalised and personalised across all of those who are seen to be members of a particular ethnic minority group. But such explanations, which are based on racialised identities, have rarely been tested. In fact, a reorientation of the public health focus to one that considers the social character of ethnicity, and the socially and economically determined nature of health, could help the development of meaningful policy in this area.

In fact, there is now considerable evidence that the social and economic inequalities faced by ethnic minority people make a substantial contribution to ethnic inequalities in health. As the other chapters in this book demonstrate, inequalities in economic position across ethnic groups are marked and complex, covering economic activity, employment levels, educational outcomes, housing, geographical location, area deprivation, racism and discrimination, citizenship and claims to citizenship. This complexity requires a challenging and multi-faceted examination (Nazroo, 1998). Indeed, the few studies that attempt to address the complexity of the economic inequalities faced by ethnic minority people demonstrate that much, if not all, of ethnic inequalities in health are the product of social and economic inequalities (Nazroo, 1998, 2001a). And there is now clear evidence that morbidity and mortality within all ethnic groups – regardless of the condition focused on – is strongly patterned by socio-economic position. For example, richer South Asian people have low rates of cardiovascular disease rather than the high rate that is presumed to be present regardless of socio-economic position (Nazroo, 2001b). This variation within groups indicates the lack of an inherent link between ethnic (minority) category and disease outcome. Explanations that are reductive to a cultural or genetic root are not sufficient.

There is also a growing body of evidence that both physical and mental health are adversely affected by: experiences of racial harassment; fear of experiencing racial harassment; experiences of discrimination; and the belief that there is general prejudice and discrimination against ethnic minority people (Krieger et al, 1996; Karlsen et al, 2002; Williams et al, 2003). These 'indicators' of racism and discrimination reflect general perceptions of society as racist (belief that minority groups are discriminated against, fear of racism), personal threat (fear of racism and experiences of harassment), and experiences of events that undermine status and identity (experiences of harassment and experiences of discrimination). And these effects have been found to accumulate across domains of exposure to racism and discrimination, and over time (Wallace et al, 2016).

Related to this, there is also evidence that the aggregation of ethnic minority people in areas with those of similar ethnicity is beneficial, particularly for mental health, once the effects of area deprivation are controlled for (Bécares et al, 2009). This is likely to operate through a combination of feelings of increased security (lower exposure to racial harassment and discrimination) and increased social support. Indeed, there is some evidence demonstrating that ethnic minority people rate the areas where they live much more highly than would be implied by official indices of deprivation precisely because these are locations where a sense of inclusive community for people like them has developed (Bajekal et al, 2004).

So, although a concern with the detailed aetiology of specific conditions occurring at higher rates for particular ethnic groups might lead to a focus on the putative proximal causes of biological change (genetic and behavioural differences), research on distal social and economic causes shows clearly that these are key drivers of ethnic differences in health. But this is not just a simple reflection of class disadvantage, the complex and multidimensional nature of the economic and social inequalities faced by ethnic minority people reflects the processes of racialisation faced by ethnic minority people. This requires specific policy responses if such inequalities are to be addressed, but effective responses require a fundamental rethink of approaches to race, ethnicity and migration.

Policy frameworks

Key policy initiatives in the last decade have been via the Race Relations Amendment Act 2000; the Equality Act 2010; the NHS Equality Delivery System (EDS), revised in 2013 (NHS, 2013a) to become EDS2; and the Workforce Race Equality Standard (WRES) (NHS, 2016a) developed in 2015 (discussed in section 4 of this chapter, on employment). The government also launched the Public Health Outcomes Framework in 2010 (NHS England Analytical Services, 2017), following the Marmot review. The framework uses a series of indicators to assess key aspects of health over time, but it does not have a focus on ethnicity. Public Health England also produce 'Outcome Framework Equity Reports' (Public Health England, 2017). These reports focus on 18 key indicators of health and determinants of health selected by Public Health England's (PHE) Health Equity Board to form a dashboard of indicators that include core overarching health outcomes, public health priority areas and social determinants of health. One of the difficulties with this approach is that the narrative to accompany the measures is descriptive and lacks the socio-political analysis needed to consider ethnic inequalities.

Also, NHS organisations need to heed the equality requirements of the NHS Constitution, the Care Quality Commission Standards[1] and a range of other tailored assurance frameworks. For example, there is an assurance operating manual for Clinical Commissioning Groups (CCGs)[2] which includes a suite of equality indicators designed to hold them accountable to NHS England on employment practice (via the WRES), providing equitable and fair services, and 'reducing the inequality challenge for their population' (NHS England, 2017).

The Care Quality Commission inspection framework has 11 standards and within these there are equality considerations, such as person-centred care that meets individual needs and preferences; and dignity and respect, which includes ensuring everybody is treated as equals. Additionally, the Care Quality Commission have published *Equally Outstanding* (2017) and *Our Human Rights Approach for Our*

Regulation of Health and Social Care Services (2014). These publications are about promoting human rights and ensuring equity in access, experience and outcomes.

Thus, health and social care agencies have needed to attend to a wide range of indicators of ethnicity and equality over time. However, these policies may be misdirected, or insufficiently targeted. Progress is slow and ethnic inequalities in health outcomes have persisted. This is perhaps because, as argued earlier, the practices of health and social care agencies tend to essentialise ethnicity rather than deal with the complexity of socio-economic factors or the experience of racism. It is also apparent, from a review of health and social care organisations' websites, that equality policies and practice vary in quality and in what they cover. There is a tendency to approach legal and policy requirements in a linear way rather than use a considered analysis of all requirements, overarching intentions and contexts. This can lead to an introspective and selective examination of ethnic health inequalities. Unless broader attention is paid to the structural and societal factors that cause ethnic inequalities in health, progress on reducing them will be minimal.

The Care Quality Commission says that to tackle equality and human rights at a service level:

> Health and social care leaders need to look beyond provider boundaries. They need to ensure the community involvement of individuals. They need to develop broader, more holistic services that meet the needs of diverse communities. (Care Quality Commission, 2017)

However, beyond the involvement of communities and vague calls for holistic services, there is a need for attention to be paid to the impact of discrimination and racism and their impact on health. While there are some academic texts and third sector race equality organisations which do recognise this, there are no policies that adequately focus on this issue.

Access to, experience of, and quality of health (and social care) services

In 2010 the NHS' EDS was created with one of its four sections designed to ensure equitable access. The Equality Act 2010 requires that health organisations show how they are providing equality of opportunity. Interestingly the UK's scores on 'responsiveness' and 'measures to achieve change' in the Migrant Integration Policy Index for Health 2016 (Johnson and Jayaweera, 2017) are the highest in the EQUI-HEALTH sample of 34 countries. However, since 2010, and even more so post-Brexit, there has been:

> Firm political determination to eliminate any possibility that migrants might 'exploit' the NHS (even those who pay taxes and NI contributions into it like everybody else) [and this] has reduced entitlements, and many measures to bridge the gap between migrants and health services have lapsed into disuse. (Johnson and Jayaweera, 2017: 26)

It is possible that where ethnic minority people have a poorer experience or receive poorer quality health care, this contributes to ethnic inequalities in health. In the UK there remains (almost) free universal access to health care and this is reflected in an equal or greater use across ethnic minority groups of primary care health services (except possibly in the case of Chinese people), although some inequalities exist for use of hospital services and marked inequalities exist for dental services (Nazroo et al, 2009). Similarly, for conditions managed in primary care it seems that the outcomes of care (levels of undiagnosed or poorly managed illness) are as good for ethnic minority people as they are for White English people (Nazroo et al, 2009). Nazroo suggests that the provision, through the NHS, of publicly funded primary care with universal access and standardised treatment protocols has resulted in greater equality of access and outcomes across ethnic groups. This suggests that quality of health care does not contribute to ethnic inequalities in health. Nevertheless, the *experience* of care seems poorer for ethnic minority people. In primary care, ethnic minority people are more likely to be dissatisfied with various aspects of the care received (Rudat, 1994; Airey et al, 1999), to wait longer for an appointment (Airey et al, 1999), and to face language barriers during the consultation (Rudat, 1994). And there is a convincing body of evidence suggesting that the higher admission rate of Black people for severe mental illness is disproportionate and reflects the ways in which they are racialised (Nazroo, 2015). Later we consider some examples of access to and experience of health care, which demonstrate that a more nuanced approach to assessing access and experience can point to how inequalities in ethnic minority health outcomes may arise. This is followed by a consideration of the additional layers of institutional racism that ultimately add to the failure to address inequalities in health outcomes.

Access to and experience of health services

Szczepura, writing in 2005, was concerned to show that providing services was not the same as providing equity of access or quality of experience. She proposed three important factors that were necessary conditions for quality experiences of health care: having equal access via appropriate information (which may be reflected in uptake of service); having access to services that are relevant, timely and sensitive to the person's needs (perhaps reflected in satisfaction levels); and being able to use the health service with ease and with the confidence that you will be treated with respect (which may also be reflected in satisfaction with services).

This approach can be applied to studies of ethnic minority patients' experiences of health services. One example is the National Cancer Experience Patient Survey (2016), which worryingly reported that ethnic minority people see the GP several more times than the White British people before they get referred to a hospital. Potentially this means detecting cancer later. Further, for nearly every question in the survey, the experience was reported as significantly less good for ethnic minority groups than for the White British group.

Applying Szczepura's first point, it could be that patients do not have appropriate information in order to know what to say about their symptoms and so present information in a way that registers with the GP, or it could be that health services are not giving appropriate information to help people of different ethnicities recognise symptoms. In any case the result is that services, particularly as experienced by Asian people, are less 'timely' or 'sensitive to needs' (Szczepura's second point) than others. With regard to her third point, ethnic minority people scored lower than White people for both respect and overall experience – see Figures 4.3 and 4.4.

This deeper look under the surface of access to cancer services reveals that while there may be no explicit barrier in general access, there is a differential in access to the *right service and treatment*, which could in turn lead to differential (and poorer for ethnic minority people) health outcomes. Similarly, there may be evidence of equity of access in primary care with regard to GPs, but the GP Experience Survey 2017 shows that on almost every measure (out of 50 questions) ethnic minority people report less good experiences than White British

Figure 4.3: Rating of the experience of respect and dignity while in hospital for patients with cancer, percentage of people answering 'good' or 'better'

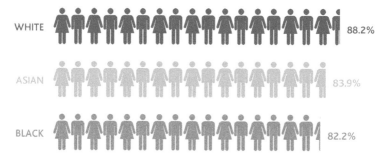

Source: National Cancer Experience Patient Survey (2016).

Figure 4.4: Experience of overall care for patients with cancer, average score

Source: National Cancer Experience Patient Survey (2016).

people. This is particularly marked for Bangladeshi, Pakistani and Chinese groups, as shown in Figure 4.5.

Equitable access to health and social care services does not mean, therefore, that there is equity of experience or even outcomes. Further, as discussed later in this chapter, discrimination and institutional racism also impact negatively on the quality of care.

Racialisation, institutional racism and the impact on access to and quality of care

Stereotyping, discrimination, racism and cultural incompetence can be detected across health and social care services. In the following sections three examples are given of the different ways in which this impacts on the lives of ethnic minority people.

Figure 4.5: Rating of GP care and concern: proportion reporting an overall positive experience

Source: GP Experience Survey (2017).

Severe mental illness

Ethnic minority people, particularly those in Black groups, are over-represented among those with a diagnosis of severe mental illness, are more likely to have adverse pathways into care, more likely to receive compulsory treatment (to be sectioned) and more likely to experience adverse outcomes of care (Nazroo, 2015). In 2003 an inquiry was conducted into the death of Rocky Bennett in a mental health institution. It concluded that institutional racism was present in mental health institutions and that the experience of racism and racist abuse had precipitated the struggles Rocky had had with other patients and staff and that ultimately led to his death. Following the Bennett inquiry, a five-year 'Delivering Race Equality (DRE) in Mental Health Care' programme was established (Department of Health, 2005). However, the DRE failed to address underlying factors relating to racism and socio-economic factors, its objectives were insufficiently specific and allowed an in-practice reframing of the problem as one of cultural competence For example, the inquiry report recommended that to reduce and eliminate ethnic inequalities in mental health service experience and outcome it would be important to:

> develop the cultural capability of mental health services; and to engage the community and build capacity through Community Development Workers (CDWs). (Department of Health, 2005)

It might be expected that, although the policy response did not adequately recognise race and racism, there might have been some improvements in access, a reduction in disproportionality of diagnosis and in sectioning of Black people. However, evidence from the most recent, and the last, in-patient census designed to monitor progress in ethnic inequalities in treatment reported:

> Overall, the findings of the sixth Count me in census[3] show little change from previous years. They continue to show differences in mental health admission and detention rates between Black and minority ethnic groups and white groups, and also differences within minority ethnic groups. Although the total numbers of mental health inpatients have fallen since 2005, ethnic differences in rates of admission, detention under the Mental Health Act and seclusion have not altered materially. (Care Quality Commission, 2011)

These findings were an echo of the 2010 annual report from the Care Quality Commission. Indeed, in 2016 the *Five Year Forward View on Mental Health* (NHS, 2016b) stated that the DRE programme concluded with no improvement in the experience of people from ethnic minority communities receiving mental health care. And it went further to say that data since 2010 showed little change. However, it made no specific recommendations to address these inequalities, reflecting a broader policy vacuum in this area, as noted by the commission set up to review the provision of acute in-patient psychiatric care for adults (NHS, 2016b), which stated that:

Since 2010, there has been no targeted national policy aimed at improving mental health care for ethnic minority communities and campaigning groups have expressed concern that mental health services lack a sense of strategic direction for reducing inequalities in ethnic minority mental health. (NHS, 2016b)

So, although theoretically there is equitable access to mental health services, the experience and quality of those services is discriminatory. Further, fear of racism, which could lead to incorrect diagnoses or inappropriate compulsory treatment, may delay access, precipitating the involuntary admission feared in the first place. Health professionals for their part may stereotype or misunderstand symptoms. The *Breaking the Circles of Fear* report had picked up on this in 2002:

> Black people mistrust and often fear services, and staff are often wary of the Black community, fearing criticism and not knowing how to respond, and fearful of young Black men. (Sainsbury Centre for Mental Health, 2002)

As the Bennett inquiry said in 2003:

> At present people from the Black and minority ethnic communities, who are involved in the mental health services, are not getting the service they are entitled to. Putting it bluntly, this is a disgrace. The NHS is national. (Sallah et al, 2003)

Interpreting services

Although not a legal right, interpreting services are necessary for basic clinical practice and in order to meet the professional standards set by the Care Quality Commission and the NHS Equality and Delivery System. However, the increasing emphasis in the last decade on proficiency in English before citizenship is granted has allowed a drift from attempts to provide high-quality translation services to a rapid decline in these justified by the expectation of fluency in English and by an argument around prioritising resources. This means that the provision of interpreting services is patchy. For example, a study by Healthwatch Islington (2017) found that respondents were not always aware that there was a service and when they did receive it, it was not always a quality service. Among the responses, one woman reported that she did not feel comfortable discussing gynaecological conditions through a male interpreter; others said the dialect or accent was difficult to understand, and that sometimes racial profiles were used to make assumptions that a certain interpreter was needed when they were not.

Johnson and Jayaweera (2017), when writing about interpreting services for migrants, said:

> The best provision is still in London, but even there, it is not universal or always of 'gold standard.' Central & North-West London NHS Trust maintains a bank of paid interpreters, many of whom would not be legally recognised as qualified interpreters by the national body (National Register of Public Service Interpreters), being trained only to level 3. There is a very large reliance on the linguistic skills of the very diverse mix of staff in the NHS, and many Trusts do maintain registers of language competent staff, not all of whom are medically or linguistically qualified, and few of whom are paid or insured for this role.

This means that the quality of health care offered by the NHS is compromised by inadequate resourcing of interpreting services, leading to poor coverage, poor quality of the service, stereotyping of patients and their needs, and a lack of respect for the individual needs of patients.

Sickle cell and thalassaemia disorders

It has taken years of joint efforts from campaigning groups, such as the Organisation for Sickle Cell Anaemia Research (OSCAR) and researchers, to ensure attention is paid to the treatment of sickle cell and thalassaemia disorders within the NHS. Screening of newborn children for sickle cell only started in 2003, even though it has been shown to be highly effective in preventing mortality and unnecessary pain. However, although there is now an annual update of those registered with sickle cell disease and improved screening and understanding of the disorders, a lack of resources or appropriate awareness has been a consistent issue with severe consequences. For young people, painful episodes can lead to significant periods away from school. Section 100 of the Children and Families Act 2014 in England places a duty on the appropriate school authority, who must make arrangements for supporting pupils at the school with medical conditions, but a lack of resources and understanding can mean that affected young people don't get the care they need. Dyson et al (2016) described how stereotypical and racist perceptions of the people involved can be a barrier to accessing services and add to the pain and misery of the disease. Additionally, this connects with broader claims that immigration presents a 'drain' on the NHS.

Summary

From the preceding considerations of access to and experience of cancer and GP services, mental health and interpreting services, and attention paid to sickle cell disorders, it becomes apparent that access alone tells us very little about the quality of the experience. The latter is important to the impact of health services on health outcomes for ethnic minority groups. However, even when the data clearly point to poorer experiences for ethnic minority people, responses tend not to locate analyses or responses beyond the service provider and focus on 'cultural considerations'. Given what is known about institutional and structural racism and discrimination, and the impact of socio-economic status on health, this is an insufficient response if the issues are to be tackled with any effectiveness.

Employment

As an employer, the NHS has the opportunity to provide significant leadership. For example, in 2017 the NHS directly employed 1.2 million people, indirectly many more, so employment practices within the NHS are able to impact on the labour market nationally and regionally. However, while ethnic minority people are over-represented in the NHS workforce – 22% of NHS staff, compared with 13% of all workers – there are marked ethnic inequalities in terms of grades and location of employment. To address this the Department of Health introduced its Race Equality Action Plan (Department of Health, 2005), which had been developed as a result of the Macpherson inquiry's findings of institutional racism in public sector and the subsequent requirements of the Race Relations (Amendment) Act (RRAA) 2000. However, it seems that little progress has been made.

Kline (2014, 2015) showed significant ethnic differentials in pay bands, representation among senior staff and representation on boards. Although his study was largely focused on London, he found the picture to be very similar elsewhere in England. His finding that representation at senior levels of the NHS was getting worse, despite several years of employment monitoring and other initiatives, including the Equality Act 2010 and the NHS EDS2, is perhaps of most concern. He found that:

- The proportion of London NHS Trust Board members from an ethnic minority background was 8%, an even lower proportion than was found in 2006 (9.6%).
- The proportion of chief executives and chairs from an ethnic minority background had decreased from 5.3% in 2006 to 2.5% in 2014.
- There had been no significant change in the proportion of non-executive ethnic minority Trust Board members, continuing the pattern of under-representation compared to both the workforce and the local population.
- The proportion of senior and very senior managers who were from an ethnic minority background had not increased since 2008, when comparable grading data were available, and had fallen slightly since 2011.
- The likelihood of White staff in London being senior or very senior managers was three times higher than it was for ethnic minority staff. (Kline, 2014)

Partly as a result of this report, the NHS introduced the Workforce Race Equality Standard (WRES) in 2015. There have now been three years of reporting against this standard and some of the key findings of the latest WRES data on senior level employment showed that the proportion of very senior managers (VSMs) from ethnic minority backgrounds increased from 5.2% in 2010 to 6.7% in 2016. Although in percentage terms this is a meaningful improvement, it does not reflect the proportion of NHS staff who have an ethnic minority background (22%) and while there are nearly 14 White staff per trust on a VSM grade, on average just over one ethnic minority member of staff per trust is on VSM grade, and in many trusts there are none. That, in turn, impacts on the likelihood of executive board members being from ethnic minority backgrounds, which remains significantly lower than ethnic minority representation in both the overall NHS workforce and in the local communities served. Board membership percentage across England was 7.1% and, significantly, 43.5% (84) of trusts reported having no ethnic minority board members.

Other concerns highlighted by the WRES data in 2016 (NHS, 2016a) are that ethnic minority staff have a less good experience of being employed than their White counterparts. For example: ethnic minority staff in the NHS are significantly more likely to be disciplined than White staff members and remain significantly more likely to experience discrimination harassment, bullying or abuse from other staff at work from colleagues and their managers. It is of note that the WRES seems to recognise that there is deep-seated resistance within the NHS to criticisms and that there may be excessive reliance on training, processes, and individuals raising concerns, rather than employers proactively identifying and addressing problems.

Conclusion: the need for policy development

It is clear that there has been little policy development to specifically address ethnic inequalities in health at a national level, only occasional and fragmented implementation of policy at a local level, and no real evaluation of the impact of targeted, or general, policies on ethnic inequalities in health. Where policy has been developed and implemented, it has largely been concerned with addressing questions of accessibility to and delivery of services, typically with a focus on language and communication and equity of access. But as we have seen, equity of access is an insufficient indicator of the quality of health care or outcomes for ethnic minority people.

However, there is not a policy 'vacuum', rather there has been a series of reactive NHS policies since 2000 which have all failed to make significant progress in tackling differentials in health care. In part this is due to an over-emphasis on personal, cultural and sometimes organisational factors, rather than addressing relevant social and economic inequalities. Turning attention from economic or societal problems by locating the kernels of the problems in the 'other' is a typically divisive tool for maintaining the power of a government to implement controlling measures that more often than not penalise poorer and disadvantaged people. Recent discourses around culture, community and segregation that are populist and that disregard the evidence base do nothing to help tackle social inequalities. Indeed, they are likely to aggravate ethnic inequalities by increasing economic disadvantage, prejudice, and experiences of racism and discrimination.

This manifests in a policy leaning toward an emphasis on the importance of cultural assimilation to a White British norm that, together with the securitisation agenda, vehement anti-immigrant feeling and Brexit, has meant that it is now even more difficult to find or initiate responses to the impact of racism and discrimination on the health of ethnic minority people. Rather than trying to challenge this agenda, it has perhaps been easier for policy leads and senior managers to find explanations for differentials in health care in cultural or lifestyle factors. So, for example, it is well known that ethnic minority groups are up to six times more likely to develop diabetes than White people, however, there is a need to look beyond the typical focus on diet and exercise for solutions. For example, Patel et al (2016) identified socio-economic barriers to healthy behaviours, such as prioritising work over physical activity to provide for the family; different perceptions of a healthy body weight and fear of racial harassment or abuse when exercising. In addition, it is likely that socio-economic factors operating across life courses and over generations contribute significantly to this greater risk.

Discourses which locate the causes of ethnic inequalities in health, access to health care, and employment experiences in the NHS in essentialised notions of ethnicity as culture or genetics will inevitably be insufficient for finding solutions. There is a need for social accounting as well as economic (and environmental) accounting within the NHS. And there is a need for long-term policies that promote equitable life chances and that address racism and the marginalisation of ethnic minority people. Attention to reforming institutional cultures, including politics and government, is crucial. There is a need to tackle more complex and seemingly intractable issues of economics and racism at the interdependent structural, institutional and personal levels.

Notes

[1] The Care Quality Commission inspects health and social care providers.
[2] CCGs play key roles in addressing equality and health inequalities as commissioners of services across a local area, as employers and as local and national system leaders.
[3] In 2010 the last Count Me In survey was completed and information was obtained from 32,799 patients (including 2,959 outpatients on a community treatment order) at 261 NHS and independent health care organisations in England and Wales. Twenty-three per cent of the patients were from ethnic minority groups.

5

Ethnic inequalities in the state education system in England

Claire Alexander and William Shankley

Key findings

- The demography of the pupil population in state education in England shows the pupil population is more diverse than the broader population. The same is true for Wales, Scotland and Northern Ireland.
- The 2016/17 GCSE grades data for England show that there is disparity in attainment between different ethnic groups: Chinese and Indian pupils were the most likely to achieve A★ to C in maths and English; meanwhile, Black Caribbean, Pakistani and Gypsy and Irish Travellers were the least likely to achieve A★ to C grades in maths and English.
- The 2016/17 data show rates of permanent exclusion continue to be a significant issue for Black and Gypsy and Irish Traveller pupils compared to other ethnic pupil groups.
- Recent Prevent policies targeting radicalisation have been criticised for producing highly racialised surveillance of Muslim and South Asian pupils, threatening the relationships between local communities and schools.
- The 2016/17 data show that White British continue to be over-represented in apprenticeship schemes compared to ethnic minority people.
- In contrast to apprenticeship schemes, ethnic minority pupils disproportionately enter further or higher education. Ethnic minority groups constitute 26% of all undergraduate students in England. However, they are less likely to attend Russell Group Universities, with the Black group particularly under-represented.
- The 2016/17 data show that all ethnic minority groups are less likely than White students to receive a 'good' (2:1 or first class) degree. However, ethnic minority students who attend Russell Group

universities achieve a higher proportion of good degrees than those who attend New Universities.

- The 2016/17 data of those working in higher education institutions show an under-representation of academic staff from all UK-born ethnic groups, notably from Black and Muslim groups. There is an over-representation of non-UK national staff from Chinese, Indian, and Black African groups compared to the low representation of non-UK staff from Bangladeshi, Black Caribbean, Mixed and Other Black groups.
- The 2016/17 data highlight the under-representation of ethnic minority women, particularly at professorial level in higher education institutions.
- The UK Race Equality Mark offers the potential for higher education institutions to improve conditions for ethnic minority staff and students in a similar way to the Athena Swan Award. However, it is not compulsory and not linked to other metrics of academic rigour or teaching excellence.

Introduction[1]

Education has long been a key site in the struggle for racial and ethnic equality in Britain. Seen as both a mechanism for social mobility and a means of cultural integration and reproduction, schools (as institutions) and schooling (as a practice) lie at the heart of the pursuit of a successful future for an equal multi-ethnic Britain. Nevertheless, 35 years on from the Swann report (Department of Education and Science, 1985), which argued for *Education for All*, and 20 years after the *Future of Multi-ethnic Britain* report (Parekh et al, 2000), issues of racial and ethnic inequality in our schools are as pertinent as ever. Education remains a primary arena for both the maintenance of entrenched racial stereotyping and discrimination, on the one hand, and anti-racist activism, on the other. Concerns over structural racism, low educational attainment, poor teacher expectations and stereotyping, ethnocentric curricula and high levels of school exclusions for some groups remain entrenched features of our school system. While there has been progress and change, recent years have seen the erosion of the fragile gains made in the wake of the Macpherson report (1999) and the Race Relations Amendment Act 2000, which imposed a duty on schools to promote race equality. In their place we have seen a refocusing on 'fundamental British values', a narrowing of the curriculum, the embedding of the Prevent agenda in schools and universities, and the use of schools as internal border sites, focusing on new migrant and asylum seeking children and families (Alexander et al, 2015). These measures have introduced a 'hostile environment' within schools, and imposed an exclusionary and utilitarian version of citizenship, which has pushed issues of race equality and diversity to the margins.

At the same time, the face of Britain's schools is changing. Nearly 17% of children aged 0−15 in England and Wales are from Black and minority ethnic backgrounds, making up 26% of primary and secondary schools in England in 2018 (DfE, 2018d).[2] Patterns of settlement mean that in urban areas, the school population will often be predominantly Black and Asian. The picture is complicated by the dramatic increase of white non-British pupils, now the second largest ethnic minority in schools (at nearly 8% in primary schools and 6% in secondary schools), while ethnic minority composition is increasingly diverse, with growing numbers of Black and Asian Others and an increasing Mixed population (over 5% in primary and secondary schools).

Recent figures (DfE, 2015a) suggest that educational attainment for ethnic minority young people is improving, with Indian and Chinese young people consistently outperforming White British students, Bangladeshi and African descent young people achieving near or above the national average for GCSE attainment, and African Caribbean and Pakistani descent young people showing clear gains in the past decade. These changes are reflected in the increasing numbers of ethnic minority young people going on to university. Nevertheless, ethnic minority young people are over-represented in pupil referrals units and exclusions and, while they enter higher education in greater numbers, they remain under-represented at Russell Group universities (Alexander et al, 2015) and on apprenticeship schemes, and over-represented in the figures for unemployment and the prison system (see Chapters 3 and 6 on the criminal justice system and the labour market respectively).

Education thus marks a key point of transition, between family, community and broader society, and into the world of work, which has implications for the maintenance and future transformation of inequalities in housing, health and wellbeing, employment and so on. This chapter maps the changes in racial and ethnic inequalities in education, focusing on primary, secondary and tertiary/higher education. It will examine the changing patterns of educational inequality, and the policy contexts in which these are embedded, focusing on diversity within and across ethnic groups, and across the educational life cycle. It will also focus on issues of staffing as well as on pupils and students, to explore the institutional framework of the education system and how inequalities may be replicated over time.

The availability of data and the disproportionate concentration of ethnic minority people in England result in this chapter focusing mainly on educational inequalities in England. Where possible, and where the data are available, this chapter will compare the patterns across ethnic groups in the other constituent countries of the UK. The chapter will show that there remain significant ethnic inequalities in the education system at all levels and that, in understanding the nature of these inequalities, it is important to be attentive both to the diverse experience of different ethnic minorities but also to questions of class and gender.

A brief history of race and education policy: from SENs to Prevent

Ethnic and racial inequalities in education in Britain should be situated within broader debates and policies around the expansion of education to all children in the postwar period. These debates have focused on the inequalities between private and state education systems and, from the 1960s, on the educational divide between grammar and secondary modern schools, with many concerned that the bipartite, selective system of education had led to 'two nations in education' (Mays, 1962, cited in Tomlinson, 2014: 18), entrenching social divides centred on family and class. The Labour government's policy of comprehensive education in 1964 retained exemptions for private and religious educational establishments (Tomlinson, 2005). Under the Conservative administration, with Margaret Thatcher presiding first as education minister and then Prime Minister, the 1970s saw the rolling back of comprehensive education, giving local education authorities (LEAs) the choice to provision comprehensive education or retain grammar schools. This already complex picture was radically transformed further with the proliferation of free schools, academies and faith schools from the 1990s onwards (Byrne and De Tona, 2019).

The position of ethnic minority pupils within the mainstream education system, whatever its form, has been recognised to be one consistently defined through disadvantage and discrimination, with Black and minority ethnic (BME) pupils often placed under separate provision to address 'Special Educational Needs' (SEN) (Coard, 1971; Rattansi, 1992). However, it was not until the 1980s that 'underachievement' became a central policy focus, first with the Rampton report (1981) and then with the Swann report (1985), titled *Education for All*. These interventions should be understood against the backdrop of the 'riots' of 1980 and 1981, and again in 1985, which focused attention on second-generation Black Caribbean young people and broader structural inequalities, but also the wider policy shift away from 'assimilation' to 'integration'. In the education arena, this was particularly framed through a move towards 'multicultural' education (Rattansi, 1992; Tomlinson, 2014). Moreover, the Swann report, in 1985, showed a stronger awareness of issues of socio-economic conditions, and of differences between ethnic groups, in structuring the experience of ethnic minority pupils. The report made 71 recommendations about the role of education in a 'complex and diverse multicultural society – and indicated a positive policy position towards race in the education system' (Tomlinson, 2014: 38). The report's insistence on 'Education for All' reflected both a recognition of the need for measures to tackle racial inequality in schools, and a shift towards a multicultural ethos aimed at mandatory teacher training and developing more inclusive curricula (Tomlinson, 2014). However, as Rattansi (1992) has argued, the report promoted understandings of inequality as stemming from an ethnically essentialist view of identity, which perpetuated a division between 'West Indian' underachievement stemming from deprivation and racism and 'Asian' achievement, arising from 'culture'.

The establishment of the National Curriculum for England and Wales in 1988 took as a central concern the ways in which it should 'take account of the ethnic and cultural diversity of British society and the importance of the curriculum in promoting equal opportunity for all pupils, regardless of ethnic origin or gender' (in Parekh, 2000: 142). The 1990s saw a strong focus in education policy on targeting inequalities in attainment across ethnic groups, with the 1997 White Paper 'Excellence in Schools' reiterating the government's 'core commitment to equality of opportunity and high standards for all' (Department for Education and Employment, 1997: Foreword and 6) and stressing the need for schools to take 'practical steps to raise ethnic minority pupils' achievements and promote racial harmony' However, as the Parekh report (2000: 143) noted, such policies and practices remained piecemeal and lacked national leadership and statutory power. The report noted further that ethnic monitoring was uneven and unhelpful, that the impact of diversity policies to date should be assessed, and that diversity training for teachers, governors and inspectors needed to be mandatory.

The Race Relations Amendment Act 2000 made public bodies, including schools, accountable for race equality and required them to record and monitor racist incidents (Bhopal, 2018). However, successive Coalition and Conservative governments have weakened this duty and the policy was eventually replaced with the Equality Act 2010. This legislation was rolled out across all public sector institutions in 2011 and required all public bodies to promote equality for all protected characteristics, including race (Bhopal, 2018). The dilution of a dedicated focus on race equality has been exacerbated by the fragmentation of the education system with the proliferation of academies, free schools and faith schools. The extent to which this increasing diversity of schools has the potential to exacerbate existing racial inequalities (Florian et al, 2016) remains an issue of concern, whether in view of the lack of real school choice for ethnic minority families when seeking to access them for their children (Weekes-Bernard, 2007; Byrne and De Tona, 2019), the failure of some free schools to comply with equality legislation (Gillborn, 2005), or the often difficult educational experiences that some ethnic minority pupils face within them (Gillborn, 2005). The National Curriculum has been overhauled to herald a return to 'traditional' subjects and teaching methods which have sought to overturn decades of more diverse, socially inclusive and multicultural curricula (Alexander et al, 2015; Alexander and Weekes-Bernard, 2017).

This retrenchment is nowhere more apparent than in the introduction of the Prevent Duty in schools and universities in 2015. Underpinning the Prevent Duty is a guideline which states that 'Section 26 of the Counter-Terrorism and Security Act 2015 places a duty on certain bodies' "specified authorities" listed in schedule 6 to the Act)', in the exercise of their functions, 'to have due regard to the need to prevent people from being drawn into terrorism' (DfE, 2015b; Bhopal, 2018: 74). The Prevent Duty spans multiple state institutions, but in schooling it has been formulated to support schools, early years childcare providers and later years providers to identify children who may be vulnerable to radicalisation (DfE, 2015b). In particular, schools are expected to instil 'British values' into the curriculum to help children combat the threat of extremism and radicalisation (DfE, 2015b).

The Prevent Duty has been heavily criticised as detrimental to ethnic minority groups, particularly by targeting Muslim pupils and their families (Qurashi, 2018). Some have criticised the policy as a vehicle for explicit and implicit forms of racism to be committed against non-white students under the banner of anti-terrorism (Awan, 2012; Taylor, 2018). More recently, a report by the United Nations (UN) rapporteur highlighted that the Prevent Duty could actually contribute to extremism rather than deter it by singling out specific ethnic/religious groups (Alston, 2018). As Bhopal notes

(2018), the Prevent Duty has painted ethnic minority pupils as a threat to social order. Moreover, the Prevent Duty has ruptured the traditional teacher–student relationship as it has forced teachers to monitor children they believe are at risk of radicalisation and, as a consequence, threatened the trust and the pastoral element of this relationship (Bhopal, 2018).

Ethnicity and schooling in Britain: a contemporary portrait

Access

The most recent data from the Department for Education show that for the school year 2016/17, 7.05 million pupils were registered as attending state-funded primary, secondary and special schools across England and Wales. This covers the years of compulsory schooling in the UK, from the ages of 4 to 16. However, in the past ten years, compulsory education has been extended across the UK to the age of 18 (Gov.uk, 2018b).

Figure 5.1 shows the demography of the pupil population in the state education system (primary and secondary) in England for 2015/16 versus the population of England broken down by ethnicity. It shows there are significant demographic changes to the school-age population in England compared to the ethnicity of the broader population for England from the 2011 Census. Figure 5.1 shows the pupil population was comprised of 69% White British, 10% Asian, 6% Black, 6% Other White, 5% Mixed and 0.4% Chinese, with White British pupils making up a lower share of the pupil population compared to their broader share of the English population. In comparison, all ethnic minority groups, except the Chinese, make up a larger share of the pupil population than their share of the English population.

More generally, in England, ethnic minority people are unevenly residentially concentrated in urban centres, particularly London (Finney and Simpson, 2009), and this has implications for school demography. Policymakers regularly question the so-called 'London effect' and why attainment levels in the capital are significantly higher than the national average (Burgess, 2014). According to Burgess (2014), the success of London schools can be attributed to their above national average share of ethnic minority and immigrant pupils, who, as we can see in other sections of this chapter, perform on average higher than White British pupils.

By comparison, the ethnic profile of the student population across the other constituent countries of the UK is different from England.

Figure 5.1: School population (England) and 2011 Census of population (England) by ethnicity

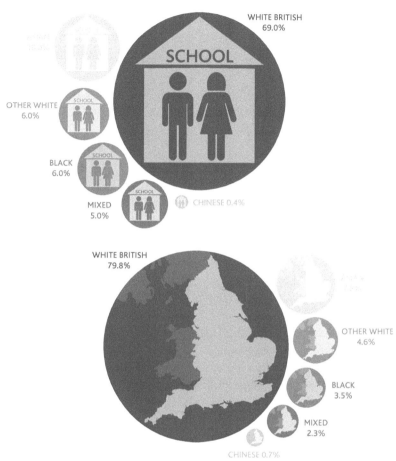

Source: School attendance and absence, Race Disparity Audit (Gov.uk, 2017b).

Scottish Statistics (2017b), for example, suggest 85% of pupils were White Scottish or White Other British (including White Welsh and Northern Irish), with the largest ethnic minority groups being the White Other (5%), Asian Pakistani (2%) and Mixed (1%) groups. Moreover, the statistics also indicated that the Gypsy and Traveller pupils had increased by 52% from 737 in 2011 to 1,121 in 2017. Meanwhile, in Wales, the 2011 Census suggests that the ethnic minorities' population now makes up 4% of the Welsh population, with the student population showing 91% of pupils are recorded as White British in 2015 and the other 9% comprised of over 100 ethnic groups (Lewis and Starkey, 2015). In Northern Ireland, the share of the ethnic minority population is relatively small compared to England, although the country has experienced an increase of White diversity as the result of the expansion of the European Union (EU) in 2004 and 2007(Burns et al, 2015).

Attainment

As already noted, a primary focus of education policy around racial inequality in schools has focused on perceived 'underachievement' of ethnic minority pupils – most usually linked to a deficit model of ethnic minority pupils, families or 'cultures'. At the same time, the picture of differential attainment of ethnic minority pupils has changed, and become more complex over time and according to place. Educational attainment is an important measure of ethnic inequality in the education system, and provides a lens through which we can observe how inequality emerges at key stages through a pupil's schooling career (Key Stage 1 and 2, GCSE and A level). The attainment of pupils by their ethnicity can tell us about the disadvantage across different groups at various points during their compulsory education, although comparison over time can be hindered by changes in these forms and levels of assessment.

Even as early as the Rampton report (1981), there was an awareness of differences between Black and Asian children, and in performance within 'Asian' groups, notably between Pakistani and Bangladeshi pupils, and Indian and East African Asian pupils. There were differences, too, between the attainment of girls and boys. More recent studies have illustrated an even more complex picture, with Indian and Chinese pupils, often outstripping their White British counterparts, the improvement of Bangladeshi and Black African pupils, while the Black Caribbean, Gypsy and Irish Traveller and Pakistani groups consistently and significantly underperform (Gillborn et al, 2017). This picture is complicated further by the growth of mixed populations and of increased ethnic 'superdiversity' in Britain's classrooms, with the arrival of new migrant and asylum seeking communities, which as yet are not fully reflected in the data.

GCSE

GCSE (General Certificate of Secondary Education) and GNVQs (General National Vocational Qualifications) are taken towards the end of compulsory schooling at the age of 16. The data from 2016/17 show that in total 527,859 pupils took GCSE examinations at the end of Key Stage 4 in England in state-funded schools and, of these pupils, the ethnicity was known for 99% of the sample. Of the pupils taking GCSE examinations in 2016/17, 77% were White, 10% were

Asian, 5% were Black, 5% were Mixed, 1.5% were Other ethnicity and, finally, 0.4% were Chinese.

Historically, there has been a consistent rise in the patterns of GCSE attainment between 1993 and 2013; with the proportion of students achieving at least five higher grade GCSE passes almost doubling (Bosworth and Kersley, 2015; Gillborn et al, 2017). GCSE attainment over time, and recently, across ethnic groups highlights great variation across ethnic groups but also signs of improvement across all groups (Gillborn and Gipps, 1996; Gov.uk, 2018b). Data from the Department for Education 2016/17 show that Chinese and Indian students were the most likely ethnic groups to achieve A$\star$ to C in maths and English, a pattern well established since the late 1980s (Demack et al, 2000). Meanwhile, data show the Black Caribbean, Pakistani and Gypsy and Irish Traveller students were the least likely to achieve A$\star$ to C in English and maths (DfE, 2018a; Gov.uk, 2018b). Significantly, Bangladeshi pupils (a group who have historically performed poorly) overtook their White British peers in 2011. Similar progress has not been observed for the Pakistani, group who continue to be the lowest achieving South Asian group.

The major story, however, has been the poor performance of the Black Caribbean and Gypsy and Irish Traveller pupils at GCSE level, which has been consistently lower than other ethnic groups (Tomlinson, 2014; Bhopal, 2018). While Black Caribbean pupils' GCSE performance has steadily improved over time, there is still a distinct gap between their attainment compared to that of White British pupils and ethnic minority pupils from the Chinese and Indian groups. There is unlikely to be a single factor responsible for Black Caribbean attainment. Demie (2018) has suggested array of factors, including: poor leadership by headteachers on matters of equality; stereotyping; the low expectations of teachers for Black Caribbean pupils; as well as the exclusionary nature of the curriculum (Doharty, 2015). Socio-economic disadvantage and the broader impact of poverty, poor housing and institutional racism also needs to be taken into account (Demie, 2018). By comparison, the patterns of GCSE attainment for the Black African pupils present a more positive picture, with their attainment levels overtaking White British pupils in 2013. The most recent GCSE attainment data (2016/17) show that Black African students perform relatively well compared to other ethnic groups.

The GCSE attainment levels of Gypsy and Irish Traveller pupils are also consistently lower than other ethnic groups. Bhopal (2004) attributes Gypsy and Irish Travellers' poor GCSE attainment to a range of issues: for example, a transient lifestyle, discrimination and racism by education institutions and wider British society (Lymperopoulou

Figure 5.2: Percentage of pupils attaining English and maths grades (A*–C) by ethnicity, 2016/17

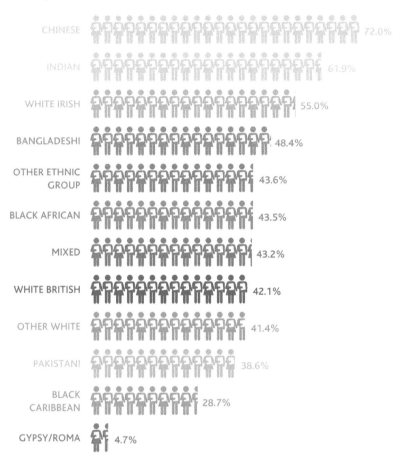

CHINESE 72.0%

INDIAN 61.9%

WHITE IRISH 55.0%

BANGLADESHI 48.4%

OTHER ETHNIC GROUP 43.6%

BLACK AFRICAN 43.5%

MIXED 43.2%

WHITE BRITISH 42.1%

OTHER WHITE 41.4%

PAKISTANI 38.6%

BLACK CARIBBEAN 28.7%

GYPSY/ROMA 4.7%

Source: Key stage 4 and multi-academy trust performance 2017 (DfE, 2018e).

and Shankley, 2018), a lack of familiarity with the education system or an open dialogue with teachers and other staff at schools, as well as issues related to class. In terms of GCSE attainment, Gypsy and Irish Traveller students can also be limited in obtaining good GCSE grades by the high levels of illiteracy among adults, which affects their ability to navigate the education system and to help and support their children's studies (Bhopal, 2004).

Ethnicity, gender and class

While it is clear that there are differential patterns of GCSE attainment across ethnic groups, this picture is complicated by gender and class.

Figure 5.3: Percentage achieving attainment 8 scores by ethnic group and gender

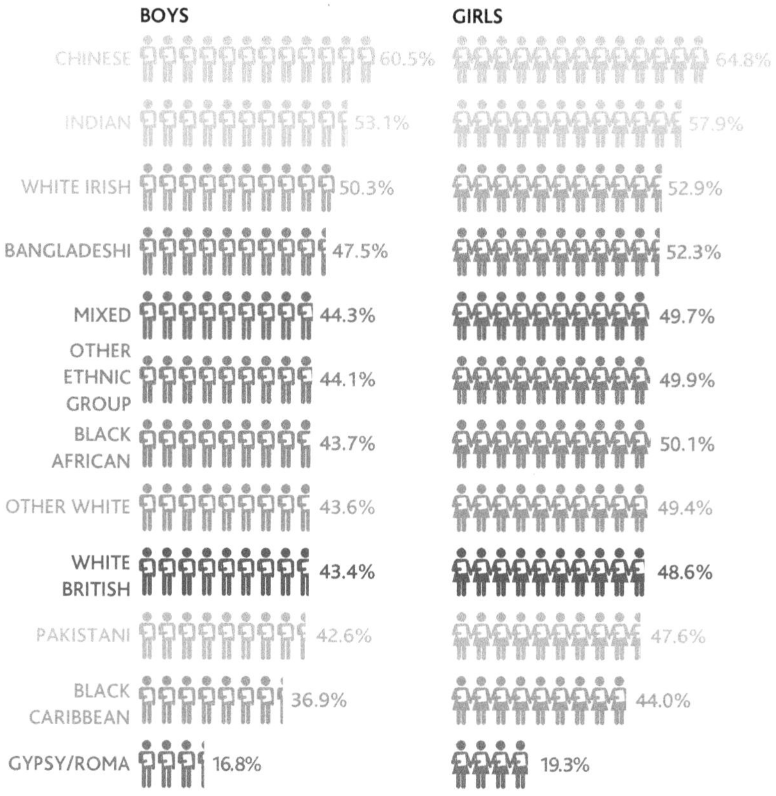

	BOYS	GIRLS
CHINESE	60.5%	64.8%
INDIAN	53.1%	57.9%
WHITE IRISH	50.3%	52.9%
BANGLADESHI	47.5%	52.3%
MIXED	44.3%	49.7%
OTHER ETHNIC GROUP	44.1%	49.9%
BLACK AFRICAN	43.7%	50.1%
OTHER WHITE	43.6%	49.4%
WHITE BRITISH	43.4%	48.6%
PAKISTANI	42.6%	47.6%
BLACK CARIBBEAN	36.9%	44.0%
GYPSY/ROMA	16.8%	19.3%

Source: Key stage 4 and multi-academy trust performance 2017 (DfE, 2018e).

Broader patterns of GCSE attainment over time consistently show that girls overall outperform boys at GCSE level (Gillborn and Mirza, 2000; Tomlinson, 2014). Recent data (2016/17) show on average, GCSE (attainment 8 – which measures pupils' performance in eight GCSE level qualifications[3]) scores were higher for girls than boys across all ethnic groups, with girls achieving on average a score of 49.0, compared with 43.7 for boys. More specifically, the data show girls from the Chinese ethnic group achieved the higher average score out of all ethnic groups and among boys and girls. By comparison, the data show that boys from a Black Caribbean background scored the lowest average score, at 36.9, compared to Black Caribbean girls who scored 44. There is a range of explanations for the gender differences in educational attainment between girls and boys that include issues of differences in gendered expectations, the difference in the way teachers treat girls and boys, and the importance of role models (Gillborn and Mirza, 2000; Tomlinson, 2014).

Class has also frequently been used to explain the differences between not only ethnic minority pupils' GCSE attainment but also the differences in educational attainment among the broader population. The broader patterns of GCSE attainment suggest that pupils from a higher socio-economic background performed better on average. Gillborn and Mirza (2000: 18) analysed the historical patterns of educational attainment by a student's class and found on average that 'children from the most advantaged backgrounds were more than three times as likely to attain five or more higher grades at GCSE than their peers at the other end of the spectrum'. Gillborn and Mirza's study used free school meals (FSM) as an indicator of class, and while FSM is generally viewed more as a measure of household poverty, it is a useful if imperfect measure to examine broadly how class could affect educational attainment. Their results showed pupils who were eligible for FSM performed worse than those not eligible for FSM. The 2016/17 data show that when FSM is used in combination with ethnicity, the Gypsy and Irish Traveller students were the ethnic group most eligible for FSM and were also the least likely to achieve an A★ to C in maths (7%) or English (7%). While it seems clear that class and gender are significant factors that explain some of the pupils' attainment, Gillborn and Mirza (2000) found that, even when class and gender were controlled for, ethnic differences were still evident.

A levels/vocational training

Since 2015, the Education and Skills Act has made education compulsory in England until the age of 18 and requires students to continue in full-time education, start an apprenticeship/traineeship, or spend at least 20 hours or more volunteering while in part-time education/training (Gov.uk, 2018b). This change to compulsory education has not extended to Scotland, Wales or Northern Ireland. Department for Education data for 2016/17 show 222,084 students were entered for at least one A level or applied A level, with the ethnicity known for 181,348 of the students (82%). The data show that 76% of the students are White, 12% are Asian, 5% are Black, 5% are Mixed, 1% are Chinese and 2% are from Other ethnic groups. Again, compared to each group's share of the population, ethnic minorities are over-represented.

Considering the broader data (including students for whom the ethnicity was not known), 13.4% of students achieved three A grades or better at A level. In specific ethnic minority groups, 22.5% of the Chinese group achieved three A grades or better, which was the highest

Figure 5.4: Attainment 8 scores by eligibility for free school meals across ethnic groups

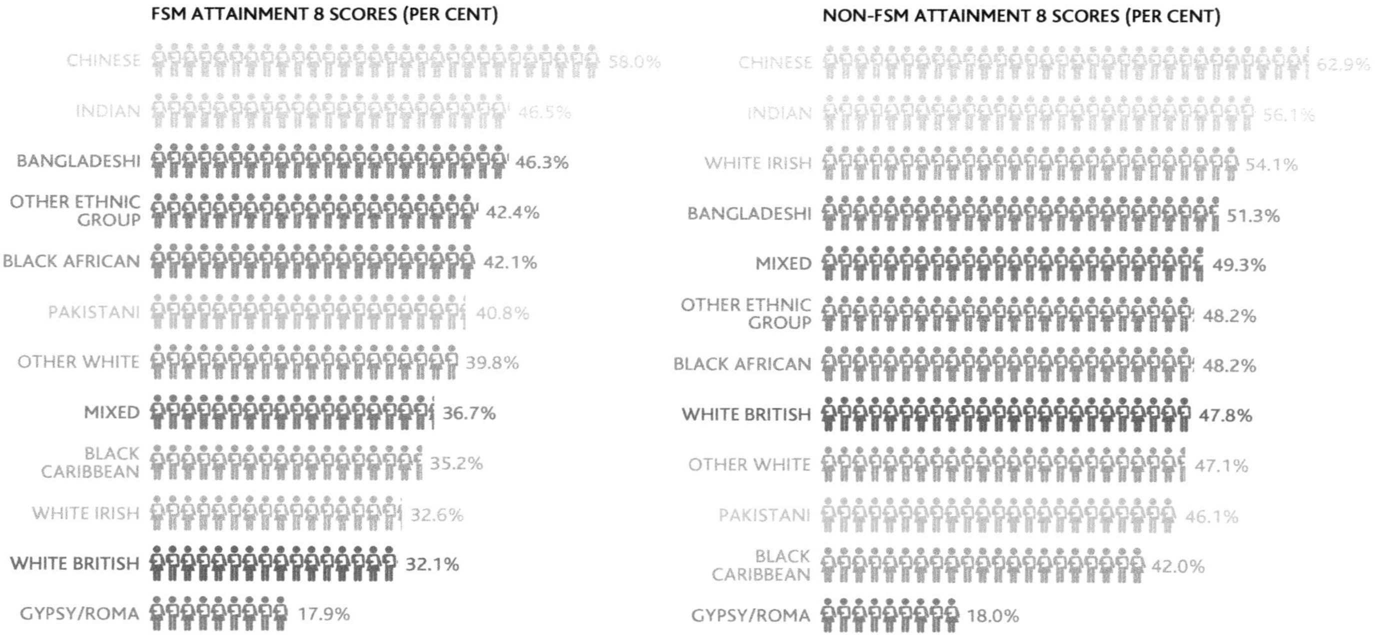

FSM ATTAINMENT 8 SCORES (PER CENT)

CHINESE — 58.0%
INDIAN — 46.5%
BANGLADESHI — 46.3%
OTHER ETHNIC GROUP — 42.4%
BLACK AFRICAN — 42.1%
PAKISTANI — 40.8%
OTHER WHITE — 39.8%
MIXED — 36.7%
BLACK CARIBBEAN — 35.2%
WHITE IRISH — 32.6%
WHITE BRITISH — 32.1%
GYPSY/ROMA — 17.9%

NON-FSM ATTAINMENT 8 SCORES (PER CENT)

CHINESE — 62.9%
INDIAN — 56.1%
WHITE IRISH — 54.1%
BANGLADESHI — 51.3%
MIXED — 49.3%
OTHER ETHNIC GROUP — 48.2%
BLACK AFRICAN — 48.2%
WHITE BRITISH — 47.8%
OTHER WHITE — 47.1%
PAKISTANI — 46.1%
BLACK CARIBBEAN — 42.0%
GYPSY/ROMA — 18.0%

Source: Key stage 4 and multi-academy trust performance 2017 (DfE, 2018e).

across all ethnic groups. A similar pattern was found for Chinese school leavers in Scotland (2016/17) where 90.8% of leavers achieved one or more passes at Scottish Credit and Qualifications Framework (SCQF) level six or better. This result was far higher than the percentage for White Scottish leavers (60.5%) (Gov.scot, 2017b). As with GCSE level examinations, a combination of their immigration history, socio-economic and socio-demographic profile may explain their high levels of attainment compared to other ethnic groups (see Chapter 1). Nonetheless, we need to be careful in the interpretation the data on the Chinese students as they remain disproportionately represented in the private education system in the UK (Gillborn and Mirza, 2000). Therefore, to determine if their attainment is consistent across education at this level would require data from the private and state school system, which is difficult to obtain. A level attainment across other ethnic groups shows variable results with, for example, the Indian group achieving 15.3%, Pakistani 7.3%, Black African 5.6%, and finally 3.5% of Black Caribbean students (Figure 5.5). The data also show that no Gypsy and Irish Traveller student in 2016/17 achieved three A grades or better at A level (there were only 13 students in this group).

Racism in schools

A key element of the experience of ethnic minority pupils in schools, but one which has perhaps been less examined or monitored, is the everyday experience of racism. This may arise in relationships between pupils, but also in the relationships between pupils and teachers, and in wider issues around the curriculum and the 'hidden curriculum' in schools' cultures (as discussed earlier in relation to the Prevent agenda) (Doharty, 2015; Richardson, 2015; Tomlinson, 2014).

The concern around racism between pupils is a long-standing one – an early example, which influenced policy, was the murder of 13-year-old Ahmed Iqbal Ullah in the playground of Burnage High School in Greater Manchester in 1986. The types of racism that have been documented in schools include physical fighting and name calling as well as verbal abuse against pupils and their families (see Varma-Joshi et al, 2004; Tomlinson, 2005; Cemlyn, 2009). However, data on racist incidents are unevenly monitored; the limited data that exist on cases of racist incidents reported are confined to hate crime statistics. Bulman (2018) found that between September 2016 and July 2017, 919 incidents of hate crimes were reported in or around schools in England. This equated to five offences occurring per day, of which 71% were attributed to race and ethnicity. Bulman (2018) found that compared

Figure 5.5: Percentage of students achieving at least three A grades at A level by ethnicity

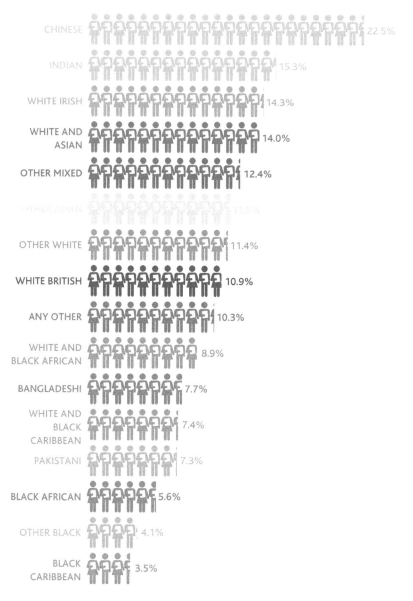

Source: A level and other 16 to 18 results: 2017 to 2018 (DfE, 2018f).

to the previous year there had been an increase in the number of hate crimes occurring in schools from 568 to 919. However, it is unclear if this is an issue of an increase in racism in schools or of reporting, and it is likely these figures are only the tip of the iceberg.

What is clear, however, is the relative inability of schools to address racist events, with studies by the Department for Education Statistics (2004), Myers and Bhopal (2015) and Andreouli, Greenland and Howarth's (2015) illustrating variation in reports of racism between institutions and localities. Although the Race Relations Amendment Act 2000 required all schools to report racist incidents (Hart, 2009), these studies revealed the differences in racist incident reporting practices across different locations. While there is limited quantitative data concerning the exact extent of racism in schools, these studies have found that, particularly in schools with largely white populations, there may be limited awareness of racism and a lack of staff knowledge about how to prepare children for a cultural and ethnically diverse society (Department for Education Statistics, 2004). Staff are unwilling or ill-equipped to deal with racist incidents, as it was not covered adequately in their teacher training (Maylor, 2015). Andreouli et al (2015) and Myers and Bhopal's (2015) studies revealed that teachers often felt that racism was located elsewhere (in multi-ethnic urban environments only) or in a different period (pre-Macpherson), while parents of ethnic minority children who attended schools in rural areas were viewed as troublemakers and their claims played down as minor incidents (Myers and Bhopal, 2015). The experience of ethnic minority students outside urban centres is increasingly important as ethnic diversity spreads geographically across the country.

However, racism is not confined to the way schools as institutions enact anti-racist legislation, it has also been found in the fashion in which teachers treat pupils from different ethnic backgrounds. Again, this has been a source of long-standing concerns and activism from black parents (Rattansi, 1992), and a focus of research on teachers' stereotypes and low expectations, particularly of Black Caribbean pupils. In recent years, similar concerns have emerged around the stereotyping of Muslim pupils, reflecting the broader climate which views Muslims as a social problem (Bhattacharyya, 2008; Mac an Ghaill and Haywood, 2014) – a perspective consolidated by the Prevent duty, as discussed earlier.

Racism and exclusions in schools

A particular indication of racism within schools may be the exclusion rates of ethnic minority groups compared to the White British population (Gillborn and Demack, 2018). School exclusions refer to times pupils are removed from schools for either a permanent or fixed period for up to 45 days in a school year (Gov.uk, 2018b).

As noted earlier, the exclusion of ethnic minority pupils in schools has been a long-standing issue of concern, particularly with Black Caribbean communities (Mac an Ghaill, 1988; Gillborn et al, 2017; Richardson, 2018). These trends have been exacerbated in recent decades by the marketisation, increased selectivity and target pressures across the school system. Gordon (2001) suggests exclusions from state educational institutions have been on the rise since the early 1990s, with BME students showing a greater than average rate of exclusion (both temporary and permanent) compared to White British pupils (Bhopal, 2018; Gillborn and Demack, 2018). The pattern of Black exclusions appears consistent from Early Year Foundation Stage (ages 4 and 5) through to Key Stage 4 (ages 15 and 16). However, it seems the issue is more pronounced during the final three years of compulsory secondary education, when students are due to sit their GCSE exams (Gillborn and Demack, 2018), raising concerns around 'off-rolling'. Figure 5.6, using the data from Gov.uk (2018b), shows the Irish

Figure 5.6: Ethnic composition of state school exclusions in England

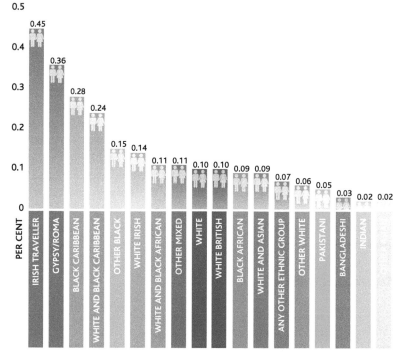

Note: The data for the Chinese group have been removed because the cell count was too small and therefore removed to protect the anonymity of the pupil/pupils.
Source: RDA 2016/17.

Traveller, Gypsy/Roma and Black Caribbean groups have the highest rates of permanent exclusions, with the level of fixed exclusions for the Black Caribbean group three times that of the pupil population as a whole (Bhopal, 2018: 69). By comparison, Figure 5.6 shows that pupils from the Asian (Asian Other, Indian, Bangladeshi and Pakistani) groups have the lowest rates of exclusions. Moreover, Crenna-Jennings (2017) suggests that students with special education needs and disability (SEND) are more likely to be permanently excluded than non-SEND students. When ethnicity, gender and SEND intersect, the most recent data indicate that Black Caribbean boys with SEND are 168 times more likely to be excluded than White girls who are non-SEND.

The disproportionality of exclusions among Black students has been attributed by Parsons (2018) to racist attitudes and stereotyping by teachers and school administrators. According to Crenna-Jennings (2017) the disproportional exclusion rate of Black pupils is deeply entrenched within statutory categories which were formulated in the 1960s and 1970s. These categories were conceived and assigned to children thought to be of so-called limited ability and perceived to have a tendency to experience mental health issues. More recently, Joseph-Salisbury and Connelly (2018) have also shown how the stigmatisation and pathologisation of hairstyles racialised as Black can lead to the disciplining and exclusion of Black students. Crenna-Jennings (2017) also suggests that exclusion rates may link to broader inequalities some ethnic groups experience, in the labour and housing market for example. Exclusion has serious knock-on effects for opportunities in the labour market (IPPR, 2017; Demie, 2019), However, we can also see the resilience of ethnic minority communities in setting up supplementary education (Reay and Mirza, 1997) and also increases in home schooling as a response to high rates of exclusion (D'Arcy, 2014; Bhopal and Myers, 2018).

Ethnic minority employment in education

Mac an Ghaill and Haywood's (2014) study found evidence that young people of all ethnic groups perceived a clear social distance between ethnic minority pupils and the demographics of staff in state schools in England. This is centred on class and also ethnicity. Studies show that this can have an effect on how the pupils are treated, but also the expectations of teachers with regards to pupils' behaviour and attainment. Recent data from the Department for Education Statistics for 2016/17 suggest there were 498,100 teachers in state-funded schools in England (including classroom teachers, headteachers, deputy and

Table 5.1: Ethnicity of the teaching workforce in state schools (primary and secondary) in England compared to each group's share of the working-age population, by gender, 2016–17

	PERCENTAGE OF TEACHER WORKFORCE	PERCENTAGE OF MALE TEACHER WORKFORCE	PERCENTAGE OF FEMALE TEACHER WORKFORCE	PERCENTAGE OF WORKING AGE POPULATION
WHITE BRITISH	86.2	86.2	86.3	78.5
OTHER WHITE	3.8	3.3	4.0	5.6
INDIAN	1.9	1.5	2.0	3.0
WHITE IRISH	1.6	2.0	1.5	1.0
PAKISTANI	1.1	1.1	1.1	2.0
BLACK CARIBBEAN	1.0	1.0	1.1	1.2
BLACK AFRICAN	0.8	1.3	0.7	1.9
OTHER ASIAN	0.6	0.7	0.6	1.7
ANY OTHER ETHNIC GROUP	0.6	0.6	0.6	0.7
BANGLADESHI	0.5	0.6	0.5	0.8
OTHER MIXED	0.5	0.4	0.5	0.5
OTHER BLACK	0.3	0.4	0.3	0.5
WHITE AND ASIAN	0.3	0.4	0.3	0.5
WHITE AND BLACK CARIBBEAN	0.3	0.3	0.3	0.6
CHINESE	0.2	0.2	0.2	0.9
WHITE AND BLACK AFRICAN	0.1	0.1	0.1	0.2

Note: Arab and Gypsy and Irish Traveller ethnic groups are not included because they were not sampled in the survey on the ethnicity of the teaching workforce in state schools in England.
Source: School workforce in England: November 2017 (DfE, 2018g).

assistant heads). For the academic year 2016/17 (England), the data suggest that 86.2% of staff were White British (401,400 teachers) with 13.6% coming from all other ethnic groups (including White minority groups). In addition, there were more female teachers than male teachers across almost all ethnic groups (Gov.uk, 2018b).

Table 5.1 shows, for 2016/17, teachers from the White British ethnic group make up the majority of teaching staff in state schools in England and are over-represented compared to their share of the working-age population from the 2011 Census. Data from Gov.uk (2018b) on the ethnicity of headteachers in England, for example, show that 93% of headteachers (20,700) were White British. Table 5.1 also shows all other ethnic groups are under-represented in the teaching profession apart from the White Irish and the Other Mixed group. Statistics Scotland (Gov.scot, 2017a) suggests for 2016/17 that only 7% of school teachers in Scotland recorded a non-white ethnic background, with the majority stating they were from a white ethnic background (93%). Nonetheless, a significant issue is that currently there are no publicly available data to disaggregate the ethnicity of the workforce by primary and secondary education as well as by region.

The lack of ethnic minority teachers in the sector has become a cause for concern, particularly in non-STEM (science, technology, engineering and mathematics) subjects (see, for example, the Royal Historical Society report by Atkinson et al, 2018). The Why Isn't My Teacher Black? campaign, for example, refers to a collection of writing and blog posts that highlight the issue in the education sector (Peacock, 2014; Young, 2018; *The Guardian*, 2018). In their study of recruitment practices in initial teacher education, Wilkins and Lall (2011) found that while ethnic minority recruitment has been increasing, rates of completion of training for ethnic minority recruits were lower than for White British trainees. According to Wilkins and Lall (2011), some of the reasons for the lack of completion by ethnic minority recruits were linked to their fears of social isolation in the teaching profession as well as some of the stereotypical attitudes they encountered from some White British peers, as well as instances of overt racism, particularly while they were on school placement.

Leaving school: race, ethnicity and non-compulsory education

Once students finish their A levels or training, they can enter the labour market or apply to higher education courses at a university or further education institution. Recent decades have seen a significant increase in the proportion of young people who enter into higher education, from an elite 5% of young people attending university in the 1960s to a current 40% of working-age adults with a college or university degree (Gibney, 2013). In 1999, New Labour introduced the Widening Participation Scheme to increase the number of young people who attended university to 50%. This move was intended to get more people from different social backgrounds into higher education, and as a consequence increased the number of ethnic minority students who were able to attend university and gain a university degree (Department for Education Statistics, 2004; Bhopal, 2018). The data show this trend, with ethnic minority groups disproportionately entering further or higher education.

The data (Figure 5.7) show that all ethnic minority groups (apart from Gypsy/Roma) have higher levels of continuing education after Key Stage 5 than their White British counterparts. The highest levels are found among the Chinese (84%), Black African (80%) and the Indian (79%) groups, whereas the lowest levels of continuing in education are found in the Gypsy/Roma (39%). Correspondingly, the highest levels of entry into employment after Key Stage 5 are among the White British (25%), Gypsy/Roma (24%) and Mixed (18%) whereas the lowest levels of entry into employment after Key Stage 5 are among the Chinese (5%), Black African (8%) and Bangladeshi (9%) groups. Finally, data show the highest levels where non-sustained education or employment are accessed after Key Stage

Figure 5.7: Destinations of school leavers Key Stage 5 (16–18) by ethnic group, 2017

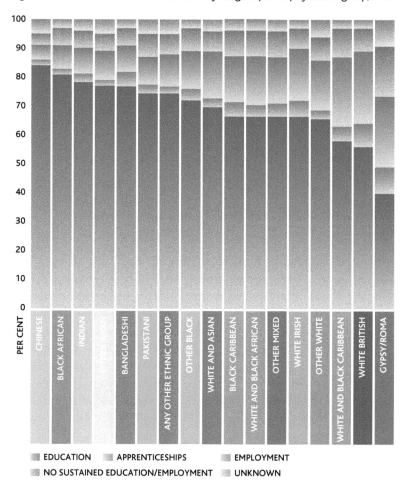

Note: Ethnic groups shown in increasing order of share of the ethnic group that continued on in the education system. Figures overlain on each section of the bars show the per cent of each ethnic group who pursued education, apprenticeships, employment, no education/employment or unknown after Key Stage 5. Source: DfE (2018).

5 are for the Irish Traveller (17%) group whereas the lowest is for the Chinese (4%), Black African (6%), Indian (6%) and Bangladeshi (6%) groups. Considering the data by order, we can see low levels of continued entry into education after Key Stage 5 are apparent for all white groups. Khattab (2018) argues that one of the reasons for the over-representation of ethnic minorities pursuing further or higher education after Key Stage 5 is a strategy to counterbalance the anticipated labour market discrimination and ethnic penalties they will experiences as well as their perception of the value of education as a means for social mobility.

Figure 5.8: Ethnic composition of apprenticeships from 2002/03 to 2017/18, England and Wales

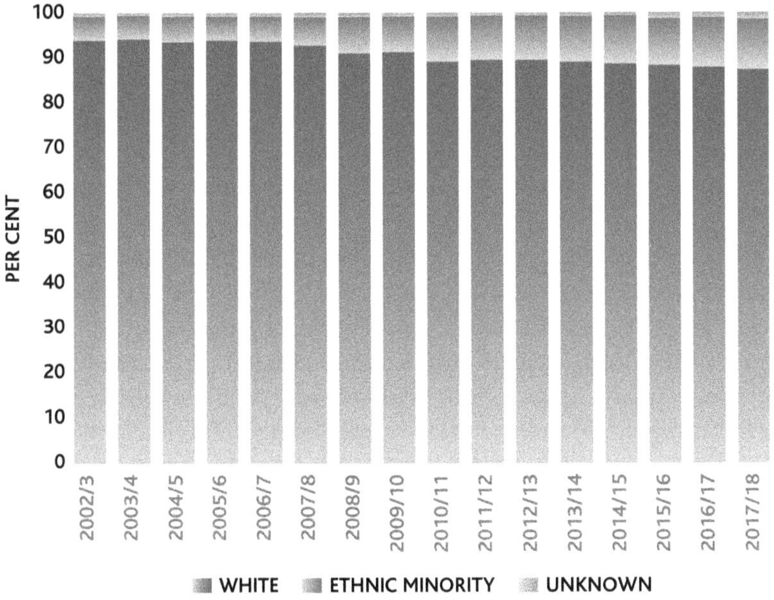

Source: Education and Skills Funding Agency (ESFA).

Further education

One option for students after Key Stage 5 is to enter into vocational training to learn a specific skill or trade. In April 2017, the apprenticeship levy was introduced across the UK, and required all UK employers with a pay bill over £3 million per year to pay the levy, to be spent on training and assessment (Powell, 2019). Further education provides a pathway to train in many vocational subjects. Data from the Department for Education (2018b) suggest that in 2016/17, 11.2% of those starting an apprenticeship were from an ethnic minority background, which is below their share of the population.

Even though the number of apprenticeships has increased since 2008, this increase has not been reflected in a parallel increase in the numbers of ethnic minority people who have started apprenticeships (Frumkin and Koustsoubou, 2013). Crucially, Figure 5.8 shows that only 10.6% of apprentices were from an ethnic minority background, which is below the 13% share of the population of England and Wales in the 2011 Census. However, the data from the Department for Education (2018b) show that the percentage of ethnic minority people who start apprenticeships has increased from 5.3% in 2002/03 to 11.2%

in 2017/18, with the number of ethnic minority apprentices growing from 8,900 (2002/03) to 42,230 (2017/18). A study by the Black Training and Enterprise Group (2019) that looked at the differences in ethnic minority participation in apprenticeships (2016/17) found that 0.9% of Black Caribbean, 1.5% Black African, 1.1% Indian, 1.1 Pakistani, 0.8% Bangladeshi and 1.9% from the Mixed groups successfully completed a course. The statistics suggest an increase in ethnic minority people's participation on apprenticeship programmes. Nevertheless, the dramatic growth of apprenticeships in England has been overwhelmingly taken up by White British young people (Frumkin and Koustsoubou, 2013). Some of this differential take up may be related to different levels of awareness of the apprenticeship route and also the higher proportion of ethnic minority groups that continues on to higher education. However, given the known patterns of discrimination and exclusion in employment, it is likely that racial discrimination is also operating in the distribution of apprenticeships. More research is needed in this area (Black Training and Enterprise Group, 2019).

Aiming higher: race, ethnicity and inequality in universities

As noted, the majority of ethnic minority school leavers elect to enter higher education (Blanden and Machin, 2004; Boliver, 2011; Alexander and Arday, 2015). Data from AdvanceHE for 2016/17 show that 26% of all undergraduate students in England are from ethnic minorities, with 43% of these from Asian, 31% from Black (Caribbean and African), 16.4% from mixed ethnicity, and 3.7% from Chinese backgrounds (Table 5.2).

More detailed analysis shows that there is variation within racial group, with larger proportions of African-, Indian- and Pakistani-descent students than other groups.

Access

However, it is crucial to be attentive to the types of institutions where ethnic minority students are found (Boliver, 2015, 2018; Tatlow, 2015) as this can be revealing of issues of inequalities in access across the higher education landscape. The proportion of ethnic minority students who attend Russell Group versus New Universities is commonly used as an indicator of equality of access. This is because Russell Group universities are viewed as more prestigious

Table 5.2: UK-domiciled students by country of institution and ethnic group (2016/17)

	PERCENTAGE OF UK-DOMICILED STUDENTS				
	ENGLAND	NORTHERN IRELAND	SCOTLAND	WALES	UK
WHITE BRITISH	74.0	96.6	91.7	89.8	77.3
BME	26.0	3.4	8.3	10.2	22.7
BANGLADESHI	1.5	0.1	0.2	0.8	1.2
INDIAN	3.9	0.5	0.9	1.4	3.4
PAKISTANI	3.3	0.3	1.6	0.9	2.9
BLACK AFRICAN	6.0	0.5	1.5	1.9	5.2
BLACK CARIBBEAN	1.8	0.1	0.1	0.4	1.5
OTHER BLACK	0.4	0.1	0.1	0.1	0.4
CHINESE	0.9	0.4	0.7	0.5	0.8
OTHER MIXED	4.1	0.7	1.8	2.4	3.7
ARAB	0.6	0.1	0.3	0.2	0.5
ANY OTHER ETHNIC GROUP	1.1	0.2	0.4	0.6	1.0

Source: HESA data for 2016/17 (2018).

research-driven universities and have the most resources (Tatlow, 2015). Historically, Russell Group universities have lower levels of student admissions from people from ethnic minority backgrounds, as well as students from state schools and low-income backgrounds, indicating stratification within the higher education system in Britain (Bhopal, 2018). The disparity across ethnic groups as to who attends Russell Group versus New Universities has been linked to ethnic minority people's lack of familiarity with the Russell Group admissions process, and broader issues of lack of recognised social and cultural capital (Bhopal, 2018), as well as concerns around discrimination in the admissions system (Boliver, 2015, 2016).

Figure 5.9 highlights that the Black group is under-represented in Russell Group institutions compared to other ethnic minority and White groups. A more detailed analysis by Boliver (2016) found that ethnic minority applicants are more likely to choose oversubscribed courses and are less likely to receive offers from Russell Group universities than equally qualified white applicants 'even when the numerical competitiveness of courses have been taken into account' (Boliver, 2016: 261). Furthermore, Boliver's (2016: 261) analysis also found that ethnic inequalities in admissions were greater for degree subject areas at Russell Group universities where 'the percentage of ethnic minority applications is higher'. While data restrictions imposed by UCAS (Universities and Colleges Admissions Service) have limited analysis of the exact mechanisms, Boliver (2016: 262) suggests that one explanation 'is that, consciously or unconsciously, some admissions selectors might be unfairly rejecting some ethnic minority applicants in order to achieve an entering class with an ethnic mix that is ultimately representative of the ... wider

Figure 5.9: Ethnic composition of UK-domiciled higher education student enrolment by university type (Russell Group versus New University) and ethnicity

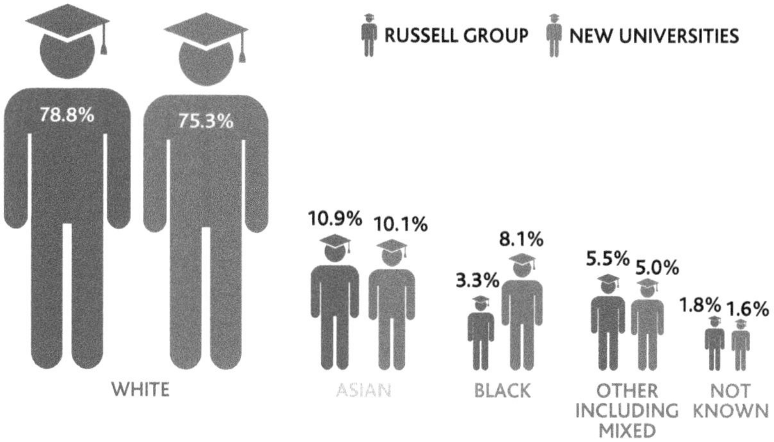

Source: HESA data for 2016/17 (2018).

population'. Boliver (2016) argues that more research, particularly qualitative research, is needed into admissions selectors' decision making to ascertain the exact mechanisms underpinning this form of ethnic inequality.

Attainment

As well as differences in university type, and degree programme, there are also stark differences in degree attainment by ethnicity, and in particular by differences in 'good degrees' (that is first or upper second classifications) (Richardson, 2018). The difference in the percentage of students who receive a 'good' degree classification compared to their white counterparts is known as the 'attainment gap'. This gap is found across ethnic minority groups

There is, however, a clear difference in the ethnic attainment gap between Russell Group and post-1992/New institutions, and across degree subjects (Richardson, 2018). Figure 5.10 shows that all ethnic minority groups' students who attend Russell Group universities achieve a higher proportion of good degrees than those who attend New Universities. Figure 5.9 also shows the most notable attainment gap within a specific ethnic minority group and between institution type is for Black African followed by Black Caribbean groups. For example, 77.82% of Black students who attend Russell Group universities achieve a good degree compared to 66.33% of Black students who attend New Universities in Britain; a percentage point

Figure 5.10: Proportion of students from each ethnic group who obtained a 'good degree' split by Russell Group and New Universities (2016/17)

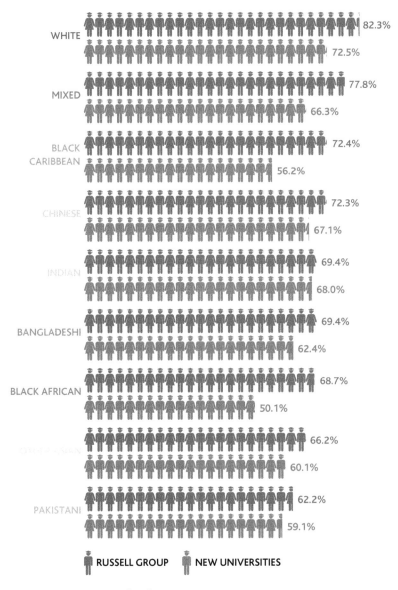

Source: HESA data for 2016/17 (2018).

difference of 11.49%. While there is a difference in the number of ethnic minority students who attend New Universities compared to Russell Group universities, the findings suggest the type of university a student attends continues to affect the likelihood of their achieving a good degree at graduation.

However, it is important to bear in mind the difference in access/ attendance between institution types: for example, only 2,210 Black students graduated from Russell Group universities in 2016/ 17 compared to 19,020 Black students who graduated from New Universities. Once graduated, ethnic minority students then face the challenge of converting their degrees into access and entry into the labour market (Li, 2015).

HESA (Higher Education Statistics Agency) 2016/17 (2018) data show the earning differences across ethnic groups a year after graduating. The data suggest graduates from the Indian and Chinese ethnic groups had the highest average earnings one year after graduation, at £21,900 and £21,700 respectively. Meanwhile, graduates from the Other Black and Bangladeshi ethnic group had the lowest average earnings one year after graduation, at £17,400 and £17,900. Moreover, ten years after graduation, graduates with highest average earnings were from Asian Other and Indian groups, at £33,200 and £33,100; those with the lowest average earnings were from the Pakistani (£24,700) group. Furthermore, comparing the destinations after graduation, HESA (2018) data for 2015/16 suggest that White graduates had the highest percentage of sustained employment, further study or both, one year after graduation (87.4%), followed by graduates from the Indian (86.3%) and Black Caribbean (86.0%) ethnic groups. Meanwhile, graduates from the Other Black (13.1%), Pakistani (12.2%) and Black African (11.5%) ethnic groups were the most likely to have no sustained destination compared with all other ethnic groups. (For a more comprehensive overview of the differences across ethnic groups see Chapter 6 on ethnic inequalities in the labour market.)

Employment in higher education

As with primary and secondary schooling, racial and ethnic inequalities in higher education can also be measured by looking at the demography of the staff who work within higher education institutions, and has been highlighted in recent years by the high-profile student-led Why Isn't My Professor Black? campaign (Joseph-Salisbury, 2019), and the establishment of the Race Equality Chartermark (Bhopal and Pitkin, 2018; Bhopal and Henderson, 2019). Data from HESA (2018) for 2016/17 show the breakdown of academic and non-academic staff working in higher education in the UK. There are two ways to look at ethnic inequalities in higher education: first, the representation of ethnic minorities in the workforce as a whole and, second, the representation of ethnic minorities at different levels of the workforce (for example, professorial versus non-professorial). It is apparent that ethnic minority academics are under-represented in higher education, with less than 10% of academic staff of ethnic minority origin.

Looking at the workforce within higher education as a whole, we can see that staffing varies significantly by ethnic group and UK/non-UK nationality. Table 5.3 shows that, among non-UK national staff, Chinese, Indian, Other Asian and Black African groups are over-represented compared to their proportion of the UK population. Meanwhile, Bangladeshi, Black Caribbean, Mixed and Other Black groups are under-represented. However, all BME groups are under-represented in relation to their proportions of the working-age population (See Table 5.1).

The profile of staffing becomes starker at more senior levels, with a marked disparity at professorial level, with only 8.4% ethnic minority professors, meaning 91.6% of professors in the UK are from White backgrounds. As Figure 5.11 illustrates, there are small numbers of Black professors (4.6%), and an over-representation of Chinese professors (15.8%). Again, this is likely to be skewed by the presence of non-UK professors. As Figure 5.11 shows, there is a significant difference between men and women in both professorial and non-professorial grades in higher education by ethnicity (Wright et al, 2017; Solanke, 2018). Figure 5.11 shows ethnic minority women are particularly poorly represented in professorial roles in higher education in the UK and White groups dominate all academic roles across men and women. Considering

Table 5.3: Ethnic composition of UK/non-UK staff, percentage of total

	UK NATIONALS	NON-UK NATIONALS	ALL STAFF
ASIAN	42.9	36.8	40.3
BANGLADESHI	3.7	1.5	2.8
INDIAN	23.3	15.5	20.0
PAKISTANI	7.7	3.1	5.8
OTHER ASIAN	8.2	16.6	11.7
BLACK	21.5	14.6	18.6
BLACK AFRICAN	9.6	11.4	10.4
BLACK CARIBBEAN	10.4	1.6	6.7
OTHER BLACK	1.5	1.6	1.5
CHINESE	10.4	25.2	16.6
MIXED	17.3	9.6	14.1
WHITE AND ASIAN	5.3	1.7	3.8
WHITE AND BLACK AFRICAN	1.6	1.1	1.4
WHITE AND BLACK CARIBBEAN	3.5	0.5	2.2
OTHER MIXED	6.9	6.6	6.3
OTHER	8.0	13.8	10.4
ARAB	1.3	2.7	1.9
ANY OTHER ETHNIC GROUP	6.7	11.1	8.6

Source: HESA data for 2016/17 (2018).

Figure 5.11: Ethnic composition of UK academic staff by gender, professorial category

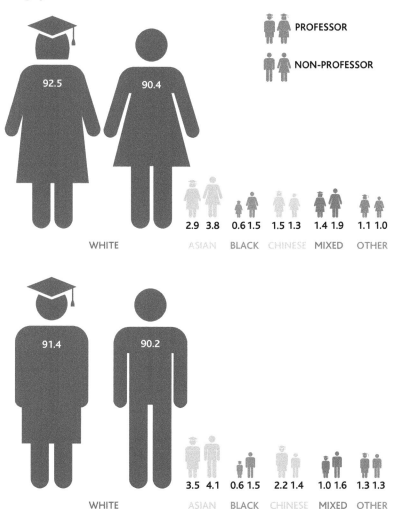

Source: HESA (2018).

the percentage of each ethnic group in the working-age population, Figure 5.11 shows that all ethnic minority groups are under-represented compared to their share of the working-age population and at different levels of the academic hierarchy (professorial and non-professorial level). In addition, the 2017/18 Higher Education Statistics Agency staff record suggests an ethnic disparity among non-academic staff, with 84.34% of the staff reporting they were from a White background, 2.90% Black, 5.50% Asian, 2.38% Other and 5.88% not known (HESA, 2018). Here we can see that the Black and Other group are over-represented in non-academic roles compared to their share of the working-age population, whereas the White and Asian groups were under-represented compared to their share of the working-age population.

Arday (2015) explains the poor levels of representation of ethnic minorities in higher education as a consequence of recruitment practices, but there are also broader perceptions around universities as 'white' spaces (Arday and Mirza, 2018; Joseph-Salisbury, 2019). These exclusionary practices also explain the restrictions on ethnic minority staff members progressing to more senior positions, with many early career researchers describing the existence of a glass ceiling, which prevented many of them from progressing further in their disciplines. In addition, Bhopal (2015: 38) found among ethnic minority staff respondents, that many experienced 'covert exclusionary processes that relate to their ethnicity'. Many felt they experienced differential treatment compared to their White counterparts, as well as more overt incidents of racism (Atkinson et al, 2018). Moreover, some experienced feelings of a lack of trust, questions over their credibility as well as 'over-scrutinisation' which their white colleagues did not experience (Bhopal, 2015; Mirza, 2015; Rollock, 2019).

It is significant that while the numbers of ethnic minority students have increased over time, the proportion of ethnic minority academics has not increased at a similar rate. Importantly, the presence or absence of ethnic minority staff members can affect the experience of ethnic minority students attending their institutions as they can provide informal support and role models (Arday, 2015; Joseph-Salisbury, 2019).

Campaigning for equality

While the ethnic inequality of the workforce in schools and universities has become a recent focus in academic writing (Arday and Mirza, 2018), it has also become an issue for students, activists and the media – for example in the high-profile campaigns Why Isn't My Professor Black?, Why Is My Curriculum White?, I Too Am Oxford and the Rhodes Must Fall campaign.

Two charter schemes have been introduced in higher education aimed at tackling inequality around gender and race in the sector. The Athena Swan award was introduced in 2005 and requires universities to demonstrate their commitment to gender equality to receive an award. The second, more recent scheme has been the Race Equality Mark, introduced in 2016, which provides a framework specifically to address matters of race in higher education where universities demonstrate their commitment to racial equality in their institutions to receive an award (Bhopal et al, 2015; Bhopal and Pitkin, 2018; Bhopal and Henderson, 2019). However the Race Equality Mark is not compulsory or linked to any metric of academic rigour or success such as the Research Excellence Framework (REF) or Teaching Excellence Framework (TEF). It is likely that universities will only sign up if they believe it a benefit in terms of their reputation (Bhopal, 2016) and it is startling that in its first year only 21 institutions applied, and only 8 were awarded. This latter number has only risen to 12 institutions in 2019. The growth of the award has been much slower than its sister, Athena Swan award, and it seems unlikely to gain the same traction (Bhopal and Pitkin, 2018; Bhopal and Henderson, 2019).

Conclusion

This chapter clearly illustrates that ethnic inequalities persist across the education system in Britain, despite changing demographics in UK schools. One enduring concern has been the attainment gap between white and (some) ethnic minority pupils in state schools in Britain – a pattern that has been consistent across GCSE and A level examinations. New data from 2016/17 show us that there is now great variation across groups, with Chinese and Indian pupils outperforming other groups at both GCSE and A level examinations, whereas Black Caribbean, Pakistani and Gypsy and Irish Traveller groups perform consistently poorly compared to other groups. Analysing attainment by intersecting characteristics of gender and class highlights that girls continue to perform better than boys, and those from a higher class background perform better than those from a lower class background: nevertheless ethnic differences remain.

While attainment is a significant concern, schools continue to be viewed as a significant site where the British government believes it can solve social problems, with the most recent example being embedded in the Prevent policy. However, the policy has been criticised for disproportionately targeting Muslim and/or South Asian pupils. Its use has been blamed for creating a chasm of mistrust between schools and Muslim communities across the country, with little focus on other forms of radicalisation. The role of schools as site of internal border controls for migrant and asylum seeking children also needs greater scrutiny.

These issues are replicated in the further and higher education sectors, with ongoing concerns around under-representation in apprenticeship schemes and ethnic inequality in access, attainment and employability at universities. Campaigns such as Why Isn't My Professor Black? point to the inadequate representation of ethnic minorities among academic staff, as well as a lack of diversity across ethnic groups and, particularly, by gender. These campaigns have sought to highlight the structural barriers that have prevented ethnic minorities' representation and visibility across institutions. The campaigns to 'decolonise the curriculum' have also brought attention to ethnic inequality and exclusions in the curriculum, and sought to improve the representation and role that ethnic minorities have in the formation and pursuit of knowledge.

Finally, the introduction of the Race Equality Charter Mark (REC) could be a positive change to the higher education landscape in Britain. Similar to the Athena Swan Award (which has increased the representation of women in STEM subjects), the REC has the potential to bring about institutional change across higher education institutions that commit to this scheme, demonstrating the sector's commitment to racial equality. Nevertheless, to date, few universities have signed up to the scheme and/or received the bronze award. It remains to be seen if the REC will have the same traction and commitment as Athena Swan, and whether it will have the force to achieve broad cultural change within higher education institutions.

Notes

[1] The authors would also like to thank David Gillborn, Kalwant Bhopal, Bridget Byrne and Remi Joseph-Salisbury for comments on the chapter.

[2] DoE, Schools, pupils and their characteristics: January 2018, https://assets. publishing.service.gov.uk/government/uploads/system/uploads/attachment_data/ file/719226/Schools_Pupils_and_their_Characteristics_2018_Main_Text.pdf

[3] A student's Attainment 8 score is calculated by adding up the points for their eight subjects and dividing by 10 to get their Attainment 8 score. Students don't have to take eight subjects, but they score zero for any unfilled slots.

6

Ethnic minorities in the labour market in Britain

Ken Clark and William Shankley

Key findings

- Labour Force Survey (LFS) data show significant differences in levels of economic activity across ethnicity groups and, within groups, by gender, including a sustained ethnic penalty in earnings suffered by some groups. (1) While the LFS shows variation across ethnic groups by gender, there is evidence of employment rate gaps between white groups and non-white groups narrowing over time. Removing students from the analysis also narrows the employment rate gap; (2) Self-employment rates differ between men and women, with Pakistani men and Chinese women showing the highest rate of self-employment. High rates of self-employment for non-white groups can be linked to discrimination in the paid labour market which makes self-employment an attractive alternative.
- Broader economic and labour market policy has been found to disproportionately impact on ethnic minority workers and households. (1) The introduction of Universal Credit disproportionately affects ethnic minority groups particularly women. Their immigration history and socio-economic profiles reduce their resilience to any sanctions imposed; (2) Despite higher coverage rates, the national minimum (or living) wage may not be paid to individuals from some ethnic minority groups (particularly Bangladeshis, Pakistanis and Chinese). This is partly the result of non-compliance by employers.
- There is great variation in the representation of non-white workers in the public sector, with the state education system (primary and secondary), armed forces and non-medical positions in the National Health Service (NHS) dominated by white groups, while ethnic minority groups are well represented in medical roles in the NHS. Future policy needs to address exclusionary practices in specific institutions rather than the public sector as a whole.

- Key pieces of public policy, such as the Ethnic Minority Employment Task Force (EMETF) and the McGregor-Smith review, have attempted to reduce ethnic labour market disadvantage, however these have had, at best, limited success to date.

Introduction[1]

In February 2017 an independent UK government review highlighted the continued disadvantage that ethnic minority people face in the labour market compared to their White British counterparts (McGregor-Smith, 2017). Such disadvantage has been a notable feature of the experience of non-white workers for decades and can be seen in measurements of different dimensions of labour market outcomes such as activity, employment, self-employment and earnings. Much scholarly attention has been devoted to this issue and new data sources have become available. It is now more widely understood that differences between different non-white groups can themselves be substantial and there is a more nuanced awareness of the differences between groups. It is less clear, however, that the enhanced portfolio of evidence has been matched by successful policy action to address ethnic inequalities. While policymakers have attempted to address inequalities in a variety of ways, the continued disadvantage that we observe suggests that their efforts so far have been limited at best.

In this chapter, we provide an up-to-date snapshot of how individuals from ethnic minority backgrounds in the UK compare in their labour market behaviour to those from other groups including the White British majority. This is contextualised by a discussion of how a number of powerful external drivers have changed, and continue to change, the nature of work and labour markets. We then discuss two major policy initiatives from central government which were specifically designed to address ethnic labour market inequalities, as well as other policy developments, with a view to assessing what has or has not worked in the past and what is likely to be effective in the future. We also consider public sector employment as a particular site where the government can have a direct influence on employment and work conditions and where a moral responsibility to promote equality can be exercised by the state.

The labour market is fundamental to individuals' life chances and welfare. National living standards depend ultimately on productivity, which in turn depends on the size of the workforce and its quality, in terms of human capital. Equally important to questions of fairness in society and social cohesion is the question of how labour and its rewards are distributed between different groups. It is with this perspective in mind and amid a landscape of transforming labour markets, increasing precarity and the uncertainties associated with Brexit that we position our analysis of the labour market experiences of ethnic minority groups.

The changing UK labour market

The period since mass migration from former colonies first led to sizeable non-white populations living in the UK has seen the British labour market undergo considerable change driven by a number of interrelated developments at both national and international levels. Deindustrialisation has been a constant theme, driven in part by globalisation and technological change which, in turn, have contributed to rising wage inequality and polarisation in job types. Women have joined the labour market in larger numbers and the issue of workplace diversity has become a more central concern. Wider economic and social trends have led to a legislative change which has simultaneously reduced worker protection in some areas, such as trade union activity, but which has also strengthened protection against discrimination (for example the Equality Act 2010). A transforming labour market impacts all workers but it need not impact them all equally and each of these wider developments has played a particular role in influencing how workers from particular ethnic backgrounds participate in, and benefit from, work.

Long-term patterns of deindustrialisation and the move to a service-based economy have led to the offshoring of a substantial proportion of traditional manufacturing industry. There is a certain irony in the fact that while manufacturing jobs were moving from the UK in the global North to rising economies in the global South, the UK was experiencing waves of Commonwealth immigration in the opposite direction. Kalra (2000) notes how South Asian workers who came to Britain prior to the 1980s were employed in industries which were in long-term decline, and how the employment experience of men from this group was a journey from 'textile mills to taxi ranks'. While labouring in manufacturing industry could be intensive and physically demanding, there was a regularity to the hours, some degree of employee protection and rights, and a lower degree of risk compared to the more precarious world of marginal service sector employment and self-employment as taxi drivers or in takeaways.

In tandem with the offshoring of industrial employment, technological change in the form of the increasing use of information technology and automation in the workplace has had a profound effect on the demand for labour. Many jobs traditionally undertaken by workers are now done by computers or machines and further technological disruption to labour markets is a recurring theme for writers who attempt to predict the future of work (Brynjolfsson and McAfee, 2014). However, it is clear that the development of technology affects some sectors more than others. For instance, while the textile sector saw many jobs lost to automation, a need for health and social care to respond to the ageing population is likely to remain. In occupations like these, automation and outsourcing cannot occur to the same extent as manufacturing because they require specific 'human' skills such as empathy or levels of manual dexterity that machines cannot at present replicate. Such jobs in many countries have often attracted non-white immigrants and are often a route into the labour market for women.

The feminisation of the workforce has also impacted on labour markets more generally. The employment rate for women in the UK was 53% in 1971 compared to around 71% in 2018, however there is substantial ethnic differentiation in this rate as noted later in this chapter (ONS, 2019). Many women entered the labour market in low-paid, part-time employment, where they were in competition with younger male workers and those from ethnic minority backgrounds. As well as more egalitarian social attitudes, the growth of the service sector has increased female labour force participation and, as noted by Goos and Manning (2007), there is a link to the increasing educational attainment of women. Male educational attainment has also increased on average, with the expansion of higher education and increases in minimum school leaving ages. Again, the degree of human capital investment and the returns it generates have not been uniformly distributed across ethnic groups.

The increasing supply of skills in the labour market associated with greater educational participation is in part a response to the needs of an economy in which automation, technological change and globalisation have fundamentally changed patterns of labour demand. The implications of this for workers include rising wage inequality, particularly in the period between the late 1970s and the early 2000s, and polarisation of the occupational structure of the labour market. Skill-biased technical change (Goos and Manning, 2007), the idea that technological innovations disproportionately increase the demand for skilled workers relative to the unskilled, presents a convincing argument for increased wage inequalities and has been used to explain why some ethnic minority groups perform better than others (McCall, 2002).

There has also been a series of shifts in the relationship between the employer and employee over the period, driven in part by changing patterns of work but also facilitated by policy changes, which have reduced the strength of worker protection legislation. Unionisation has been in decline in the UK since the late 1970s when the proportion of employees who were members of a union was over 50% compared to 23% in 2017 (DBEIS, 2018a). In line with further globalisation and technology-driven connectedness, recruitment agencies now play an increasing role (locally, nationally and internationally) as an intermediary or conduit by connecting prospective workers with employers. Recent years have also seen increasing concern about non-standard, less formal patterns of paid employment, such as the use of so-called 'zero-hours' contracts and the rise of the 'gig' economy (Kuhn, 2016). While some legislation, such as that to limit trade union activity, might be thought to work against securing improvements for ethnic minorities in the labour market, there has also been a suite of legislation specifically directed at reducing discrimination in a range of contexts including employment. The Equality Act 2010 collated and superseded four previous Acts of Parliament and other statutory provisions and protects people against discrimination on the grounds of nine protected characteristics one of which is race. Such concern with fairness in the workplace is consistent with an increased interest from business in workplace diversity and its perceived benefits (Clark, 2015a).

A snapshot of ethnic minorities in the labour market

Tables 6.1 and 6.2 present a snapshot of the labour market outcomes for different ethnic groups by sex in the UK based on the quarterly LFS. The data set refers to men aged 16 to 64 and women aged 16 to 59 who were interviewed between January 2015 and June 2018. A range of labour market indicators is presented including the activity (or participation) rate, employment rate, unemployment rate, self-employment rate and the mean weekly earnings of those in employment. The employment rate is also re-calculated excluding students from both the numerator and denominator of the calculation. This follows the approach taken by Clark and Drinkwater (2007) to account for differential rates of educational participation between different ethnic groups. If a large proportion of a group is in education then these people are counted as non-employed which tends to reduce the employment rate measure. Nonetheless, those who continue in post-compulsory education have higher employment rates on graduation than those who do not; hence including students may bias our measure of ethnic differences in employment rates where there are

Table 6.1: Labour market characteristics of ethnic minority groups in the UK (men)

MEN	ECONOMIC ACTIVITY (%)	EMPLOYMENT (%)	EMPLOYMENT (NO STUDENTS) (%)	UNEMPLOYMENT (%)	SELF-EMPLOYMENT (%)	MEAN EARNINGS (£/WEEK)
WHITE BRITISH	82.2	79.9	83.6	4.0	14.3	651.0
WHITE IRISH	84.7	83.8	85.1	2.5	17.4	853.5
OTHER WHITE	90.9	88.3	92.4	2.6	18.2	647.2
INDIAN	84.2	80.4	87.3	4.5	13.3	720.4
PAKISTANI	77.9	71.5	81.4	6.9	23.3	507.7
BANGLADESHI	77.8	71.9	81.7	6.6	17.5	385.6
CHINESE	68.7	66.5	82.2	3.6	13.5	744.8
BLACK AFRICAN	79.0	71.6	83.0	8.0	11.6	489.9
BLACK CARIBBEAN	81.9	73.7	77.9	10.0	12.7	505.6

Notes: Variables used: ETHEWEUL, SEX, ILOEFR (economic activity), INECACO5 (self-employed), GRSSWK (wages), men (ages 16 to 64)/women (ages 16 to 59).
Source: Quarterly Labour Force Survey (merged data from 14 waves of data, January 2015 to June 2018).

Table 6.2: Labour market characteristics of ethnic minority groups in the UK (women)

WOMEN	ECONOMIC ACTIVITY (%)	EMPLOYMENT (%)	EMPLOYMENT (NO STUDENTS) (%)	UNEMPLOYMENT (%)	SELF-EMPLOYMENT (%)	MEAN EARNINGS (£/WEEK)
WHITE BRITISH	78.8	75.6	78.8	3.5	7.9	408.2
WHITE IRISH	79.9	76.2	78.7	3.8	6.9	619.0
OTHER WHITE	78.9	74.9	78.5	4.6	10.2	443.4
INDIAN	72.0	67.5	72.0	5.9	6.8	469.0
PAKISTANI	41.1	37.8	41.1	12.8	5.1	329.0
BANGLADESHI	41.3	34.9	37.1	13.8	3.2	355.9
CHINESE	61.8	60.1	73.1	3.2	10.6	531.1
BLACK AFRICAN	69.1	60.2	68.3	10.3	4.4	377.5
BLACK CARIBBEAN	77.0	71.5	76.7	6.5	5.4	428.0

Notes: See notes to Figure 6.1.
Source: Quarterly Labour Force Survey (merged data from 14 waves of data, January 2015 to June 2018).

large disparities in rates of educational participation between groups (see Chapter 5 on education for more details).

Economic activity

A basic indicator of how well different groups are integrated into the labour market is the level of labour market participation or economic activity. A respondent to the LFS is classified as active if they are either working or not working but looking for work. Among men, Table 6.1 suggests that the ethnic minority groups that show the highest levels of economic activity are the Indian and white groups (White Irish and White Other) whereas the groups that show the lowest levels of economic activity are the Chinese (68.7%), Bangladeshi (77.8%) and Pakistani (77.9%) groups. Among women, Table 6.2 suggests that the non-British white groups again have the highest rates whereas the lowest levels of economic activity are for the Bangladeshi (41.3%) and Pakistani (41.1%) groups. There are a number of explanations for the ethnic and gender differences across ethnic minority groups with regard to their economic activity. One reason for the high activity rate among the white ethnic minority groups is their relatively high proportion of labour migrants, their relatively young average age and their lack of caregiving commitments. Meanwhile, many families from South Asian groups (Indian, Pakistani and Bangladeshi) are responsible for caregiving (child and adult dependents) in line with traditional attitudes to gender roles. Cumulatively, these themes explain the high levels of economic inactivity, particularly for women, in Pakistani and Bangladeshi groups (Khoudja and Platt, 2018). Moreover, Carter et al (2015) find that ethnic and gender norms are prevalent in minority business structures and can act to prevent women from becoming entrepreneurs. Inactivity may also reflect that some individuals are 'discouraged workers' who have dropped out of the labour market because of a perceived lack of employment opportunities. Students and those who are long-term sick or ill are also classified as inactive, which means that groups with high proportions of students tend to have lower activity rates. This is particularly so for the Chinese group.

Employment

Employment rates are often used as a measure of labour market success. Joblessness is a powerful predictor of poverty and the analysis of employment rates can shed light on welfare disparities across ethnic groups. For this reason, reducing the employment rate gap between white and non-white workers was one of the central ambitions of UK government policy in the 2000s. The raw employment rates in Figures 6.1 and 6.2 measure the percentage of the age group who are either in paid employment or are self-employed. The data suggests that there is a high level of variation in employment rates between groups. For men these range from 88.3% for the White Other group to 66.5% for the Chinese. Most of the largest non-white ethnic groups have lower employment rates than the majority White British group, the exception being the Indians. For women, reflecting the previous discussion of participation rates, the variation in outcomes between groups is even wider than for the men. The Pakistani and Bangladeshi women are notable for the employment rates which are less than half those of White British women. Indeed all the non-white groups have lower employment rates than the White British.

Figure 6.1: Employment rates for men, 16–64, 2001–18

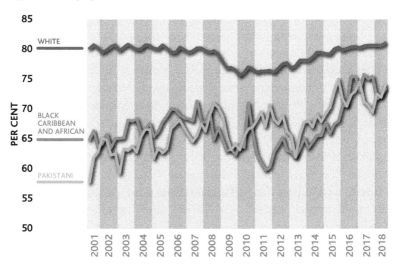

Source: 2001–18 Labour Force Survey.

Figure 6.2: Employment rates for women, 16–64, 2001–18

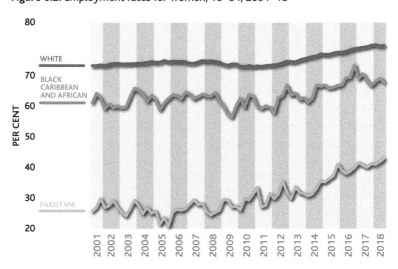

Source: 2001–18 Labour Force Survey.

Excluding students from the employment rate calculation to account for differential rates of educational participation between groups makes a considerable difference to the observed patterns and demonstrates the usefulness of this approach. The gap between White British and other ethnic groups is substantially reduced. For example, excluding students increases the White British employment rate by 3.5 percentage points but the equivalent figure for Pakistani men is nearly 10 percentage points higher. This has the effect of reducing the employment rate gap between these groups from 6.8 percentage points to 0.6 percentage points. A similar pattern exists for the Bangladeshi men. The most dramatic increase in the employment rate is for Chinese men where the rate jumps from 66.5% to 82.2%. This reflects the relatively young age structure of these groups and the resulting high proportions in education. For example, analysis of the LFS shows that 7.1% of White British, 3.2% of White Irish, 7% of White Other, 9.2% of Indian, 14.8% of Pakistani, 14.7% of Bangladeshi, 21.5% of Chinese, 19.9% of Black African and 9.6% of Black Caribbean men are full-time students. The ethnic minority women who show the highest levels of employment (excluding students) are the White British (78.8%), White Irish (78.7%) and White Other (78.5%) groups. Gaps remain between the White British women and non-white ethnic groups even after removing students from the calculation, especially for the Pakistanis and Bangladeshis.

Taking account of the large proportions of students in some ethnic groups does close the gaps between those groups and the majority group. Similarly, there is some evidence of employment gaps closing over time. Comparing Figure 6.1 with similar calculations undertaken by Clark and Drinkwater (2007), which used data from 1991 Census microdata, show considerable improvement in the position of non-white groups, particularly for Pakistani and Bangladeshi men where their (raw) employment rates have increased by around 20 percentage points. Figure 6.1, drawn from a longer run of LFS data illustrates a similar pattern for Pakistani men and men from Black Caribbean and Black African backgrounds. Despite a dip around the time of the financial crisis, the long-run trend has been for the employment rate gap to close.

Figure 6.2 performs the same exercise for women and finds that while the employment rate for Black Caribbean and Black African women has remained fairly constant over time, Pakistani women have begun to close the gap with White women, particularly since 2005.

Rates of unemployment

Among those active in the labour market, the proportion that are unemployed is a key measure of barriers to labour market success. The unemployment rate can also reflect the riskiness or precarity of their employment situation. Sandhu (2016) notes that high rates of unemployment among ethnic minority men and women can have disproportionate effects on their welfare given how the benefits system, and in particular the new Universal Credit regime, penalises larger families. Among men, Table 6.1 suggests that the ethnic minority groups that experience the highest rates of unemployment in the UK are the Black Caribbean (10%) and Black African (8%) groups whereas the lowest rates of unemployment are among the White Irish (2.5%) and Other White (2.6%) groups. By comparison, among women, Table 6.2 suggests the highest rates of unemployment are for the Black African (10.3%) group whereas the lowest rates of unemployment are among the Chinese (3.2%) and White Irish (3.8%) groups. The low levels of unemployment found among the Chinese and the White Irish groups can partly be explained by their high rates of employment in routine, low-skilled and poorly paid employment (Clark et al, 2018).

Unemployment has negative consequences for workers of all ethnicities, however higher rates for some groups compared to others can have particularly pernicious and long-term consequences. Li and Heath (2008) note the hypercyclicity of non-white employment rates. This means that during recessions, when there is a reduction in the demand for labour, non-white unemployment rates rise faster than those of the white majority group. Thus during these periods, the ethnic differential in unemployment rates grows. Heath and Li (2018) find similar ethnic-specific effects in the form of more pronounced 'scarring' effects of unemployment on some ethnic groups. Scarring is the idea that experiences of unemployment can have longer-term consequences for the labour market outcomes of workers as it leads to a loss of human capital or can act as a negative signal to future employers. Heath and Li (2018) find that Bangladeshi and Black Caribbean men, as well as Pakistani and Black African women, experience greater scarring effects that their white peers.

Di Stasio and Heath (2019) examined the hiring practices of UK employers by applying for jobs using fake CVs which differed only by the ethnicity of the applicant (ethnicity was signalled by name). The results suggested that ethnic minorities needed to send 60% more applications to get a positive response from employers than a white British person, with discrimination particularly high against

Pakistani applicants (Di Stasio and Heath, 2019). The implication is that discrimination continues to exclude ethnic minorities, to different degrees, from accessing the labour market, and the different levels of discrimination that various minority groups face appear to contribute to their differential rates of unemployment.

Comparing the different regions in Britain, unemployment rates across ethnic minority groups vary, with the disparity between unemployment rates more stark in London (where 9% of ethnic minority groups including men and women are unemployed compared to 4% of white groups), the West Midlands (where 11% of ethnic minority groups are unemployed compared to 5% of white groups) and finally, the north–west region (where 9% of ethnic minority groups are unemployed compared to 5% of white groups). These regional disparities may reflect different geographical and sectoral concentrations of ethnic minority groups (Lymperopoulou and Finney, 2016).

For all workers, regaining access to jobs while unemployed can be a challenge. A report by Hall et al (2017) for the Runnymede Trust showed that ethnic minority women faced the biggest challenges following the most recent recession and subsequent austerity measures. A significant issue is that funding cuts have impacted training courses used by ethnic minority women to improve their access to the labour market. The introduction of the Universal Credit system has further penalised women who participate in these courses as the courses are not counted within the formal criteria to receive Job Seekers Allowance. A particular challenge is the type of work ethnic minority women participate in, which the report shows is predominantly part-time (73.3%). Issues of caring responsibilities and obligations (both child and adult dependents) are a major barrier to women's employment levels, as well as the types of employment they can access. Benefit cuts have exacerbated the financial challenges facing working women with these having a disproportionate impact on non–white women.

Self-employment

Table 6.1 shows the ethnic minority men who show the highest levels of self-employment are the Pakistani group (23.3%) whereas the group that shows the lowest levels of self-employment is the Black African (11.6%) group. In comparison, Table 6.2 shows that the ethnic minority women who show the highest levels of self-employment are the Chinese (10.6%) and Other White (10.2%) groups. High rates of self-employment, particularly for men, are frequently observed for immigrant and minority groups in a variety of countries (Clark, 2015b) and are often viewed as a sign of dynamism and economic progress. However, closer inspection suggests that much of the self-employment undertaken by South Asian men in the UK is low-status, low-reward work, such as taxi driving or running small food outlets. Indeed Clark and Drinkwater (2007) suggest that the high rates of self-employment for non-white men in the UK are due to racial discrimination in the paid labour market, which makes self-employment relatively more attractive; ethnic minority men are pushed out of paid employment rather than pulled towards self-employment by its inherent merits.

Earnings

Another measure of the socio-economic attainment of ethnic minority groups is their earnings. Among men, Table 6.1 reports mean weekly earnings from the LFS and suggests that the ethnic minority groups who show the highest average (mean) weekly wages in the labour market are the White Irish (£854), Chinese (£745) and Indian (£720) groups, whereas those with the lowest mean weekly wages are the Bangladeshi (£386) and Black African (£490) groups. By comparison, among women Table 6.2 suggests the ethnic minority groups that show the highest mean weekly wages in the labour market are the White Irish (£619) and the Chinese (£531), whereas those with the lowest mean weekly wages are the Pakistani (£329) and Bangladeshi (£356) groups.

These are dramatic disparities and will reflect many differences between the groups, including the age structure of the group, educational qualifications, region of residence, occupation and a host of other differences. Using statistical methods to control for these factors can establish the extent to which average differences in the characteristics of different groups contribute to the observed gaps in earnings. Many such statistical studies have been done in the UK over the last thirty years and a consistent pattern emerges where Pakistani, Bangladeshi, Black African and Black Caribbean groups have lower average earnings, even after differences in other factors thought to affect earnings are taken into account. Thus it cannot be claimed that the observed ethnic differences in pay are wholly the result of a difference in education or the age structure of the relevant populations, and the inescapable conclusion is that an important 'ethnic penalty' exists. A recent study by the Resolution Foundation (Henehan and Rose, 2018), for example, shows that, after controlling for a wide variety of personal and occupational factors including age, education, sector, industry and job tenure, Black male non-graduates had hourly wages around 9% less than equivalent White workers. The equivalent figure for graduates was even higher at around 17%. For Pakistani non-graduates the ethnic pay penalty was around 14% and that for graduates 12%. For women graduates and non-graduates, there were pay penalties of up to 10% for Black, Pakistani/Bangladeshi and Indian groups relative to White women.

Public policy and ethnic minorities in the labour market

Two significant pieces of labour market policy have attempted to address the access to and position in the labour market of ethnic minority groups in Britain. The first is the EMETF, instituted by the New Labour government in 2003. The second is the McGregor-Smith review established by the Cameron government in February 2016 and which reported under the May government in 2017. In the period between the review being commissioned and its report being published Theresa May also established the Race Disparity Audit – an initiative to gather data on the different experiences of people from different ethnic groups across a range of public services. The first audit results were published in October 2017.

The EMETF was a response to a 2003 Cabinet Office report by the Prime Minister's Strategy Unit titled *Ethnic Minorities and the Labour Market* (Clark and Drinkwater, 2007; Bloch, 2008). The report provided a comprehensive overview of how ethnic minority groups fared in the labour market and concluded that many groups showed high rates of unemployment, comparatively low levels of income among those working, and underachievement in the labour market as well as poor self-esteem. Collectively these factors were shown to have a negative effect on national income and economic growth but, more personally, on ethnic minority individuals' social and economic inclusion (Bloch, 2008).

The EMETF, which was a cross-departmental initiative, identified three main policy strands. First, it sought to build the employability of ethnic minority individuals by enhancing their human capital. Second, it aimed to identify and remove the barriers to ethnic minority employment by connecting ethnic minority individuals more effectively with employers. Finally, it intended to reduce the discrimination ethnic minority people faced from employers and to support a broader equal opportunities framework in the labour market. The EMETF was a high-profile initiative, which engaged stakeholders and advisors from business, the trade unions and academics. Its provenance in the Strategy Unit ensured that, while housed in the Department for Work and Pensions (DWP), it had impact and influence across government and the DWP was given a specific target in the form of a Public Service Agreement (PSA) to reduce the employment rate gap between white and non-whites.

The authors are not aware of any comprehensive government or academic evaluation of the EMETF. As noted, there was some convergence in the employment rates, the chosen measure of success, across the period when the Task Force was operational. However, the Public Accounts Committee (PAC) of the House of Commons was critical of the department's progress towards its employment target (PAC, 2008). In particular, the PAC noted that the employment rate gap between whites and non-whites remained 'unacceptably high' (PAC, 2008: 5) and that it had fallen only by 2.8% despite the expenditure of £40 million per annum. The PAC also criticised the DWP for failing to consolidate or learn from the various pilot projects that it had run in various parts of the country with a view to developing the three policy strands outlined earlier. Finally, PAC (2008: 7) noted that in spite of the DWP's work through the EMETF, 'discrimination remains a significant barrier to employment'.

The McGregor-Smith review (2017) provided an up-to-date and large-scale review of the significant challenges ethnic minority groups continue to face in the labour market. The review recommended 26 improvements to address ethnic inequalities workplaces and the labour market. The recommendations included the following:

(2)   Publicly available data: Listed companies and all businesses and public bodies with more than 50 employers should publish a breakdown of employees by race and pay band.

(5)   Free unconscious bias training: All organisations should ensure that all employees undertake unconscious bias training.

(10) Reverse mentoring: Senior leaders and executive board members should undertake reverse mentoring with individuals from different backgrounds, to better understand their unique challenges as well as the positive impacts of diversity.

(12) Challenge school and university selection bias: All employers should critically examine entry requirements into their business, focusing on potential achievement and not simply which university or school the individual went to.

(18) Transparency on career pathways: New entrants to the organisation should receive a prior induction, including basic and clear information on how the career ladder works, pay and reward guidelines and how promotions are awarded.

(19) Explain how success has been achieved: Senior managers should publish their job history internally (in a brief, LinkedIn style profile) so that junior members of the workforce can see what a successful career path looks like.

(22) A guide to talking about race: Government should work with employer representatives and third sector organisations to develop a simple guide on how to discuss race in the workplace.

(26) One year on review: Government should assess the extent to which the recommendations in this review have been implemented, and take necessary action where required. (McGregor-Smith, 2017: 32)

As this list of recommendations shows, the focus of the review is very clearly on employers who are viewed, if not as the ultimate cause of 'the problem' then at least as the most effective site for policy action. There is, in comparison to the EMETF, much less focus on the human capital of minority groups themselves, or the role of local and national government in either funding initiatives in specific localities to help non-white workers there or, indeed, to strengthen and enforce anti-discrimination law.

The review's recommendations were made relatively recently so it is perhaps not surprising that initial evidence suggests that there may have been only a limited impact. A government-commissioned progress report one year on noted that on a 'scorecard' of ten areas where the action had been recommended only two had seen positive progress, eight had seen no change and one had actually gone backwards (DBEIS, 2018c). On the other hand, the review's proposal to publish ethnicity pay gaps in the same way as gender pay gaps has gained some traction, with a government consultation in progress to consider how this should be implemented (TUC, 2019; DBEIS, 2018d).

More widely, a variety of other types of policy, which are not specifically targeted at ethnic minority groups, might nevertheless have disproportionate effects on ethnic minority workers. As already noted, Hall et al (2017) examine how the changes to the Universal Credit system affect ethnic minority people, with a particular focus on women. The authors forecast that by April 2021 anyone in employment, and who lives in a household that claims Universal Credit, will be approximately £1,200 worse off than under the previous system. Hall et al (2017) explain this loss is the result of cuts, primarily to the work allowance that contributes to 57% of the benefits total. Furthermore, Hall et al (2017) find that claimants who are unemployed would be approximately £500 a year worse off. The report also suggests that families with children will be worse off than those without children. However, ethnic minority people are not the only marginal group that Universal Credit affects and the changes also affect working class and physically and mentally impaired claimants. The report also finds that social and cultural factors (for example, language and digital exclusion) are important. They create barriers for ethnic minority people and limit their resilience against broader changes, such as the implementation of the Universal Credit system, by making it harder for them to navigate and work around problems that arise in the system.

Another policy with the potential to affect the labour market situation of ethnic minority groups, given their relatively low earnings, is the National Minimum Wage (NMW, latterly rebranded as National Living Wage, NLW). Indeed the Low Pay Commission (2018) reports that coverage of the NMW/NLW is higher for ethnic minority workers at 13.2% of workers compared to 9.6% of white workers. However, data analysed by Peters (2015) suggest that non-compliance with the NMW by employers is a particular problem for minority groups. Specifically, he suggests that, among hourly paid workers between 2000 and 2013, 10.6% of Pakistani workers and 17.8% of Bangladeshi workers reported being paid at less than the statutory minimum. Peters speculates that this is due to the nature of the employment undertaken by such workers, which may be concentrated in relatively informal types of activity particularly in the catering sector. Ram et al (2017) confirm this conjecture using case study evidence from small firms in four low-paying sectors including restaurants, clothing, food manufacture and processing and food retail. Ram et al note that many firms do not comply with the minimum wage and may rely on 'helpers', who are paid below the legal minimum and who are often recruited through co-ethnic friendship or other informal networks. Lordan and Neumark (2018) attempted to identify whether those jobs, which were most vulnerable to offshoring or automation, were most at risk of being lost in response to increases in the statutory minimum wage. While she found that overall the displacement effects of increases in the minimum were small, one group that was particularly at risk was the group of non-white, low-skilled workers in vulnerable jobs. This emphasises that while ethnic minority workers being in low-paying jobs means that increases to the wage floor are more likely to benefit such groups, to the extent that there are negative employment effects as a result of job displacement it is also such workers who are most at risk.

Ethnic minority groups and the public sector

As well as its role in developing and implementing labour market policy, it is important to consider the government's role as a major employer – the public sector accounts for around 17% of total UK employment. Evidence from the private sector has highlighted the benefits of having an ethnically diverse workforce for businesses. An influential McKinsey and Co. (2015) report highlighted how businesses with ethnically diverse workforces permit a diverse array of voices to play a role in the decision-making process, particularly at a senior level, and how this can contribute to increased profitability. There is no reason to assume that any enhanced productivity due to the diversification of the workforce should be restricted to private firms so the same benefits should also be evident in the public sector. Diversifying the public sector workforce, therefore, offers the opportunity to improve how public services are delivered but also, since the government can more easily influence the terms and conditions of employment, there exists an opportunity to directly address racial and ethnic inequalities in the workplace.

There is considerable diversity in the representation of non-white groups in the public sector in the UK, both between parts of the sector as a whole and between different groups. The 'public administration, education and health' category in official statistics gives some information on this, although it should be noted that this is a wider classification than the public sector per se. Most non-white groups exhibit a slightly higher tendency to work in this sector compared to white workers. The notable exception is the Black group (comprising both Caribbeans and Africans), 43% of whose total employment is in this sector compared to 30% overall (DBEIS 2018b). The only minorities significantly more likely to find employment in the private sector are the Pakistani and Bangladeshi groups, which are particularly prominent in the distribution, hotel and restaurant sectors. Within different parts of the public sector there is considerable variation: in 2017 around 14% of civil servants were non-white compared to 7% in the armed forces, 6% in the police and 5% in the Fire Service. Eighteen per cent of NHS staff were classified as non-white, rising to 41% of doctors (Browning and Uberoi, 2019).

Within the NHS, 2018 data from the Race Disparity Audit (RDA) show that, for medical roles in NHS hospitals (excluding General Practitioners [GPs]), doctors classified as 'White' made up 58% of senior roles and 56% of junior roles. Non-white doctors were therefore slightly more highly represented at a junior level. What is most notable about these figures however is how well doctors classified as 'Asian' are represented in the doctor workforce. Asians make up 31% of senior doctors and 27% of junior doctors. By comparison, doctors classified as 'Black' make up a relatively small proportion of hospital doctors – 3% of senior doctors and 5% of junior doctors. Unfortunately, the RDA data do not allow us to break down either the Asian or Black group into its constituent ethnic minorities.

Appleby (2018) investigated the pay gap between doctors of different ethnicities and found very small or non-existent ethnic pay gaps for most categories of doctor. The only exception was the consultant level, where white doctors earned 4.9% more than non-white doctors. This gap varied between 3.5% for Black or Black British doctors and nearly 5% for Asian or Asian British doctors. It is worth noting that it is not possible to break down the GP workforce by ethnicity in a similar way. However, Esmail et al (2017) find that practices which included more than 40% GPs who obtained their medical qualifications outside the European Economic Area (EEA), a group that comprises 23% of practices, were more likely to be in deprived areas and had lower average pay per patient than practices with fewer such GPs.

By comparison, the data for allied health professionals (these include, for example, physiotherapists and speech and language therapists) show that 77.5% are White and this represents the highest proportion of white employees in a medical grade role. In higher pay grades, data indicate that ethnic minorities make up a lower percentage of middle management roles (bands 5 to 7), senior grades (bands 8a and 9) and very senior management roles (grades 1 to 4). Crucially, there is a clear difference with respect to the ethnic minority diversity between medical and non-medical roles and between junior and senior leadership roles in the NHS (see also Chapter Five for further discussion).

Considering the demography of the civil service, data from 2016 (ONS, 2016) show that 88% of civil servants are White, 5.8% are Asian, 3.1% are Black, 1.4% are Mixed, 0.3% are Chinese, and finally, 0.5% are from the Other ethnic group. Regionally, the data show London has the highest percentage of staff from an ethnic minority background, with 16.3% Asian, 11.8% Black, 3.0% Mixed, 0.7% Chinese and 1.2% Other. Breaking down the data by gender, the results show that male civil servants are more likely to be White (90.1%) than female civil servants (87.8%). In terms of salary, Asian staff show the lowest median salary (£25,000). Consequently, the results show that, unlike the NHS, white employees dominate the civil service and have a higher share of jobs than their share of the population of working age (86%). Furthermore, the RDA data also show that ethnic minority groups (not including white minorities) are poorly represented in the Armed Forces and represent only 2.4% of officers. Data on the Army also show, when comparing the different sectors of the armed forces, that the Army employs the highest percentage of officers and other ranked employees from an ethnic minority background.

In social services, the 2017 RDA data suggest that 73% of the workforce is White British compared to 10.6% of staff from an ethnic minority background. Moreover, 5.3% of staff come from an Other White background, and this represents the largest ethnic group after the White British group. Meanwhile, in the police force, 2017 data show that 93.7% of police officers are from a White background and only 6.3% of officers are from ethnic minority backgrounds (see Chapter 3, where Shankley and Williams show further evidence of an ethnic disparity in the police and judiciary). Even though strides have been made to increase the recruitment of ethnic minority officers, the latest police statistics show there remains an ethnic pay gap. This is partly the result of new recruits entering junior positions and therefore data will continue to show evidence of an ethnic disparity until they have had the opportunity to progress into more senior roles.

Finally, 2016 data show that 86.5% of all teachers in state-funded schools in England (primary and secondary education) are White British, whereas 13.4% are from an ethnic minority background. Furthermore, 93% of headteachers were White British. It is useful to contextualise this by noting that the proportion of non-white children in state primary schools is 25.3% (Asian 11%, Black 5.5%, Mixed 6.2%, Chinese 0.5% and Other 2%) and 24.2% (Asian 11%, Black 5.8%, Mixed 5.2%, Chinese 0.4%, Other 1.8%) in state secondary schools (DfE, 2018d). Thus while the classroom teacher workforce is not drastically different from the working-age population in terms of ethnicity, it does not reflect the ethnic mix of pupils. Chapter 4 discusses the differences in the demography of different stages of the state education system and some of the challenges ethnic minority staff face.

There is considerable variation in the patterns of representation and reward found for ethnic minority workers in the public sector. Albeit data limitations may disguise the fact that some subgroups do not do as well as others, there is a positive message in the figures for medical roles in the NHS, where some ethnic minority groups are well represented. However, a general, and less benign, pattern emerges in a number of parts of the public sector whereby the representation of non-white groups diminishes the further up the seniority hierarchy one looks. More senior leadership and non-medical roles in the NHS, as well as in institutions such as the state education system or the armed forces, show much more of a glass ceiling effect. Our ability to know about these patterns and to observe employment data across the public sector has benefited from the RDA. It is vital that statistical bodies continue to publish data on the ethnic make-up of public sector institutions to show changes to the patterns across different ethnic minority groups. This information is invaluable not only for auditing purposes but also because it raises public awareness of the continued inequalities certain ethnic minority groups face. It is also important to make sure that these data are as detailed as possible since the consideration of the labour market as a whole shows very clearly that, for example, combining groups such as Indians and Pakistanis into a single Asian category is very likely to provide a misleading picture. A similar point holds for Black, and potentially for Mixed, groups.

Interpreting the impact of policies such as those proposed in the McGregor-Smith review is difficult. However, the initial signs in some institutions such as the police force are of modest progress. It is too early to tell if there will be any lasting impact on ethnic minority diversity because it will take some time before these employees have been allowed the opportunity to advance to more senior positions. Moreover, with respect to future policy, the variation across institutions beckons future policy decisions to incorporate these differences and target the specific practices within certain institutions to provide a bespoke policy to improve the access ethnic minority employees have to specific job roles at different pay grades and levels of seniority.

Conclusion

This chapter has documented well-established, persistent patterns in the labour market disadvantage of ethnic minorities in the UK. These patterns have been studied extensively over several decades, are well known in policymaking circles and, indeed, have been the focus of a variety of initiatives by local and central government. In the face of this attention, it is the persistence of the broad patterns and trends that is the most striking feature of the snapshot of the current data presented here. While it is possible to find some evidence of progress, particularly in the convergence of employment rates and some reductions in the earnings gap, the essential picture of a labour market in which there is no level playing field for ethnic minority workers remains.

To some extent, this surface-level stasis disguises deeper and changing currents. Educational attainment and the demography of non-white groups might suggest hope for improved employment and earnings prospects for ethnic minority workers in the future. Against this, technology-driven deindustrialisation and new work patterns, a largely non-interventionist model of labour market policy which has reduced employment protection and social security, and relatively lax immigration policy have made progress more difficult.

Policy measures specifically aimed at this problem have grabbed headlines but it is not entirely clear what their impact has been or will be other than to keep the issue, sporadically, in the headlines. The question of 'what works' for improving the position of ethnic minorities in the labour market remains substantially open. It is striking that a recent attempt to make policy recommendations (Weekes-Bernard, 2017) echoes very closely some of the recommendations of the EMETF, which reported nearly fifteen years earlier. Both reports emphasise the importance of skills and human capital, and the need to improve the matching of potential employees with prospective employers. To the extent that we accept that these are the right policies, the question of why there is such an apparent 'implementation gap' is raised.

The government's particular role in the labour market, not only as the source of policymaking and implementation but as an employer, assumes importance here. There is even some evidence that the private sector may be moving ahead on this issue more quickly than the public (Clark, 2015a). Adequate leadership, both by example, and by properly implemented and evaluated policymaking is the challenge made by this analysis to the UK government.

Note
[1]   With thanks to Karen Chouhan for initial work on this chapter.

7

Ethnic minorities and housing in Britain

William Shankley and Nissa Finney

Key findings

- Ethnic inequalities in housing stem from the particular settlement experiences of postwar migrants to the UK in terms of the location and housing access afforded to them. This is consolidated by dramatic changes to the UK's housing landscape over recent decades, which have, to a large extent, exacerbated housing disadvantage for minorities. Evidence reveals stark and persistent ethnic inequalities in housing: (1) Census data analysis shows differences across ethnic minority households in housing tenure and overcrowding; (2) At least 1 in 3 households of some ethnic groups (Bangladeshi, Pakistani, Black African) live in overcrowded conditions compared to 1 in 20 white households; (3) Ethnic minority households are over-represented as statutory homeless in Britain and a person's ethnicity is one of the key characteristics that increases the likelihood of experiencing homelessness; (4) New migrant groups show an overwhelming concentration in the private rented sector with associated vulnerability to housing precarity.
- Housing law, systems and practices create disadvantage for minorities and migrants in the UK: (1) Practices of discrimination and racism exist in housing, for example in restricting ethnic minority households from entering specific housing tenures in Britain; (2) The tragedy of the Grenfell Tower fire in 2017, which disproportionately befell ethnic minorities and migrants, has shed light on the challenges for the social rented sector including the lack of housing supply. The tragedy also exposes the systemic failures of existing social housing structures to maintain quality housing and to provide clear processes of accountability for tenants; (3) Policy changes such as the 'Right to Buy' have significantly reduced the social housing stock and this has had an adverse impact on specific ethnic minority groups; (4) Policies such as the 'Help to Buy'

scheme have helped many ethnic minority households enter owner-occupied housing but have also increased the financial risk that these first-time homeowners encounter by granting them mortgages that they would have previously been denied; (5) Recent changes to immigration law have disadvantaged minorities in housing, for example, the 'right to rent' procedures.

- Addressing ethnic disadvantage in housing requires better data and increased research investment to understand experiences, causes of disadvantage and impacts of recent policy changes. It also requires political commitment and collaborative action to make use of this evidence to bring about more equitable housing systems and practices.

Introduction

On 14 June 2017 fire took hold of the 24-storey Grenfell Tower in central London. Seventy-two people were killed. Of these, the vast majority were ethnic minorities, and many were international migrants. The fire in this public housing block was so devastating because of substandard building practices combined with the failure of the landlord, the local government Royal Borough of Kensington and Chelsea, to take heed of residents' concerns. The tragedy of the Grenfell Tower fire brings ethnic inequalities in housing in the UK into stark relief: why were ethnic minorities so disproportionately affected?

Only a partial answer to this question is possible because of a relative neglect of attention to ethnic minorities in housing research in recent decades. Although there is a well-established body of literature on minorities and housing in continental Europe that includes work on housing policy, housing practices and the experiences of minorities in the housing market (Musterd and Andersson, 2005; Musterd and Van Kempen, 2009; Bolt et al, 2010; Van Ham et al, 2016) comparable work is lacking in the UK (Markkanen and Harrison, 2013). Housing studies in Britain is in dire need of up-to-date research that explores how increasing diversity coupled with strains in the housing market differently affect black and minority ethnic households.

This chapter draws on existing evidence and data, which is admittedly limited, to point to ethnic differences in housing experiences in the UK and reasons for this. The chapter provides an overview of historical migrant settlement and housing experiences to illustrate the long roots of housing disadvantage; it identifies changes in the UK housing landscape over recent decades that culminated in the contemporary housing crisis with particular implications for minorities; and it evidences inequalities in housing using the most robust data available. What is clear from this review is that housing is an arena in which there are vast differences in the experiences of ethnic groups and, given that housing experience is so vital to other life opportunities and wellbeing, much greater attention to this is required from researchers, activists and government.

Migrant settlement and housing experiences

Postwar migrants to the UK, being predominantly labour migrants from (former) British colonies entering manual and public sector occupations in urban areas, settled to a large extent in poor, central areas of the largest cities, often occupying neighbourhoods vacated by suburbanisation (Harrison and Phillips, 2010). The location of specific employment opportunities in particular parts of the country, such as in the textile industries of Lancashire and Yorkshire, also brought migrants to smaller towns and cities. Within these towns and cities, the exact place where migrants lived, and the degree of difficulty they faced establishing stability, was strongly shaped by the availability of and access to housing and their ability to navigate housing systems (Finney and Simpson, 2009; Harrison and Phillips, 2010; Lukes et al, 2018). For example, Patterson (1963) argued that early Caribbean migrants were steered by housing providers to specific neighbourhoods in East London where there was available social housing stock to which they, as British subjects, were entitled.

Discrimination and racism have been found to shape the housing experiences of migrants and minorities historically (Rex and Moore, 1969; Dahya, 1974; Harrison and Phillips, 2010). In the private rented sector and owner-occupied sectors, discrimination and racism by private landlords and estate agents have restricted ethnic minority people from entry in specific areas (Rex and Moore, 1969; Robinson, 1986). In the social rented sector (SRS), discrimination and racism by local authorities have resulted in specific social renting practices whereby ethnic minorities have been allocated the least desirable housing in the least favourable estates (see Lukes et al, 2018). These practices amounted to the concentration of some ethnic minority groups in social rented housing in specific areas but also created barriers to them moving from this specific tenure. Such were the housing challenges that ethnic minority households faced in the 1970s and 1980s that specific policies and ethnic minority-led housing movements and associations were set up to increase ethnic minority groups' access to good quality housing and entry into more desirable neighbourhoods

(Ratcliffe, 1996). In addition, policies were drafted under New Labour in the late 1990s and early 2000s to decrease the obstacles that certain groups had to overcome, specifically in the SRS (De Noronha, 2018a).

Recent migrants, including those from European Union (EU) accession countries, have been subject to policy changes which, combined with their dominance in routine and low-paid employment with fixed-term contracts, has resulted in their concentration in private rental accommodation (Robinson, 2010; Bone, 2014; Lukes et al, 2018). For example, they must be resident for three months before having any entitlement to social housing (Shelter, 2008). Moreover, the increase in recruitment agencies as intermediaries between employers and employees in low-skilled positions has had a substantial effect on the housing patterns and experiences of new migrant groups. For example, 'tied-in' employment and housing arrangements mean that a migrant's housing is dependent on their continued worker status (Shelter, 2008). In these cases, if a migrant's employment ceases, their housing is also lost. These practices are particularly evident in industries such as agriculture and construction, where housing availability in specific geographical locations might be sparse and there is a need to accommodate short-term and transient migrant populations (Shelter, 2008).

A quite separate set of issues (which we do not address here) is evident for forced migrants (asylum seekers and refugees), who are often placed in precarious and temporary accommodation, in dispersed locations where they have no connections, while they await their asylum outcome. They then have to navigate a complex housing system, often with very limited economic and social capital, when they obtain refugee status (Perry 2012). This precarity is exacerbated by turbulent housing landscapes, including increasing privatisation of accommodation provision for forced migrants (Darling, 2016). See Chapter 2 for further discussion.

Changes in UK housing and the 'housing crisis'

> We are in a housing crisis that extends from the homeless on the street well into the middle class. (Cohen, 2013: 1)

The UK's housing landscape has changed drastically over recent decades from an era when residents had considerable choice and social housing provision adequately met the needs of those who required it, to a situation of a shrunken, under-resourced social housing system, fragmented private rented sector, inflated prices in the ownership market and limited investment and strategy for housing provision nationally (Meen, 2018). Thus, Cohen's (2013) observation of a housing crisis affecting all but the very well off seems insightful but worrisome.

Lukes et al (2018) provide a useful overview of changes to the UK housing terrain in the postwar period and point to its intersection with immigration policy. Four policies, or policy approaches, with particularly significant implications for ethnic minority households, can be picked out. First is the 'Right to Buy' policy that was introduced by Thatcher's Conservative government in 1974. The policy was instigated to permit tenants of local authorities and social housing associations the legal right to buy (at a large discount) the council houses in which they were resident. Proponents of the policy argue that it has given millions of households, including ethnic minority households, the opportunity to buy their own homes thus providing them with an asset of future security for their families. However, critics of the policy have voiced that it has contributed to the widespread social housing shortage across the country. This is because it was not paralleled by policy to build additional social housing or to fund programmes to maintain the existing social housing stock. Thus, supply did not meet demand and tenants were steered towards private renting. The impact of the contraction of social housing is hard to measure among ethnic minority households due to the paucity of data but for those with relatively high participation in social housing, such Black Caribbeans, it has brought an increased risk of housing insecurity (Lukes et al, 2018).

The second housing policy with notable implications for ethnic minorities is the 'Help to Buy' policy brought in by George Osborne and the Conservative government in 2013. Dorling (2015) articulates that the policy was intended to address housing inequality and the widening need for housing that had developed in the country in the previous two decades. Rising housing prices and the unstable and competitive labour market had made it hard for many people, particularly the young, to buy a home. For many ethnic minority households, the 'Help to Buy' scheme has offered the financial leverage to enter into the owner-occupied tenure of the housing market. However, the policy has been criticised for granting mortgages to those who previously would not have been afforded them, thus increasing their risk of loan default (Gimson, 2013). Dorling (2015) argues that policy would have been better focused on building more housing to contribute to the lack of social housing stock rather than increasing people's entry into home ownership through mortgage approval.

The third housing policy that has noteworthy implications, particularly for migrants is the 'Right to Rent', which was brought in as an embedded part of the Immigration Act 2016. Crawford et al (2016) describe how part 2 of the Immigration Act extends the 2014 Immigration Act's article on the 'Right to Rent' for England. It is noteworthy that in Britain housing policy is a devolved matter and the 'Right to Rent' from the Immigration Act 2014 did not extend to Scotland, Wales or Northern Ireland (Crawford et al, 2016). The act introduces a provision to make it harder for migrants to live and work in the UK without official documentation. For example, it is easier for private landlords to evict migrant tenants without appropriate documentation, incentivising landlord checks and also making the practice of renting to undocumented tenants a criminal offence. The amendment to Britain's housing policy was part of broader changes sought to make the UK a more hostile environment towards migrants and ultimately steer undocumented migrants towards leaving the country (see Chapter 2 for further discussion). In March 2019, in a case brought by the Joint Council for the Welfare of Immigrants with supporting interventions from the Equality and Human Rights Commission, the Residential Landlords Association and Liberty, the High Court ruled that the Right to Rent scheme requiring landlords to carry out immigration checks of tenants was incompatible with human rights law. The scheme was found to directly cause racial discrimination in the housing rental market.

The barriers that ethnic minority households face in the housing landscape in Britain were well illustrated by the 2018 *Windrush* generation scandal. In this case incompetence by the Home Office in issuing passports or official documentation for long-term leave to remain resulted in some British citizens and long-term residents who arrived as part of the postwar *Windrush* generation facing exclusionary and discriminatory practices (such as being refused tenancy in the private rented sector or allocation of social rented sector housing) (Grant, 2018; Wardle and Obermuller, 2018). It seems that the Immigration Act 2016 pushes migrants and some ethnic minority households further into precarious living in a context that the UK Collaborative Centre for Housing Evidence (Meen, 2018) suggests is becoming increasingly unaffordable for low-income households.

Finally, the fourth aspect of policy that has implications for ethnic minorities and migrants is the promotion of gentrification, which Bridge et al (2011: 1) define as 'the movement of middle-income people into low-income neighbourhoods causing the displacement of all, or many, of the pre-existing low-income residents'. A recent example of gentrification has occurred at the former Olympic Village development in East London. Part of the London 2012 bid to host the Olympics was that after the event the area would be regenerated and add a mixture of housing to respond to the needs of the local area. However, the so-called regeneration effort has been marred by criticism that it has become a gentrification project. Rather than adding much-needed housing for existing residents, the project has (financially) excluded many marginal groups that include ethnic minority households and migrants. It has forced some to leave the area in search of more affordable housing, some to distant neighbourhoods in Essex (Bernstock, 2016).

Efforts to gentrify specific areas and create social mixing have gained further momentum following the use of terms such as *sink housing estate* that Slater (2018: 877) articulates has been a label 'invented by journalists, amplified by free market think tanks and converted into policy doxa by politicians in the United Kingdom' to justify current housing policy initiatives. Rhodes and Brown (2018) similarly argue that (negative) connotations of diverse 'inner cities' have been employed as a rationale for gentrification. These initiatives have gained further political clout when they have been considered as part of the broader and negative narratives associated with ethnic segregation (Finney and Simpson, 2009; Bridge et al, 2011). It seems that rather than improve housing availability, particularly for vulnerable and local residents, regeneration projects have in many cases left the voices of ethnic minority groups out of the decision-making processes that affect their local areas (Markkanen and Harrison, 2013; Finney et al, 2018b). Rhodes and Brown (2018) suggest that given these new patterns and processes of diversity in Britain, it is necessary for us to rethink and re-theorise race and ethnicity over the cityscape and how housing security and precariousness are spatialised for marginal groups.

Evidence of ethnic inequalities in housing

A paucity of evidence

Although housing is a major social issue, there has been relatively little recent work on the experience of ethnic minorities, and there is also a paucity of data available for research purposes (Lukes et al, 2018). The main quantitative sources giving national coverage are the census and the English Housing Survey. The strength of the census is its breadth, covering as it does the whole population and geographical landmass, but it has limited information, on tenure and overcrowding. The English Housing Survey has greater detail but analysis for ethnic groups is restricted because of the sample size of the survey (12,000 households), use of crude ethnic categories and the lack of an ethnic boost sample (UK Data Service, 2017). Other surveys, including the UK Household Longitudinal Study, suffer from the same issues of sample size for examining ethnic minorities, especially over time or with any geographical detail. Administrative data sets are limited in the information they provide, as they are not designed for academic endeavour; and commercial data have samples that are difficult to calibrate to any population baseline. The 2017 release of the Race Disparity Audit (RDA), the government's review of ethnic inequalities, provides the opportunity to look at ethnicity and housing in greater detail. It uses a combination of the English Housing Survey; the COntinuous REcording (CORE) social housing lettings data, Ministry of Housing data as well as Communities and Local Government data on homelessness. While there are benefits from the use of multiple data sources, the RDA relies heavily on the English Housing Survey and this limits analysis for the reasons stated earlier. The 2017 disaster at the Grenfell Tower evidences the need for quality data on ethnicity, migration and housing but, unlike other academic interests (for example, education or health), housing scholarship is a small constituency in the UK, and there have not been comparable campaigns for improving data.

Ethnic minority households and housing tenure

An important indicator of housing situation in the UK is tenure, for which robust data are available. Traditionally, three types of housing tenure are measured within the housing market in Britain. First, is 'owner-occupied' housing where households own or partly own (with use of a mortgage) their homes. Second, is the social rented sector (SRS), where households are provided housing through local authorities or housing associations and rents are subsidised by the state. The third type of tenure is the private rented sector (PRS), where tenants live in houses owned by private landlords and pay the rent for their tenancy to these landlords. Additionally, when we talk about each of the housing tenures it is important to recognise that these broad categories comprise varied housing in type, quality, cost and management. For example, in the SRS, which has been traditionally delivered by local authorities, housing associations play a major and increasing role in providing and maintaining housing. Housing associations are private and non-profit making organisations that reinvest any income surplus into maintaining existing homes or financing of new homes. They are also tightly regulated by the state and receive a large amount of their funding from the state. In recognition of the specific needs of ethnic minority tenants, there are ethnic minority-specific housing associations in the UK that operate as a collective through BMENational.[1]

To aid the interpretation of the data, it can generally be understood that owner occupation is the most desirable tenure in the UK as it is presumed to provide 'greater security, more freedom, financial advantage and therefore higher housing satisfaction' (Elsinga and Hoekstra, 2005: 401; Woods, 2017), whereas social housing does not provide the quality or security it once did, and private renting can be precarious and is largely unregulated (Shelter, 2008). While home ownership is generally considered the most appealing tenure, it should be noted that preferences may vary between (and indeed within) ethnic groups (Peach and Shah 1980; Phillips and Karn, 1992; Hamnett and Butler, 2010).

Statistics on housing show that 9.8 million people in England and Wales – 19% of the population – are living in privately rented accommodation compared to 12% a decade ago (Dorling, 2015). The shift equates to an additional 1.6 million households privately renting in 2011 compared to 2001. Changes to the housing landscape have affected ethnic minority households but it is important to note that these changes have not affected all groups equally and there are also substantial within-group differences. The 2011 Census for England and Wales is used for Figure 7.1 to examine the levels of each ethnic group's home ownership, and concentration in the PRS and SRS. The analysis is a reproduction of the work by Finney and Harries (2015) and is used in this case to examine the intergroup differences across 18 ethnic groups.

Figure 7.1 shows that the ethnic minority groups with the highest levels of private renting are the Other White (51%), Arab (49%) and Other Asian (39%) groups whereas the lowest levels of renting are among the Black Caribbean (15%), White British (15%) and White Irish (17%). The high figure for the Other White group is unsurprising given that this group includes EU migrants who arrived to Britain during the 2000s and adopted, in the first instance at least, housing in the PRS on account of its accessibility and flexibility (Pemberton, 2009). Finney and Harries (2015) summarise that all ethnic groups saw a proportional increase in their concentration in the PRS between 2001 and 2011 and this is evident in Figure 7.1, particularly for African, Other White and Chinese ethnic groups.

Analysis of the English Housing Survey (2014 and 2016 combined) shows the percentage of ethnic groups in the private rented sector as

Figure 7.1: Type of housing tenure (private renting, social renting, ownership) by ethnic group and variation between the 2001 and 2011 Censuses (England and Wales)

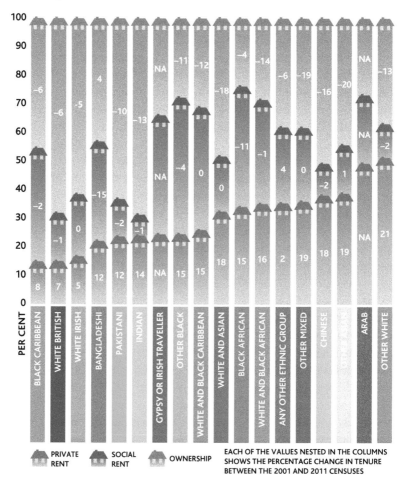

Note: Ethnic groups shown in increasing order of Owner Occupied. Figures overlain on each section of the bars show the absolute per cent change in proportion of the ethnic group in the tenure between 2001 and 2011. There are no data on tenure for the Arab and Gypsy/Irish Traveller ethnic groups prior to the 2011 Census and therefore their percentage change is 'N/A' across all tenures.

Source: 2001 and 2011 censuses for England and Wales – per cent of each ethnic group (household reference persons).

an up-to-date indicator of the exposure that each ethnic group has to precarity in the housing market Table 7.1 suggests that the ethnic minority groups that show the highest levels of private renting (2015/16 and 2016/17) are the Other White (59%), Chinese (53%) and Any Other ethnicity (46%) groups whereas the lowest levels of renting are among the White British (16%), Mixed White and Asian (17%), and

Table 7.1: Percentage of households privately renting their home by ethnicity (England, 2001–2011–2016)

	PRIVATE RENTING (PER CENT)		
	2001	**2011**	**2016**
WHITE BRITISH	9	15	16
WHITE AND ASIAN	20	32	17
WHITE IRISH	11	17	20
BANGLADESHI	12	22	21
OTHER MIXED	22	36	22
INDIAN	13	24	23
OTHER BLACK	11	25	24
WHITE AND BLACK AFRICAN	23	35	31
BLACK AFRICAN	20	34	31
PAKISTANI	15	24	32
WHITE AND BLACK CARIBBEAN	14	26	34
BLACK CARIBBEAN	8	15	34
ARAB	N/A	49	39
OTHER ASIAN	19	39	46
CHINESE	21	38	53
OTHER WHITE	30	51	59
ANY OTHER ETHNIC GROUP	34	35	59

Note: Ethnic groups shown in increasing order of Private Renting in 2016.
Source: English Housing Survey combining data from 2015/16 and 2016/17, England; and Census 2001 and 2011.

Black Caribbean (18%). Considering the data by rank we can see that the Chinese and Arab groups have become highly concentrated in private renting and thus at increased risk of housing precarity. Table 7.1 shows, by comparing the levels of private renting across the ethnic groups between 2011 and 2016, that levels of private renting have grown noticeably for the Chinese (+15%), Pakistani (+8%), White Other (+8%), Mixed White and Black Caribbean (+8%) and Asian Other (+7%) groups, with a notable decrease for the Mixed White and Asian (-15%), Other Mixed (-14%) and Arab (-10%) groups. Table 7.1 shows that for all other groups, including Indian, Bangladeshi and Black African, the levels of private renting have remained relatively stable between 2011 and 2016.

For social renting, as shown in Figure 7.1, it is the Other Black (48%), Mixed White and Black Caribbean (43%) and African groups (42%) who have highest levels whereas the lowest levels of social renting were among the Indian (7%), Chinese (11%) and Other White (12%) groups. All ethnic groups witnessed a decrease in the proportion in social renting between 2001 and 2011 (Figure 7.1), and this was particularly marked for the African and Bangladeshi groups, reflecting the uneven effects of contraction of social housing.

In 2011 the highest levels of home ownership (owner-occupied housing) were among the Indian (69%), White British (68%) and Pakistani (63%) groups, and the lowest levels were among the African (24%), Arab (27%) and Other Black (28%) groups (Figure 7.1). All ethnic groups experienced a decrease in representation in owner occupation over the 2000s except for the Bangladeshi group who experienced a small increase in their representation in this tenure (4%). For example, in 2001 8 out of 10 people of the Indian ethnic group lived in houses which they owned; by 2011 this was 7 in 10, with the difference being evident in an increase in the PRS (10% in 2001 to 24% in 2011).

In recent years there have been concerns over a 'generation rent' phenomenon developing in Britain, where young adults are particularly disadvantaged in terms of purchasing a home in the current economic climate (Meen, 2018). Dorling (2015: 149) asserts that 'competition for employment, stagnant incomes and the rising price of houses coupled with more restricted access to mortgages' after the housing crisis of 2008 has closed off specific tenures of the housing market to younger households. For young adults trying to enter the owner-occupied section of the housing market, Coulter (2017) identifies that parental (financial) support is a major factor that can significantly affect young adults' transition into the tenure. The extent of the financial support offered to young adults by their parents can inhibit or facilitate social mobility, and inequalities in intergenerational wealth transmission contribute to housing inequalities. In fact, Coulter (2017) finds that the amount of financial support young adults receive from their parents is vital particularly in a housing market with increasing housing prices: young adults' housing outcomes are 'persistently stratified by parental class and tenure' (Coulter, 2018: 1). It seems that young adults' housing outcomes are shaped by parental tenure, with the children of those who rent becoming less likely to enter home ownership and more likely to privately rent. Thus, private renting has implications for the housing careers of children of those who rent as well as the persistence of housing inequality.

There is concern that the broader effect of 'generation rent' might have a heightened impact on some ethnic minority groups. For example, Finney and Harries (2015) looked exclusively at young ethnic minority households (25–43 years old) and found that levels of home ownership were lower for ethnic minority young adults compared to their peers. In addition, the levels of young adults from ethnic minority groups in PRS housing were higher than for the population as a whole. For example, PRS housing was higher for

Other White, Arab and Chinese young adults than other groups, potentially reflecting the high prevalence of recent migrants and students in these groups. However, there were also high levels of home ownership for young adults in specific ethnic groups particularly for the Pakistani (52%), White British (46%) and Indian (44%), which may reflect long-standing cultures of home ownership and parental investment in housing

Ethnic minority households and overcrowding

Another significant issue of ethnic minority housing relates to overcrowding. Finney and Harries (2015) define it in line with official definitions, as a situation where a household has too few bedrooms to meet the needs of the household. Overcrowding can affect housing conditions and has substantial physical and mental health implications. Replicating one of Finney and Harries's (2015) analyses of the 2011 Census, the findings in Figure 7.2 show that Bangladeshi (41%), Pakistani (32%) and Black African (32%) households demonstrate the highest levels of overcrowding compared to White British (5%) and White Irish (6%) households, which have the lowest levels of overcrowding. That a third or more of some ethnic minorities live in overcrowded conditions compared to 1 in 20 White households is striking. Furthermore, the results show that the Pakistani group exhibits the largest percentage increase in overcrowding between 2001 and 2011 (+7% to 32%) while the Black African demonstrates the largest percentage decrease in overcrowding between 2001 and 2011 (43% to 32%). It is difficult to discern the causes of overcrowding but what can be concluded from these analyses is that housing provision is not meeting the needs of certain ethnic minority groups in Britain.

Homelessness

Although housing is a major issue, little work has been done on the links between housing and homelessness that considers ethnic minority households and their risks and transitions into housing precarity. The RDA confirms that ethnic minority households are more likely to experience homelessness than white households.

The 2016/17 data paint a disturbing picture with 59,100 households considered to be 'statutory homeless' and, of those, 35,890 (61%) are white households (including White ethnic minorities). The data suggest that 16% of all homeless households were Black, 9% were Asian, 3% were from a Mixed ethnic background and 5% were from the Other

Figure 7.2: Percentage of households (household reference persons), by ethnic group, in under-occupied, required size and overcrowded accommodation, and change between 2001 and 2011 Censuses (England and Wales)

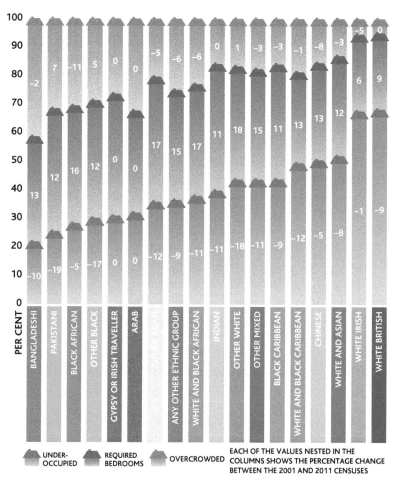

Note: Reproduction of Finney and Harries (2015) analysis that is ordered by decreasing per cent of overcrowding. Figures overlain on each section of the bars show the absolute per cent change in proportion of the ethnic group in the category of overcrowding between 2001 and 2011.
Source: 2011 and 2001 censuses for England and Wales – per cent of each ethnic group (household reference persons).

ethnic group; ethnicity wasn't known for the further 6% of homeless households. This is concerning given that 80% of the population are White British: ethnic minority households are over-represented as statutory homeless in Britain. Indeed, Bramley and Fizpatrick (2018) find that a person's ethnicity is one of the key characteristics (alongside poverty, local labour market variations and gender) that increase the likelihood of experiencing homelessness. Crucially, while ethnic minority households are over-represented among those who are homeless, these numbers could, in fact, be an undercount because of the way in which homelessness is conceptualised and operationalised in administrative and official statistics. The official definition (Gov.uk, 2018f) demarcates a person as *statutory homeless* only if the household is unintentionally homeless and demonstrates a priority need, for example through having dependent children. Multiple reports by Shelter (for example 2004, 2017) note that these criteria overlook many homeless people as the definition does not include single homeless people with specific vulnerabilities (migrants and asylum seekers, for example) or people who do not approach local authorities to seek help (Shelter, 2004; Gov.uk, 2018f).

It seems there is a plethora of factors that explain the over-representation of ethnic minority households classified as homeless. A collection of reports by the charity Shelter (for example 2004, 2017) suggest these factors include overcrowding, which is more pronounced among ethnic minority households as shown earlier. Furthermore, the problems that some ethnic minority households face in buying their own homes, such as poverty and low wages, reduce their housing security and increase their risk of precarity and homelessness. Poverty, racism and discrimination by local authorities in the SRS, or racism and discrimination by private landlords may further strain ethnic minority people in accessing quality and affordable housing. Changes to Britain's housing terrain, with a broader decrease in home ownership, have accelerated across ethnic minority households in particular, as shown earlier. In addition to the housing-related disadvantages that ethnic minority residents face that have been discussed in this chapter, the ongoing multiple impacts of austerity affect ethnic minority and other marginal households more than White British households (Runnymede Trust, 2017a) making them particularly vulnerable to finding themselves without a home.

Marginalisation in housing debates

A significant problem continues to be that race and ethnicity are marginalised from housing debates (Finney et al, 2018b), and as a result black and ethnic minorities' needs and voices tend to be excluded from housing planning and provision, with the implication that housing does not adequately cater for a diverse society. Previously black and ethnic minority housing groups have been integral to gains made in relation to social housing but these groups are marginal (Harrison et al, 2005; Robinson, 2002; Beider, 2012). The housing association sector has grown and seen more commercially orientated housing associations merge (Finney et al, 2018b; Lukes et al, 2018), which has a negative effect on those black and ethnic minority housing associations that have been vital to ethnic minorities' access to social housing. This is particularly the case in a housing market that, as highlighted, is characterised by the inadequate supply of social housing and a growing ethnic minority population, some of whom are highly dependent on social housing. Although ethnic minority housing associations, under the umbrella of BMENational, are undertaking pioneering work to engage with questions specific to migrant and minority housing needs (Lukes et al, 2018), specialist housing associations such as these are facing strategic and financial challenges as larger organisations increasingly secure contracts for housing provision.

Housing initiatives, such as gentrification, that marginalise minorities, illustrate that ethnic minorities have limited voice in housing decisions, with policies that in some cases work against ethnic minority communities, dismantle local areas and exclude ethnic minorities from housing in specific areas (Markkanen and Harrison, 2013). Moreover, tragic events such as the fire that happened at the Grenfell Tower in 2017 raise questions about the way in which ethnic minorities (alongside other groups including working-class council tenants, migrants, refugees and Muslims) have been negatively represented and how this is compounded by the stigmatisation of people who live in tower blocks (Madden, 2017). This negative representation works to silence certain housing concerns, delay improvements to housing conditions and exacerbate inequalities between ethnic groups.

Conclusion

This chapter has mapped out the changes to Britain's housing landscape over the past thirty years, demonstrating how those who are marginalised, including ethnic minority groups, have been detrimentally affected. Housing policies that have aimed to increase owner occupation (for example 'Right to Buy' and 'Help to Buy') have, we have argued, exacerbated the disadvantage of migrants and minorities, for example through discriminatory practices, exposure to financial risk and reduction of social housing stock. The housing disadvantage of minorities is consolidated by requirements in the PRS (for example 'Right to Rent') that encourage discriminatory landlord practices.

Furthermore, there is evidence that gentrification projects, which ostensibly benefit local residents have, conversely, contributed to some ethnic minority households facing greater housing insecurity by steering households out of certain neighbourhoods, fragmenting communities and disrupting local connections. For example, the gentrification project at the former Olympic Park in East London had the potential to build newer and more suitable housing for the needs of the diverse local communities but had the effect of local residents not being able to afford the newer housing available and subsequently steering them further east to find more affordable accommodation.

A recurring theme of cases of minority housing disadvantage is the execution of change (or lack thereof) without the inclusion of residents' voices. This was true of the 2017 tragedy at the Grenfell Tower, where the concerns of residents (regarding the safety of the building) were largely ignored. It has taken a horrendous event for the government to focus its attention on social housing, particularly the conditions people experience living in tower blocks. More broadly, the tragedy shows the persistent discrimination that marginal groups (ethnic minorities, minorities and working class) face in the housing sector where their voices are not heard and their concerns not dealt with adequately. It also highlights how stigmatisation results from racialisation of groups housed in precarious conditions in the social rented sector. There needs to be a substantial shift, from viewing these residents as passive to bringing them into decision making to influence social housing policy.

The national shortage of available housing in the SRS is a particular concern for specific ethnic minority households. For example, the Black Caribbean group are concentrated in this tenure as a consequence of their immigration history and socio-economic profile at the time of their arrival. Britain's decision to leave the EU in 2019 poses a considerable question about the future social housing landscape and projects to build new social houses. This is because leaving the EU system excludes the country from receiving European Investment Bank (EIB) funding, which has been vital to sustain many social housing building projects (Maclennan and Gibb, 2018). We currently do not know if the government will match the EIB funding for social housing post-Brexit. If they fail to do so this poses a considerable threat for ethnic minority households. A lack of new social housing could potentially steer many more ethnic minority households into the PRS, which is already characterised by poor housing conditions, minimal regulation and unscrupulous landlord housing practices. For the most vulnerable ethnic minority households it could also steer them into homelessness. Given that ethnic minorities are already over-represented in homelessness, steps should be taken to avoid this inequality growing.

The chapter has illustrated a broad pattern of ethnic minorities experiencing a shift from the SRS and home ownership towards the PRS. This has a number of implications, particularly given the government's continued pursuit of a 'hostile environment' aimed to dissuade migrants from moving to Britain. The Immigration Act 2016 moves Britain's borders into the hands of gatekeepers such as private landlords: renting to a tenant who is unlawfully living in Britain is now a criminal offence. This has, by default, supported racist practices, with landlords discriminating against anyone they believe might be living in the country illegally or using falsified documents to rent a house. A collection of cases have come to light that relate to *Windrush* generation migrants, which show that private landlords have discriminated against British citizens in order to avoid the perceived risk of potential prosecution.

This chapter has revealed many worrying aspects of ethnic minorities' and migrants' housing experiences in the UK. Ethnic minority disadvantages in housing appear to be growing with potential implications for many other life domains including employment and health. However, there is also a dearth of evidence about the exact nature of the disadvantages; how they might vary across the country and between household types and generations; what their implications are now and in the longer term; what institutional and structural practices are exacerbating or mitigating them; and what good practice can be identified to reduce them. The data presented here from the 2011 Census and 2016 English Housing Survey are useful but they can only tell us limited information about ethnic minority households' experiences of the housing market. Investment in housing data and robust research is vital as is political commitment and collaborative action if more equitable housing systems and practices are to be achieved.

Note

[1] https://ethnicminoritynational.wordpress.com/about/

8

Arts, media and ethnic inequalities

Sarita Malik and William Shankley

Key findings

- Ethnic minority people are less likely than white Britons to work in the creative industries and are more likely to experience unemployment from precarious labour in the creative industries.
- Ethnic minority people represent 6% of workers in design; 9.1% in film, TV and radio; 6.7% in music and performing and the visual arts, compared to 14.1% of the overall population for England and Wales and 40% in London, where there is a high concentration of cultural and creative industries (Warwick Commission, 2015).
- There is a paucity of data available to examine the demography of ethnic minority groups in the cultural and creative industries. Where data are available, for example, from the BBC or Channel 4, they are organisation-specific and show a clear need for organisations to increase the number of ethnic minority people in their workforce.
- The BBC Census (2017/18) revealed that 14.8% of staff are from an ethnic minority background. Nonetheless, only 10.4% of the senior leadership roles are filled with people from an ethnic minority background, indicating a wider problem of the under-representation of ethnic minority people in decision-making roles in the sector.
- The BBC and Channel 4 (in 2018 and 2015 respectively) published new diversity charters with the main aim of reflecting the diversity of the workforce of each organisation.
- The discursive shift in how diversity is understood and approached in arts and media has led to a shift in cultural policy where funding bodies (such as Arts Council England) now require applicants to demonstrate their commitment to diversity in order to be funded.
- Cultural policy seems to focus exclusively on the demography and representation of ethnic minority people in the creative industries workforce with the assumption that more diversity in the workforce leads to more diversity in cultural production. However, the relationship between these areas is unclear.

Introduction

The growth of the cultural and creative industries (CCIs) in the past thirty years has coincided with an increase of research on inequality in the sector. This has included how ethnic minority people are involved in, represented by and experience the CCIs in Britain. The Warwick Commission (2015) found that the CCIs account for £77 billion in added value and this corresponds to 5% of the economy, with 1.7 million people employed in these industries. There are three main areas that we concentrate on in this chapter and these relate to the concepts of *cultural production*, *cultural consumption* and *cultural representation*, as well as policy responses to ethnic inequalities in the industry. These three areas are marked by several linked factors in relation to ethnic minority concerns, including ongoing problems with a lack of employment, differential audiences and problematic representations. While there are various problems with data in each of these three areas, such as research gaps, the inconsistency of terminology and variation of categories, this chapter will reference relevant data in what still remains a largely under-researched area, even in studies of racial inequality. This is of concern because of the significant role that the field of cultural production plays in shaping everyday society and culture, how ethnic minority people see themselves and are seen by others and in how the nation, literally, narrates itself. The field of cultural production and representation, therefore, has real social effects.

In the first section of this chapter, we consider matters of cultural production where we review what the census data tell us. We discuss sector specific figures on ethnic minority involvement in production as well as discussing the recently growing concern around privilege and inequality in the cultural sector, and how this links with issues of cultural production. In the next section, we consider cultural consumption. In this section, we discuss the audiences that cultural products and content attract, and question if this maintains and reproduces ethnic inequalities in this field. We then move on, in the third section, to consider cultural representation, exploring how media content provides a window into the way ethnic minority groups are constructed in wider British society. In order to consider the complex interplay between cultural production, consumption and representation, we use the final section to consider industry funding and policy responses. Here, we use a case study approach, looking at the BBC and Channel 4, to outline how cultural and creative policies in broadcasting, a highly influential and popular area of cultural production, have evolved and changed and how this, in turn, affects ethnic minority groups in this prominent sector of the cultural industries.

Cultural production: ethnic disparities in employment in the industry

In Chapter 6 on ethnic inequalities in the labour market, Clark and Shankley, highlight how data from 2017/18 show that ethnic minority people are under-represented across public sector institutions compared to the White British population, and with respect to their share of the broader population. A similar accusation has been levelled against the cultural industries and suggests that ethnic minority people are under-represented in sectors ranging from television to advertising. As with other sectors, there is a paucity of data, particularly recent data, to enable us to explore the extent of this inequality and its marked affect in specific sectors in finer detail.

Considering the cultural industries as a whole, data from CIC (2019) suggests that in 2017 the number of jobs in the UK creative industries overtook 2 million for the first time, and this had increased faster than the growth of the rest of the UK economy. If creative jobs outside the creative industries are taken into account, this represents 3,121,000, or a 2.8% rise year on year. According to Consilium (2013), ethnic minority workers in the creative industries in 2011/ 12 accounted for 7% of cultural industry jobs. Furthermore, Morris (2017) found that this had risen to 11% in 2016/17, representing a 4% increase over a four-year period. Of all jobs in the creative economy in 2016, ethnic minority workers filled 11%, a similar level to their representation in the labour market as a whole (11.3%) (Department of Culture Media and Sport, 2016). Moreover, since 2011 there has been a 38.2% increase in the number of ethnic minority jobs in the creative economy compared to an 18.5% increase in the jobs for white groups (Department of Culture Media and Sport, 2016). While it seems the creative economy and jobs for ethnic minority people in the creative industries are expanding, a specific look at individual sectors within the creative industries shows contradictions and tensions in the diversity across individual sectors.

Figure 8.1 shows that a large proportion of ethnic minority workers in the cultural sector work in IT, software and computing. This is also the area that has had the largest increase in ethnic minority workers between 2011 and 2015. In other areas, the numbers of ethnic minority workers have either remained static or decreased.

Figure 8.1: The proportion of ethnic minority workers in sectors in the creative industries over time, 2011–15

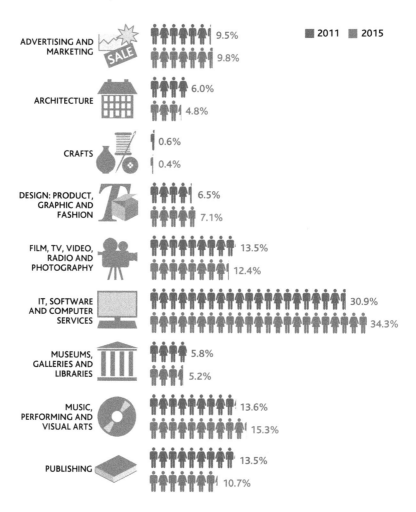

Source: Department of Culture, Media and Sport (2016).

Film and television

A recent BFI (2015: 5) report focusing on the representation of ethnic minority people in the film industry in Britain noted that the sector generated approximately £6 billion for the economy in 2013, which included a £1.5 billion investment overseas. Nonetheless, the film industry continues to under-represent ethnic minority people, women and people with disabilities within employment. A review by CAMEo (2018) showed that ethnic minority employment across the sector had steadily declined between 2006 and 2012, from 7.4% to 5.4%, with different levels of ethnic minority workers in different sectors. For example, ethnic minority workers in the animation sector comprised only 3.5% of the workforce. As with other sectors, issues of access to information and social networks appear to be particularly important in the animation sector (Creative Skillset, 2014).

In television, the findings are slightly better and ethnic minority people account for 7.5% of the workforce, which is marginally higher than the industry average at 5.6%. Ofcom (2018) recently published a report that shows that across the five main broadcasters in the UK, Viacom (which owns Channel 5) has the highest proportion of ethnic minority people among its employees (19%) compared to ITV which has the lowest representation among its employees (9%) (Figure 8.2). However, the report publishes data on the protected characteristics of its workforce separately. This prohibits any examination of the intersectional characteristics of the workforce of the different broadcasters being available.

Specific data from the BBC (the UK's main public broadcaster) show that 14.8% of its employees come from an ethnic minority background in 2018 (Ofcom, 2018). While the equitable representation of ethnic minority people extends across middle and junior management positions as well as non-management levels, it decreases significantly among employees in senior management roles (10.4%) (BBC, 2018a). In spite of the proportion of ethnic minority people in junior-level roles being slightly higher than their share of the UK working-age population (12%), Ofcom (2018) found that ethnic minority people continue to face a mean pay gap of 4% in 2018 compared to their white colleagues (Ofcom, 2018). While broadcasting represents a sector in the CCIs with a relatively good representation of ethnic minority people among its workforce

Figure 8.2: Employees across the five main broadcasters in the UK by ethnic group

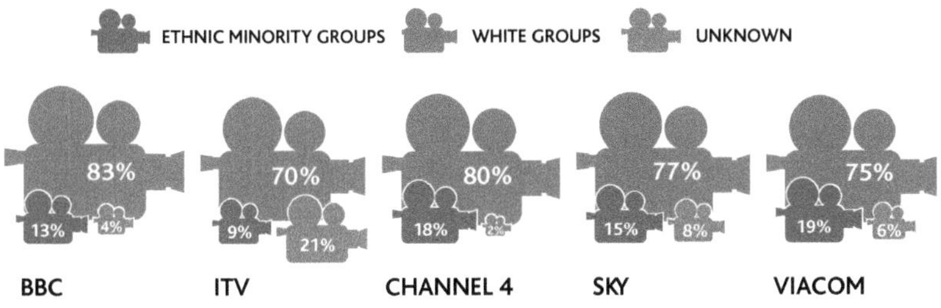

ETHNIC MINORITY GROUPS   WHITE GROUPS   UNKNOWN

BBC	ITV	CHANNEL 4	SKY	VIACOM
83%	70%	80%	77%	75%
13% 4%	9% 21%	18% 2%	15% 8%	19% 6%

Source: Ofcom (2018) on the period April 2017 to March 2018.

compared to other sectors, particularly at junior levels, more needs to be done to target the sector's working conditions to ensure pay parity extends evenly across all ethnic groups.

In the film sector, the percentage of ethnic minority workers employed (4.4%) fell short of the industry average of 5.6%. In director positions, for instance, ethnic minority people represent only 3.5% – suggesting a serious under-representation of ethnic minority people in senior leadership positions or opportunities (Grugulis and Stoyanova, 2012). Meanwhile, in the video game sector, the proportion of ethnic minority people increased in 2012 to 4.7% – which again fell short of the industry average. Finally, there is a dearth of current data available on the representation of ethnic minority workers in the visual effects sectors, with raw figures, however, indicating that they only constitute 1% of employees (CAMEo, 2018).

The current data suggest that television has higher representation of ethnic minority people among its workforce, compared to employees in the film, video game and visual effects sectors. Yet, there is currently a lack of research to explain *why* television has moved at a faster pace than other sectors within the film and television industry. In the absence of UK-based research, the Hollywood Diversity Report (2019) suggests that broadcasting executives are aware that their audiences are declining and therefore prioritise the need to attract newer audiences (see discussion later in the chapter). This may affect their employment practices.

Journalism and publishing

In journalism, there is evidence that ethnic minority people face barriers to entry into the profession and face an ethnic penalty. A report published in 2016, for example, found that 94% of journalists were white compared to 91% of the total working-age population. This suggested that ethnic minority people continue to be under-represented among the workforce. Geographically, the under-representation of ethnic minority people in the newspaper and magazine sector is heightened by the majority of the sector being located in London, where only 60% of the population is white, suggesting that white employees are over-represented and disproportionately occupy jobs in the sector. Explanations for ethnic minority people's under-representation links to findings that black and Asian journalist students are particularly likely to face discrimination and racism that prevent them entering the profession compared to white graduates (Thurman,

2016) Meanwhile, black students only have an 8% chance of finding employment in the sector altogether. If magazines and newspapers are reluctant to employ minority journalists, this creates a vicious cycle in which 'unreflective newsrooms continue to produce unreflective editorial and cover content, further alienating readers from different backgrounds' (Hirsh, 2018).

The wider publishing industry shows a similar lack of diversity. According to Shaffi (2016), of the thousands of titles published in 2016 in the UK, fewer than 100 were by British authors from a non-white background, although publishers do not keep data on the ethnic background of authors. Noting this deficit, the publisher Penguin Random House has set a company goal to hire and produce books that better reflect 'social mobility, ethnicity, gender, disability, and sexuality' (Akbar, 2017: 1705). The 100 top selling books of 2018 had only one British non-white author, although, interestingly, this was on the subject of race (Reni Eddo-Lodge's *Why I'm No Longer Talking to White People about Race*). There is a particular lack of ethnic minority representation among senior publishing executives (Shaffi, 2016).

Leadership in the CIC

While recent statistics highlight that the lack of ethnic diversity is endemic across the cultural industries, a recent survey by Arts Council England (2019) examined the nature of diversity of decision makers and those in senior positions in the creative industries. These roles included the Chief Executives, Artistic Directors and Chairs of organisations. The Arts Council England (2019) report examined 663 arts organisations in its national portfolio, with Figure 8.3 showing only 9% of chief executives, 12% of artistic directors and 10% of chairs of organisations came from an ethnic minority background.

Some research considers why the lack of representation endures in the creative industries and some of the structural challenges inherent within these industries. Koza (2008) explored the way ethnic minority people are required to 'act white' – to behave in a certain manner to be included and accepted into certain cultural professions and the elite educational institutions in which practitioners are trained. For example, in opera, ballet and certain genres of music, cultural norms exist that restrict ethnic minority people's entry. These predominantly white spaces inhibit ethnic minority people from participating, as they are often excluded from the knowledge and/or expected behaviours that are needed for entry (*The Stage*, 2017).

Figure 8.3: Ethnic diversity of leadership in arts organisations in England

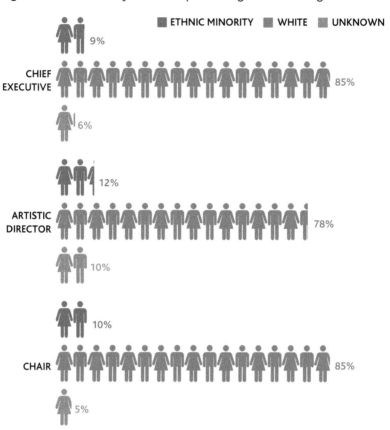

ETHNIC MINORITY   WHITE   UNKNOWN

CHIEF EXECUTIVE
9%
85%
6%

ARTISTIC DIRECTOR
12%
78%
10%

CHAIR
10%
85%
5%

Source: The ethnicity of workers in leadership positions at National Portfolio Organisations (NPOs) and Major Partner Museums (MPMs) taken from the *Equality, Diversity and the Creative Case: A Data Report, 2017–2018* (Arts Council England, 2019).

Arts teaching

This section examines the representation of ethnic minority people in arts teaching and studies. Art schools with ethnic minority teaching staff are important as those in senior positions, as well as those involved in admissions, can act as gatekeepers to the industry. According to Snow (2017), who used the workforce data from the UK's 13 leading drama schools for 2015/16, only 6% of teachers come from an Asian, black or minority ethnic background. Act for Change found in the same year that ethnic minority graduates made up a total of 17.5% of total drama school leavers from 17 major drama schools (*The Stage*, 2017). Unpacking the challenges that ethnic minority staff and students continue to face in drama schools, *The Stage* magazine ran a collection of interviews with minority students and found many experienced snobbishness, racism and practices of exclusion from the predominantly white teaching body. The experiences of some minority students suggest that a culture of exclusion runs the risk of alienating ethnic minority people from attending drama education and threatening those that do attend drama education in their successful transition into the CCI sectors of the labour market, reproducing the ethnic inequalities in the wider workforce.

Oakley and O'Brien (2016) discuss the possible links between higher education and inequalities in the creative industries. They argue that as increasing numbers of graduates are leaving university with a degree in media studies or related creative degrees, more people are attempting to enter into the creative industries, where ethnic minority people face particular barriers. Ashton and Noonan (2013) have shown how many graduates from arts degrees participate in an array of extracurricular activities to increase their employability. These pursuits are marked by class as well as ethnic inequalities. According to Lloyds (2006), the cultural industries have developed an internal industrial culture where creative workers, particularly those starting their careers, subsidise their creative work by working at other jobs. Others describe the blurring of the boundaries between work and life. For instance, this is present in the design of the offices of many creative industry professions, such as marketing and advertising, which infuse work life with social life (Nixon and Crewe, 2004). These aspects are particularly important in the creative industries where a lot of people work freelance and the social dimension is vital as it is where people find out about future possible employment and funding opportunities. This risks solidifying a culture where people have to perform being social in a specific way and can never truly switch off from work (Banks, 2007). Expecting workers to perform a specific type of social interaction is exclusionary, particularly for ethnic minority people, as it assumes that people have the same access to knowledge of the lay of the industry, as well as the time to work both in and out of work to build their industry profiles in order to maintain their careers in the creative industries. It also has clear gendered implications.

Eikhof and Warhurst (2013) also identify a collection of structural features that are significant to the exclusion of ethnic minority people in the creative industries. These included wage instability and the phenomenon of unpaid internships. Access to the creative sector in particular often requires following an unofficial route, which includes unpaid internships and utilising social networks to gain entry via contacts already working in the sector. Current data from other chapters suggest that ethnic minority people are often more likely not to have the same financial capital as white groups to resource these routes (Friedman et al, 2017). Entrants to the creative industries are predominantly from middle- and upper-class privileged backgrounds and have access to the economic capital to be able to undertake internships and cope with fragmented employment and unstable wages (Friedman et al, 2017). Moreover, many ethnic minority people do not have the same social networks to draw upon. Consequently, many of the sectors exist as predominantly white spaces where exclusionary mechanisms inhibit ethnic minority entry. Research is lacking in this area but is greatly needed in order to move beyond the simple idea that a boost in diversity of the workforce demographic creates better diversity outcomes. As research indicates, internal industrial culture and patterns of exclusion persist, even for those working within the sector, suggesting that data also need to be compiled around attrition rates, retention and career progression.

Cultural consumption: ethnic minority audiences

We can see from the previous section a variable picture has emerged with respect to how well ethnic minority people are represented in the different sectors within the cultural industries. Nonetheless, what is relatively unclear and under-researched is a focus on *who* consumes the different outputs from the creative industries and *how* ethnic minority people feature as consumers of cultural content.

Participation in the arts

A report by the Warwick Commission (2015) used the 'Taking Part' data to measure how many ethnic minority people took part in the creative industries. The findings showed that, in spite of an overall increase in the number of minority people taking part in the creative industries between 2005/06 and 2012/13, the gap between the majority White British and ethnic minority participation continued to widen. More recent data from the RDA suggests that in 2017/18, 78.9% of people aged 16 and over had taken part in the arts at least once in the past year (Gov.uk, 2018a). The levels of participation had remained relatively stable since the 2013/14 (Figure 8.4). The data also indicated that a higher percentage of those who fell into the 'mixed ethnic' category took part in the arts than people from all other ethnic groups (Figure 8.4). The data also showed that Asian people were

Figure 8.4: Percentage of people aged 16 years and over who took part in arts in the past year, by ethnicity over time (two specified years)

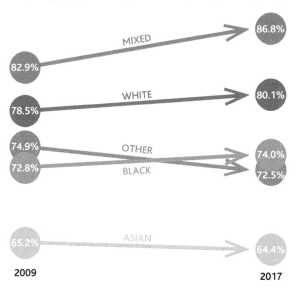

2009

2017

Source: DCMS (2019).

significantly less likely to take part in arts than white people (including white ethnic minority people and black people); across the two years. The findings supported the idea that ethnic minority people are relatively under-represented as consumers of th e arts.

The reasons for the relative lack of consumption of and participation in the arts are likely to be complex and would include questions of representation (discussed in the following section); perceptions of *who* art is produced for as well as economic factors which prohibit participation in the arts. According to the Pulse survey (*Arts Professional*, 2018), an ongoing question relates to how to increase the diversity among those engaging with the arts and what strategy should be pursued by the wider creative industries? Collecting data from the 509-strong UK-based respondents who completed an *Arts Professional* Pulse survey (2018), respondents were asked how they would achieve diversity in their sector. The survey data suggested that those working in theatre and music were the most likely to see audience diversity as a priority. This seemed to be the result of respondents recognising the lack of diversity of their audiences and seeing that their existing audience were typically white and middle class and, on average, older than the population as a whole. The following section examines what is known about television audiences.

Television audiences

As we have established in other chapters, the ethnic minority population of Britain is growing and has a younger age profile than the White British population. In the creative industries, for organisations such as the BBC, the growth of the young ethnic minority audience has raised questions of diversity. Broadcasting organisations are worried their audience is declining because of an increase in choice and because their programmes fail to reflect the interests of newer audiences. This is reinforced by the BBC's own statement of purpose to 'reflect, represent and serve the diverse communities of the UK's home nations and regions' (BBC, 2017b: 8). In order to accommodate difference, the BBC needs to avoid ethnic tropes and negative stereotypes to better engage with ethnic minority audiences if they are to maintain and grow their audience base. However, the paucity of data in the UK on audience dynamics has resulted in little being known about the ethnic minority consumption of channels such as the BBC.

Recent data from the BBC's audience team suggests that ethnic minority people use BBC services significantly less than the national average (Figure 8.5), suggesting a need for the BBC to produce more programmes that better reflect ethnic minority audiences and their interests. A recent report by Kantar Media (2018: 11) found among audiences who took part in multiple focus groups that the BBC was seen as 'establishment, stiff, white, middle-class and politically correct' and did not represent ethnic minority people well or in a positive light. Other respondents suggested that alternative broadcasting outlets such as Netflix and Amazon Prime catered more to ethnic minority people's tastes and represented them better throughout their programming content (Kantar Media, 2018). As we will see later in this chapter, the newest BBC and Channel 4 diversity policies attempt to increase the ethnic diversity of their broadcasting with respect to the workforce but also the content of their programmes. However, while it seems apparent that ethnic minority audiences are key to the future strategy among mainstream broadcasters, the increasing selection of outlets, for example, digital and social media, Netflix and other digital streaming options, are also offering new opportunities for content and programming. These newer digital streaming services such as Netflix show more diverse programmes and therefore offer competition to mainstream broadcasting with respect to content that depicts ethnic minority characters (Kantar Media, 2018). Therefore, if broadcasters (public and private) want to retain and grow their audiences, it is imperative that they keep up with the diversity of the broader

Figure 8.5: Ethnic minority audience of the BBC, 2016–17

■ ETHNIC MINORTIY   ■ ALL AUDIENCES (AGED 16 AND OVER)

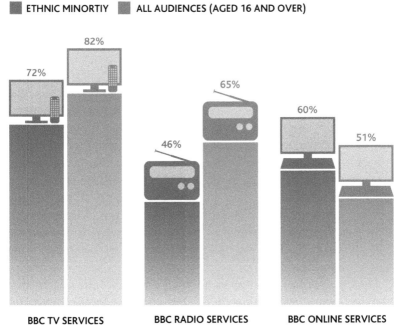

BBC TV SERVICES   BBC RADIO SERVICES   BBC ONLINE SERVICES

Source: Internal BBC data, 2016–17.

population. As Levin (2018) explains, ethnic minority audiences are more likely to watch television shows that depict ethnically diverse casts. The following section examines the question of cultural representation.

Cultural representation

As stated, cultural representations matter because they influence how we see and understand ourselves and the world, and how social understandings are formed. Cultural representation is, therefore, a powerful social force that shapes civil society, its politics and discourses. This is especially pertinent when it comes to race and ethnicity because of the history of cultural representations of racial and ethnic populations that have depended on racialised tropes and stereotypes. Thus, questions of cultural representation go beyond numbers and the proportion of ethnic minority people represented on-screen in film and TV or non-white characters in books for example. It is important to examine how ethnic minority characters are represented. The Riz Test (www.riztest.com), for example, is an intervention that seeks to dismantle well-rehearsed stereotypes and ideologies underpinning

Islamophobia, in order to broaden public perceptions of a much-vilified sector of UK society. Improving the cultural representation of ethnic minority people is important for building a more inclusive society, ascribing identities and a sense of place, as well as generating new forms of political participation in which more diverse forms of cultural and artistic content can be generated.

If existing quantitative data offer us some information about the inequalities that exist in relation to cultural production (employment) and cultural consumption, they have very little to demonstrate in the area of cultural representation. This is partly because it is challenging to quantify ethnic minority representation across different genres and cultural sectors. However, although there are methods available to enable this quantification, we still lack the studies and data to fully examine ethnic minority representation. Nonetheless, there have been some local, small-scale quantitative studies that take a particular cultural industry, such as publishing, and try to examine representation using different metrics.

The lack of ethnic minority authors in the publishing bestsellers chart was discussed in an earlier section. Data compiled by the Centre for Literacy in Primary Education (CLPE, 2018) titled *Reflecting Realities*, revealed the stark lack of diversity in children's books. The report examined 9,115 children's books published in the UK in 2017 and found only 391 of them featured a character with an ethnic minority background. This accounted for only 4% of children's books overall, with a further examination finding only 1% of these books featured the ethnic minority character as the main character. Thus, not only were ethnic minority characters under-represented they were marginalised in the different stories published for children. The CLPE's (2018) analysis of the specific genres where ethnic minority people featured prominently found that the majority of ethnic minority characters featured in 'contemporary realism' books or those set in a modern-day landscape. A further 10% of the characters featured in books labelled as 'social justice', with only one book defined as a 'comedy'. In terms of audience, the data revealed that 26% of the non-fiction books that contained an ethnic minority character were aimed at an early years audience, leaving older children even more under-served. The CLPE (2018) report sheds light on the missing narratives of different ethnic and migrant groups' experiences that were edited in a specific way to exclude accounts of suffering and trauma. Many topics that could enrich the children's books and pay particular attention to ethnic minority groups' experiences with respect to current affairs and themes of conflict and the refugee experience have been excluded. What is needed are more books that embrace a range of topics to adequately represent the diversity of ethnic minority experience and the backing to promote them into the mainstream.

Similarly, a survey on the content of glossy magazines revealed that printed content was another area where ethnic minority people were under-represented (Hirsh, 2018). Recent statistics gathered by *The Guardian* newspaper suggest that of the 214 women's magazine covers by 19 of the bestselling glossy magazines in 2017, only 20 featured an ethnic minority person (Hirsh, 2018). This accounted for a meagre 9.3%, well below the 13.7% share of ethnic minority people in the broader population (ONS, 2016b). Comparing similar representation among children's magazines (where ethnic minority people comprise more than a quarter of school children in England), *The Guardian* found that representation was even more limited, with 95% of cover models being white. The same was true for men's magazines, where only *GQ* featured two black cover models and *Men's Health* only featured one. In addition, neither of the men's magazines featured cover models from any other ethnic minority background (Hirsh, 2018). Therefore, cumulatively across the spectrum of women, men and children's magazines, it is clear that ethnic minority people were poorly represented.

According to Hirsh (2018), the lack of representation that is endemic across the publishing sector is reinforced by the sector's unwillingness to change. This was most telling in a quote by Alexandra Shulman (former editor-in-chief of *British Vogue*), who stated in 2012 that 'in a society where the mass of the consumers are white and where, on the whole, mainstream ideas sell, it's unlikely there will be a huge rise in the number of leading black models'. Nevertheless, change has been afoot in *British Vogue* more recently, with the recruitment of its first black editor-in-chief, Edward Enninful, who launched his premier cover featuring the British Ghanian model Adwoa Aboah and has included a recent edition featuring more non-white models, including Halim Aden, the first woman to wear a hijab on the magazine's cover. Enninful's hiring, and specific response to publishing's historic resistance to change, represents a small and important step that opens up a space for the sector to do more to increase the representation of ethnic minority people.

Finally, in broadcasting, Cumberbatch and colleagues (2018) analysed the on-screen presence of ethnic minority people across BBC One and BBC Two programming. Their study found that ethnic minority people made up 12.5% of both channel's television population (between 2016 and 2017), which is slightly lower than the ethnic minority share of the

British population (14%). They also found a slight difference in the on-screen presence of ethnic minority people between BBC One (13.8%) and BBC Two (10.9%). Further, by examining the on-screen presence of ethnic minority people by gender, they found that ethnic minority men (54%) were represented more than ethnic minority women (46%). While the results suggested a gender difference, in fact, ethnic minority women's on-screen representation is actually better than the national average of the representation of all women, where men outnumber them by a ratio of 2:1 (Cumberbatch et al, 2018). Moreover, examining the on-screen presence of ethnic minority people by age category, the results showed that ethnic minority people tended to be young, with nearly half (44%) being under the age of 35 compared to less than one third (31%) of the television population more broadly (Cumberbatch et al, 2018).

Funding and industry policy responses: a focus on diversity in public broadcasting

It is abundantly clear that descriptive representation of ethnic minority people is a problem among many of the creative industries, and there are calls for industry-wide cultural change and matters of diversity to be foregrounded. In broadcasting, Sharon White, a black British woman, was appointed as the new CEO of the broadcast regulator, Ofcom. White, who became one of the most influential decision makers in the CCIs (she left Ofcom in Autumn 2019), has pledged to make diversity a priority (Albury, 2016). The growth of the creative industries in the UK has expanded Ofcom's remit to regulate the entire broadcasting sector and as a result more businesses and organisations have encountered the regulators' commitment to diversity and inclusion. Previously Ofcom had done very little to support broader diversity and a particular problem with their lacklustre approach has centred on their reluctance to push for more data to be gathered to audit and monitor the representation of ethnic minority people and other protected characteristics in broadcasting (Albury, 2016). In a talk in January 2019 by Sharon White at the launch of the Ofcom Annual Plan 2019/20, she suggested the government's Department for Culture, Media and Sport had rejected the media regulator's request to have greater powers when collecting data on diversity in broadcasting (Ofcom, 2018). Without a collective will to address this disparity and a greater drive to collect more precise data on the representation of ethnic minority people in the industry, the ambition to target ethnic inequality as a whole could disappear. Karen Bradley, then Secretary of State, explained that the government's stalling on the issue was partly due to the broader concern over the country's pathway through Brexit that had precluded a focus on many domestic issues. If Ofcom wants to see a significant improvement in terms of diversity, they should introduce a set of minimum standards with respect to diversity, increase their commitment to transparency and make diversity data freely available to monitor change within broadcasting.

Box 2: DIAMOND

One apparatus that shows broadcasters' (public and private) commitment to different types of diversity is the new DIAMOND monitoring system. DIAMOND is an initiative that seeks to capture diversity across the major TV channels. It aims to assess the diversity of those who create programmes (diversity in cultural production) and the representation of diversity within programmes. The BBC's specific involvement with DIAMOND has also come under scrutiny by BECTU, the union for creative industry workers in non-performance roles, and the Writers' Guild of Great Britain because both unions accused the corporation of not being transparent enough with respect to publishing data (for example, data on gender, on jobs and on the grades of staff working in the corporation) (*The Stage*, 2017). The BBC's response was that it could not publish certain demographic data because of data protection restrictions. The unions subsequently criticised this stance as being the main obstacle that has prevented increasing ethnic diversity. This is because, the unions argued, a few gatekeepers at DIAMOND tightly controlled the essential data necessary to audit the patterns of diversity across different broadcasters (*The Stage*, 2017). This restricted DIAMOND from being able to make any meaningful change, and its power and control over production and access to diversity data regulated the speed at which any progress was made in the sector (if at all). The unions called for DIAMOND to publish the quality monitoring data by production so that they could identify which production companies or broadcasters have the most diverse workforce and can learn what works and what does not, to improve them for ethnic minority workers. The unions subsequently argued that without this information new ethnic minority recruits would experience challenges in retaining their position in the sector. As Ofcom's Sharon White said to the Digital, Culture, Media and Sport Select Committee in May 2019, DIAMOND 'started with very, very good intentions and there have been challenges in terms of the reach and the quality and the depth of data' (DCMS, 2019). White went on to say that this is one reason why Ofcom have used their statutory powers to collect from diversity data across TV and radio but that even Ofcom has limits to accessing this.

Diversity policy in public broadcasting

As highlighted in the work of Herman Gray (2016: 242), public service television is 'a key location where diversity is practiced materially and symbolically'. According to Malik (2018), something of a transformation has occurred within the cultural industries, which have seen issues of diversity change from being primarily a social concern to being considered a matter significant to businesses as a profit incentive. Under this new guise, corporate owners have come to view engaging with diversity issues as one way of diversifying the audiences they target. Corporate owners, for example, will often finance the production of output (programming, for example) that is not to their tastes in order to make a profit (Hesmondhalgh and Saha, 2013). The business case for diversity suggests that businesses benefit from the diverse skill set of their increasingly diverse employee base, which has come in particular use when they are targeting products at new markets (DBIS, 2013). While the business case helps explain why the private sector has so readily internalised diversity into their recruitment and content, change has also been evident in public funded arts and creative industries by steering public sector funding in a specific way to support diversity.

In the public sector, a later Arts Council England report, *Equality, Diversity and the Creative Case* (ACE, 2019) mentions how the call for diversity in the arts and media sector has directly affected how projects are funded. New applications made to Arts Council England (one of the four UK arts councils) have to ensure they support the council's three interlocking themes (equality, recognition and new vision). The approach not only seeks to diversify the arts and media workforce but also change creative processes and working arrangements. Malik (2018) suggests that a problem with the prescribed framework for 'creative diversity' is that it produces and reproduces a specific type of diversity rhetoric and expectation. While the shift in the creative industries has raised awareness of the inequalities that exist in the industry and the steps that need to be taken, a substantial barrier is that the four different arts councils in the UK take different approaches to how diversity can be achieved in new funding applications. Creative Scotland, for example, requires organisations and individuals wishing to apply for funding to ensure that diversity is reflected across the application. This includes how the art is produced, the staff and working environments, and the audience and/or participants of the programme/project as well as the buildings and spaces used (Creative Scotland, 2018). By comparison, the arts councils for Northern Ireland and for Wales support diversity in their future strategies but are less stringent in the precise ways that diversity needs to be included in arts funding applications. The different approaches and the lack of definition with respect to how diversity can be included in art projects can obfuscate how to ensure ensuring the profile of ethnic minority people is raised uniformly throughout different areas of the creative industries and in equal measure across the four nations.

Pressure to endorse ethnic diversity in the labour market from reports such as that of McGregor-Smith (2017) has seen a focus on ethnic diversity filter into the business structure and the framework of the content that these organisations produce. Focusing on the broadcasting sector, it is interesting to see how the broader shift in diversity policy has impacted on a specific sector, and, in turn, how the policies have endorsed addressing ethnic inequality in various forms in specific institutional policies. The newest manifestation of cultural policy towards ethnic diversity in broadcasting is now being framed as *creative diversity*. This has differed from previous cultural policies, which were targeted directly at ethnic minority issues. According to Malik (2013), we have seen a policy shift away from a focus on multiculturalism to creative diversity, losing a specific focus on ethnic inequalities and arguments around social justice. She argues that this is linked to the state rejection of multiculturalism, which has run parallel to the marketisation of the cultural industries.

An issue with the new approach related to how 'creative diversity' would be operationalised in public policy. Creative diversity, as a new approach to diversity in broadcasting, was charted as being composed of four principles: access, excellence, education and economic value (Garnham, 2005). The argument here is that this policy framing focuses on creativity rather than a concern for ensuring equity in the demography of the cultural industries and the representation of ethnic minority people in its content. It was in the early 2000s that both Channel 4 and the BBC put forward their diversity strategies, taking a much broader approach to diversity than had previously been applied in separate policy approaches to different social identities such as race and ethnicity, gender, sexuality and class. There also appeared to be a change in tone in media circles towards diversity and the new *cultural* and then *creative* diversity that placed significant emphasis on the idea of *widening access*.

Examining the existing work on diversity policy in the UK in a specific industry (public broadcasting) and how it responds to ethnic minority populations can thus tell us a lot about their position and status in the creative industries. Briefly looking at two examples in broadcasting, we can see how influential changes to diversity policy have been for ethnic minority employment and representation. The first example is the *BBC Equality Information Report* (2017b) and the second example is Channel 4's 360° Equalities Strategy.

British Broadcasting Corporation

The BBC, as the largest public broadcasting channel in the UK, released its diversity policy titled the *BBC Equality Information Report 2016–17*. The report described the corporation's commitment to a 'Diversity and Inclusion Strategy'. The policy's aim was, first, to increase the representation of ethnic minority people, women, disability and LBGT employees across its workforce. Second, it aimed to include more diverse voices in its programming content. The *BBC Equality and Information Report* (2017b) highlighted the BBC's already diverse workforce compared to other broadcasting organisations in the UK; however, it also sheds light on areas the corporation could improve upon. The corporation commended itself in its report for several of its programmes already being dedicated to increasing the ethnic diversity in its broadcasting. For instance, shows such as *Damilola: Our Loved Boy* (2016), *The People v. O.J. Simpson* (2016) and *Black is the New Black* (2016) demonstrate more diverse content. Additionally, it has developed a number of schemes to help increase the ethnic diversity of its employees in several areas, for example, a scheme to recruit more ethnic minority employees among the directors of its programmes, with the 2016 cohort admitting 5 out of 12 trainees from an ethnic minority background (BBC, 2017b).

A more recent report by the BBC in 2018 focused on the career progression and culture for staff from minority backgrounds at the corporation (BBC, 2018b). The report was compiled from the comments of many ethnic minority staff members (over 200 staff members) and made a number of recommendations. First, the BBC should increase the ethnic diversity of its leadership team and, second, it should build a solid and sustainable ethnic minority mid and senior leadership pipeline to get minority people channelled into higher positions. Third, the BBC should enhance accountability and trust and, fourth, it should develop a modern, agile and culturally intelligent workforce. Finally, the BBC should review areas with specific ethnic diversity issues. Examples of specific recommendations include the BBC introducing a policy to ensure that shortlists for all jobs include at least one ethnic minority candidate, to 'increase the [ethnic minority] representation across the interview panel backed by performance monitoring' and to 'develop specific action plans based on further analysis of all divisions with less than 10% [ethnic minority] representation or below par employee survey results including radio, Newsroom, Newsgathering, English regions and the World Service' (BBC, 2018b: 1). In 2019 it was announced that the BBC's dedicated Head of Diversity role would be split into two jobs, the Director of Creative Diversity and the Head of Workforce Diversity and Inclusion, suggesting a separation between approaches to diversity into two distinct areas of content/output and workforce.

Channel 4

Channel 4 also launched its 360° equalities strategy in 2015 and the charter stated the organisation's commitment to record and report diversity and remain transparent about its current levels of diversity among its workforce. Similar to the BBC's strategy, the internal diversity policy sheds light on diversity for public service broadcasting. In the UK the BBC is publicly funded from the licence fee; meanwhile, Channel 4 is publicly owned but commercially funded. Channel 4's current strategy celebrates a number of key diversity achievements. An audit of the channel's workforce shows that the organisation is relatively ethnically diverse at junior levels compared to the BBC; however, there is work still to be done in terms of its senior positions. As a result, Channel 4's strategy has been aimed at recruiting and training ethnic minority and other subgroups in progressing into senior leadership positions. Furthermore, a central strategy with regard to ethnic minority employment is to diversify new joiners by 50% by 2020. The policy is clear in stating it aims to increase the representation of ethnic minority people in its workforce. However, their diversity strategy is not limited to race and ethnicity, but also shows the organisation's commitment to gender equality, disability visibility and inclusion, and regionality, suggesting an acknowledgement of the single legal framework of the Equality Act 2010. The diversity strategy goes further and recognises that it is necessary to foster diversity at all levels of the organisation, from commissioners to writers and those who are interns to the headhunters who search for talent. The strategy is also focused on increasing diversity in the content of programming and this will be achieved by a number of schemes and targets that Channel 4 is committed to (including a career development model that focuses on exposure, education and experience) focused on increasing the presence on screen of ethnic minority people, women, disabled people, voices from different regions and social mobility.

While it is clear that both channels have made positive moves towards increasing diversity among their respective workforces as well as diversity in their programmes, there are still questions about how suitable the one-size-fits-all *creative diversity* approach is in producing meaningful ethnic equality.

Conclusion

The cuts to the funding of public arts and creative sector industries as well as the uncertainty created by Brexit are impacting on the creative industries. It remains to be seen whether the emerging commitment the creative industries have shown towards increasing ethnic diversity intensifies or is thwarted by their focus moving elsewhere. As Nicholas Serota, CEO of Arts Council England stated in 2017, a major obstacle in tackling inequality in the cultural industries is that many arts and cultural organisations are failing to supply data about diversity and inclusion. There is deep variance across the CCIs, so that while there are signs of increasing ethnic minority representation in terms of leadership and content in theatre in London, for example, the wider picture shows a deep level of unevenness across different sectors within the CCIs and across the UK.

The chapter has particularly focused on public service broadcasting where there has been an acknowledgement of the marginalisation of ethnic minority people. This has led to a number of policy initiatives that have specifically focused on improving the numbers of ethnic minority people working in the industry (such as BBC's and Channel 4's diversity strategies). But more diverse ethnic minority representation with regard to content is not a proven outcome of more diverse representation in the workforce. The problem is that even though ethnic diversity in certain organisations increases, ethnic minority workers too can revert to modes of cultural production that depend on familiar, racialised representations, 'thereby reproducing stereotypical representations of race.' (Hesmondhalgh and Saha, 2013: 192). These strategies still revolve around the assumption that increasing the ethnic diversity of the workplace necessarily produces an increase in the ethnic diversity of the content produced. While channels may increase the diversity of their workforces, there is little evidence to show that those cultural workers have the will, power or persistence to implement change in the content of programmes or the audiences who watch or listen to content. More ethnic minority representation within sector employment does not guarantee more creative freedom.

9

Politics and representation

Maria Sobolewska and William Shankley

Key findings

- Following decades of very slow progress, the last three general elections saw large increases in numbers of ethnic minority MPs, leading to more than a tripling of their numbers in less than 15 years.
- The major political parties had to utilise different strategies to increase the numbers of ethnic minorities in Westminster, crucially leading to the fielding of ethnic minority candidates in many predominantly 'white' seats.
- Standing ethnic minority candidates in 'white' seats ends the era of ethnic ghettoisation of ethnic minority politicians and signals a qualitative change in ethnic minority representation in Britain.
- Despite the huge progress, minorities remain under-represented and recent data show that ethnic minority candidates still face discrimination at the stage of candidate selection.
- The majority of the 52 ethnic minority MPs elected in 2017 came from a similar class background to their white counterparts and therefore continue not to represent a broad range of voices among the ethnic minority electorate.
- Voting of British ethnic minorities has not changed as much in the last decades as political representation, with a majority still loyal to the Labour party.
- The Conservative party continues to make very slow, but steady progress with British Indian voters, despite some headline grabbing news announcing that progress has been dramatic.
- The Liberal Democrats have lost the vast majority of their ethnic minority vote, since minorities returned to Labour after a short period of voting Lib-Dem in protest over the Iraq war.
- Ethnic minority voters have always been thought to participate in politics less than white Britons, yet research now agrees that the main problem is in the rates of electoral registration, with many

ethnic minority residents unsure and unaware that they can vote in British elections.

- A non-negligible proportion of ethnic minority voters voted to Leave the European Union (EU) in the 2016 referendum, but the majority supported Remain.

Introduction

The last decade has seen revolutionary progress in political representation of ethnic minorities. Yet we are still short of an exact match between the proportion of ethnic minorities living in the UK (at the last census in 2011 which was estimated at 14%) and the percentage of ethnic minority MPs in Westminster, which at the time of writing stood at 8% (52 MPs). Although progress was very slow until the 2005 election, in the 2010 general election the numbers of minority MPs nearly doubled, and advances were made in 2015 and 2017 as well, meaning that between 2005 and 2017, the number of ethnic minority MPs more than tripled. One in ten of the MPs elected in the 2019 general election are non-white; however, all non-white MPs represent English seats. The story of how and why political representation improved is the most dynamic story to be told about race in politics. The other aspects of politics have been marred – as before – by scarce or poor-quality data. The glimpses into the other aspects of politics that are available given the scarcity of data in this area focus on persistent Labour party loyalty among minorities, their patterns of electoral participation and, last but not least, their vote in the 2016 EU referendum. The main challenges for the future remain studying the still very under-researched substantive representation, and working towards equal opportunity in politics, particularly issues around candidate selection and voter registration.

Representation

Historically, Britain has lacked ethnic diversity in Westminster (Saggar and Geddes, 2000; Bird et al, 2010). Since 1987, when the first four self-identifying ethnic minority MPs were elected, progress has been very slow, with the numbers added in each election remaining in single digits. Nevertheless, the 2010 general election was a critical election in this regard, when the number of ethnic minority MPs elected to Parliament nearly doubled, from 16 to 27. The main reason why the 2010 election proved critical was a step-change in the way the main political parties approached candidate selection of ethnic minorities.

The newly employed party strategies not only continued to lead to an increase of numbers of ethnic minority MPs in the 2015 and 2017 elections, but also represent a watershed moment for minority politicians, as they were no longer limited to standing in ethnically diverse constituencies (Sobolewska, 2013). The 2010 general election provided a good opportunity for the major parties to increase their diversity as a record number of incumbents were retiring (Labour 102; the Conservatives 37; Lib Dems 10) (Criddle, 2010; Sobolewska, 2013). Individually, all the major parties had an internal interest in growing their ethnic minority representation. The Conservative party, for example, wanted to overhaul their image as the 'nasty party' as well as attempt to court the ethnic minority voter, who historically had showed a tendency to vote for the Labour party in the postwar era (Evans, 2008). Meanwhile, Labour and the Lib Dems wanted to increase their representation to reflect the changing structure of their party's support and broader pressure to diversify (Norris et al, 1992; Sobolewska, 2013). Some argued that Labour needed to increase ethnic minority representation in order to retain their vote and avoid complacency, particularly as a sizeable number of voters had defected to the Lib Dems previously following Labour's position on the Iraq war in 2003 (Le Lohé, 2004; Curtice, 2005).

While the 2010 general election opened up a number of new seats, structurally each party suffered with both demand- and supply-side problems in selecting ethnic minority candidates for these vacant seats, and had to use different strategies to accomplish this aim. Four main strategies were used: centralisation of the selection process, recruitment from the outside of the party, selecting local ethnic minority candidates, and standing ethnic minority candidates in 'white' seats. The first of these strategies was designed to overcome a by-product of the British decentralised candidate selection model, which has been the very low success rate for ethnic minority candidates (and women; see Norris and Lovenduski, 1995; Durose et al, 2012). Many have argued that this was a direct result of the homophily in the local party selectorate, who were more likely to select candidates who were similar to them: white men to a large extent. Some level of centralisation of selections had already worked in the past to increase the number of women candidates for the Labour party, as the party National Executive Committee had an existing power to make any newly vacant seat consider an all-women shortlist.

The Conservative party attempted to make their processes more centralised in the run-up to the 2010 election, by creating an 'A list' of priority candidates, which they envisaged will be used as a basis of local candidate selection, and which contained a number of ethnic minority politicians. In the event, the 'A list' was dropped in the face of overwhelming opposition, but the indirect result of this has been that many of the politicians on the 'A list' were in fact selected and elected in safe Conservative seats. Conservatives also trialled open primaries in these elections, which were thought also to overcome the biases of the local selectors. Out of all the new Conservative ethnic minority candidates selected to stand for 2010 elections, one quarter were previously on the A list or were selected via open primaries, indicating that the party's efforts were paying off. Although the Labour party has always fielded much greater numbers of ethnic minority candidates, they too struggled to select them into winnable and safe seats. Thus, Labour's efforts to centralise in 2010 were also detectable, and yielded a third of their new ethnic minority candidates (see Sobolewska, 2013).

However newer research from Representative Audit of Britain 2015 suggests that candidates of minority origin still face a significant number of obstacles, having to apply for more vacancies to get a nomination for example, as well as having to be on more shortlists, and having to interview more times to get nominated (see Sobolewska, 2017). Many fewer ethnic minority candidates also reported that they were encouraged to stand for election by their own party. However, in the run-up to the 2017 snap general election centralisation of candidate selection was introduced to some extent by both Labour and Conservatives, and it seems that yet another increase in ethnic minority MPs elected offers yet more evidence that centralisation is helpful, if not necessary, for parties to increase the ethnic diversity in Westminster.

Finding the right ethnic minority candidates to stand for election has also been a struggle for parties, again particularly for the Conservatives who have fewer ethnic minority voters and thus a smaller pool to draw from, so again the 2010 election has seen some new strategies to recruit more ethnic minority candidates, which Representative Audit of Britain from 2015 confirms are continuing (Sobolewska, 2017). These two strategies are trying to find local ethnic minority candidates and selecting them from the outside of the party itself. Being a local candidate is perceived as desirable thing for all politicians (Campbell and Cowley, 2014), and it might be especially important for non-white candidates who feel the pressure to fulfil many more criteria of being a perfect fit to overcome their perceived 'otherness' (Durose et al, 2012). There is some evidence that the minority candidates at the 2010 election were to a large extent local (Sobolewska, 2013), although it is unclear whether this is a trend that continued in 2015 or 2017. Recruitment from outside of party politics carries a special importance, as it seems to have continued in 2015 as well as 2017, with ethnic minority candidates having on average only around half the years of party membership of white candidates before getting selected, were less likely to have been a party official than white candidates, and were also less likely to have held an elected office at the local level before standing for a seat at Westminster (Sobolewska, 2017). All of this is evidence that they were being fast-tracked in order to overcome a shortage of more experienced ethnic minority candidates.

The final strategy, which proved to be the most revolutionary in the 2010 election, was to select ethnic minority candidates for what are usually considered 'white' seats, where the ethnic minority population constitute less than 20%, or even 10%. This strategy was particularly important for the Conservative party, which has few safe and winnable seats in areas with high ethnic diversity. Thus, in order to elect new ethnic minority MPs at all, the Conservatives had to select them for their best safe seats, especially in the face of evidence that ethnic minority candidates still face a small electoral penalty from voters (discussed later in this chapter), and these seats are, for the Conservatives, predominantly 'white'. This was a very successful strategy, as out of the 27 ethnic minority MPs who were returned in 2010 election, only 7 represented seats that had more than 40% minority residents, and 10 represented seats in which minorities amounted to less than 10% of the population. This strategy has continued with the 2015 and 2017 elections, again particularly within the Conservative party. What this strategy has achieved, however, is a symbolic shift in how ethnic diversity is perceived, in what amounts to a paradigm shift in the study of representation. There are three main consequences. First, the racial ghettoisation of ethnic minority MPs seems to be a thing of the past, with ethnic minority politicians no longer seemingly limited to being the spokespeople for ethnically diverse constituencies and very narrowly defined 'ethnic' issues, which used to limit their aspirations and political careers, as well as the types and number of constituencies in which they were able to stand and win (Saggar and Geddes, 2000). Second, both main parties now offer meaningful levels of ethnic diversity, which challenges the traditional link between ethnic representation and left-wing politics and throws open the party competition over voters of non-white origin wider than it has ever been before (although more on this later). Third and finally, as a result of both ethnic minority MPs coming from non-left-wing parties and their no longer being 'ghettoised' in the most diverse seats, an assumption of an almost automatic link between descriptive representation and substantive representation needs reassessing (more on this later). But before we turn to the consequences of the rapid increase of ethnic diversity in Parliament, let's look at what it means in terms of evidence of discrimination from the white voters.

Does the recent dramatic increase in the number of ethnic minority MPs, and the fact that they are no longer elected in the most ethnically diverse seats mean there is little or no prejudice against non-white candidates at the ballot box? Analysis of the voting patterns for ethnic minority and majority voters in the 2010 and 2015 general elections, as well as an analysis of aggregate election results, gives us some indication on whether or not ethnic minority candidates suffer an ethnic penalty at the ballot box.

Traditionally, the aggregate-level evidence indicates that non-white candidates suffer a small ethnic penalty, losing around 3% of the vote in comparison to the general performance of their party in that election (Ford et al, 2010; Stegmeir et al, 2013). At the individual voter level, studies are much more rare, but generally show that the ethnicity of the candidate does not usually make a statistically significant difference. Evidence from the 2010 general election showed that white British voters were significantly less likely to vote for an ethnic minority candidate only if that candidate was Muslim (Fisher et al, 2015). However, even for Muslim candidates, the influence of party was much stronger than the impact of candidate's ethnicity and, where present, the ethnic penalty appeared to be rather small and limited to particular segments of the white voting population. This matters in contests where the winning majority is small, but should not matter in so-called safe seats, where the majority exceeds this percentage vastly. As a result, it once again underlines that candidate selection, and not the prejudices of the electorate, is more decisive in driving – and preventing – fair ethnic minority representation.

Before celebrating the rising numbers of ethnic minority MPs, and a seemingly small levels of opposition to them from white majority voters, we need to assess whether the increase in the number of such MPs in parliament means that the interests of ethnic minorities are better represented. There has always been an assumption, both in the academic literature and in real-life politics, that descriptive, numerical representation leads to substantive representation: whereby a point of view, or interests, are brought into Parliament by the representative who comes from the under-represented group her or himself. However, the empirical evidence for this has previously been hard to come by, because almost all of the ethnic minority MPs were also members of the Labour party, thus it was impossible to see whether their behaviour was caused by their party ideology or their ethnicity. The finding that white Labour party MPs were also likely to substantively represent minority interests in Westminster, especially if they had a very ethnically diverse constituency, has been well established (Saalfeld and Bischof, 2012).

However, with the recent increase not only of the absolute numbers of ethnic minority MPs, but also ethnic minority MPs from both Labour and Conservative parties, we have a much better chance of discovering if non-white MPs are more likely to represent minority voters. Although there are no current in-depth studies of substantive representation of ethnic minorities, research into attitudes of ethnic minority candidates and MPs suggests that we can now disentangle the influence of party and ethnicity. Based on the Representative Audit of Britain survey of candidates and MPs, Sobolewska and others (2018) show that while all ethnic minority politicians have higher levels of motivation to represent ethnic minority interests than white politicians, there are significant party differences. Conservative ethnic minority candidates and MPs are much less eager to represent fellow minorities (although still more so than white Conservative politicians) than Labour party ethnic minority candidates and MPs. In addition to the directly expressed motivation and will to represent, this study asked the politicians if they felt that racism held back British black and Asian minorities. This is a crucial attitude to hold if one is expected to try and overcome racism and represent the minority interests. Again, all ethnic minority prospective and actual representatives were more likely to think this than their white party colleagues. However, again, the Conservative ethnic minority politicians were less likely to believe this than their Labour counterparts. Finally, the demographic composition of the constituency has a clear impact on how ethnic minority politicians think about their motivation to represent and whether they perceive racism as a problem. Those who represent, or seek to represent, very diverse areas score much higher on both, which makes them more likely to represent ethnic minority people in Parliament. Given that, as already documented, the number of ethnic minority politicians who represent less diverse areas increased dramatically, this is certain to have an impact on representation of minority interest by minority politicians. This offers a check on the assumption that all ethnic minority politicians will let ethnic minority voices be heard in Westminster.

This change in the nature as well as the volume of representation of ethnic minorities in parliament raises many new questions that future academics and politicians will have to grapple with. Particularly, is ethnic diversity an end in itself, or does it need to be linked to substantive representation of interests and points of view, to be valuable?

Local representation

As representation in Westminster receives a lot of scrutiny from the media and civil society organisations such as Operation Black Vote and Runnymede Trust, we have much more detailed data on its progress over the years. In contrast, local government largely escapes such scrutiny and little is known about how diverse local representatives really are. Existing studies focus either on a particular ethnic minority (such as Muslims, see Dancygier, 2017) or localities (see Muroki and Cowley, 2019). As a result, the most recent published data are from 2013, and put the percentage of ethnic minority councillors at 4% (Rallings et al, 2013), which is a huge shortfall. The Centre on the Dynamics of Ethnicity's (CoDE's) own, more recent figures show that in early 2019 this figure was at 7.5%, representing an improvement comparable to progress at national level. What this research also shows is that the local presence of ethnic minorities is the main explanatory factor for under-representation of minorities in local government. As the majority of local authorities do not have large numbers of minority residents, they do not usually have any ethnic diversity on local councils. However, more ethnically diverse areas usually do have substantial levels of non-white MPs.[1]

Intersectionality

It is often alleged that the focus on increasing representation of ethnic minorities competes directly with a focus on increasing gender representation. This has been shown to be true for local representation of Muslim minorities by Dancygier (2017), who provides evidence that Muslim women candidates struggle to win selections for parliamentary office from parties trying to recruit Muslim candidates. However, the picture seems less convincing for all minorities at the national level. Allegations that all-women shortlists, instituted by the Labour party to increase female representation, have been predominantly white (Krook and Nugent, 2016) are undermined by the fact that they are in fact a lot less 'white' than normal shortlists, with 17% ethnic minority candidates on all-women shortlists as opposed to 5% on regular Labour shortlists (Krook and Nugent, 2016: 626). Also, looking at the gender profile of ethnic minority MPs, we find little evidence of a larger gender imbalance than among white MPs. According to the House of Commons Library, out of the 52 minority MPs elected in 2017, 50% were female, and the overall figure for Westminster was 32% (Cracknell, 2017).

Voting behaviour

The positive efforts that the Conservative party made on representation have quite clearly been designed to banish the label of 'the nasty party'. Although some of this effort was aimed at white liberal voters, the party had hoped that it would either win them some ethnic minority voters or, at the very least, banish the notion that the Conservatives are a no-go party for ethnic minorities. In contrast, Labour's historic popularity among ethnic minorities has been further cemented over the last decades by the party passing all major legislation that supports their rights and opportunities and offers ways of addressing discrimination (Heath et al, 2013). With the growing number of ethnic minority voters in the electorate this was becoming a crucial electoral problem for the Conservatives. As a result, the party has renewed their efforts (the last such attempt being in the early 1990s) to fix their relationship with ethnic minority voters. Clearly promoting ethnic diversity within the parliamentary party has been one of the foundation stones of this tactic. In 2015, a slew of front-page headlines seemed to confirm that their efforts have started to pay off. A Survation poll commissioned by the think tank British Future announced that in 2015 general election the Conservatives captured a significant number of ethnic minority voters from Labour. However, a closer look at this result showed that the Conservatives have made much less dramatic inroads, and these were limited to those of Indian origin, a group that was already more likely to support the Conservatives (Ford et al, 2015). However, even among this group, almost 60% supported Labour in 2015.

The problem that British Future encountered is that data on attitudes and political behaviour of the ethnic minority population in Britain is scarce and of very poor quality. Since academic polling is very expensive, the last in-depth study of this type was done in 2010, and most other reliable data sets do not contain many political questions. It is predominantly because the ethnic minority population tended to be younger than the White British population, concentrated geographically, and many have poorer levels of English language that they are less likely to be included in the usual polling samples. A more recent analysis by Martin (2019) confirms this analysis of 2015 and 2017 general elections (Martin and Khan, 2019). It seems that, despite all efforts to aggressively recruit ethnic minority politicians, the Conservatives cannot get through to ethnic minority voters.

Using Understanding Society survey (waves 3, 5 and 7), Martin and Mellon (2018) also found that the advantage that Labour has with minorities is unlikely to fade because ethnic minorities aged 20 to 30 have much higher levels of party identity than White British people. In fact their level of partisan attachment is comparable levels to those of White British people aged 50. People who identify with and feel attached to a party are more likely to vote for that party consistently. To explain how this pattern arose, Martin and Mellon (2018) suggest that partisanship among ethnic minorities was shaped by parental views. Partisanship was therefore transmitted predominantly during socialisation processes. Unlike White British voters, ethnic minority voters continue to transmit strong signals about politics and the parties to their children, and this explains why partisanship is higher among ethnic minorities.

Participation

Historically, the enduring link between ethnic minorities' vote and the Labour party has been carefully maintained by Labour, which has relied in many places on the so-called 'ethnic bloc vote'. The party has therefore always cared about high turnout in areas where the percentage of minority residents has been substantial. In fact, against the picture of slightly lower than average national turnout figures for many minority voters, it has been shown that people who live in high concentration areas of (particularly South Asian) minorities, had higher than average turnout. However, recently, a dark side to this pattern has been more publicly acknowledged, and it paints a picture of political exclusion and disenfranchisement of large proportions of ethnic minority voters. Research on electoral fraud, which has been increasingly associated with areas of high concentration of South Asian origin minorities, which were previously thought to have high levels of political engagement, exposed a pernicious problem. In 2015 a study commissioned by the Electoral Commission (Sobolewska et al, 2015; Hill et al, 2017) showed that in those areas the high levels of participation are often actually artificial, as the reality is that women and younger people are often excluded from the political process through the influence of kinship networks and breaches of the secrecy of voting. However, both Sobolewska et al (2015) and Peace and Akhtar (2015) show that many, particularly younger, members of the South Asian communities in Britain, reject such influence and look to the political parties to help them eradicate it.

In addition to these problems, ethnic minority political participation is further marred by issues around electoral registration. Following the

2010 general election, the Ethnic Minority British Election Study uncovered much lower levels of electoral registration among non-white communities than the British average. As many as 28% British Africans were not registered to vote (Heath et al, 2013) and other minority groups were also affected more than the white majority population. The main cause of this under-registration has been due to lack of knowledge about eligibility: the majority of non-white British residents come from countries of the Commonwealth and thus can vote in all elections upon arrival, but a huge number of them do not know this.

In 2014 there was a change to the electoral registration system, which further threatened the number of ethnic minorities eligible to vote. The change saw a move from household to individual electoral registration (IER), with the former previously allowing one member of a household to register all of the people resident at the same address, while the new system required each person to register individually and, most importantly, to provide evidence of their identity such as their National Insurance Number (NIN) (Electoral Reform Society, 2019). This was a particularly risky change for many ethnic minority women, whose workforce participation is lower so they might not have a NIN, and who were previously registered by their husbands. While the move was designed to increase the accuracy of the register and tackle registration fraud, the Electoral Commission recognised the potentially negative impact on ethnic minority voters. These voters were also vulnerable not just because of their ethnicity but also because they were likely to belong to other groups that were likely to be negatively affected. These included students, private renters and young adults, groups known from previous research to be in specific danger of not registering to vote. For ethnic minorities, who, as shown in other chapters in this book, are overwhelmingly younger than the white majority population and are more likely to rent privately than their white counterparts, the electoral change might have negatively impacted on their political participation. Further research on this issue is imperative.

Brexit

With the most salient political development in British politics, the unexpected decision to leave the EU referendum, dominating the political and news agenda, we must ask to what extent ethnic minorities supported the decision to leave and what impact Brexit is likely to have on non-white people in the UK.

Much of the commentary on who has chosen to support Britain's exit from the EU focuses on white voters who have been the losers of globalisation and have experienced relative decline in social and economic status over past decades. They are often characterised as 'left behind' and their seeming socio-economic exclusion has led to attitudes of disenchantment and alienation from existing political options. But, as the chapters in this collection make clear, ethnic minority groups are not only suffering from many socio-economic disadvantages, they also, as we saw earlier in this chapter, are often excluded and alienated politically. Many people in working-class jobs or with a low return on their human capital are not white, but from ethnic minority backgrounds, and yet the possibility that they also voted to leave the EU is largely ignored and discounted. Recent research that aims to fill this gap shows that while ethnic minority voters were less likely than white people to vote to leave the EU, the vote differed according to ethnicity (just like party choice, with Indian Britons more likely to have voted Leave). It is possible that some minorities have been persuaded by the leave campaign's claims that post-Brexit immigration policy is less likely to be racially discriminatory, as white European migrants will face the same entry requirements as non-white migrants.

In addition, non-white people who match the description of 'left behind' were more likely to vote leave, just as among white voters (Martin et al, 2019). Ethnic minorities who believed that they cannot 'get ahead' in the UK were also more supportive of Brexit, suggesting that the subjective sense of deprivation, just as for white 'left behind' voters, correlated with the leave vote. This undermines the assumption that the phenomenon of the 'left behind' is a uniquely white phenomenon, but also raises the question of why ethnic minority people are excluded from these narratives and the subsequent efforts by politicians to reach out to the 'left behind'. One answer comes from the work on what contributed to the result of the referendum, which consistently finds that attitudes towards ethnic diversity were a good predictor of the leave vote among white people: that is, these who were uncomfortable with racial equality were more likely to vote leave (Sobolewska and Ford, 2019). The many racial elements of the campaign are discussed further in Chapter 10 of this volume. The politicians who only include white people in their definition of the 'left behind' voters are effectively leaning in to this highly racialised tendency (Kinnock cited in Hughes, 2016).

Despite the fact that some ethnic minority voters supported leaving the EU in the 2016 referendum, Brexit is likely to affect ethnic minority communities negatively (something which is also true for many poorer white leave voters). Although the Conservative party since 2010 has placed ethnic equality near the top of their legislative agenda, with both David Cameron and Theresa May speaking on the issue in their first speeches as Prime Minister, and in fact they delivered some efforts in this direction (for example, Theresa May's Race Disparity Audit in 2017), Brexit now seems set to derail any legislative effort in this direction. What exact impact leaving the EU has remains to be seen, but we must stay attuned to how it impacts on racial disadvantage in Britain, as well as more general effects it may have on the economy.

Conclusions

Although the story of race in politics in Britain is generally one of progress, with record numbers of MPs of ethnic minority origin now sitting on both sides of the Westminster aisle, there is still no equality in politics. The 2011 Census suggests that 14% of Britain's population comes from an ethnic minority background and therefore, in political terms, to achieve accurate descriptive representation the number of ethnic minority MPs would need to increase from 65 to 84 MPs out of a total of 650 MPs in Westminster. Moreover, some groups are still extremely under-represented. While there are many MPs of Black African origin and a growing representation of Muslim Britons, the under-representation of people of Chinese origin and those of Black Caribbean backgrounds is very severe. This chimes in well with findings that candidate selection remains a major hurdle for candidates from non-white groups. Research also points out that ethnic minority MPs are more likely to be at the margins of Westminster, with fewer influential positions in government, the shadow cabinet and select committees (English, 2018) although with the Home Secretary and Shadow Home Secretary both of ethnic minority backgrounds (at the time of writing), clearly progress is being made here too. All these changes stand in stark contrast to the almost unchanged image of ethnic minority party choice, with the Conservative party making very small strides in an Indian community that was already more likely to vote for them.

Apart from continuing the effort to diversify the political parties in Parliament, other challenges include closing the ethnic gap on electoral under-registration and issues around fraud in British politics. It is also still uncertain whether the growing ethnic diversity of MPs will translate into these MPs tackling the persistent disadvantage minority people face in the UK – or will the dominant parties use them as a fig leaf to distract from and excuse inaction, or even worse, to pander to racially conservative white voters? Finally, the dark cloud of Brexit continues to hang over British politics and there is a worry that the continued uncertainty and political oscillations of politicians over Brexit might hijack the agenda, distracting from other important policy priorities such as tackling race inequality.

Note

[1]   The purpose of this research, and reflecting the lower age profile of ethnic minorities in Britain, we assumed that in areas where ethnic minorities constituted less than 10%, any local representation was unlikely.

10

Racisms in contemporary Britain

William Shankley and James Rhodes

Key findings

- Racisms are embedded in historically and politically determined systems of domination and work to exclude, marginalise and inferiorise groups on the basis of purported physical, cultural, and symbolic differences.
- The UN Special Rapporteur, reporting in 2018 found 'striking' levels of 'structural socio-economic exclusion of racial and ethnic communities in the UK' as well as 'growth in the acceptability of explicit racial, ethnic and religious intolerance'.
- Racism and prejudicial attitudes and practices, while improving in some ways persist, with Muslims and Gypsy-Traveller communities in particular facing high levels of prejudice. Acts of bias, discrimination and racial violence remain a pervasive feature of everyday life for ethnic and religious minority groups, evident in hurtful statements, and forms of aggression, bullying and harassment.
- There have been increases in reported hate crime every year since 2013.
- The shift from recognition of institutional racism to a concern with 'unconscious bias' risks excusing governments, institutions and organisations from tackling structural and social causes of racism and inequality.
- Religion has become central to contemporary articulations of racism, impacting most markedly on Muslims. Counter-terrorism policies, including Prevent, have introduced state surveillance in which Muslims are positioned as 'suspect' communities, exacerbating Islamophobic sentiment.
- There has been an increasing political mobilisation of racism and xenophobia in fringe parties and the political mainstream. This affected the Brexit campaign and its social and political aftermath.

Introduction

In 2018, the United Nations Special Rapporteur visited the United Kingdom, with a stated aim to 'assess the situation of racism, racial discrimination, xenophobia, and related intolerance' (Achiume, 2018). In an interim statement based on preliminary observations and prior to the final report (due summer 2019), she presented a complex picture of the contemporary landscape of racism. On the one hand, the UK was praised for the development of relatively robust governmental policies and structures through which to address racial equality and racially motivated hate crime. Similarly, the intention behind the publication of 2016's Race Disparity Audit (RDA), which outlined racial and ethnic inequalities across various domains, was praised as 'worthy of emulation by governments all over the world' (Achiume, 2018: 11–12). However, the statement also points to the pervasiveness of racism, xenophobia and discrimination in contemporary Britain. It identifies the 'striking' levels of 'structural socio-economic exclusion of racial and ethnic communities in the UK' in areas such as housing, employment, policing and health, as other chapters in this volume have shown. It concluded that race and ethnicity, 'continue to determine life chances in ways that are unacceptable, and in many cases, unlawful' (Achiume, 2018: 19). Compounding this, the rapporteur, Tendayi Achiume, lamented, 'the absence of a comprehensive, inter-governmental policy co-authored with civil society and racial and ethnic minority communities to ensure that the grave disparities documented ... are fully addressed' (Achiume, 2018: 13).

More widely, her statement also noted an increasingly charged social and political climate in the UK. Conducting her visit in the midst of the scandalous treatment of the '*Windrush* generation' and the government's wider 'hostile environment' immigration policy (see Chapter 2), she pointed to the negative impacts this exerted on both immigrants and established black and minority ethnic groups. She also highlighted the exacerbation of 'Islamophobic sentiment, policy and action', producing a political culture characterised by 'anti-Muslim panic' (Achiume, 2018: 41–2). Furthermore, Brexit was cited as revealing how political concerns around race, immigration and nation remain persistent features of the contemporary political landscape. Achiume stated that: 'The discourses on racial equality before, during and after the 2016 referendum in which Britain voted to leave the EU, as well as the policies and practices upon which the Brexit debate has conferred legitimacy, raise serious issues' (Achiume, 2018: 58). She pointed to rising hate speech and violence in the wake of Brexit, the emboldening of far-right and extremist politics, and a widespread sense that such sentiments have gained ground within the political mainstream. The result of this, Achiume concluded, is 'the growth in the acceptability of explicit racial, ethnic and religious intolerance' (2018: 62).

Exploring these issues further, this chapter considers the contemporary landscape of racism in Britain. The chapter begins by defining racism, setting out how the concept is being understood and used, and considering the different scales at which racism animates contemporary British society, with a focus on the individual and interpersonal as well as the institutional and societal. The second part of the chapter examines the morphing landscape of racism in contemporary Britain. Given that racisms continually evolve through time and space in relation to changing social, economic and political contexts, the chapter traces and situates key shifts in racialised discourse, considering emerging forms of racism such as Islamophobia and 'xeno-racism' (Fekete, 2009) alongside the persistence of established forms of hostility and discrimination such as 'anti-Black racism' (Anthias and Yuval-Davis, 1992) and antisemitism. The final part of the chapter examines contemporary political mobilisations around 'race'. The last two decades have seen the rise of far-right and right-wing populist parties that have sought to both cultivate and capitalise upon a range of concerns pertaining to race, nation, multiculturalism and immigration (Vieten and Poynting, 2016). Groups such as the British National Party (BNP), English Defence League (EDL), Britain First and the UK Independence Party (UKIP), have garnered significant levels of both political support and influence, forged around an agenda that is both forcefully anti-Muslim and anti-immigrant. The chapter concludes with a discussion of Brexit, considering what the referendum campaign and the response to it reveals about contemporary racisms and political mobilisation.

Racism, discrimination and disadvantage

Before we can offer a review of racism in Britain today, we need first to define it. Racism exists not in static or singular form but as plural and heterogeneous, evolving with and through changing socio-historical, cultural and political contexts (Golash-Boza, 2016; Garner, 2017). Racisms are embedded in historically and politically determined systems of domination and work to exclude, marginalise and inferiorise groups on the basis of purported physical, cultural and symbolic differences (Golash-Boza, 2016). They operate as part of wider processes of racialisation in which racial/ethnic collectivities are constituted and given meaning, status and value within particular societies. Here racial groups are seen to exist as observable realities, and are assigned a range of features and qualities on this basis. Indeed, while race categories have no scientific basis, either physically or intellectually, they remain important social markers of identity, and play a key role in shaping ideas of collectivities and groups. Racisms represent these groups as 'other' in a variety of ways. While historically, racisms drew heavily on notions of biology, in more recent times, notions of ethnic and cultural difference are drawn on more heavily and racism 'has come to be grounded in anthropology rather than biology; it is the matter of the [purported] way of life of a group of people, rather than the way in which those people came to life' (Kinnvall, 2017: 2).

Racisms operate not simply as a set of ideas but through the forms of inequity and marginalisation that they sponsor and sustain, as racisms inform a range of social policies and practices that produce differential outcomes for racialised groups (Garner, 2017). As Tanya Golash-Boza (2016: 131) states:

> Racism refers to both (1) the ideology that races are populations of people whose physical differences are linked to significant cultural and social differences and that these innate hierarchical differences can be measured and judged and (2) the micro- and macro-level practices that subordinate those races believed to be inferior.

Racism therefore results from how 'racial categories … are used in ways that are psychologically and materially harmful', and the mutually reinforcing links between 'racist ideologies and racist structures'. It also operates across different scales, ranging from the individual and the interpersonal, through to the institutional and the structural or systemic (Golash-Boza, 2016; Garner, 2017).

Racism has been a defining feature of postwar Britain and endures in the contemporary period, across various domains and levels of society. Post-1945, the arrival of New Commonwealth immigrants from Africa, the Caribbean and the Indian subcontinent, was met with widespread popular and political anxiety, and a range of discriminatory attitudes and practices. Shaped by ideas of Empire and Britain's colonial history, as well as the media, 'black' immigrants were viewed through a range of tropes, stereotypes and prejudices that saw their presence as both alien and threatening, linking the 'non-white' presence to a range of social ills such as crime, poor health, and competition for jobs and housing (Gilroy, 1987b; Solomos, 2003; Small and Solomos, 2006). Related to this, discriminatory practices in areas such as housing, employment and criminal justice produced a deeply unequal society, in which black and minority communities have been disproportionately concentrated in more deprived areas, in poorer quality housing, and within low-wage and insecure employment. In the contemporary period, as racial and ethnic diversity continues to increase in more complex configurations, a range of racial attitudes and practices continue to shape the experiences not just of established black and minority groups from Britain's former colonies, but also of more recent citizens and migrants (Bhopal, 2018).

Individual and interpersonal racism

Racism importantly comprises sets of attitudes and individual and interpersonal behaviours towards racial and ethnic difference. Such prejudices, stereotypes and orientations continue to be observable today, working to demarcate racialised groups as 'other', informing and legitimating forms of inequality. Indeed, while there is some evidence to suggest growing tolerance of racial and ethnic difference, this has been tempered by the persistence of negative and discriminatory attitudes (Kelley et al, 2017; Storm et al, 2017). Research by Storm et al (2017) suggests that a combination of the increasing diversity of the population, a growing acceptance of this fact, rising educational levels and shifts in norms and values which reject explicit forms of racism, have produced some positive developments in relation to racial and ethnic prejudice. For example, they argue that between the 1940s and 1990s, attitudes regarding intermarriage improved significantly. However, they also observe the perpetuation of collective notions of racial and ethnic hierarchies which position the White British majority at the top and Muslims at the bottom.

Other research also indicates that attitudes towards racial and ethnic difference have remained relatively stable if we focus on the last few decades. This stasis becomes even more marked when compared to the development of more 'liberal' attitudes evident towards, for instance, same-sex relationships (Kelley et al, 2017). Kelley et al (2017: 6), based on evidence from the British Social Attitudes Survey, found that between 1983 and 2013, the proportion of the population that describe themselves as 'very' or a 'little racially prejudiced' has remained between one quarter and one third of the population. The figure has never fallen below 25%, and has increased since 1996 (see Figure 10.1). When the same question was asked in 2017, 26% of respondents described themselves as 'very' or a 'little racially prejudiced'. Those who described themselves in these terms were associated with being male, a

Figure 10.1: Trends in prejudice over time

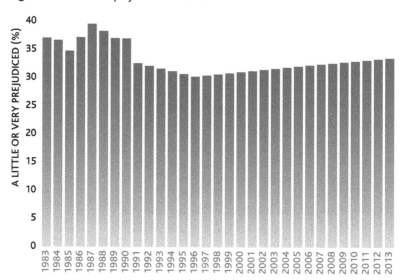

Source: British Social Attitudes Survey.

Conservative party supporter, and a leave voter in the 2016 referendum (Kelley et al, 2017: 7). Similarly, while attitudes towards inter-racial/ ethnic marriage have improved among the general population, in 2013, 21% of respondents still said they would 'mind if a close relative were to marry' an Asian person, and 22% would 'mind if a close family member married a black person' (Kelley et al, (2017: 10). Most strikingly, 44% stated they would mind if a close relative married a Muslim person (Kelley et al, 2017: 11). Storm et al (2017) also found that racial and ethnic prejudice was most directed towards Muslims, with more negative attitudes held towards this group relative to other minorities. Worryingly, Kelley et al also draw on findings from the 2014 European Social Survey, which indicated that 18% of UK residents agreed with a statement that asked whether 'some races or ethnic groups are born less intelligent' (Kelley et al, 2017: 8).

Racism and prejudicial attitudes and practices also continue to shape interpersonal relations in the UK, with acts of bias, discrimination and racial violence remaining a pervasive feature of everyday life for ethnic minority groups, evident in hurtful statements, and forms of aggression bullying and harassment. A Guardian/ICM survey commissioned in 2018 found evidence of significant levels of everyday racial bias across a range of social domains and types of interaction. Those from ethnic minority backgrounds were three times more likely to report having been thrown out of or denied entrance to restaurants, bars or clubs in the last five years, with two thirds believing Britain had a problem with racism. Of those from ethnic minority backgrounds, 38% said they had been wrongly suspected of shoplifting compared with 14% of white people. Furthermore, approximately 1 in 8 survey respondents reported hearing racist language directed towards them in the previous month (Booth and Mohdin, 2018). These 'micro-aggressions' are defined by Golash-Boza (2016: 131) as 'daily, commonplace insults and racial slights that cumulatively affect the psychological wellbeing of people of colour'.

A recent poll conducted in 2019 by Opinium also suggests that in the wake of the European Union (EU) referendum, and within an increasingly charged political atmosphere, these experiences of overt racial abuse and discrimination are intensifying. Between January 2016 and February 2019, the proportion of those from Black and Asian backgrounds reporting they have experienced discrimination increased from 58% to 71%. During the same period, the proportion of those stating that they had been targeted by strangers increased from 64% to 76%. Social media also appears to offer a significant outlet for the expression of racist sentiment and, between 2016 and 2019, the proportion of people who saw racism on social media on a daily basis increased from 37% to 50%, and that figure is even higher for ethnic minority people between the ages of 18 to 34 (Booth, 2019). Another recent report by the National Society for the Prevention of Cruelty to Children (NSPCC) stated that incidents of racial abuse and bullying directed at children have increased by around 20% since 2015/16, with 10,571 incidents committed against children recorded as racist by police in 2017/18 (Dodd, 2019).

Recent statistics indicate increases in race-hate crime. Home Office figures show that racially motivated hate crime has risen every year since 2013. In 2018, 71,251 such crimes were reported in England and Wales, and the number of hate crimes – of which racially motivated attacks comprise the vast majority – more than doubled from 2013 (Home Office, 2018a). While the Home Office attributes some of this increase to more effective police recording it also accepts that, 'there [have] been spikes in hate crime following certain events such as the EU Referendum and the terrorist attacks in 2017'. Similarly, despite increases in recorded hate crime the number of completed prosecutions fell from 14,480 in 2016/17 to 14,151 in 2017/18 (Home Office, 2018: 7).

Institutional and societal racism

As observed, racisms exist not solely through individual and interpersonal beliefs and acts, but are also manifest in more institutionalised and

Figure 10.2: Variations in reports of racist victimisation by ethnic/religious group (%)

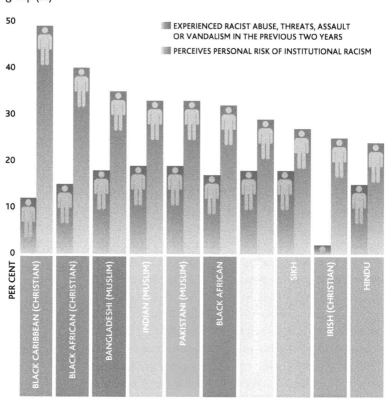

Note: Amended table from Karlsen and Nazroo (2014).
Source: 2002 EMPRIC & 2008/09 Home Office Citizenship Survey: sample – 10,000 adults and 4,000 booster sample – 16–74 years old.

systemic forms. The state and other key societal institutions, also play an active and decisive role in shaping the experiences and inequalities faced by ethnic minority groups (Phillips, 2010). In postwar Britain, successive Race Relations Acts in 1965, 1968 and 1976, highlighted racial discrimination in the realms of housing, education and employment. However, it was not until the publication of the Macpherson report (1999) that 'institutional racism' was identified as existing within public bodies. Responding to the police investigation of the murder of black British teenager Stephen Lawrence in 1993, Lord Macpherson concluded that the conduct of the Metropolitan Police was symptomatic of institutional racism. Macpherson defined this as:

> The collective failure of an organisation to provide an
> appropriate and professional service to people because of

their colour, culture or ethnic origin. It can be seen and detected in processes, attitudes, and behaviour which amount to discrimination through unwitting prejudice, ignorance, thoughtlessness, and racist stereotyping which disadvantage minority ethnic people. (Macpherson, 1999: 6.34)

While there has been intense debate about the definition offered, importantly, Macpherson recognised that racism does not result simply from overt or intentional forms of action or inaction, but is also present in the form of more covert and indirect policies and practices that produce racially uneven outcomes. More broadly, the report also made general recommendations on policies pertaining to race relations, education and social policy. In response to the inquiry, the then Labour government introduced the Race Relations (Amendment) Act in 2000, which placed a statutory duty on all public authorities to prevent acts of racial discrimination before they occur and to act with 'due regard to the need to eliminate unlawful racial discrimination, and to promote equality of opportunity and good relations between persons of different racial groups' (cited in Solomos, 2003: 92).

As the UN Special Rapporteur has argued, such legislative measures, alongside stated commitments to respect the equality of groups on the basis of protected characteristics (race, ethnicity, national origin, gender, disability), offer a robust framework through which racial inequality can be addressed (Achiume, 2018). However, two decades on from the Macpherson report and the Race Relations (Amendment) Act, racial inequalities and discriminatory practices remain. The 2016 RDA revealed widespread racial disparities in contemporary society, and it is clear that institutions continue to operate in ways which systematically disadvantage ethnic minority groups, and which have been covered in other chapters in this volume.

The perpetuation of these disparities questions the attempts to address racial inequality and exclusion in Britain. The UN Special Rapporteur noted that, despite existing legal frameworks to tackle these issues, there appeared to be a lack of commitment and coordination across state institutions and through engagement with ethnic minority communities (Achiume, 2018). Recently, Bourne (2019) also notes that there has been a move away from discussions of 'institutional racism'. Instead, training initiatives aimed at reducing 'implicit' or 'unconscious bias' have become the dominant approach to address racial and ethnic inequalities in institutions. Bourne (2019) argues that this represents an ineffective strategy, and one that situates racism as residing within the often unconscious attitudes of individuals rather than as a wider social problem. She states that within this approach, 'racism is covert not overt; it is psychological not social; it is individual not structural; it is subconscious not conscious. Hence, it effectively exonerates governments, institutions, organisations, even individuals, for it is unconscious, inevitable' (Bourne, 2019: 71).

This appears to be symptomatic of a wider reneging on commitments to address institutionalised and systemic racism and discrimination, with central government policy itself complicit in compounding such exclusions and inequalities. In 2012, the government rejected mandatory commitments to equality impact assessments, and the 2010 Emergency Budget, which introduced large-scale austerity policies making drastic cuts to welfare and public services, and the 2017 Budget were not subject to assessments of their impacts on equality. This despite evidence which points to the disproportionate impacts such policies have had on black and minority ethnic communities. A report for the Runnymede Trust, for instance, stated that the reforms to welfare and services would see the living standards among the poorest fifth of society decline (where household living standards are defined as the value of household disposable income plus the use-value of public services), with a loss of 11.6% and 11.2% for Black and Asian families respectively, compared to 8.9% for white households (Hall et al, 2017). These impacts are particularly damaging for black and minority women, who are disproportionately living in poor households, more heavily reliant on benefits and public services, and are concentrated in low-wage and insecure work. The research estimated that, by 2020, Asian women in the poorest third of households will have lost 19% of their income, while black women will lose 14%. The UN Special Rapporteur went as far to state that, 'Austerity measures today appear to function inadvertently as a prime instrument of racial subordination', as she called for the reinstatement of equality impact assessments (Achiume, 2018: 32).

Alongside this, Achiume also observed the disproportionate impacts that immigration control and counter-extremism and counter-terrorism measures have on black and minority ethnic communities, and how they are both informed by and feed wider sentiments of racial animosity (see Chapter 2). She lamented the failure to include the impacts of such policies in the RDA, and called for equality impact assessments to be considered in relation to these policies. Beyond the legislative implications, it is also clear that such policies and associated rhetoric continue to position both immigrants and established ethnic minority communities as precariously and contingently belonging to the nation, linking them to a range of social problems.

The changing landscape of racism

Racism clearly continues to be evident in a range of forms and at various scales in contemporary Britain. However, as racial and ethnic diversity increases and as social and political contexts shift, the targets of racist discourse and practices are also evolving, in ways that reveal both the persistence of deeply rooted, alongside more emergent, forms of racism. In postwar Britain, much racial discrimination and hostility can be captured by what Anthias and Yuval-Davis (1992) describe as 'anti-Black racism' as 'non-white' migrants from the New Commonwealth were the targets of racist opprobrium that identified them as 'others' primarily on the basis of skin colour. Within such discourses and actions, the term 'immigrant' became synonymous with 'black', encompassing both migrants and subsequent generations of UK citizens with backgrounds in South Asia, Africa and the Caribbean. Here 'older' conceptions of biological difference and hierarchy have more recently interacted with 'newer' forms of racism, which draw upon notions of cultural incompatibility to construct these groups as both 'alien' and 'threatening' to the nation and its integrity (Gilroy, 1987b; Solomos, 2003; Small and Solomos, 2006). Such views became institutionalised in successive immigration policies that enshrined 'colour-coded' forms of exclusion, which favoured white migrants.

Clearly racisms predicated on skin colour continue to be directed at Black Caribbean and African and South Asian populations and, in comparison to the White British, they are exposed to greater levels of inequality, institutional racism, as well as racial harassment and victimisation. The recent *Windrush* scandal continues to highlight their more insecure claims to citizenship and belonging, and the 'hostile environment' has also seen a number of high-profile deportation cases that have targeted black and minority ethnic groups in particular. Similarly, as Chapter 3 demonstrates, long-standing racialised tropes that link young black men in particular with violence and criminality – for instance through associations to knife crime and 'gangs' – continue to inform widespread negative media and popular stereotypes as well as disproportionately punitive institutional practices.

Islamophobia

Over the course of the last few decades, religion has also become central to contemporary articulations of racism, impacting most markedly on Muslims. As Karlsen and Nazroo (2014: 373) argue, 'religion has become an increasingly important marker of difference as racist sentiment has moved from anti-Asian and anti-Arab to anti-Muslim/Islamophobic interpersonal and institutional prejudice and violence'. In 1997, a report by the Runnymede Trust brought attention to the growing challenge of Islamophobia. In the wake of the Rushdie Affair, the Gulf War, and the criminalisation of young South Asian Muslim males, it identified growing prejudice, hostility, violence and discrimination towards the Muslim population across a range of domains, including the media, criminal justice system and labour market.

In the intervening period, anti-Muslim racism or Islamophobia has increased significantly, becoming deeply entrenched within British society and across Europe, as states including Britain have moved away from the promotion of multiculturalism to an emphasis on integration. Here, the 2001 riots in Bradford, Burnley and Oldham, and the attacks of 9/11 and 7/7 were pivotal events informing this hardening of attitudes and practices (Poynting and Mason, 2006; Kundnani, 2007; Pantazis and Pemberton, 2009; Jackson, 2018; Kallis, 2018). An understanding of Muslims as a 'suspect community' (Pantazis and Pemberton, 2009) has taken hold within contemporary popular and political conceptions. Muslims are widely viewed as a 'threat' to the nation (whether through associations with terrorism, criminality, grooming, sharia law and so on), as not, or only contingently belonging to the nation, and as bearers of sets of values deemed irreconcilable with the values of Britain's asserted status as a liberal democracy (Poynting and Mason, 2006; Runnymede Trust, 2017b; Jackson, 2018). These established tropes work to deny the heterogeneity of Muslims in terms of nationality, ethnicity, religious practice, place, social and economic positions, and gender. Alexander has noted, 'an intensification and banalization of Islamophobic sentiment, policy and practice in Britain, alongside the increased targeting, both violent and mundane, of British Muslims' (in Runnymede Trust, 2017b: 13).

These anti-Muslim sentiments are manifest in various forms of hostility, discrimination and exclusion. Perhaps most prominently, the introduction of the government's Prevent agenda through the Terrorism Act 2006 has introduced a form of state surveillance in which Muslims are positioned as 'suspect' communities linked to the increased use of police stop-and-search powers (Karlsen and Nazroo, 2014; Runnymede Trust, 2017b; Jackson, 2018). Kundnani (2009) has argued that the policy has undermined attempts to improve community relations through the specific targeting of Muslims, and has been approached in a top-down manner which does not engage effectively with local organisations or communities. In 2015, the Counter-Terrorism and

Security Act placed a statutory duty on a range of public bodies, including schools and hospitals, to monitor those they came into contact with for signs of radicalisation. According to Cohen and Tufail, this has normalised Islamophobia while also serving to heighten a sense of suspicion from Muslims about public institutions. They argue that the legislation breaches existing equalities legislation through its disproportionate impacts on Muslims, curtailing free speech and citizens' rights, particularly in terms of political engagement within civil society (in Runnymede Trust, 2017b: 41–2). Indeed, while Prevent is described as a policy to tackle all forms of extremism, figures indicate that in 2015–16, a person from a Muslim background was 40 times more likely to receive referrals compared to others (Kallis, 2018: 680–1). As the UN Special Rapporteur concluded, counter-terrorism law 'has vastly exacerbated Islamophobic sentiment' (Achiume, 2018).

At the level of national government and politics, Baroness Warsi has also accused the Conservative party of institutional racism, and there have been a number of instances of party members engaging in Islamophobic behaviour (Kallis, 2018). In May 2019, the Equality and Human Rights Commission announced an investigation into Islamophobia within the Conservative party. The discrimination and exclusion facing Muslims is also evident in other ways. Muslims are disproportionately concentred in the poorest areas of the country and face significant barriers within the education system and labour market, while also being subject to negative media representations. A report by the Social Mobility Commission (Stevenson et al, 2017: 19) found that almost half (46%) of Muslim households live in the most deprived 10% of neighbourhoods. Muslims are also most likely to live in overcrowded housing (42% compared to a national average of 12%) (Runnymede Trust, 2017b: 23). These forms of marginalisation are particularly evident in the lives of young Muslims in Britain, who face severely constrained prospects for social mobility. The commission concluded that young Muslims, 'are excluded, discriminated against, or failed at all stages of their transition from education to employment', with 'Islamophobia, discrimination and/or racism … ever present and pervasive' (Stevenson et al, 2017: 2).

Islamophobia is also particularly evident in the form of marked levels of racial harassment and violence, with increasing attacks on mosques and Islamic centres, as well as individuals (Home Office, 2018). Figure 10.2 shows that religious hate crime rose by 40% between 2016/17 and 2017/18. Tell Mama recorded 1,201 Islamophobic and anti-Muslim incidents between January and December 2017. More than two thirds of these incidents occurred at street level (most frequently in public spaces and on public transport) and included abuse, physical threats and threatening behaviour, with these types of victimisation increasing 30% compared to 2016. Between 2015 and 2016, such incidents increased 46.9% (Tell Mama, 2018b: 1–2). The remaining third of Islamophobic incidents recorded by the organisation took place online, marking an increase of over 16% from 2016 (Tell Mama, 2018b: 1). The study reveals a number of important findings. First, the prevalence and severity of these attacks is triggered by national and international events. Instances increased significantly during the reporting period in the wake of events such as the Manchester and London Bridge attacks. In the week following the attacks at the Manchester Arena in 2017, incidents increased by 700% (Tell Mama, 2018b: 7). Second, attacks also disproportionately target Muslim women, with 57% of victims in 2017 being female, and 64% of perpetrators male. Of those committing such acts, 73% were white men (Tell Mama, 2018b: 9). This phenomenon has been referred to as 'gendered Islamophobia', which references how women, particularly those wearing the veil or headscarf and therefore 'visibly Muslim women', are targeted (Awan and Zempi, 2015; Tell Mama, 2018a). An investigation into the impacts of such incidents on Muslims found that they produce emotional distress, depression and fear, leading to profound disruptions of a sense of safety and belonging (Awan and Zempi, 2015).

In the context of rising hostility towards Muslims, there has been significant debate about the appropriateness of the term 'Islamophobia'. For some the term is problematic, given the way it is seen to suggest pathological fear or mental illness rather than indicating discriminatory practices (Runnymede Trust, 2017b; Jackson, 2018). Other contestations have focused on whether or not this constitutes a form of racism. Some, including far-right and right-wing populist movements, have argued that as Muslims constitute a 'religious' rather than a 'racial' group, and this is a voluntary rather than an ascribed identity, anti-Muslim sentiment is not a form of racism (Meer and Modood, 2009). It has been suggested that hostility is directed towards Islam as a religious ideology and set of practices rather than Muslims. This distinction appears untenable. Alexander has warned against 'the separation of anti-Muslimism from the longer and broader historical and social context of racial discrimination and racism' (in Runnymede Trust, 2017b: 13). A range of scholars point to how racisms have always been based upon, not just perceived physical, but also ethno-religious and cultural differences, citing the example of antisemitism. In this way, Islamophobia is widely understood as a form of cultural racism, drawing less on notions of biological hierarchy and instead on ideas of cultural heritage (Meer and Modood, 2009; Karlsen and Nazroo, 2014; Runnymede Trust, 2017b; Jackson, 2018).

The 2017 Runnymede Trust report defines Islamophobia as 'anti-Muslim racism', characterised as:

> Any distinction, exclusion, or restriction towards, or preference against, Muslims (or those perceived to be Muslims) that has the purpose or effect of nullifying or impairing the recognition, enjoyment or exercise, on an equal footing, of human rights and fundamental freedoms in the political, economic, social, cultural or any other field of public life. (Runnymede Trust, 2017b: 7)

In 2019, the Labour party and Liberal Democrats adopted an official definition of Islamophobia resembling the definition offered by Runnymede Trust, although the Conservative party, as of January 2020, has refused to adopt this. The importance of identifying Islamophobia as a form of racism is not simply a semantic issue, as it has real political consequences. In 2006 the government expanded existing legislation on racial hatred to include religious discrimination, through the Racial and Religious Hatred Act, which made it unlawful to incite hatred on the basis of religion as well as race. This was an important piece of legislation given that, unlike Jews and Sikhs, Muslims are categorised as a 'religious' rather than a 'racial' group within the law. However, significant issues with this remain. The UN Special Rapporteur noted that while race-hate crimes 'require no showing of racist intent' to be recorded as such, religiously motivated hate crimes exhibit a different legal standard which requires intent to be established (Achiume, 2018: 9). This likely leads to significant under-recording of religiously motivated hate crime, and this is of particular import for Muslims, given that statistics show that over half of all such crimes in 2017/18 targeted Muslims (Home Office, 2018).

Immigration, xeno-racism and antisemitism

Alongside the intensification of Islamophobia, another important development in the evolving landscape of racism has been the increasing racist, anti-immigrant and xenophobic sentiment directed towards migrants, refugees and asylum seekers, including ostensibly white migrants and communities. During the 1990s, in the context of globalisation, geopolitical conflict and instability, and rising economic and cultural insecurity, there emerged across Europe both populations and regimes increasingly hostile to immigrants and refugees (Kundnani, 2001; Solomos, 2003; Small and Solomos, 2006; Fekete, 2009). Kundnani argues that during the 1990s, popular animosity directed towards asylum seekers from countries such as Somalia, Iraq and Kosovo, represented an emergent form of 'common sense racism'. Central to this were discourses that linked these migrants with notions of illegality, criminality, disease, and position them as 'bogus' economic migrants. Kundnani describes this hostility as being driven by a, 'vicious circle logics of suspicion and deterrence, by the racism that turns human beings into numbers. This mindset migrates from the corridors of the Home Office to the streets, the schools, the pubs; carried there by tabloid newspapers eager to play up to fears of an "influx"' (Kundnani, 2001: 42).

For Fekete (2009: 2), such sentiments mark the development of a form of 'xeno-racism', which she describes as 'a non-colour coded institutionalised racism', that targets migrants, particularly those from poorer countries, and often from outside of the EU. Borrowing from the work of Sivanandan, the term reflects xenophobic sentiment which excludes or marginalises people on the basis of national origin, and is often constructed as a fear of strangers, with forms of stigmatisation, segregation and expulsion that have historically characterised racism (Fekete, 2009: 19–20). Fekete argues that increasingly restrictive state legislation regulating immigration and asylum, and a growing far-right political presence produced a 'new pan-European racism directed at asylum seekers and migrant workers' (Fekete, 2009: 1). The trend Fekete identifies is evident in contemporary Britain, in the creation of a 'hostile' immigration environment, and negative attitudes towards migrants and refugees evident within both the media and the public opinion (see Chapter 2).

These notions have assumed prominence again in the context of the economic recession of 2008–9 and, importantly, the 2015 European 'migrant crisis' (Anderson, 2017; Gupta and Virdee, 2018), that is, the increasing arrival of displaced peoples within the EU from countries such as Syria, Afghanistan, Libya, and Iraq. For Gupta and Virdee, the specificities of this series of events, 'morphed into a generalised anxiety about immigration and the presence of immigrants, in fact exacerbating long-simmering sensitivities about religious and cultural as well as "racial" difference' (2018: 1750). A European Commission Against Racism and Intolerance (ECRI) report in 2016 noted how terms such as 'swarms' of immigrants had been employed by both UKIP and the Conservative party. According to this document, 'The

UN Special Representative of the Secretary General for International Migration accused politicians of adopting a "xenophobic response" to the migrant crisis and said their language had been "grossly excessive"' (ECRI, 2016: 17). With many of these migrants hailing from majority-Muslim countries, this hostility towards migrants has heavily rested upon their conflation as Muslim, as xenophobic and Islamophobic sentiments have interacted (Gupta and Virdee, 2018).

A 2018 Report from the Migration Observatory at the University of Oxford found significant levels of anti–immigrant sentiment. Based on a range of data sources including the British Social Attitudes Survey and the European Social Survey, they found that 58% of Britons favoured reducing the number of immigrants, with almost one third agreeing that it should be 'reduced a lot'. The briefing suggests that this sentiment has declined since 2015, when 71% of people desired a reduction in immigration, although it remains a defining contemporary political issue and was significant in the period prior to the EU referendum. Between 2015 and 2016, 56% of respondents ranked immigration as the most salient political issue (Blinder and Roberts, 2018). Indeed, during the referendum campaign anti-immigrant rhetoric was a defining feature of the 'leave' campaigns (Burnett, 2017; Virdee and McGeever, 2018)

As Fekete notes, xenophobic and anti-immigrant sentiment also targets white Europeans, particularly those from Eastern Europe. Antagonism towards certain white migrants has a long history in Britain, as evidenced through the antipathy directed towards groups such as Irish and Jewish people for instance. These sentiments have also emerged as a significant issue in the context of changing patterns of European migration with the enlargement of the EU in 2004 and 2007 (see Chapter 2). While state regimes continue to favour white migrants (Fox et al, 2012; Garner, 2017) and public attitudes demonstrate a preference for white rather than non-white migrants, particularly when they are skilled and English-speaking, (Blinder and Roberts 2018), it is evident that within the media, popular opinion and policy, negative and hostile attitudes are also directed to these groups (Fox et al, 2012; Anderson, 2017; Garner, 2017). This became particularly evident in the wake of the EU referendum as race-hate crimes were also directed at white people who were identifiable as migrants or non-nationals, something which has been noted as a more recent development in contemporary manifestations of racial exclusion (Burnett, 2017; Virdee and McGeever, 2018; Rzepnikowska, 2019). Research conducted by Rzepnikowska with Polish migrants in Manchester found that since the 2008 recession, and in the wake of the referendum, attitudes

Figure 10.3: Ethnic hierarchy of immigration preferences by leave / remain: percentage that would allow some / many migrants move to the UK

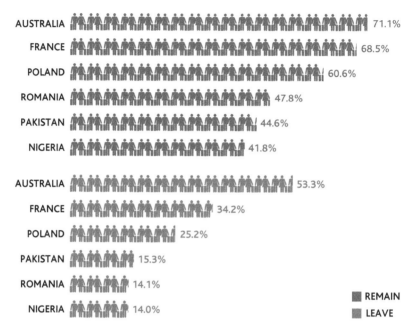

Source: See Carl et al cited in Blinder and Richards (2018).

towards Polish migrants have become more hostile, with media and public discourses framing them as competitors for jobs and resources. She found that in this context Poles have been increasingly subject to racist abuse both before and after the EU referendum. Finally, Carl et al (2018) looked at differences in social attitudes expressed by the electorate (remain versus leave) towards immigration to unpack why there had been an increase in hostility towards migrants. Figure 10.3 shows a stark difference between leave and remain voters, with 61% of remain voters stating they would continue to allow 'some' or 'many' migrants move to the UK, compared to only 25% of leave voters. The study also sought to analyse if there existed an implicit preference that discriminated between different groups of white migrants and thus uncovered why some new white migrants faced increasing incidents of discrimination compared to other groups. The results uncovered a preference towards migrants from Australia compared to migrants from Poland or Romania. This confirmed the existence of an implicit hierarchy of whiteness whereby Commonwealth migrants and migrants from Western European countries are viewed more favourably and thus their immigration is viewed in a more positive fashion to migration from central and Eastern Europe.

Within contemporary forms of 'xeno-racism', particular hostility is also reserved for Roma and Gypsy-Traveller populations (Fekete, 2009; Anderson, 2017). Data from the 2015 Eurobarometer Survey showed that across the EU28, only 63% of respondents stated they would feel 'comfortable' if a work colleague was from a Roma background, compared to 93% of respondents asked about a white co-worker. In the UK, 79% stated they would be comfortable with a Roma colleague compared to a figure of 95% if the colleague was white (Kinnvall, 2017: 1). Forms of racial discrimination and exclusion are also evident in the position and experiences of Gypsy-Traveller communities in Britain. The ECRI report noted the hostile and negative discourses perpetuated by the media, which it described as perpetuating 'hate speech', as well as those emanating from mainstream politicians (ECRI, 2016: 18). Gypsy-Traveller communities also exhibit significant degrees of inequality and institutional marginalisation and exclusion, as discussed in Chapter 5 in this volume. The 2016, ECRI (2016: 34) report called for the development of a national strategy to address the disadvantages experienced by these communities.

Antisemitism represents another form of racism with long historical antecedents that has increased in recent years, both in the UK and throughout Europe (ECRI, 2016; Kinnvall, 2017). In the UK, there has been a marked rise in attacks at Jewish people, as well as cemeteries and religious institutions, and this has increased in the wake of the EU referendum. According to a report by the Community Security Trust (2019: 4–5), there were 1,652 incidents of antisemitism in Britain in 2018, the highest number ever recorded, and an increase of 16% from 2017, with three quarters of incidents occurring in London and Greater Manchester, home to the two largest Jewish communities in the UK. The figures for 2018 represent the third consecutive year in which record-high totals have been recorded, indicating 'a sustained pattern' of intensification, and figures have increased by more than 300% since 2012 (Community Security Trust, 2019: 13). The report suggests that this spike has coincided with when the accusations of antisemitism levelled at the Labour party were at their most intense, and the Community Security Trust recorded 148 incidents in 2018 that were examples of, or related to arguments over, alleged antisemitism in the Labour Party (Community Security Trust, 2019: 5). In recent years, Labour has faced a number of accusations of antisemitic behaviour. In 2016, Shami Chakrabarti conducted a review into antisemitism within the party, however the findings have been widely criticised for failing to engage seriously with these issues.. In May 2019, the Equality and Human Rights Commission launched a formal investigation into antisemitism within the Labour Party.

Antisemitic prejudices and attitudes also remain in evidence among the general population, although research suggests this has declined in recent years. A YouGov study commissioned by the Campaign Against Anti-Semitism (CAA) found that between 2015 and 2017, antisemitic prejudice among British adults declined from 45% to 36% of people endorsing what are seen to be antisemitic stereotypes about Jewish people. Clearly, however, this remains a sizeable proportion of the population holding such views. Alongside this, one in three British Jews reported having considered leaving the country, and only 59% reported feeling welcome in the UK. More than half of Jews, also felt that the Crime Prosecution Service were not sufficiently combating antisemitism (CAA, 2018: 4).

Racism, nationalism and political mobilisation

The changes in the landscape of racism in contemporary Britain outlined in the previous section have occurred in the context of increasing political mobilisations around race and nation. Britain has a long history of far-right, nationalistic politics, evident through the British Brothers League (BBL) during the early 1900s, the British Union of Fascists (BUF) in the 1930s, and the National Front (NF) which rose to prominence in the 1970s (Solomos, 2003). Over the past two decades, across Europe far-right and right-wing populist parties have experienced growing support (Vieten and Poynting, 2016; Kinnvall, 2017). Britain has been no exception, as a range of parties and movements such as the British National Party (BNP), the English Defence League (EDL), Britain First, and the UK Independence Party (UKIP) have gained increasing political prominence and traction, particularly in the context of the EU Referendum vote in 2016.

As elsewhere in Europe the rise of these forms of nationalistic and exclusionary politics has mobilised a range of racialised anxieties centring principally upon immigration, terrorism, multiculturalism and the perceived economic, cultural and political marginalisation of the 'indigenous' white population (Solomos, 2013; Vieten and Poynting, 2016). Vieten and Poynting (2016: 533) see the rise of 'right wing racist movements' as characterised by, 'nationalist, anti-immigration, anti-asylum seeker, anti-Muslim politics'. In the context of economic recession, the 'migrant crisis' and the perceived threat of Islamic terrorism, Kinnvall (2017) has argued that such movements draw upon and help to create notions of risk and 'ontological insecurity'. She argues that, '[t]he far right has been successful in mobilising such anxieties and fears, and has often used the notion of "others" – immigrants, foreigners, Muslims – to spur a development towards exclusion and deportation of unwanted "others"' (Kinnvall, 2017: 1).

In Britain, such political mobilisations have also been closely aligned with both anti-immigrant and anti-Muslim sentiment. The EDL, which emerged as a street-protest movement in 2009 led by Stephen Yaxley-Lennon ('Tommy Robinson'), developed with the specific aim of countering what was seen as the inexorable rise of, and existential threat posed by, Islamic extremism and the purported 'Islamification' of the nation. The movement has engaged in protests against 'Islamist' terrorism, but also issues such as sharia law, child sexual exploitation ('grooming') and the construction of mosques across the country (Copsey, 2010; Allen, 2011; Bartlett and Littler, 2011; Goodwin, 2013; Kassimeris and Jackson, 2015; Pilkington, 2016; Jackson, 2018). Research into the nature of EDL support has found that hostility towards Muslims and black and minority ethnic groups is the most decisive factor. Support for the movement is also concentrated disproportionately among male workers, those with lower levels of education, and those who tend to vote for more right-wing parties, with 40% of EDL sympathisers also identifying with the Conservative Party, and who also register significant disaffection towards the existing political system (Goodwin et al, 2016: 10). Elsewhere Goodwin (2013: 1) has argued that the negative views of Muslims on which the EDL thrives find wider public support in a context in which, 'few mainstream voices in Europe are actively challenging counter-Jihad narratives, or the surrounding reservoir of anti-Muslim prejudice among the general public'.

Britain First, founded in 2011, has also pursued a strongly anti-Muslim agenda, committed to what it views as preserving Christian values and identity in the face of the rise of 'Islam', multiculturalism and immigration (Davidson and Berezin, 2018). Identified as more aggressive than the EDL, it pursues street-level demonstrations including 'Christian patrols', which have seen invasions of mosques and Muslim-owned businesses (Allen, 2014; Burke, 2018). In the wake of the *Charlie Hebdo* attacks in Paris in 2015, the movement also launched 'safety patrols', with the declared aim of protecting Jewish communities. For both Britain First and the EDL, anti-Muslim sentiment has been used to assert their 'legitimacy' and to distance themselves from previous extreme right movements. Kassimeris and Jackson note how movements like the EDL position themselves as advocates of LGBT and 'human rights'. Here, 'the new far right, in actively distancing itself from neo-Nazi and antisemitic themes, represents a departure from traditional far-right concerns but employs a culturally racist ethno-nationalist xenophobia which has the same exclusionary effects on target groups' (Kassimeris and Jackson, 2015: 175–6).

Both the EDL and Britain First have made significant use of the internet and social media to garner support (Bartlett and Littler, 2011; Goodwin, 2013; Kassimeris and Jackson, 2015; Pilkington, 2016; Burke, 2018). Highlighting growing concerns about the role of social media in providing a platform for racist political views, in 2019 both Facebook and YouTube introduced policies to ban far-right content from its sites. Emerging research has identified social media as significant in helping to diffuse far-right and right-wing populist sentiment, and the spread of anti-Muslim attitudes in particular (Awan, 2016; Davidson and Berezin, 2018; Froio and Ganesh, 2018). Davidson and Berezin (2018: 485), in their study of how Britain First and UKIP have utilised social media, argue that far-right movements 'have used new technologies to generate an unprecedented amount of popular support and to attempt to influence the political mainstream'. A 2019 report also highlighted how prevalent this was, with social media being crucial in elevating the profile of figures such as 'Tommy Robinson' (Hope Not Hate, 2019).

The rise of such movements and sentiments both online and offline is linked to wider concerns about the marked growth in far-right extremism, with the murder of Jo Cox in June 2016 by a white extremist bringing a growing focus on the rise of racist political violence. Recent years have also seen the emergence of violent neo-Nazi movements such as National Action, which was founded in 2013 and advocated for 'white jihad', openly supporting the killer of Jo Cox. The movement was proscribed in 2016 and, following a court case in 2018, members were charged with plotting to kill a police officer. Home Office data published in 2019 indicates a significant rise in white extremism, with white extremists comprising the largest proportion of terror arrests during the 12 months up to March 2019, the highest percentage since 2004, with Brexit identified as a contributory factor (Giordano, 2019). A report by the anti-racist organisation Hope Not Hate (2019) argued that as the protracted negotiations for the UK to leave the EU go on, interactions between racism and xenopohobia and high levels of political disaffection have served to cultivate a fertile environment for the far right to exploit. They point to a far right that is becoming more extreme and younger in its composition (Hope

Not Hate, 2019). Further reports suggest that these sentiments are particularly concentrated in economically marginalised areas with relatively smaller populations compared to the large cities, and among those with lower educational levels (Carter, 2018)

Alongside these more street-based movements, Islamophobia and anti-immigrant sentiment has also been central to the emergence of right-wing, nationalistic electoral mobilisations. The far-right BNP, which has pursued both an anti-immigrant and anti-Muslim agenda, made a series of local political breakthroughs during the 2000s in locations such as Burnley, Barking and Dagenham, and Stoke-on-Trent. It also secured representation on the Greater London Assembly in 2008. In more recent years, UKIP, often defined as a 'radical right' or 'right-wing populist' party, has drawn upon the linkages between anti-immigrant feeling and rising Euroscepticism, securing significant amounts of political support (Ford and Goodwin, 2014). In the 2014 European elections, the party gained over 4.3 million votes, amounting to a share of over 25%, while it polled over 12% of the vote, representing almost 4 million votes, in the 2015 general election in the UK. The party's former leader, Nigel Farage, was a central figure in the political campaigning to leave the EU in the 2016 referendum, going on to form the Brexit Party in 2019.

Central to the appeal of UKIP have been calls for withdrawal from the EU, the restoration of national sovereignty, and tighter immigration controls (Ford and Goodwin, 2014; Geddes, 2014; Anderson, 2017). Research on the attitudes of UKIP supporters has found that hostility towards immigration and anxieties about its impacts on British society are central drivers for the party and right-wing populism more broadly (Ford and Goodwin, 2014; Goodwin and Milazzo, 2017). Ford and Goodwin (2014) argue that these sentiments have resonated particularly with a 'left behind' constituency, with UKIP support concentrated among older, less educated males, disproportionately located in the former industrial heartlands of the Midlands and the North. At the same time, the party has also been able to attract more affluent voters, with Ford and Goodwin's work indicating that almost one third of UKIP supporters are drawn from the middle-classes.

In recent years, UKIP has moved further to the political right, and Islamophobia has become more central to the rhetoric of the party and its supporters. In the context of the 2015 'migrant crisis', UKIP's 2015 manifesto made specific links between immigration, 'foreigners' and crime. The fact that at that moment most of these migrants were from majority-Muslim countries reveals the 'conflation between "Muslim" and "migrant" (Gupta and Virdee, 2018: 1756). A study of the social media activity of UKIP followers in the wake of the EU referendum found that many UKIP supporters frequently justified calls to leave the EU through the expression of grievances towards Islam and Muslims. The research also found significant online connections between followers of Britain First and UKIP, suggesting that this has influenced the party's move to a more explicit anti-Islam agenda (Davidson and Berezin, 2018; see also Hope not Hate, 2019)

Brexit and mainstreaming racism and xenophobia

If the past two decades have witnessed an increasing political mobilisation of racism and xenophobia, the political struggle around Brexit illustrates how such sentiments animate not just the margins but the political mainstream in contemporary society. While the vote for Brexit comprises diverse political constituencies and political views, it is clear that questions of race, nation and immigration were central within it, made evident not simply in the campaign rhetoric or the evidence about the drivers of support for Brexit, but also in its social and political aftermaths.

While the two key political campaigns promoting Britain's exit from the EU drew on a range of issues to stake their claims, Virdee and McGeever (2018: 1804) argue that the way in which they 'carefully activated long-standing racialised structures of feeling about immigration and national belonging' was central. While 'Vote Leave' drew on nostalgic notions of Empire and British global dominance, the 'Leave.EU' campaign, led by Nigel Farage, placed immigration at its heart. Citing the use of the 'Breaking Point' poster, which pictured refugees from the Middle East queuing to enter European territory, Virdee and McGeever (2018) note how 'migrants' were cast as both an economic threat, through competition for jobs and other key resources and public provisions such as health care, as well as a 'security' threat, through links made between immigration and terrorism, and the apparently sexual predatory behaviour of migrants. The EU was charged with failing to protect its member states and citizens, disabling nations from being able to control their own borders and immigration levels.

These xenophobic and Islamophobic sentiments clearly resonated with large swathes of leave voters. A study by Swami et al (2018) found that those expressing voting preferences for Brexit were distinct from other respondents by virtue of being more likely to demonstrate Islamophobia and a belief in Islamophobic conspiracy theories, with 'perceptions of threat to political and economic power posed by Muslim immigrants ...

directly associated with the intention to vote to leave the EU' (Swami et al, 2018: 170). Similarly, research has revealed that immigration was the most significant issue for Brexit supporters. Using data from the British Election Survey, Goodwin and Milazzo (2017) found that anti-immigrant sentiment was a key driver of support to leave the EU, along with the notion that such a vote would allow the nation to 'regain control' of immigration. They also noted a correlation between the proportion of leave voters in an area with increased rates of immigration and ethnic change in the years immediately preceding the vote.

If the campaign and the vote itself indicated the wide appeal of racialised political rhetoric and an emboldening of racism and xenophobia, this became particularly apparent in the marked rise in racial violence and abuse in the immediate aftermath of the referendum, targeting both migrants and established black and minority ethnic communities (Komaromi and Singh, 2016; Burnett, 2017; Virdee and McGeever, 2018; Rzepnikowska, 2019). Tell Mama (2018b: 7) recorded a 475% increase in the number of offline anti-Muslim incidents reported in the week following the referendum. Similarly, in the midst of the referendum campaign between 16 and 30 June 2016, more than 3,000 hate crimes were reported to the police across the UK, representing a 42% increase on the same period in 2015 (Burnett, 2017: 87). Jon Burnett has argued that Brexit has served to embolden racially exclusionary forms of belonging and entitlement. A report which investigated 'post-referendum racism and xenophobia', based on testimonies from ethnic minority and migrant communities, also identified 'an increasing normalisation of xeno-racist narratives' and the manifestation of the 'hostile environment principle' (Komaromi and Singh, 2016: 1). Their analysis, based on a total of 636 individual reports of incidents of racist and xenophobic hate crime, found that abuse targeted anyone deemed to be 'foreign' or 'other', with nearly one third of incidents aimed at ethnic minority communities, particularly South Asians (Komaromi and Singh, 2016: 5). A study conducted by the Migrants' Rights Network (2017), examined the experiences and attitudes of migrants in areas registering particularly high levels of leave votes. Migrants reported increasingly negative views of immigrants in the wake of Brexit as well as a rise in reported experiences of hate incidents, prejudice and discrimination, including from employers.

Conclusion

This chapter has illustrated the persistence, prevalence and transformation of racism in contemporary Britain. As has been argued, racisms exist in multiple forms, evident in forms of individual and interpersonal prejudice and discrimination, but also through institutionalised and structural forms of racial and ethnic exclusion and marginalisation. Ethnic minority communities remain disproportionately subject to negative views and forms of racist victimisation, with research suggesting that exposure to such incidents has increased in a charged social and political climate. Similarly, the same communities remain structurally disadvantaged, more likely to be concentrated in poorer areas and to experience more negative outcomes in relation to their engagement with and employment within key social and political institutions, including the criminal justice system and labour market. While the UK has historically developed policies and structures aimed at addressing racial inequalities, it is clear that significant challenges remain and, worryingly, recent years seem to have marked a retreat from any meaningful pursuit of racial equality, evidenced for instance in the destructive and racially exclusionary impacts of Brexit and the government's 'hostile environment' policies.

As argued, racisms are dynamic and become transformed through changing social, economic and political contexts. While established ethnic minority communities continue to face racism on the basis of skin colour and their status as 'immigrants' and descendants of 'immigrants', religion has also emerged as a significant marker of racial difference. Muslims navigate an increasingly hostile and discriminatory landscape as Islamophobia has increased notably in recent decades, evident in racist attacks, widespread negative stereotypes and tropes, and through institutional and state practices, particularly those such as Prevent, initiated under the auspices of counter-terrorism policies. Alongside these developments, emergent forms of xeno-racism directed towards migrant groups such as Roma and Eastern Europeans have both informed and gained increasing traction within a context of rising Euroscepticism and anti-immigrant sentiment. These political impulses have been mobilised since the turn of the century by a range of far-right and right-wing populist actors who have pursued forms of discourse and action that call for a rejection of multiculturalism, for greater immigration controls, and promote hostility towards black and minority ethnic communities. The Brexit vote has served in many ways to simultaneously mobilise and intensify these sentiments, representing the further development of a social and political climate marked by racial and ethnic inequalities, intolerances and enmities.

Conclusion

Omar Khan, Runnymede Trust

Without data we cannot understand, much less respond to, social phenomena, including long-standing and extensive injustices such as racism. But the persistence of racism and other injustices shows why data by itself cannot tackle those injustices.

This may seem an odd or inapt conclusion from long report built on data, especially from the director of a race equality think tank that was founded 50 years ago to use evidence to 'nail the lie' on racism.

As this book outlines in successive chapters, there is no shortage of evidence about the extent of racial inequalities in Britain in 2019 – from education to employment, and from housing to health. Or, from birth to death. This evidence is still too poorly understood, and many of the data sets that include ethnicity are still insufficiently studied by researchers as well as policymakers, a gap this book seeks to fill.

But this book isn't just about data. It's about interpreting or understanding those data, and providing historical and policy background to explain why racial inequalities persist, change and in some cases improve. Better public and policymaker understanding of this background is the only way that we won't simply be 'nailing lies', but ending racial inequalities over the next 50 years.

Bringing together the common themes of the book highlights what is now a relatively consensual view about race in Britain today, at least among academics and researchers. At the end of this conclusion we also outline a number of recommendations, more or less organised in response to the findings outlined in each chapter. The gap between the analysis of these chapters and the failure to implement these recommendations partly reflects the gap between understanding racism among those who work on the topic, and the policymakers and wider public who don't.

The first theme is that history matters. Understanding our history matters for its own sake, so that Britain doesn't provide a partial or inaccurate account of who we were and what we did. History also matters in the context of understanding inequalities in Britain because those inequalities are not *randomly* patterned. When someone with an

African- or Asian-sounding surname but the same qualifications has to send in more CVs in 2019 just to get an interview, this is because of the stereotypes about the relative capacities and talents of people because of their race or ethnicity. And those stereotypes were developed some four centuries ago to justify the inhuman treatment and economic domination of people from Africa and Asia.

In Britain we don't ordinarily have a difficult time understanding that how we memorialise the past corresponds to and provides support for who we are and the values we believe in today: whether the First World War, the Holocaust or Srebrenica. Only by acknowledging how Britain not only failed to stand up to racism, but practised and believed in racist policies, can we understand why racial inequalities persist today. This is not about apportioning blame, but instead about understanding the source of the persistent and extensive racial inequalities outlined in this book.

Britain is of course far from alone in failing to recognise the role of history in explaining current injustices. Earlier this year the *New York Times* initiated a '1619 project' to highlight the extent of the influence of slavery on the United States. It is notable that the date being commemorated – when the first Africans were brought to North America by English ships – was when the North American colonies were part of the British or English empire. There was no United States of America in 1619, there would not be one for another 150 years, during which time *English* ships transported more enslaved Africans (over 3 million) than any other country. During the hundreds of years of Empire the distinctive intellectual, cultural and economic aspects of our culture developed, underpinned by denying equality on the basis of race even as Britishness consumed and absorbed idea and practices as well as resources from Asia, Africa and the Caribbean. And, as the last year has shown, these are not ancient wrongs, but have a direct impact in the present, whether in terms of the *Windrush* injustice or the issues raised by Northern Ireland for the Brexit negotiations.

A second theme is the need to defend but also build on anti-discrimination law and policy. Considering the extent of evidence of racial inequalities across different domains of everyday life, this book's chapters indicate how Britain's public services are instrumental in producing racial inequalities. Runnymede Trust's work with the Women's Budget Group has shown that government's budgetary policies have hit the poorest black and Asian women hardest, further increasing already existing inequalities. This is not to say that public services never address or reduce inequalities. However, if equality legislation was working as intended – in particular the public sector equality duty – public service and wider social outcomes would today be less unequal over 50 years on from when that legislation was first passed.

This raises a wider or more profound question: even if the anti-discrimination approach has been weakly or poorly implemented, is it sufficient to tackle racial inequalities? In recent years there is increasing criticism that 'equality and diversity' initiatives focus more on supporting ethnic minority people, and less on changing institutions. In place of this incrementalist approach, we instead need a more comprehensive redesign of our institutions and practices, if not revolution, to realise and deliver race equality, and equality generally. We don't need to 'fix the person' so that they can better navigate Britain's institution, but rather to 'fix our institutions' so that they provide fair chances and outcomes to everyone.

The challenge looks sharper still. Across this volume's chapters there is evidence that tackling racial inequality will require tackling inequalities more generally. The term 'intersectionality' may seem academic but it's obvious enough that simply tackling racial inequalities won't address the various ways in which people are disadvantaged, and that the response to those complexities will require targeted as well as universal measures.

It is worth contrasting the ways in which policymakers and even activists on the left have thought about tackling race compared to class inequalities. Simplifying, race (and sex) inequality has principally been viewed through the lens of an 'anti-discrimination' policy approach. The movement to challenge class inequalities (notably trade unions), however, instead focuses on macroeconomic policies and the nature of our economy, including how it distributes rewards or benefits. It is worth drawing this distinction a bit too sharply because it highlights how little of the thinking on 'redesigning the economy' has taken into account the need to address racial inequalities; or how it's just assumed that addressing class will necessarily involve tackling race. We need, instead, to ensure that any thinking and policy development on redesigning the economy addresses race at the level of first principles; or, putting it a different way, that our approach to tackling racism foregrounds structural thinking about the economy. This doesn't mean we should throw out the anti-discrimination approach. In fact, our thinking about and response to class may conversely require looking at the ways in which *discrimination* against working-class people now pervades our public services and institutions, and whether economic policies can alone tackle class inequalities. In policy terms, this would mean making class a 'protected characteristic' for the purposes of discrimination law.

A third and final theme is the question of how tackling race equality relates to our collective or democratic politics, and indeed to our identity. There has been much talk of 'British values' of democracy, equality and the rule of law. With her reference to 'burning injustice', former Prime Minister Theresa May is not alone in including non-discrimination and tackling racism among our 'British values'.

If race equality is a British value it has only become one recently, and is one whose affirmation is some way off in practice. Framing British values in this way is also a further barrier to reflecting properly on our history, making it seem that racial inequalities were an incidental or anomalous feature of our past, rather than one that was intrinsic to the nature of the British state and society for hundreds of year.

To the extent that we can talk about race equality becoming more of a social norm, that has happened in large part due to the efforts and struggles of a generation of black and minority ethnic Britons who arrived and grew up in this country in the 1960s. The legislative and policy changes were probably more reforming than is sometimes acknowledged, not least because English common law has no free-standing right to equality. Enoch Powell may have crafted a more poisonous way of putting this, but the idea that Magna Carta allowed Englishmen to discriminate on whatever grounds they wished was a very widespread one, and deployed by the Conservative opposition in objecting to race relations legislation. The notion that discrimination was justifiable if distasteful was arguably correct from a legal if not a moral point of view until the campaign to challenge it. To the extent that we now see equality and non-discrimination as British values, this is only because people – especially black and minority ethnic people – highlighted just how pervasive and unjust racism was.

These three themes help us outline how we better deliver on race equality, developing policies as well as a positive narrative that appeals as broadly as possible. As Chapter 10 outlines, there are different forms of racisms, and although this has long been understood among those who study race and racism, the social and political implications have only recently become apparent.

There is here a tension between acknowledging and explaining the diverse range and origin of racial inequalities in Britain today, while also requiring a shared analytic frame for understanding those inequalities. Just as importantly, how we analyse racism (or any issue for that matter) then has implications for how we respond to it, both in terms of policy design and in terms of mobilising social change to combat it.

Building on Alexander and Byrne's introduction, there are two ways of analysing race and racism: an 'ethnic studies' approach that focuses more on the particular characteristics, history and cultural practices of different groups in Britain, with a focus then on how we build a common society through integration while still respecting difference. The 'anti-racism' approach instead focuses on issues of power and inequality, and how these are reproduced generationally through institutions that have been marked by that racism for decades if not centuries. On this approach, we should address inequalities of power, especially how that power is exercised and reproduced through institutions.

Generally speaking Runnymede Trust has sought to advance both approaches, with a slightly stronger emphasis on the second, anti-racism, approach. This is in part because of our analysis of how racial inequalities persist, and in part because this perspective is almost completely missing from the policy response to racism.

Yet one of the striking findings of this report is just how much racial inequalities differ, whether in terms of education, housing, health, employment or the criminal justice system. And although the fit is not perfect, the pattern is clear: Black people (that is people of African descent), Bangladeshi, Pakistani and Gypsy, Roma and Traveller groups do worse than Indian and Chinese group, who in some domains (especially secondary education) outperform White British groups.

This is not simply a question of analysis, but of how we *respond* to racism, whether in terms of organising or mobilising socially against it, or in terms of designing public policy. If groups vary too much in how they experience racism, that makes it more challenging to build alliances, to resist people creating hierarchies of racism, and to find an umbrella frame of analysis, or a banner under which everyone can march. This is of course what 'political blackness' provided in the 1970s, and although it is difficult to see how that particular framework could now be revived, the conceptual and social purpose it serves still remains.

Getting beyond this stalemate is an absolute priority in the current environment. As Chapter 8 outlined, the UN found a 'striking' level of 'structural socio-economic exclusion of racial and ethnic communities in the UK' as well as the growth in the 'acceptability of explicit racial, ethnic and religious intolerance'. We've seen an increase in hate crime, and increased airing of far-right grievances and hatred, a phenomenon that is connected to wider international mobilisations of white nationalism. And yet the most common institutional response has been to develop 'equality and diversity' initiatives or 'unconscious bias' training instead of directly tackling racism and its ongoing consequences.

One more positive development has been the increase in representation of ethnic minority voices, or in ensuring 'lived experiences' or 'marginalised voices' are better heard. The value of lived experience is two-fold. First, it explains how racism operates, by affording those most affected by racism the opportunity to explain their experience of injustice. By listening to those who are differently positioned in systems or institutions, we better reveal the nature of those institutions, and how it feels as a person to be subjected to indignities or contempt, or just ignored. This can lead to a wider understanding of and focus on tackling inequalities in institutions without relying on overly academic arguments about power and positionality.

This indicates the second way 'lived experience' can matter: by changing outcomes. A good example is the *Windrush* injustice. Charities including Runnymede Trust had been arguing for many years that the 'hostile environment' was discriminatory and unjust. Yet however persuasive or well evidenced those claims, they were ignored by a government that was committed to driving down immigration numbers as a matter of principle. Any disagreement or dissent was quickly dismissed by politicians and policymakers as do-gooders seeking to undermine a government policy priority.

When those affected by the injustice – Anthony Bryan, Paulette Wilson, Sarah O'Connor, Sylvester Marshall, Elwaldo Romeo – stood up to explain their experiences, however, the government could no longer ignore the consequences of their actions. The public was soon outraged by how people were treated: being denied employment, housing and health care, and in some cases detained and deported. Without this direct confrontation with the lived experience, change would probably not have happened. By speaking clearly about the horrors of their lived experiences, they benefited not just those who stuck their heads above the parapet and were asked to reveal their terrible treatment to millions on live TV, but the entire *Windrush* generation.

There are, however, limitations to lived experience as a way of building the arguments and social change necessary to tackle racism. People experience racisms differently, and it is necessary and legitimate to foreground and understand the specific forms of different kinds of racism. It's also legitimate for people to challenge those forms of racism that most affect them, and to organise with others with similar experiences.

However the very embeddedness of lived experience, the detailed and personal knowledge of a particular form of racism, can make people misunderstand or even be tone-deaf to other forms of racism. Given that racisms differ, it won't actually be true that a lived experience of one kind of racism will inevitably help people understand or be sensitive to other forms of racism. So while it's justifiable and understandable that people start from their lived experience, tackling all forms of racism will require supporting experiences and changes that won't directly relate to our lived experience, and instead are based on an in-principle commitment to anti-racism.

We cannot simply pretend that this is happening already, or that it will be easy to provide the social support necessary for the policies and wider social change necessary to tackle racism. If Runnymede Trust is still around in another 50 years, it will be because we haven't succeeded in developing the narrative, policies and social pressure to combat the inequalities outlined in this book.

To get there we must first acknowledge that things haven't always been positive, and admit that Britain has often believed in and supported racism as a matter of policy and practice. Recognising that we haven't always lived up to our values will allow us to better frame and deliver on a positive vision for the future. The various chapters in this book provide a strong outline of what that vision must include. It must of course recognise the contributions and value of different ways of life and communities, and of the value of every one of us being able to lead the lives that we ourselves choose. But those aims can only be achieved by acknowledging and addressing racism more directly.

By way of a conclusion, we've suggested a number of recommendations to respond to the key findings of each chapter. These indicate what needs to change for the positive vision of a Britain free of racism and other forms of injustice to become a reality. The recommendations also provide a way for us to hold government and other decision makers in the public, private and charitable sector to account. We have the luxury to think about and analyse the problem of racism; we owe it to those whose work we've built on and to those who continue to stand up to these injustices to provide a way of tackling racial inequalities in the world in a practical way, and assessing whether progress is being made.

Recommendations

Omar Khan, Runnymede Trust

The following recommendations are directed at all institutions and individuals who have the responsibility and ability to implement them. This includes government and public sector bodies, as well as the private and charitable sectors. It also includes all of us, who have a responsibility to ensure that racism is confronted wherever it appears, and to act with others to work towards a better society.

Some recommendations, however, are more explicitly targeted at public institutions, whose democratic and legal role requires them to address racial discrimination, promote equal opportunities and encourage 'good relations' between different ethnic groups.

General

1) Improve the collection of mandatory data on race and ethnicity (and religion/belief). Ensure that public data sets have consistent annual data collection, and continue to adapt ethnic categories to capture increasing complexity and demographic changes.
2) Training should be required on tackling *racism*, not only on 'equality and diversity' nor only on 'unconscious bias'. The responsibility for equality lies with the institutions and not just individual employees.
3) Organisations and managers should set targets to hire and progress ethnic minority employees in line with national and local benchmarks. Where managers fail to meet targets to reduce racial inequalities, this should affect their appraisals and progression decisions.
4) Ensure equality law is applied, so that existing provisions are respected and applied in relation to all policy areas and decisions. Follow the spirit of the law by strengthening the 'due regard' clause in the public sector equality duty, which applies to all public bodies from central government to local authorities to hospitals and universities.
5) In response to the extensive inequalities outlined in the government's Race Disparity Audit, the government should adopt a race equality

strategy across all public policy areas. This strategy should be led by a senior minister who regularly attends and reports directly to the Cabinet.

Citizen rights and immigration

6) All children should be taught an accurate and inclusive history of Britain, including the history of migration, enslavement, empire and decolonisation, and the history of racism and the struggle for equality in Britain.

7) Racial discrimination legislation should apply more widely to immigration law and policy.

8) Level up rights of non-European Union (EU) migrants, creating equality in rights and access to services and benefits with EU and UK citizens.

9) Lift the ban: give people seeking asylum the right to work, so that they can use their skills and live in dignity. Everyone deserves a chance to contribute to the economy and to integrate into our communities.

10) Re-introduce birthright citizenship as part of a wider review into race, immigration and citizenship law and policy. Revoke the 'no recourse to public funds' provision and allow for a quicker (3–5 year) path to citizenship, and an end to extortionate citizenship fees.

11) Scrap 'hostile environment' immigration policies: the monitoring of the right to work by private individuals and non-immigration specialist organisations such as landlords, General Practitioners and teachers.

Criminal justice

12) The government should set a target that 20% of new police recruits and prison officers are from an ethnic minority background. There should be an additional target that 20% of promotions are from ethnic minority backgrounds by 2025.

13) Stop-and-search powers should not be extended and instead curtailed, especially the use of section 60. The government should establish national youth and community panels, and equivalent panels for each police force, to scrutinise the use and outcomes of stop-and-search powers.

14) The government should institute a formal review into race and the youth criminal justice system, including the racially discriminatory nature of ideas of 'the gang' and the use of 'joint enterprise'.

15) There must be an independent review of counter-terrorism legislation including Prevent, including to determine whether the policy is racially discriminatory. The review announced in August 2019 is not sufficiently independent.

16) The Angiolini report's recommendations on deaths in police custody must be implemented (2017).

Health

17) The National Health Service (NHS) should establish targets to reduce health inequalities and improve health outcomes for ethnic minority people. There should be clear action plans to achieve these targets.

18) The NHS Equality Objectives 2016–20 should be built upon. Race and ethnicity need to be more explicitly monitored, and action plans developed where data suggest representation and staff satisfaction remains unequal.

19) The NHS should continue to develop and implement the Workforce Race Equality Standard (WRES). The aim of 'enabling people to work comfortably with race equality' should be further embedded in the 2019 report and beyond.

20) The NHS should set a target of at least 20% of new NHS Trust board appointees to be from an ethnic minority background, with all trusts set a target to reach the proportion present in their local area population by 2030.

21) The NHS should set targets for staff progression, to ensure that promotions better match the proportion of ethnic minority staff in the health service.

Education

22) A government action plan should be initiated to tackle long-standing and persistent ethnic inequalities in education, particularly for Black Caribbean and Gypsy, Roma and Traveller children.

23) Policy should seek to reduce racial inequalities in school exclusions. Parents and children should be supported to know their rights.

24) Schools should better address racist bullying in schools, and support teacher training in this area.

25) Ofsted (the Office for Standards in Education) should develop a number of basic race equality measures as part of their assessment of schools. A school should not be 'outstanding' if any ethnic minority group has poor outcomes, and any racial inequalities in attainment, exclusions, staffing or governance should be made transparent to all parents.

26) The government should establish a target that 20% of all apprentices should be from an ethnic minority background.

27) All universities should establish an action plan for tackling black and minority ethnic (BME) attainment gaps. This should include the proportion awarded a first-class degree, as well as those getting a 2:1.

28) Universities and research councils and other funders should establish targets for graduate studies, to ensure that 20% of PhD and postdoctoral positions are filled by people with a BME background to address concerns over the 'pipeline' into the academy.

29) Universities should also establish targets for staffing at all levels, in hiring as well as progression in academic and professional appointments, as well as monitoring probation and promotions.

30) The Race Equality Charter should be adopted on an equal footing to Athena Swan, including financial penalties for institutions that fail to meet benchmarks in two successive years.

Employment

31) Employers with over 50 employees must monitor all hiring, promotion, disciplinary and pay decisions by ethnicity.

32) The Equality Act 2010 provision for all employers with over 250 employees to publish gender pay gap data should be extended to ethnicity gap data.

33) Better enforcement of the minimum wage, to ensure employers are compliant. Adopt a genuine living wage; the current national living wage (for those over 25) is £8.21, £0.79 less than a genuine living wage. In London the living wage needs to be £10.55.

34) Adopt the Institute of Employment Rights' 'Manifesto for Labour Law' (2018) to improve the security, pay, conditions and bargaining power of workers. This includes establishing a Ministry for Labour to rebuild and promote collective bargaining structures.

35) Relink benefits and inflation, and ensure benefits more closely correspond to the relative poverty line.

36) Re-establish child poverty targets, including a specific target to reduce disproportionately high ethnic minority child poverty.

37) Interview panels should generally have at least one BME interviewer. If necessary, this may require bringing in outside interviewers (with adequate training or support).

38) A presumption in favour of one BME person on every shortlist, especially for graduate positions where around 1 in 4 are from BME backgrounds.

39) Monitoring appraisal and promotion procedures, and disciplinary and complaint procedures, by ethnicity and taking action to ensure that line managers are equipped to effectively manage all members of their staff by providing them with anti-racist training.

Housing

40) Improve the security of housing tenure. As well as building more social housing, this will require providing more long-term, low-cost secure private accommodation (for example five-year leases with inflation-protected rental rises).

41) Tackle overcrowding, including by building more three-bedroom properties and increasing housing supply, and by placing a duty on local authorities to re-accommodate those in overcrowded conditions. Implement a policy to end homelessness.

42) Ensure local people have a real say or voice in housing decision making.

43) Implement the idea of 'universal basic services', expanding the welfare state to include housing, food, transport and internet access[1]

Arts and media

44) All creative industries need to adopt employment targets for ethnic minority people, from hiring to progression.

45) The BBC and other broadcasters need to establish more accurate targets, including for those who are employed on external production contracts, and reflecting the regional and age profile of the ethnic minority population.

46) Better and mandatory data collection and reporting on all publicly funded arts bodies to ensure diverse hiring across all roles.

47) Public funding to be withheld from arts bodies where diversity targets are not met over three years.

48) Public funding of the arts should not just focus on ensuring 'ethnic quotas' but focus on substantive work to tackle racism.

Politics and representation

49) All political parties should continue to increase the number of BME candidates in general elections and among local councillors.

50) Political parties should agree to an anti-racist 'code of conduct' during election campaigns.[2]

51) Political parties should seek to address racial inequalities in their policies as well as seek to increase representation.

Racisms in Britain

52) Race equality, and other civil society groups and organisations should work more closely together to build a common platform to challenge all forms of racism and prejudice. It is not enough for people or organisations to challenge only the form of discrimination that directly affects them; anti-discrimination and equality are universal principles that must be defended even when doing so doesn't have a direct effect on us personally. It is important to understand that different forms of racism have different attributes, whether anti-Jewish, anti-Muslim or anti-black, and that it is therefore reasonable and justifiable to understand and respond to specific forms of racism. But challenging racism requires challenging it in all its forms, and understanding anti-racism as a wider human rights and equality position entails defending other groups that experience discrimination too.

53) The government should provide a review into the far right in Britain, and the threat it poses to safety and security for ethnic minorities. This should include recommendations for action to address hate crime on the internet.

Notes

[1] See https://www.ucl.ac.uk/bartlett/igp/sites/bartlett/files/universal_basic_services_-_the_institute_for_global_prosperity_.pdf

[2] See https://www.runnymedetrust.org/uploads/publications/pdfs/Electoral%20Code%20of%20conduct%202016.pdf

Bibliography

Acheson, D. (1998) *Acheson Report*, London: The Stationery Office.

Achiume, E.T. (2018) *End of Mission Statement of the Special Rapporteur on Contemporary Forms of Racism, Racial Discrimination, Xenophobia and Related Intolerance at the Conclusion of her Mission to the United Kingdom of Great Britain and Northern Ireland*, UN Office of the High Commissioner on Human Rights, Available from: www.ohchr.org/EN/NewsEvents/Pages/DisplayNews.aspx?NewsID=23073&LangID=E (accessed 12 November 2019).

AdvanceHE (2018) *Student Statistics Report 2018*, York: AdvanceHE, Available from: https://www.advance-he.ac.uk/sites/default/files/2019-05/2018-06-ECU_HE-stats-report_students_v5-compressed.pdf (accessed 21 February 2019).

Airey, C., Bruster, S., Erens, B., Lilley, S., Pickering, K. and Pitson, L. (1999) *National Surveys of NHS Patients: General Practice 1998*, London: NHS Executive.

Akala (2018) *Natives: Race and Class in the Ruins of Empire*, London: Two Roads Publisher.

Akbar, A. (2017) 'Diversity in publishing – still hideously middle-class and white?', Available from: www.theguardian.com/books/2017/dec/09/diversity-publishing-new-faces (accessed 15 April 2019).

Albury, S. (2016) 'Diversity – what Ofcom needs to do', Available from: www.opendemocracy.net/en/ourbeeb/diversity-what-ofcom-needs-to-do (accessed 6 February 2019).

Alexander, C. (2002) 'Beyond black: rethinking the colour/culture divide', *Ethnic and Racial Studies*, 25(4): 552–71.

Alexander, C. (2004) 'Re-imagining the Asian gang: ethnicity, masculinity and youth after "the riots"', *Critical Social Policy*, 24(4): 526–49.

Alexander, C. (2015) *The Runnymede School Report 2015: Race, Education and Inequality in Contemporary Britain*, London: Runnymede Trust, Available from: www.runnymedetrust.org/uploads/The%20School%20Report.pdf (accessed 12 November 2019).

Alexander, C. (2017) 'Raceing Islamophobia', in F. Elahi and O. Khan (eds) *Islamophobia: A Challenge for Us All: 20 Years On*, London: Runnymede Trust.

Alexander C. (2018) 'Breaking black: the death of ethnic and racial studies in Britain', *Ethnic and Racial Studies*, 41(6): 1034–54.

Alexander, C. and Arday, J. (eds) (2015) *Aiming Higher: Race, Inequality & Diversity in the Academy*, London: Runnymede Trust, Available from: https://www.runnymedetrust.org/uploads/Aiming%20Higher.pdf (accessed 4 December 2019).

Alexander, C. and Weekes-Bernard, D. (2017) 'History lessons: inequality, diversity and the National Curriculum', *Race, Ethnicity and Education*, 20(4): 478–94.

Alexander, C., Weekes-Bernard, D. and Chatterji, J. (2012) *Making British Histories: Diversity and the National Curriculum*, London: Runnymede Trust. Available from: https://www.runnymedetrust.org/uploads/publications/pdfs/MakingBritishHistories-2012.pdf (accessed 2 December 2019).

Alexander, C., Weekes-Bernard, D. and Arday, J. (2015) *The Runnymede School Report: Race, Education and Inequality in Contemporary Britain*, London: Runnymede Trust.

Alexander, C., Chatterji, J. and Jalais, A. (2016) *The Bengal Diaspora: Rethinking Muslim Migration*, London: Routledge.

Aliverti, A. (2014) 'Enlisting the public in the policing of immigration', *British Journal of Criminology*, 55(2): 215–30.

Allen, C. (2011) 'Opposing Islamification or promoting Islamophobia? Understanding the English Defence League', *Patterns of Prejudice*, 45(4): 279–94.

Allen, C. (2014) 'Britain first: the "frontline resistance" to the Islamification of Britain', *Political Quarterly*, 85(3): 354–61.

Allen, C. (2017) 'Proscribing National Action: considering the impact of banning the British far-right group', *Political Quarterly*, 88(4): 652–9.

Alston, P., (2018) 'Statement on visit to the United Kingdom, by Professor Philip Alston, United Nations Special Rapporteur on extreme poverty and human rights' Office of the United Nations High Commissioner for Human Rights, Available from: https://www.ohchr.org/EN/NewsEvents/Pages/DisplayNews.aspx?NewsID=23881&LangID=E#navigation (accessed 29 July 2019).

Anderson, B. (2013) *Us and Them? The Dangerous Politics of Immigration Control*, Oxford: Oxford University Press.

Anderson, B. (2017) 'Towards a new politics of migration?', *Ethnic and Racial Studies*, 40(9): 1527–37.

Anderson, D.Q.C. (2012) *The Terrorism Acts in 2011: Report of the independent reviewer on the operation of the Terrorism Act 2000 and Part 1 of the Terrorism Act 2006*, London: The Stationery Office.

Andreouli, E., Greenland, K. and Howarth, C. (2016) '"I don't think racism is that bad any more": exploring the "end of racism" discourse among students in English schools', *European Journal of Social Psychology*, 46(2): 171–84.

Angiolini, E. (2017) *Report of the Independent Review of Deaths and Serious Incidents in Police Custody*, Available from: https://www.gov.uk/government/publications/deaths-and-serious-incidents-in-police-custody (accessed 12 November 2019).

Anthias, F. and Yuval-Davis, N. (1992) *Racialized Boundaries: Race, Nation, Gender, Colour and Class and the Anti-Racist Struggle*, London: Routledge.

Appleby, J. (2018) 'Ethic pay gap among NHS doctors', Available from: www.bmj.com/content/362/bmj.k3586?int_source=trendmd&int_medium=trendmd&int_campaign=trendmd (accessed 2 December 2019).

Arday, J. (2015) 'Creating space and providing opportunities for BME academics in higher education', *Aiming Higher: Race, Inequality and Diversity in the Academy. Runnymede Perspective*: 40–2.

Arday, J. and Mirza, H.S. (eds) (2018) *Dismantling Race in Higher Education*, Basingstoke, Palgrave Macmillan.

Arts Council (2017) *Equality, Diversity and the Creative Case: A Data Report, 2016–2017*, Available from: www.artscouncil.org.uk/publication/equality-diversity-and-creative-case-data-report-2016–17 (accessed 6 February 2019).

Arts Council England (2019) *Equality, Diversity and the Creative Case: A Data Report, 2017/18*, Manchester: Arts Council England. Available from: https://www.artscouncil.org.uk/sites/default/files/download-file/Diversity_report_1718.pdf (accessed 20 November 2019).

Arts Professional (2018) 'Pulse Report – Part 3: Diversity in audiences – what needs to change?', Available from: www.artsprofessional.co.uk/pulse/survey-report/pulse-report-part-3-diversity-audiences-what-needs-change (accessed 6 February 2019).

Ashton, D. and Noonan, C. (2013) 'Cultural work and higher education', in D. Ashton and C. Noonan (eds) *Cultural Work and Higher Education*, London: Palgrave Macmillan.

Ashton, D., Maguire, M. and Spilsbury, M. (2016) *Restructuring the Labour Market: The Implications for Youth*, Baskingstoke: Palgrave Macmillan.

Atkinson, M., Clark, M., Clay, D. et al (2001) *Systematic Review of Ethnicity and Health Service Access for London*, Coventry: Centre for Health Services Studies, University of Warwick.

Atkinson, H., Bardgett, S., Budd, A., Finn, M., Kissane, C., Qureshi, S., Saha, J., Siblon, J. and Sivasundaram, S. (2018) *Race, Ethnicity & Equality in UK History*, London: Royal Historical Society, Available from: https://royalhistsoc.org/wp-content/uploads/2018/10/RHS_race_report_EMBARGO_0001_18Oct.pdf (accessed 12 November 2019).

Au, S. and P'ng, S,T. (1997) 'Introduction', in S. Au and L. Yee (eds) *Chinese Mental Health Issues in Britain*, London: Mental Health Foundation.

Audit Scotland (2011) *An Overview of Scotland's Criminal Justice System*, Available from: www.audit-scotland.gov.uk/docs/central/2011/nr_110906_justice_overview.pdf (accessed 1 May 2019).

Awan, I. (2012) '"I am a Muslim, not an extremist": How the Prevent Strategy has constructed a "suspect" community', *Politics & Policy*, 40(6): 1158–85.

Awan, I. (2016) 'Islamophobia on social media: a qualitative analysis of Facebook's Walls of Hate', *International Journal of Cyber Criminology*, 10(1): 1–20.

Awan, I. and Zempi, I. (2015) *We Fear for Our Lives: Offline and Online Experiences of Anti-Muslim Hostility*, London: Tell Mama.

Back, L. and Sinha, S. (2015) *Migrant City*, London: Routledge

Banks, M. (2007) *The Politics of Cultural Work*, Basingstoke: Palgrave Macmillan.

Bajekal, M., Blane, D., Grewal, I., Karlsen, S. and Nazroo, J. (2004) 'Ethnic differences in influences on quality of life at older ages: a quantitative analysis', *Ageing & Society*, 24(5): 709–728.

Barlow, D.E. and Barlow, M.H. (2018) *Police in a Multicultural Society: An American Story*, Illinois: Waveland Press.

Bartlett, J. and Littler, M. (2011) *Inside the EDL: Populist Politics in a Digital Age*, London: Demos.

BBC (2017a) *BBC Annual Plan 2017/18* [online], Available from: http://downloads.bbc.co.uk/aboutthebbc/insidethebbc/howwework/reports/pdf/BBC_Annual_Plan_2017-18.pdf (accessed 19 November 2019).

BBC (2017b) *BBC Equality Information Report 2016–17* [online], Available from: http://downloads.bbc.co.uk/diversity/pdf/equality-information-report-2017.pdf (accessed 12 November 2019).

BBC (2018a) *Diversity*, Available from: http://downloads.bbc.co.uk/diversity/pdf/bbc-equality-information-report-2017–18.pdf (accessed 21 March 2019).

BBC (2018b) 'BBC publishes a landmark report on BAME career progression and culture', Available from: www.bbc.co.uk/mediacentre/latestnews/2018/bame-career-progression-and-culture-report (accessed 29 June 2018).

BBC Online (2018a) 'Windrush generation: Theresa May apologises to Caribbean leaders', BBC Online, 17 April, Available from: www.bbc/news/uk-politics-43792411 (accessed 1 June 2018).

BBC Online (2018b) 'Sajid Javid replaces Amber Rudd as home secretary', BBC Online, 30 April, Available from: www.bbc.co.uk/news/uk-politics-43946845 (accessed 1 June 2018).

Bécares, L. (2015) *Which Ethnic Groups Have the Poorest Health? Ethnic Health Inequalities 1991 to 2011*, Manchester: University of Manchester, Centre on Dynamics of Ethnicity (CoDE).

Bécares, L., Nazroo, J. and Stafford, M. (2009) 'The buffering effect of ethnic density on experienced racism and health', *Health and Place*, 15: 670–8.

Bécares, L., Nazroo, J. and Stafford, M. (2011) 'The ethnic density effect on alcohol use among ethnic minority people in the UK', *Journal of Epidemiology & Community Health*, 65(1): 20–5.

Becker, S. and Fetzer, T. (2017) *Did Easter European Immigration Cause an Increase in Anti-European Sentiment in the UK?* CAGE Online Working Paper Series, 16.

Beider, H. (2012) *Race, Housing and Community: Perspectives on Policy and Practice*, Oxford: Wiley.

Bernstock, P. (2016) *Olympic Housing: A Critical Review of London 2012's Legacy*, London: Routledge.

BFI (2015) 'UK screen content generates over £6 billion for the UK economy', Available from: www.bfi.org.uk/sites/bfi.org.uk/files/downloads/bfi-press-release-uk-screen-content-gebnerates-over-6-billion-for-uk-economy-2015-02-24.pdf (accessed 22 May 2019).

Bhattacharyya, G. (2008) *Dangerous Brown Men: Exploiting Sex, Violence and Feminism in the War on Terror*, London: Zed Press.

Bhopal, K. (2004) 'Gypsy travellers and education: changing needs and changing perceptions', *British Journal of Educational Studies*, 52(1): 47–64.

Bhopal, K. (2016) 'White academia: will the Race Equality Charter make a difference?', *British Politics and Policy at LSE* [online], 3 February. Available from: https://blogs.lse.ac.uk/politicsandpolicy/tackling-race-inequality-in-higher-education/ (accessed 12 November 2019).

Bhopal, K. (2018) *White Privilege: The Myth of a Post-racial Society*, Bristol: Policy Press.

Bhopal, R. (2015) *Migration, Ethnicity, Race and Health in Multicultural Societies*, Oxford: Oxford University Press.

Bhopal, K. and Myers, M. (2018) *Home Schooling and Home Education: Race, Class and Inequality*, London: Routledge.

Bhopal, K. and Pitkin, C. (2018) *Investigating Higher Education Institutions and Their Views*, Birmingham: The Centre for Research in Race and Education, Available from: https://www.ucu.org.uk/media/9535/Investigating-higher-education-institutions-and-their-views-on-the-Race-Equality-Charter-Sept-18/pdf/REC_report_Sep18_fp.pdf (accessed 24/06/2019).

Bhopal, K. and Henderson, H. (2019) *Advancing Equality in Higher Education: an exploratory study of the Athena SWAN and Race Equality Charters*, Birmingham: The Centre for Research in Race and Education, Available from: https://www.birmingham.ac.uk/Documents/college-social-sciences/education/reports/advancing-equality-and-higher-education.pdf (accessed 24 June 2019).

Bhopal, K., Brown, H. and Jackson, J. (2015) *Academic Flight: How to Encourage Black and Minority Ethnic Academics to Stay in UK Higher Education – Research Report*, London: Equality Challenge Unit.

Bird, K., Saalfeld, T. and Wüst, A.M. (2010) *The Political Representation of Immigrants and Minorities: Voters, Parties and Parliaments in Liberal Democracies*, Abingdon: Routledge.

Black Health Agency (2013) *State of Health, Black and Other Minority Groups: BHA Contribution to the Development of a Joint Strategic Needs Assessment*, Cardiff: Black Health Agency.

Black Training and Enterprise Group (2019) *Apprenticeships – Research and Reports*, Available from: https://www.bteg.co.uk/content/apprenticeships-research-and-reports (accessed 12 November 2019).

Blanden, J. and Machin, S. (2004) 'Educational inequality and the expansion of UK higher education', *Scottish Journal of Political Economy*, 51(2): 230–49.

Blinder, R. and Richards. L. (2018) 'UK public opinion toward immigration: overall attitudes and level of concern', Migration Observatory, Available from: https://migrationobservatory.ox.ac.uk/resources/briefings/uk-public-opinion-toward-immigration-overall-attitudes-and-level-of-concern/ (accessed 8 June 2019).

Bloch, A. (2000) 'Refugee settlement in Britain: the impact of policy on participation', *Journal of Ethnic and Migration Studies*, 26(1): 75–88.

Bloch, A. (2008) 'Refugees in the UK labour market: the conflict between economic integration and policy-led labour market restriction', *Journal of Social Policy*, 37(1): 21–36.

Bloch, A. and Schuster, L. (2005) 'At the extremes of exclusion: deportation, detention and dispersal', *Ethnic and Racial Studies*, 28(3): 491–512.

Bloch, A. and McKay, S. (2015) 'On immigration, the proposals of both Labour and the Conservatives disappoint', *LSE British Politics and Policy* [Blog] 9 April.

Bloch, A. and McKay, S. (2016) *Living on the Margins: Undocumented Migrants in a Global City*, Bristol: Policy Press.

Boliver, V. (2011) 'Expansion, differentiation, and the persistence of social class inequalities in British higher education', *Higher Education*, 61(3): 229–42.

Boliver, V. (2015) 'Are there distinctive clusters of higher and lower status universities in the UK?', *Oxford Review of Education*, 41(5): 608–27.

Boliver, V. (2016) 'Exploring ethnic inequalities in admission to Russell Group universities', *Sociology*, 50(2): 247–66.

Bolt, G., Phillips, D. and Van Kempen, R. (2010) 'Housing policy, (de) segregation and social mixing: an international perspective', *Housing Studies*, 25(2): 129–35.

Bone, J. (2014) 'Neoliberal nomads: housing insecurity and the revival of private renting in the UK', *Sociological Research Online*, 19(4): 1–14.

Booth, R. (2019) 'Racism rising since Brexit vote, nationwide study reveals', *The Guardian*, 20 May.

Booth, R. and Mohdin, A. (2018) 'Revealed: the stark evidence of everyday racial bias in Britain', *The Guardian*, 2 December.

Bosworth, D.L. and Kersley, H. (2015) *Opportunities and Outcomes in Education and Work: Gender Effects*, London: UK Commission for Employment and Skills.

Bourne, J. (2019) 'Unravelling the concept of unconscious bias', *Race & Class*, 60(4): 70–5.

Bowling, B. and Phillips, C. (2007) 'Disproportionate and discriminatory: reviewing the evidence on police stop and search', *Modern Law Review*, 70(6): 936–61.

Bradford, B. (2006) *Who Are the 'Mixed' Ethnic Group?*, London: Office for National Statistics.

Bramley, G. and Fitzpatrick, S. (2018) 'Homelessness in the UK: who is most at risk?', *Housing Studies*, 33(1): 96–116.

Bridge, G., Butler, T. and Lees, L. (2011) *Mixed Communities: Gentrification by Stealth?* Bristol: Policy Press.

Brown, C. (1984) *Black and White Britain: The Third PSI Survey*, London: Hutchinson.

Browning, S. and Uberoi, E. (2019) 'Ethnic diversity in politics and public life', Commons Briefing papers SN01156, Available from: https://researchbriefings.parliament.uk/ResearchBriefing/Summary/SN01156 (accessed 12 November 2019).

Bruce-Jones, E. (2015) 'Deaths in custody in Europe: the United Kingdom in context', in N. El-Enany and E. Bruce-Jones (eds) *Justice, Resistance and Solidarity: Race and Policing in England*, London: Runnymede Trust, Available from: www.runnymedetrust.org/uploads/Race%20and%20Policing%20v5.pdf (accessed 8 May 2019).

Brynjolfsson, E. and McAfee, A. (2014) *The Second Machine Age: Work, Progress, and Prosperity in a Time of Brilliant Technologies*, New York: W.W. Norton.

Bulman, M. (2018) 'Hate crime numbers in and around schools and colleges up 62% in a year, figures show', *The Independent*, 29 January, Available from: www.independent.co.uk/news/uk/home-news/hate-crime-schools-colleges-uk-education-rise-racism-lgbt-race-ethnicity-a8183061.html (accessed 10 December 2018).

Burgess, S. (2014) *Understanding the Success of London's Schools*, Working Paper no. 14/333, Centre for Market and Public Organisation, Available from: https://www.bristol.ac.uk/media-library/sites/cmpo/migrated/documents/wp333.pdf (accessed 7 December 2018).

Burke, S. (2018) 'The discursive "othering" of Jews and Muslims in the Britain First solidarity patrol', *Journal of Community and Applied Social Psychology*, 28(5): 365–77.

Burnett, J. (2017) 'Racial violence and the Brexit state', *Race & Class*, 58(4): 85–97.

Burns, S., Leith, R. and Hughes, J. (2015) *Education Inequalities in Northern Ireland*, Belfast: Queens University Belfast, Available from: https://www.equalityni.org/ECNI/media/ECNI/Publications/Delivering%20Equality/EducationInequality-SummaryReport.pdf (accessed 06 February 2018).

Burrell, K. (2009) *Polish Migration to the UK in the New European Union: After 2004*, Abingdon: Routledge.

Burrell, K. (2016) Polish Migration to the UK in the 'New' European Union: After 2004, London: Routledge.

Business in the Community (2015). *Race at Work 2015*, London: Business in the Community.

Butler, D. (2017) 'Theresa May's "race disparity audit" tells us nothing and offers no fresh solutions', *The Guardian*, Available from: https://www.theguardian.com/commentisfree/2017/oct/13/theresa-may-race-disparity-audit (accessed 30 November 2019).

Byrne, B. (2014) *Making Citizens: Public Rituals and Personal Journeys to Citizenship*, Basingstoke: Palgrave Macmillan.

Byrne, B. (2015) 'Rethinking intersectionality and whiteness at the borders of citizenship', *Sociological Research Online*, 20(3): 1–12.

Byrne, B. (2017) 'Testing times: the place of the citizenship test in the UK immigration regime and new citizens' responses to it', *Sociology*, 51(2): 323–38.

Byrne, B. and De Tona, C. (2019) *All in the Mix: Race, Class and School Choice,* Manchester: Manchester University Press.

Cabinet Office (2017) *Race Disparity Audit: Summary Findings from the Ethnicity Facts and Figures Website*, London: Cabinet Office.

CAGE (2019) 'Citizenship deprivations: what you need to know', Available from: www.cage.ngo/citizenship-deprivations-what-you-need-to-know (accessed 17 June 2019).

CAMEo (2018) *Workforce Diversity in the UK Screen Sector: Evidence Review*, Leicester: CAMEo Research Institute.

Campaign Against Anti-Semitism (2018) *Anti-Semitism Barometer 2017*, London: CAA.

Campbell, R. and Cowley, P. (2014) 'What voters want: reactions to candidate characteristics in a survey experiment', *Political Studies*, 62(4): 745–65.

Care Quality Commission (CQC) (2011) 'Count Me In', Available from: www.cqc.org.uk/news/releases/care-quality-commission-looks-ahead-last-count-me-census-published (accessed: 7 January 2018).

Care Quality Commission (2014) *Our Human Rights Approach for Our Regulation of Health and Social Care Services*, Newcastle upon Tyne: CQC.

Care Quality Commission (2015) *A Different Ending – Addressing Inequalities in End of Life Care – Overview Report*, Newcastle upon Tyne: CQC.

Care Quality Commission (2017) *Equally Outstanding*, Newcastle upon Tyne: CQC.

Carter, R. (2018) *Fear, Hope and Loss: Understanding the Drivers of Hope and Hate,* London: Hope Charitable Trust.

Carl N., Richards, L. and Heath, A. (2018) Support for Immigration from Six Countries of Origin: How much do Leave and Remain Voters Differ? Working paper. *Centre for Social Investigation.*

Carter, S., Mwaura, S., Ram, M., Trehan, K. and Jones, T. (2015) 'Barriers to ethnic minority and women's enterprise: existing evidence, policy tensions and unsettled questions', *International Small Business Journal*, 33(1): 49–69.

Cashmore, E. (2001) 'Behind the window dressing: ethnic minority police perspectives on cultural diversity', *Journal of Ethnic and Migration Studies*, 28(2): 327–41.

Castles, S. (2009) *Indians in Britain*. International Migration and Diaspora Studies Project Working Paper Series, 23. New Delhi: Jawaharlal Nehru University.

Catney, G. (2015) 'Has neighbourhood ethnic residential segregation decreased? Ethnic identity and inequalities in Britain', *Dynamics of Diversity*: 109–22.

Cemlyn, S., Greenfields, M., Burnett, S., Matthews, Z. and Whitwell, C. (2009) *Inequalities Experienced by Gypsy and Traveller Communities: A Review*, Equalities and Human Rights Commission Research Report 12, Manchester: EHRC.

Centre on Dynamics of Ethnicity (CoDE) (2012) 'How has ethnic diversity grown 1991–2001–2011?', Available from: http://hummedia. manchester.ac.uk/institutes/code/briefings/dynamicsofdiversity/ how-has-ethnic-diversity-grown-1991-2001-2011.pdf. (accessed 2 November 2019).

Chan, Y.M and Chan, C. (1997) 'The Chinese in Britain', *Journal of Ethnic and Migration Studies*, 23(1): 123–31.

Choudhury, T. and Fenwick, H. (2011) *The Impact of Counter-terrorism Measures on Muslim Communities*, Manchester: Equality and Human Rights Commission.

CIC (2019) 'UK has 2m creative industries jobs', Available from: www. thecreativeindustries.co.uk/uk-creative-overview/facts-and-figures/ employment-figures (accessed 8 February 2019).

Clark, K. (2015a) 'Ethnic diversity and UK PLC', *Manchester Policy Blogs*, 11 June, Available from: http://blog.policy.manchester. ac.uk/featured/2015/06/ethnic-diversity-and-uk-plc/ (accessed 3 May 2019).

Clark, K. (2015b) 'Ethnic minority self-employment', *IZA World of Labor*, 120, doi: 10.15185/izawol.120

Clark, K. and Drinkwater, S. (2007) *Ethnic Minorities in the Labour Market: Dynamics and Diversity*, Bristol: Policy Press.

Clark, K., Garratt, L., Li, Y., Lymperopoulou, K. and Shankley, W. (2018) 'Local deprivation and the labour market integration of new migrants to England', *Journal of Ethnic and Migration Studies*, 1–23.

Clarke, C., Peach, C. and Vertovec, S. (1990) *South Asians Overseas: Migration and Ethnicity*. Cambridge: Cambridge University Press.

Cohen, N. (2013) 'A coalition of the complacent', Available from: https://blogs.spectator.co.uk/nick-cohen/2013/01/a%20- coalition-of-the-complacent/ (accessed 7 January 2019).

Clinks (2018) *Clinks: Supporting the Voluntary Sector in the Criminal Justice System*, Available from: https://www.clinks.org (accessed 07 March 2019).

CLPE (Centre for Literacy in Primary Education) (2018) *Reflecting Realities: A Survey of Ethnic Representation within UK Children's Literature 2017*, Available from: https://clpe.org.uk/library-and-resources/research/reflecting-realities-survey-ethnic-representation-within-uk-children (accessed 6 February 2019).

Collins, E.J.T. (1976) 'Migrant labour in British agriculture in the nineteenth century', *Economic History Review*, 29(1): 38–59.

Commission for Racial Equality (2007) *Annual Report and Accounts*, London: The Stationery Office.

Community Security Trust (2019) *Antisemitic Incidents: Report 2018*, London: Community Security Trust.

Conservative Party (2019) Invitation to Join the Government of Britain: Conservative Manifesto, London: The Conservative Party.

Consilium Research & Consultancy (2013) *Equality and Diversity within the Arts and Cultural Sector in England*, Available from: www.artscouncil.org.uk/sites/default/files/download-file/Equality_and_diversity_within_the_arts_and_cultural_sector_in_England.pdf (accessed 3 April 2019).

Copsey, N. (2010) *The English Defence League: Challenging Our Country and Our Values of Social Inclusion, Fairness, and Equality*, London: Faith Matters.

Coulter, R. (2017) 'Local house prices, parental background and young adults' homeownership in England and Wales', *Urban Studies*, 54(14): 3360–79.

Coulter, R. (2018) 'Parental background and housing outcomes in young adulthood', *Housing Studies*, 33(2): 201–23.

Courts and Tribunal Judiciary (2018) *Judicial Diversity Statistics 2018*, Available from: https://www.judiciary.uk/publications/judicial-diversity-statistics-2018/ (accessed 4 April 2019).

Cov, S. (1963) *Dark Strangers: A Sociological Study of the Absorption of a Recent West Indian Migrant Group in Brixton, South London*, London: Tavistock.

CQC/National Statistics/NHS (2017) *2017 Community Mental Health Survey – Statistical Release – NHS Patient Survey Programme*, Newcastle: CQC.

Cracknell, R. (2017) 'Diversity in the 2017 Parliament', 13 June, Available from: https://commonslibrary.parliament.uk/insights/diversity-in-the-2017-parliament/ (accessed 7 November 2019).

Craig, G., Waite, L., Lewis, H. and Skrivankova, K. (eds) (2015) *Vulnerability, Exploitation and Migrants. Insecure Work in a Globalised Economy*, Basingstoke: Palgrave MacMillan.

Crawford, J., Leahy, S. and McKee, K. (2016) 'The Immigration Act and the "right to rent": exploring governing tensions within and beyond the state', *People, Place and Policy* 10(2): 114–25.

Creative Scotland (2018) *Equalities, Diversity and Inclusion*, Available from: www.creativescotland.com/what-we-do/the-10-year-plan/connecting-themes/equalities-and-diversity (accessed 14 May 2019).

Creative Skillset (2014) *The Creative Media Workforce Survey*. London, England: Author.

Crenna-Jennings, W. (2017) 'A black Caribbean FSM boy with SEND is 168 times more likely to be permanently excluded than a white British girl without SEND. Why?', *TES*, Available from: https://www.tes.com/news/black-caribbean-fsm-boy-send-168-times-more-likely-be-permanently-excluded-white-british-girl (accessed 7 December 2018).

Criddle, B. (2010) 'More diverse, yet more uniform: MPs and candidates', in D. Kavanagh and D. Butler (eds) *The British General Election of 2005*, Basingstoke: Palgrave Macmillan, pp 306–29.

Crombie, I., Irvine, L., Elliott, L. and Wallace, H. (2005) *Closing the Health Inequalities Gap: An International Perspective*, Venice: WHO European Office for Investment for Health and Development.

Cumberbatch, G., Baily, A., Lyne, V. and Gauntlett, S. (2018) *On-screen Diversity Monitoring: BBC One and BBC Two*, Available from: www.ofcom.org.uk/__data/assets/pdf_file/0019/124255/bbc1-bbc2-diversity-monitoring.pdf (accessed 4 May 2019).

Curtice, J., Fisher, S. and Steed, M. (2005) 'Appendix 2: the results analysed', in D. Kavanagh and D. Butler (eds) *The British General Election of 2005*, Basingstoke: Palgrave Macmillan, pp 235–59.

D'Angelo, A. and Kofman, E. (2017) 'UK: large-scale European migration and the challenge to EU free movement', in J-M. Lafleur and M. Stanek (eds) *South–North Migration of EU Citizens in Times of Crisis*, Springer: Cham.

Dahya, B. (1974) 'The nature of Pakistani ethnicity in industrial cities in Britain', *Urban Ethnicity*, 77: 118.

Dancygier, R.M. (2017) *Dilemmas of Inclusion: Muslims in European Politics*, New Haven, CT: Princeton University Press.

D'Arcy, K. (2014) 'Home education, school, Travellers and educational inclusion', *British Journal of Sociology of Education*, 35(5): 818–35.

Darling, J. (2016) 'Privatising asylum: neoliberalisation, depoliticisation and the governance of forced migration', *Transactions of the Institute of British Geographers* 41(3): 230–43.

Davidson, T. and Berezin, M. (2018) 'Britain First and the UK Independence Party: social media and movement party dynamics', *Mobilization* 23(4): 485–510.

DBEIS (2018a) *Trade Union Membership 2017: Statistical Bulletin*, London: BEIS, Available from: https://assets.publishing.service.gov. uk/government/uploads/system/uploads/attachment_data/file/712543/TU_membership_bulletin.pdf (accessed 31 October 2019).

DBEIS (2018b) 'Employment by sector', Available from: www.ethnicity-facts-figures.service.gov.uk/work-pay-and-benefits/employment/employment-by-sector/latest (accessed 31 October 2019).

DBEIS (2018c) *Race at Work 2018: The McGregorSmith Review One Year On*, London: DBEIS, Available from: https://www.gov.uk/government/publications/race-at-work-2018-mcgregor-smith-review-one-year-on (accessed 19 November 2019).

DBEIS (2018d) *Ethnicity Pay Reporting: Government Consultation, Department of Business, Energy and Industrial Strategy*, Available from: https://assets.publishing.service.gov.uk/government/uploads/system/uploads/attachment_data/file/747546/ethnicity-pay-reporting-consultation.pdf (accessed 15 January 2020).

DBIS (Department of Business, Innovation and Skills) (2013) *The Business Case for Equality and Diversity*, Available from: https://assets.publishing.service.gov.uk/government/uploads/system/uploads/attachment_data/file/49638/the_business_case_for_equality_and_diversity.pdf (accessed 21 March 2019).

DCMS (Digital, Culture, Media and Sport Committee) (2019) 'Oral evidence: the work of Ofcom, HC407', House of Commons, London.

Dearden, l. (2019) 'Shamima Begum: number of people stripped of UK citizenship soars by 600% in a year', 17 May, Available from: www.independent.co.uk/news/uk/home-news/shamima-begum-uk-citizenship-stripped-home-office-sajid-javid-a8788301. html (accessed 17 May 2019).

Delsol, R. and Shiner, M. (2006) 'Regulating stop and search: a challenge for police and community relations in England and Wales', *Critical Criminology*, 14: 241–63.

Demack, S., Drew, D. and Grimsley, M. (2000) 'Minding the gap: ethnic, gender and social class differences in attainment at 16, 1988–95', *Race Ethnicity and Education*, 3(2): 117–43.

Demie, F. (2018) 'Raising achievement of black Caribbean pupils: good practice for developing leadership capacity and workforce diversity in schools', *School Leadership & Management*: 1–21.

Demie, F. (2019) 'The Experience of Black Caribbean pupils in school exclusion in England', *Educational Review*, https://doi.org/10.1080/00131911.2019.1590316

De Noronha, L. (2018a) *Deporting 'Black Britons': Portraits of Deportation to Jamaica*, DPhil Anthropology, University of Oxford.

De Noronha, L. (2018b) *Race, Class and Brexit: Thinking from Detention*, London: Verso.

Department for Culture Media and Sport (2016) *Creative Industries: Focus on Employment*, Available from: https://assets.publishing.service.gov.uk/government/uploads/system/uploads/attachment_data/file/534305/Focus_on_Employment_revised_040716.pdf (accessed 8 February 2019).

Department for Education and Employment (1997) *Excellence in Schools*, London: HMSO.

Department of Education and Science (1985) *Education for All: Report of the Committee of Inquiry into the Education of Children from Ethnic Minority Groups (The Swann Report)*, London: HMSO.

Department for Education Statistics (2004) *Aiming High: Understanding the Needs of Minority Ethnic Pupils in Mainly White Schools*, Nottingham: DfES Publications.

Department of Health (2005) *Delivering Race Equality in Mental Health Care, an Action Plan for Reform Inside and Outside Services; and the Government's Response to the Independent Inquiry into the Death of David Bennett*, London: Department of Health.

Department of Health, Local Government Association and Public Health England (2013) *Public Health Supplement to the NHS Constitution for Local Authorities and Public Health England*, Mansfield: Department of Health.

DfE (Department for Education) (2015a) *Ethnic Minorities and Attainment: The Effects of Poverty*, London: DfE, Available from: www.gov.uk/government/publications/ethnic-minorities-and-attainment-the-effects-of-poverty (accessed 12 November 2019).

DfE (2015b) *The Prevent Duty: Departmental Advice for Schools and Childcare Providers*, London: DfE.

DfE (2018a) *Revised GCSE and Equivalent Results in England: 2016 to 2017*, London: DfE, Available from: www.gov.uk/government/statistics/revised-gcse-and-equivalent-results-in-england-2016-to-2017 (accessed 4 March 2019).

DfE (2018b) *Apprenticeships and Levy Statistics: October 2018* London: DfE.

DfE (2018c) *Apprenticeships and Traineeships Data*, London: DfE, Available from: www.gov.uk/government/statistical-data-sets/fe-data-library-apprenticeships (accessed 17 March 2019).

DfE (2018d) *Schools, Pupils and Their Characteristics*, Sheffield: DfE.

DfE (2018e) Key stage 4 and multi-academy trust performance 2017, Available from: www.gov.uk/government/statistics/key-stage-4-and-multi-academy-trust-performance-2017 (accessed 17 November 2019).

DfE (2018f) A level and other 16 to 18 results: 2017 to 2018, Available from: www.gov.uk/government/statistics/a-level-and-other-16-to-18-results-2017-to-2018 (accessed 17 November 2019).

DfE (2018g) School workforce in England: November 2017, Available from: www.gov.uk/government/statistics/school-workforce-in-england-november-2017 (accessed 17 November 2019).

Di Stasio, V. and Heath, A. (2019) *Are Employers in Britain Discriminating Against Ethnic Minorities? Summary of Findings from the GEMM Project*, Available from: http://csi.nuff.ox.ac.uk/wp-content/uploads/2019/01/Are-employers-in-Britain-discriminating-against-ethnic-minorities_final.pdf (accessed 12 November 2019).

Discrimination Law Review – Justice Student Network (2007) *A Framework for Fairness*, UK: Discrimination Law Review.

Dodd, V. (2019) 'Children whitening skin to avoid racial hate crime, charity finds', *The Guardian*, 30 May.

Dorling, D. (2015) 'Policy, politics, health and housing in the UK', *Policy and Politics*, 43(2): 163–80.

Durose, C., Richardson, L., Combs, R., Eason, C. and Gains, F. (2012) '"Acceptable difference": diversity, representation and pathways to UK politics', *Parliamentary Affairs*, 66(2): 246–67.

Dustmann, C. and Theodoropoulos, N. (2010) 'Ethnic minority immigrants and their children in Britain', *Oxford Economic Papers*, 62(2): 209–33.

Dyson, S., Berghs, M. and Atkin, K. (2016) '"Talk to me. There's two of us": fathers and sickle cell screening', *Sociology*, 50(1).

ECRI (European Commission against Racism and Intolerance) (2016) *ECRI Report on the United Kingdom*, Available from: www.coe.int/t/dghl/monitoring/ecri/Countryby-country/United_Kingdom/GBR-CbC-V-2016-038-ENG.pdf/ (accessed 12 November 2019).

Eddo-Lodge, R. (2017) *Why I'm No Longer Talking to White People about Race*, London: Bloomsbury Circus.

Eichler, W. (2017) 'Ethnic minorities "under-represented" in public sector leadership roles, PM says', Available from: www.localgov.co.uk/Ethnic-minorities-under-represented-in-public-sector-leadership-roles-PM-says/43963 (accessed 17 October 2018).

Eikhof, D.R. and Warhurst, C. (2013) 'The promised land? Why social inequalities are systemic in the creative industries', *Employee Relations*, 35(5): 495–508.

Electoral Reform Society (2019) 'Voter registration', Available from: www.electoral-reform.org.uk/campaigns/upgrading-our-democracy/voter-registration/ (accessed 28 January 2019).

El-Enany, N. and Bruce-Jones, E. (2015) *Justice, Resistance and Solidarity Race and Policing in England*, London: Runnymede Trust.

Elsinga, M. and Hoekstra, J. (2005) 'Homeownership and housing satisfaction', *Journal of Housing and the Built Environment*, 20(4): 401–24.

English, P. (2018) 'Visible, elected, but effectively nominal: visibility as a barrier maintaining the political underrepresentation of Britain's immigrant origin communities', *Parliamentary Affairs*, 72(3): 542–60.

Erens, B., Primatesta, P. and Prior, G. (2001) *Health Survey for England 1999: The Health of Minority Ethnic Groups*, London: The Stationery Office.

Esmail, A., Panagioti, M. and Kontopantelis, E. (2017) 'The potential impact of Brexit and immigration policies on the GP workforce in England: a cross-sectional observational study of GP qualification region and the characteristics of the areas and population they served in September 2016', *BMC Medicine*, 15(1): 191.

Evans, S. (2008) 'Consigning its past to history? David Cameron and the Conservative Party', *Parliamentary Affairs*, 61(2): 291–314.

Fekete, L. (2009) *A Suitable Enemy: Racism, Migration and Islamophobia in Europe*, London: Pluto Press.

Finney, N. and Harries, B. (2015) 'How has the rise in private renting disproportionality affected some ethnic groups? Ethnic differences in housing tenure 1991–2001–2011', Available from: http://hummedia.manchester.ac.uk/institutes/code/briefingsupdated/how-has-the-rise-in-private-renting-disproportionately-affected-some-ethnic-groups.pdf (accessed 2 December 2019).

Finney, N. and Simpson, L. (2009) *Sleepwalking to Segregation? Challenging Myths about Race and Migration*. Bristol: The Policy Press.

Finney, N., Lymperopoulou, K., Kapoor, N., Marshall, A., Sabater, A. and Simpson, L. (2011) *Local Ethnic Inequalities – Ethnic Differences in Education, Employment, Health and Housing in Districts of England and Wales, 2001–2011*, London: Runnymede Trust.

Fisher, S. D. et al. (2015) 'Candidate ethnicity and vote choice in Britain', *British Journal of Political Science*, 45(4): 883–905.

Florian, L., Rouse, M. and Black-Hawkins, K. (2016) *Achievement and Inclusion in Schools*, London: Routledge.

Flynn, D. (2016) 'Frontier anxiety: living with the stress of the everyday border', *Soundings*, 61: 62–71.

Ford, R. and Goodwin, M. (2014) *Revolt on the Right: Explaining Support for the Radical Right in Britain*, London: Routledge.

Ford, R. and Lowles, N. (2016) *Fear and Hope 2016: Race, Faith and Belonging in Contemporary England*, London: Hope Not Hate.

Ford, R., Curtice, J. and Fisher, S. (2010) 'Appendix 2: An analysis of the results' in Cowley, P. and Kavanagh, D. (eds) *The British General Election of 2010*, Basingstoke: Palgrave Macmillan.

Ford, R., Janta-Lipinski, L. and Sobolewska, M. (2015) 'Are the Conservatives really breaking through with ethnic minority voters?', Available from: https://yougov.co.uk/topics/politics/articles-reports/2015/06/12/are-conservatives-really-breaking-through-extend (accessed 29 October 2018).

Fox, J.E., Morosanu, L. and Szilassy, E. (2012) 'The racialization of the new European migration to the UK', *Sociology*, 46(4): 680–95.

Friedman, S. O'Brien, D. and Laurison, D. (2017) '"Like skydiving without a parachute": how class origin shapes occupational trajectories in British acting', *Sociology*, 51(5): 992–1010.

Froio, C. and Ganesh, B. (2018) 'The transnationalisation of far right discourse on Twitter', *European Societies*.

Frumkin, L.A. and Koutsoubou, M. (2013) 'An exploratory investigation of drivers of attainment in ethnic minority adult learners', *Journal of Further and Higher Education*, 37(2): 147–62.

Full Fact: The UK's Independent Factchecking Charity (2018) 'Windrush generation: what's the situation?', Available from: http:www.fullfact.org/immigration/windrush-generation/ (accessed 9 July 2019).

Garner, S. (2017) *Racisms: An Introduction*, 2nd edn, London: Sage.

Garnham, N. (2005) 'From cultural to creative industries: an analysis of the implications of the creative industries' approach to arts and media policy making in the United Kingdom', *International Journal of Cultural Policy*, 11(1): 15–29.

Gentleman, A. (2019) 'UK to pay up to £200m in compensation to Windrush victims', *The Guardian*, 3 April, Available from: www.theguardian.com/uk-news/2019/apr/03/uk-pay-windrush-victims-200m-compensation-lives-damaged-hostile-environment-policy (accessed 10 April 2019).

Gibney, E. (2013) 'Robbins: 50 years later', *Times Higher Education*, Available from: https://www.timeshighereducation.com/features/robbins-50-years-later/2008287.article (accessed 12 November 2019).

Gillborn, D. (2005) 'Education policy as an act of white supremacy: whiteness, critical race theory and education reform', *Journal of Education Policy*, 20(4): 485–505.

Gillborn, D. and Gipps, C.V. (1996) *Recent Research on the Achievements of Ethnic Minority Pupils*, London: The Stationery Office.

Gillborn, D. and Mirza, H.S. (2000) *Educational Inequality: Mapping Race, Class and Gender: A synthesis of research evidence*, London: Office of Standards of Education.

Gillborn, D. and Demack, S. (2018) *Exclusions Review 2018: Evidence on the Exclusion of Black Caribbean and Mixed: White/Black Caribbean Students*, University of Birmingham: Centre for Research in Race and Education.

Gillborn, D., Demack, S., Rollock, N. and Warmington, P. (2017) 'Moving the goalposts: education policy and 25 years of the Black/White achievement gap', *British Educational Research Journal*, 43(5): 848–74.

Gilroy, P. (1987a) 'The myth of black criminality', in P. Scraton (ed.) *Law, Order, and the Authoritarian State*, Milton Keynes: Open University Press.

Gilroy, P. (1987b) *There Ain't No Black in the Union Jack: The Cultural Politics of Race and Nation*, London: Hutchinson.

Gimson, A. (2013) 'Help to buy is immoral because it encourages ordinary people to risk ruin', Available from: www.conservativehome.com/thetorydiary/2013/11/help-to-buy-is-immoral-because-it-encourages-ordinary-people-to-risk-ruin.html (accessed 14 November 2018).

Giordano, P. (2019) 'Growing threat from far right as white extremists form largest proportion of terror arrests seen in 15 years', *The Independent*, 14 June.

Glass, R. (1960) *Newcomers: The West Indians in London*, London: George Allen and Unwin.

Golash-Boza, T. (2016) 'A critical and comprehensive theory of race and racism', *Sociology of Race and Ethnicity*, 2(2): 129–41.

Goodwin, M. (2013) *The Roots of Extremism: The English Defence League and the Counter-jihad Challenge*, Chatham House Briefing Paper, London.

Goodwin, M. and Milazzo, C. (2017) 'Taking back control? Investigating the role of immigration in the 2016 vote for Brexit', *British Journal of Politics and International Relations*, 19(3): 450–64.

Goodwin, M., Cutts, D. and Janta-Lipinski, L. (2016) 'Economic losers, protestors, Islamophobes or xenophobes? Predicting public support for a counter-Jihad movement', *Political Studies*, 64(1): 4–26.

Gordon, A. (2001) 'School exclusions in England: children's voices and adult solutions?', *Educational Studies*, 27(1): 69–85.

Goos, M. and Manning, A. (2007) 'Lousy and lovely jobs: the rising polarization of work in Britain', *Review of Economics and Statistics*, 89(1): 118–33.

Gov.scot (2017a) *Equality Evidence Finder*, Available from: https://scotland.shinyapps.io/sg-equality-evidence-finder/ (accessed 02 March 2019).

Gov.scot. (2017b) *School Education: Ethnicity and School Education*, Available from: https://www2.gov.scot/Topics/People/Equality/Equalities/DataGrid/Ethnicity/EthSchEd (accessed 29 July 2019).

Gov.uk (2017) *Race Disparity Audit*, Available from: https://www.gov.uk/government/publications/race-disparity-audit (accessed 8 December 2019).

Gov.uk (2018a) *Ethnicity Facts and Figures*, Available from: www.ethnicity-facts-figures.service.gov.uk/culture-and-community/culture-and-heritage/adults-taking-part-in-the-arts/latest (accessed 6 February 2019).

Gov.uk (2018b) *Ethnicity Facts and Figures: Education, Skills and Training*, Available from: https://www.ethnicity-facts-figures.service.gov.uk/education-skills-and-training (accessed 29 July 2019).

Gov.uk (2018c) *Criminal Courts*, Available from: https://www.gov.uk/courts (accessed 01 February 2019).

Gov.uk (2018d) *Police Workforce, England and Wales: 31 March 2018*, Available from: https://www.gov.uk/government/statistics/police-workforce-england-and-wales-31-march-2018 (accessed 02 March 2019).

Gov.uk (2018e) *Police Powers and Procedures, England and Wales, Year Ending 31 March 2018*, Available from: https://www.gov.uk/government/statistics/police-powers-and-procedures-england-and-wales-year-ending-31-march-2018 (accessed 08 March 2019).

Gov.uk (2018f) *Low Pay Commission Research 2018*, Available from: https://www.gov.uk/government/publications/low-pay-commission-research-2018 (accessed 19 November 2018).

Gower, M. (2015) 'Immigration and asylum: changes made by the Coalition Government 2010–2015', House of Commons Library: Standard Note SN/HA/5829. Available at: http://researchbriefings. parliament. UK/ResearchBriefing/Summary/SN05829# full report (accessed 12 November 2019).

ignite

Grant, M. (2018) 'The Windrush Generation have been treated appallingly. EU migrants may expect an even worse deal', *LSE Brexit* [Blog], Available from: https://blogs.lse.ac.uk/brexit/2018/04/20/the-windrush-generation-have-been-treated-appallingly-eu-migrants-may-expect-an-even-worse-deal/ (accessed 2 December 2019).

Gray, H. (2016) 'Precarious diversity: representation and demography', in M. Curtin and K. Sanson (eds) *Precarious Creativity: Global Media, Local Labour*, Berkeley: University of California Press.

Griffiths, M. (2017) 'The changing politics of time in the UK's immigration system', in E. Mayroudi, B. Page and A. Christou (eds) *Timespace and International Migration*, Cheltenham; Northampton: Edward Elgar, p 48.

Grugulis, I. and Stoyanova, D. (2012) 'Social capital and networks in film and TV: Jobs for the boys?', *Organization Studies*, 33(10): 1311–31.

The Guardian (2018a) 'NHS chiefs urged to stop giving patient data to immigration officials', *The Guardian*, 31 January, Available from: www.theguardian.com/society/2018/jan/31/nhs-chiefs-stop-patient-data-immigration-officials (accessed 31 October 2019).

The Guardian (2018b) 'Amber Rudd resigns hours after Guardian publishes deportation targets letter', *The Guardian*, 29 April, Available from: www.theguardian.com/politics/2018/apr/29/amber-rudd-resigns-as-home-secretary-after-windrush-scandal (accessed 1 June 2018).

Guild, E. (2000) 'The United Kingdom: Kosovar Albanian refugees', in J. van Selm (ed) *Kosovo's Refugees in the European Union*, London: Pinter.

Guild, E., Costello, C., Garlick, M. and Moreno-Lax, V. (2015) *The 2015 Refugee Crisis in the European Union*, Brussels: Centre for European Policy Studies.

Gupta, S. and Virdee, S. (2018) 'Introduction: European crises: contemporary nationalism and the language of race', *Ethnic and Racial Studies*, 41(10): 1747–64.

Hall, S. (2017) *The Fateful Triangle: Race, Ethnicity, Nation*, Cambridge, MA: Harvard University Press.

Hall, S., McIntosh, K., Neitzert, E., Pottinger, L., Sandhu, K., Stephenson, M.A. et al (2017) *Intersecting Inequalities: The Impact of Austerity on Black and Minority Ethnic Women in the UK*, Coventry: Women's Budget Group and Runnymede Trust.

Hamnett, C. and Butler, T. (2010) 'The changing ethnic structure of housing tenures in London, 1991–2001', *Urban Studies*, 47(1): 55–74.

Hannemann, T. and Kulu, H. (2015) 'Union formation and dissolution among immigrants and their descendants in the United Kingdom', *Demographic Research*, 33(10): 273–312.

Harding, L., Oltermann, P. and Watt, N. (2015) 'Refugees welcome? How UK and Germany compare on migration', Available from: www.theguardian.com/world/2015/sep/02/refugees-welcome-uk-germany-compare-migration (accessed 19 February 2019).

Harrison, M. and Phillips, D. (2010) 'Housing and neighbourhoods: a European perspective', in A. Bloch and J. Solomos (eds) *Race and Ethnicity in the 21st Century*, Basingstoke: Palgrave Macmillan.

Harrison, M., Phillips., D., Chahal., K., Hunt, L. and Perry, J. (2005) *Housing, 'Race' and Community Exclusion*, London: Jessica Kingsley Publishers.

Hart, A. (2009) *The Myth of Racist Kids: Anti-Racist Policy and the Regulation of School Life*, London: Manifesto.

Healthwatch Islington (2017) *Community Research 2016/2017: Black and Minority Ethnic Groups Accessing Services in Islington*, London: Healthwatch Islington.

Heath, A. and Cheung, S.Y. (2006) *Ethnic Penalties in the Labour Market: Employers and Discrimination*, DWP Research report 341. London: Department for Work and Pensions.

Heath, A. and Li, Y. (2018) 'Persisting disadvantages: a study of labour market dynamics of ethnic unemployment and earnings in the UK (2009–2015)', *Journal of Ethnic and Migration Studies*, DOI: 10.1080/1369183X.2018.1539241

Heath, A.F, Fisher, S.D, Rosenblatt, G., Sanders, D. and Sobolewska, M. (2013) *The Political Integration of Ethnic Minorities in Britain*, Oxford: Oxford University Press.

Henehan, K. and Rose, H. (2018) 'Opportunities knocked? Exploring pay penalties among the UK's ethnic minorities' Resolution Foundation, Available from: www.resolutionfoundation.org/app/uploads/2018/07/Opportunities-Knocked.pdf (accessed 11 November 2019).

Hesmondhalgh, D. and Saha, A. (2013) 'Race, ethnicity, and cultural production', *Popular Communication*, 11(3): 179–95.

Higher Education Staff Statistics (HESA) (2018) *Higher Education Staff Statistics: UK, 2016/17*, Available from: https://www.hesa.ac.uk/news/18-01-2018/sfr248-higher-education-staff-statistics (accessed 15 April 2019).

Hill, E., Sobolewska, M., Wilks-Heeg, S. and Borkowska, M. (2017) 'Explaining electoral fraud in an advanced democracy: fraud vulnerabilities, opportunities and facilitating mechanisms in British elections', *British Journal of Politics and International Relations*, 19(4): 772–89.

Hirsch, A. (2018a) *Brit(ish): On Race, Identity and Belonging*, London: Jonathan Cape.

Hirsh, A. (2018b) 'Glossies so white: the data that reveals the problem with British magazine covers', *The Guardian*, 10 April, Available from: www.theguardian.com/media/2018/apr/10/glossy-magazine-covers-too-white-models-black-ethnic-minority (accessed 12 November 2019).

Hirsch, A. (2018c) 'Britain doesn't just glorify its violent past: it gets high on it', *The Guardian*, 29 May, Available from: https://www.theguardian.com/commentisfree/2018/may/29/britain-glorify-violent-past-defensive-empire-drug (accessed 12 November 2019).

Hix, S., Kaufmann, E. and Leeper, T.J. (2017) 'UK voters, including Leavers, care more about reducing non-EU than EU migration', *The London School of Economics and Political Science*, 30 May, Available from: https://blogs.lse.ac.uk/europpblog/2017/05/30/uk-voters-including-leavers-care-more-about-reducing-non-eu-than-eu-migration/ (accessed 12 November 2019).

HM Government (2010) *Healthy Lives, Healthy People: Our Strategy for Public Health in England*, Norwich: The Stationery Office.

Hollywood Diversity Report (2019) *The Hollywood Diversity Report: 2019*, Available from: https://socialsciences.ucla.edu/wp-content/uploads/2019/02/UCLA-Hollywood-Diversity-Report-2019-2-21-2019.pdf (accessed 21 March 2019).

Home Office (2016) Immigration Act 2016, Available from: www.gov.uk/government/collections/immigration-bill-2015–16 (accessed 3 March 2019).

Home Office (2017) 'National statistics: how many people are detained or returned?', Available from: www.gov.uk/government/publications/immigration-statistics-october-to-december-2017/how-many-people-are-detained-or-returned (accessed 19 February 2019).

Home Office (2018a) 'Hate crime, England and Wales, 2017/18', *Statistical Bulletin*, 20/18, 16 October.

Home Office (2018b) 'Police workforce, England and Wales, 31 March 2018', Available from: www.gov.uk/government/statistics/police-workforce-england-and-wales-31-march-2018 (accessed 27 January 2020).

Home Office (2018c) 'Police powers and procedures, England and Wales, year ending 31 March 2018', Available from: www.gov.uk/government/statistics/police-powers-and-procedures-england-and-wales-year-ending-31-march-2018 (accessed 27 January 2020).

Home Office (2018d) 'Youth justice statistics, 2017 to 2018', Available from: www.gov.uk/government/statistics/youth-justice-statistics-2017-to-2018 (accessed 17 November 2019).

Hope Not Hate (2019) *State of Hate 2019: People Vs the Elite?* London: Hope Not Hate.

House of Commons Health Committee (2009) *Health Inequalities – Third Report of Session 2008–09*, vol. 1: *Report, together with formal minutes*, London: The Stationery Office.

House of Commons, House of Lords Joint Committee on Human Rights (2019) *Immigration Detention*, Sixteenth report of session 2017–2010, HC 1484, HL paper 278, 7 February.

House of Lords: Library Briefing (2018) 'Impact of "hostile environment"', Policy Debate 14 June.

Hughes, L. (2016) 'Labour MP Stephen Kinnock says the party has become obsessed with diversity', Available from: www.telegraph.co.uk/news/2016/11/23/labour-mp-stephen-kinnock-says-party-has-become-obsessed-diversity/ (accessed 5 April 2019).

Inquest (2018) 'BAME deaths in police custody', Available from: www.inquest.org.uk/bame-deaths-in-police-custody (accessed 8 May 2019).

Institute of Health Equality (2017) *Marmot Indicators Briefing Embargo*, UK: Institute of Health Equality.

Ip, J. (2013) 'The reform of counterterrorism stop and search after Gillan v United Kingdom', *Human Rights Law Review*, 13(4): 729–60.

Institute for Public Policy Research (IPPR) (2017) *Making the Difference: Breaking the link between school exclusion and social exclusion*, London: Institute for Public Policy Research, Available from: https://www.ippr.org/files/2017-10/making-the-difference-report-october-2017.pdf (accessed 14/11/19).

Institute of Employment Rights (2018) *Rolling out the Manifesto for Labour Law*, London: IER, Available from: https://www.ier.org.uk/sites/ier.org.uk/files/Briefing.pdf (accessed 12 November 2019).

Jackson, L. (2018) *Islamophobia in Britain: The Making of a Muslim Enemy*, Basingstoke: Palgrave Macmillan.

Javid, S. (2019) 'Letter from the Home Secretary, Windrush update to the Homa Affairs Committee', 19 March, Available from: https://www.parliament.uk/documents/commons-committees/home-affairs/Correspondence-17-19/Letter-from-the-Home-Secretary-Windrush-update-as-at-31-January-2019.pdf (accessed 30 October 2019).

Jivraj, S. and Byrne, B. (2015) 'Who feels British?', in S. Jivraj and L. Simpson *Ethnic Identity and Inequalities in Britain: The Dynamics of Diversity*, Bristol: Policy Press, pp 65–78.

Jivraj, S. and Simpson, L. (2015) 'How has ethnic diversity grown?', in S. Jivraj and L. Simpson *Ethnic Identity and Inequalities in Britain: The Dynamics of Diversity*, Bristol: Policy Press.

John, P., Margetts, H., Rowland, D. and Weir, S. (2006) *The BNP: The Roots of Its Appeal*, Essex: Democratic Audit.

Johnson, M. and Jayaweera, H. (2017) *Country Report: Migrant Integration Policy Index Health Strand*. Country Report, United Kingdom. Brussels: International Organisation for Migration.

Johnston, L. (2006) 'Diversifying police recruitment? The deployment of police community support officers in London', *Howard Journal of Crime and Justice*, 45(4): 388–402.

Jones, E. and Snow, S. (2011) 'Immigration and the National Health Service: putting history to the forefront', Available from: www.historyandpolicy.org/policy-papers/papers/immigration-and-the-national-health-service-putting-history-to-the-forefron (accessed: 7 January 2018).

Jones, H., Gunaratnam, Y., Bhattacharyya, G., Davies, W., Dhaliwal, S., Forkert, K., Jackson, E. and Saltus, R. (2017) *Go Home? The Politics of Immigration Controversies*, Manchester: Manchester University Press.

Joseph-Salisbury, R. (2019) 'Institutionalised whiteness, racial microaggressions and black bodies out of place in Higher Education', *Whiteness and Education*, 4(1): 1–17.

Joseph-Salisbury, R. and Connelly, L. (2018) 'If your hair is relaxed. White people are relaxed. If your hair is nappy, they're not happy. Black hair as a site of "post-racial" social control in English schools', *Social Sciences*, 7(11): 219.

Kallis, A. (2018) 'Islamophobia in the United Kingdom: National Report 2017', in E. Bayrakli and F. Hafaez (eds) *European Islamophobia Report*, London: Foundation for Political, Economic and Social Research.

Kantar Media (2018) *Representation and Portrayal of Audiences on BBC Television: Research Report*, Available from: www.ofcom.org.uk/__data/assets/pdf_file/0016/124252/kantar-bbc-qualitative-research.pdf (accessed 11 February 2019).

Kapadia, D., Nazroo, J. and Clark, K. (2015) 'Have ethnic inequalities in the labour market persisted?', in S. Jiyraj and L. Simpson (eds) *Ethnic Identity and Inequalities in Britain: The Dynamics of Ethnicity*, Bristol: Policy Press, pp 61–180.

Karatani, R. (2004) *Defining British Citizenship: Empire, Commonwealth and Modern Britain*. Abingdon: Routledge.

Kalra, V. (2000) *From Textile Mills to Taxi Ranks: Experiences of Migration, Labour and Social Change*, Aldershot: Ashgate Publishing.

Karlsen, S. (2007) *Ethnic Inequalities in Health: The Impact of Racism*, Better Health Briefing 3 – A Race Equality Foundation Briefing Paper, London: Race Equality Foundation.

Karlsen, S. and Nazroo, J.Y. (2002) 'The relationship between racial discrimination, social class and health among ethnic minority groups', *American Journal of Public Health*, 92(4): 624–31.

Karlsen, S. and Nazroo, J. (2014) 'Ethnic and religious variations in the reporting of racist victimization in Britain: 2000 and 2008/2009', *Patterns of Prejudice*, 48(4): 370–97.

Karyotis, G., Colburn, B., Doyle, L., Hermannsson, K., Mulvey, G. and Skleparis, D. (2018) 'Building a new life in Britain: the skills, experiences and aspirations of young Syrian refugees', Building Futures Policy Report No. 1, Glasgow: Policy Scotland.

Kassimeris, G. and Jackson, L. (2015) 'The ideology and discourse of the English Defence League: "Not racist, not violent, just no longer silent"', *British Journal of Politics and International Relations*, 17: 171–88.

Katwala, S. and Somerville, W. (2016) *Engaging the Anxious Middle on Immigration Reform: Evidence from the UK Debate*, Washington, DC: Migration Policy Institute.

Katz, J. and Jackson-Jacobs, C. (2004) 'The criminologists' gang', in Sumner, C. (ed) *The Blackwell Companion to Criminology*, Oxford: Blackwell, pp 91–124.

Kayem, G., Kurinczuk, J., Lewis, G., Golightly, S., Brocklehurst, P. and Knight, M. (2011) 'Risk factors for progression from severe maternal morbidity to death: a national cohort study', *PloS One*, 6(12): 29077.

Keeble, D. and Wilkinson, F. (2017) *High-technology Clusters, Networking and Collective Learning in Europe*, Abingdon: Routledge.

Keith, M. (1993) *Race, Riots and Policing: Lore and Disorder in a Multiracist Society,* London: UCL Press.

Kelley, N., Khan, O. and Sharrock, S. (2017) *Racial Prejudice in Britain Today*, London: NatCen Social Research.

Kelly, L. (2003) 'Bosnian refugees in Britain: questioning community', *Sociology*, 37(1): 35–49.

Khan, O. (2015) 'The future of multi-ethnic Britain: 15 years on', *Race Matters*, 9 October, Available from: https://www.runnymedetrust.org/blog/the-future-of-multi-ethnic-britain-15-years-on (accessed 30 October 2019).

Khan, O. and Shaheen. F. (2017) *Minority Report: Race and Class in Post-Brexit Britain*, London: Runnymede Trust, Available from: www.runnymedetrust.org/uploads/publications/pdfs/Race%20and%20Class%20PostBrexit%20Perspectives%20report%20v5.pdf (accessed 12 November 2019).

Khattab, N. (2018) 'Ethnicity and higher education: the role of aspirations, expectations and beliefs', *Ethnicities*, 18(4): 457–70.

Khoudja, Y. and Platt, L. (2018) 'Labour market entries and exits of women from different origin countries in the UK', *Social Science Research*, 69: 1–18.

Khunti, K., Kumar, S. and Brodie, J. (2009) *Diabetes UK and South Asian Health Foundation Recommendations on Diabetes Research Priorities for British South Asians*, London: Diabetes UK.

King, R. (2000) 'Generalizations from the history of return migration', in B. Ghosh (ed) *Return Migration: Journey of Hope or Despair?* Geneva: UN and the IOM, pp 7–55.

King, R., Christou, A. and Levitt, P. (2015) *Links to the Diasporic Homeland: Second Generation and Ancestral 'Return' Mobilities*, Abingdon: Routledge.

King's Fund (2006) *Access to Health Care for Ethnic Minority Population*, London: King's Fund.

King's Fund (2011) *Health Inequalities – Reading List*, London: King's Fund.

Kinnvall, C. (2017) 'Racism and the role of imaginary Others in Europe', *Nature Human Behaviour* 1, 0122: 1–4.

Kline, R. (2014) *The 'Snowy White Peaks' of the NHS*, UK: Middlesex University Research Repository, Available from: an open access repository of Middlesex University research. Available from: https://www.england.nhs.uk/wp-content/uploads/2014/08/edc7-0514.pdf (accessed 31 October 2019).

Kline, R. (2015) *Beyond the Snowy White Peaks*, UK: Race Equality Foundation.

Kofman, E. (2004) 'Family-related migration: a critical review of European Studies', *Journal of Ethnic and Migration Studies*, 30(2): 243–62.

Komaromi, P. and Singh, K. (2016) *Post-Referendum Racism and Xenophobia: The Role of Social Media Activism in Challenging the Normalisation of Xeno-Racist Narratives*, Available from: www.irr.org.uk/app/uploads/2016/07/PRRX-Report-Final.pdf (accessed 12 November 2019).

Koza, J.E. (2008) 'Listening for whiteness: hearing racial politics in undergraduate school music', *Philosophy of Music Education Review*, 16(2): 145–55.

Krieger, N. and Sidney, S. (1996) 'Racial discrimination and blood pressure: the CARDIA study of young Black and White adults', *American Journal of Public Health*, 86(10): 1370–8.

Krook, M.L. and Nugent, M.K. (2016) 'Intersectional institutions: representing women and ethnic minorities in the British Labour Party', *Party Politics*, 22(5): 620–30.

Kuhn, K.M. (2016) 'The rise of the "Gig Economy" and implications for understanding work and workers', *Industrial and Organizational Psychology*, 9(1): 157–62.

Kulu, H. and Hannemann, T. (2016) 'Why does fertility remain high among certain UK-born ethnic minority women?', *Demographic Research*, 35: 1441–88.

Kulu, H., Milewski, N., Hannemann, T. and Mikolai, J. (2019) 'A decade of life-course research on the fertility of immigrants and their descendants in Europe', *Demographic Research*, 40: 1345–74.

Kundnani, A. (2001) 'In a foreign land: the new popular racism', *Race & Class*, 43(2): 41–60.

Kundnani, A. (2007) 'Integrationism: The politics of anti-Muslim racism', *Race and Class*, 48(4): 24–44.

Kundnani, A. (2009) *Spooked: How Not to Prevent Violent Extremism*, London: IRR.

Kundnani, A. (2014) *The Muslims are Coming! Islamophobia, Extremism and the Domestic War on Terror*, London: Verso

Lammy, D. (2017) *The Lammy Review: An Independent Review into the Treatment of, and outcomes for, Black, Asian and Minority Ethnic Individuals in the Criminal Justice System*, London: HM Government.

Le Lohé, M. (2004) 'Ethnic minority participation and representation in the British electoral system', in S. Saggar (ed) *Race and British Electoral Politics*, Abingdon: Routledge.

Lester, A. (2003) 'Nailing the lie and promoting equality', Runnymede Trust, Jim Rose Lecture, 15 October, Available from: https://www.runnymedetrust.org/uploads/aLesterSpeech.pdf (accessed 30 October 2019).

Levin, S. (2018) 'Despite reckoning on Hollywood diversity, TV industry has gotten worse', *The Guardian*, 27 February, Available from: www.theguardian.com/tv-and-radio/2018/feb/27/tv-industry-diversity-women-people-of-color-decline (accessed 3 April 2019).

Lewis, S. and Starkey, J. (2015) *Ethnic Minority Pupils: Evidence Review and Practice in Wales*, Cardiff: Welsh Government Social Research.

Levy, F. and Murnane, R. (2007) 'How computerized work and globalization shape human skill demands', in M.M. Suárez-Orozco (ed) *Learning in the Global Era: International Perspectives on Globalization and Education*, Oakland, CA: University of California Press, pp158–74.

Li, Y. (2015) 'Ethnic minority unemployment in hard times', in C. Alexander and J. Arday (eds) *Aiming Higher: Race, Inequality & Diversity in the Academy*, London: Runnymede Trust.

Li, Y. and Heath, A. (2008) 'Minority ethnic men in the British labour market (1972–2005)', *International Journal of Sociology and Social Policy*, 28(5/6): 231–44.

Lidher, S. (2018) 'The Windrush generation: British citizenship and mobility control', *Media Diversified*, 20 April, Available from: https://mediadiversified.org/2018/04/20/the-windrush-generation-british-citizenship-and-mobility-control/ (accessed 14 November 2018).

Lievesley, N. (2010) *The Future Ageing of the Ethnic Minority Population of England and Wales*, London: Runnymede and the Centre for Policy on Ageing.

Lloyd, R. (2006) *Neo-Bohemia: Art and Commerce in the Postindustrial City*, New York: Routledge.

London, L. (2003) *Whitehall and the Jews, 1933-1948: British Immigration Policy, Jewish Refugees and the Holocaust*, Cambridge: Cambridge University Press.

Lordan, G. and Neumark, D. (2018) 'People versus machines: the impact of minimum wages on automatable jobs', *Labour Economics*, 52: 40–53.

Low Pay Commission (2018) National Minimum Wage: Low Pay Commission Report 2018, Available from: https://assets.publishing.service.gov.uk/government/uploads/system/uploads/attachment_data/file/759271/National_Minimum_Wage_-_Low_Pay_Commission_2018_Report.pdf (accessed 12 November 2019).

Lu, Y. and Qin, L. (2014) 'Healthy migrant and salmon bias hypotheses: a study of health and internal migration in China', *Social Science & Medicine*, 102: 41–8.

Lukes, S., de Noronha, N. and Finney, N. (2018) 'Slippery discrimination: a review of the drivers of migrant and minority housing disadvantage', *Journal of Ethnic and Migration Studies*: 1–19.

Lymperopoulou, K. and Finney, N. (2016) 'Socio-spatial factors associated with ethnic inequalities in districts of England and Wales, 2001–11', *Urban Studies*, doi: 10.1177/0042098016653725

Mac an Ghaill, M. (1988) *Young, Gifted and Black*, London: Open University Press.

Mac an Ghaill, M. and Haywood, C. (2014) 'Pakistani and Bangladeshi young men: re-racialization, class and masculinity within the neo-liberal school', *British Journal of Sociology of Education*, 35(5): 753–76.

Maclennan, D. and Gibb, K. (2018) *Brexit and Housing*, Glasgow: UK Collaborative Centre for Housing Evidence.

Macpherson, W. (1999) *The Stephen Lawrence Inquiry: Report of an Inquiry by Sir William Macpherson of Cluny*, London: HMSO.

MacRaild, D.M. (1999) *Irish migrants in modern Britain, 1750–1922*. Macmillan International Higher Education.

Madden, D.J. (2017) 'A catastrophic event', *City* 21(1): 1–5.

Malik, S. (2013) ' "Creative diversity": UK public service broadcasting after multiculturalism', *Popular Communication*, 11(3): 227–41.

Malik, S. (2018) 'Diversity: reflection and review', in D. Freedman and V. Goblot (eds) *A Future for Public Service Television*, London: Goldsmiths Press, pp 92–102.

Markkanen, S. and Harrison, M. (2013) ' "Race", deprivation and the research agenda: revisiting housing, ethnicity and neighbourhoods', *Housing Studies*, 28(3): 409–28.

Marmot, M. (2010) *Fair Society Healthy Lives: Strategic Review of Health Inequalities in England Post-2010*, Marmot review final report, London: University College London, Available from: http://www.instituteofhealthequity.org/resources-reports/fair-society-healthy-lives-the-marmot-review (accessed 2 December 2019).

Marmot, M.G., Adelstein, A.M., Bulusu, L. and OPCS (1984) *Immigrant Mortality in England and Wales 1970–78: Causes of Death by Country of Birth*, London: HMSO.

Martin, J. (2016) 'Universal Credit to Basic Income: a politically feasible transition?', *Basic Income Studies*, 11(2): 97–131.

Martin, N.S. (2019) 'Ethnic minority voters in the UK 2015 general election: a breakthrough for the Conservative Party?', *Electoral Studies*, 57: 174–85.

Martin, N. and Khan O. (2019) *Ethnic Minorities at the 2017 British General Election* [pdf], London: Runnymede Trust.

Martin, N. and Mellon, J. (2018) 'The puzzle of high political partisanship among ethnic minority young people in Great Britain', *Journal of Ethnic and Migration Studies* : 1–21.

Martin, N., Sobolewska, M. and Begum, N. (2019) 'Left out of the left behind: ethnic minority support for Brexit', Available from: https://ssrn.com/abstract=3320418 or http://dx.doi.org/10.2139/ssrn.3320418 (accessed 22 January 2019).

Massey, D.S. and Denton, N.A. (1988) 'The dimensions of residential segregation', *Social Forces*, 16(2): 281–315.

Maylor, U. (2015) 'Challenging cultures in initial teacher education', in C. Alexander, D. Weekes-Bernard and J. Arday (eds) *The Runnymede School Report: Race, Education and Inequality in Contemporary Britain*, London: Runnymede Trust.

McCall, L. (2002) *Complex Inequality: Gender, Class and Race in the New Economy*, Abingdon: Routledge.

McDougall J. and Wagner K. (2018) 'Don't mistake nostalgia about the British Empire for scholarship', *Times Higher Education*, April, Available from: www.timeshighereducation.com/blog/dont-mistake-nostalgia-about-british-empire-scholarship (accessed 12 November 2019).

McDougall, J., Omar, H., O'Halloran, E. et al (2017) 'Ethics and empire: an open letter from Oxford scholars', *The Conversation*, 19 December, Available from: https://theconversation.com/ethics-and-empire-an-open-letter-from-oxford-scholars-89333?utm_source=twitter&utm_medium=twitterbutton (accessed 30 October 2019).

McGregor-Smith, R. (2017) *Race in the Workplace: The McGregor-Smith Review*. London: Department for Business, Energy and Industrial Strategy.

McGuinness, T. and Gower, M. (2017) 'Deprivation of British citizenship and withdrawal of passport facilities', Briefing Paper, number SN06820, 9 June.

McKinsey & Co. (2015) 'Why diversity matters?', Available from: https://assets.mckinsey.com/~/media/857F440109AA4D13 A54D9C496D86ED58.ashx (accessed 11 February 2019).

MDSAS (2017) *National Haemoglobinopathy Registry: Annual Report 2016/17*, Manchester: Medical Data Services and Solutions.

Meen, G. (2018) *Approaches for Improving Affordability: Policy Briefing*, Glasgow: UK Collaborative Centre.

Meer, N. and Modood. T. (2009) 'Refutations of racism in the "Muslim question"', *Patterns of Prejudice*, 43(3–4): 335–54.

Meer, N. and Nayak, A. (2015) 'Race ends where? Race, racism and contemporary sociology', *Sociology* 49(6): NP3-NP20 (E-Special Issue).

Menz, G. (2011) 'Neoliberalism, privatisation and the outsourcing of migration management: a five-country comparison', *Competition and Change*, 15(2): 116–35.

Metcalf, D. (2016) *Analysis: Why 361,000 Nurses Are Not Enough to Maintain the Health of NHS England*, London: Management with Impact.

Metropolitan Police (2017) *Section 60 Criminal Justice and Public Order Act 1994*, The Metropolitan Police, Available from: https://www.met.police.uk/SysSiteAssets/media/downloads/central/advice/met/stop-and-search/section-60-stop-and-search.PDF (accessed 31 March 2019).

Miah, S. (2017) *Muslims, Schooling and Security: Trojan Horse, Prevent and Racial Politics*, Basingstoke: Palgrave Macmillan

Migrants' Rights Network (2017) *Migrants' Perspectives on Brexit and UK Immigration Policies*, London: Migrants' Rights Network.

Migration Observatory (2016) 'Characteristics and outcomes of migrants in the UK labour market, Available from: www.migrationobservatory.ox.ac.uk/resources/briefings/characteristics-and-outcomes-of-migrants-in-the-uk-labour-market/ (accessed 10 February 2018).

Migration Observatory (2017) *Migrants in the UK: An Overview*, Available from: www.migrationobservatory.ox.ac.uk/resources/briefings/migrants-in-the-uk-an-overview/ (accessed 4 March 2017).

Millar, J. and Bennett, F. (2017) 'Universal credit: assumptions, contradictions and virtual reality', Social Policy and Society, 16(2): 169–82.

Miller, J. (2010) 'Stop and search in England: a reformed tactic or business as usual?', *British Journal of Criminology*, 50: 954–74.

Ministry of Housing, Communities and Local Government (2018) 'Annual day of celebrations for the Windrush generation', press release, Available from: https://www.gov.uk/government/news/annual-day-of-celebrations-for-the-windrush-generation (accessed 30 October 2019).

Mirza, H. (2015) '"Harvesting our collective intelligence": Black British feminism in post-race times', *Women's Studies International Forum* 51: 1–9.

Moch, L.P. (2003) *Moving Europeans: Migration in Western Europe since 1650*, Bloomington: Indiana University Press.

Modood, T. (1997) *Ethnic Minorities in Britain: Diversity and Disadvantage*, London: Policy Studies Institute.

Moore, R. (2011) 'Forty-four years of debate: the impact of race, community and conflict', *Sociological Research Online*, 16(3): 1–8.

Moriarty, J., Sharif, N. and Robinson, J. (2011) *Black and Minority Ethnic people with Dementia and Their Access to Support and Services*, Research Briefing Paper 35, London: Social Care Institute for Excellence.

Morris, A. (2017) 'Lack of diversity within UK's creative industries revealed', Available from: www.dezeen.com/2017/08/07/lack-diversity-uk-creative-industries-revealed-government-report-dcms-digital-culture-media-sport/ (accessed 3 April 2019).

Muroki, M. and Cowley, P. (2019) 'Getting better, slowly: ethnicity, gender and party in London's local government', *Political Quarterly*, 90: 117–23.

Musterd, S. and Andersson, R. (2005) 'Housing mix, social mix, and social opportunities', *Urban Affairs Review*, 40(6): 761–90.

Musterd, S. and Van Kempen, R. (2009) 'Segregation and housing of minority ethnic groups in Western European cities', *Tijdschrift voor economische en sociale geografie*, 100(4): 559–66.

Mygov.scot (2018) *Understanding Criminal Justice*, Available from: https://www.mygov.scot/criminal-justice-system/ (accessed 11 November 2019).

Nair, M., Kurinczuk, J.J. and Knight, M. (2014) 'Ethnic variations in severe maternal morbidity in the UK – a case control study', *PLoS One*, 9(4): 95086.

Nair, M., Knight, M. and Kurinczuk, J.J. (2016) 'Risk factors and newborn outcomes associated with maternal deaths in the UK from 2009 to 2013: a national case-control study', *BJOG: An International Journal of Obstetrics & Gynaecology*, 123(10): 1654–62.

National Audit Office (2008) *Department for Work and Pensions: Increasing Employment Rates for Ethnic Minorities*, Available from: www.nao.org.uk/report/increasing-employment-rates-for-ethnic-minorities/ (accessed 23 January 2018).

National Audit Office (2017) *The BBC's Understanding of Its Audiences and Users*, Available from: www.nao.org.uk/wp-content/uploads/2017/12/The-BBCs-understanding-of-its-audiences-and-users.pdf (accessed 15 April 2019).

National Cancer Experience Patient Survey (2016) *National Results Survey*, Available from: www.ncpes.co.uk/index.php/reports/2016-reports (accessed: 2 February 2018).

Nazroo, J.Y. (1998) 'Genetic, cultural or socio-economic vulnerability? Explaining ethnic inequalities in health', *Sociology of Health & Illness*, 20(5): 710–30.

Nazroo, J.Y. (2001a) *Ethnicity, Class and Health*, London: Policy Studies Institute.

Nazroo, J.Y. (2001b) 'South Asians and heart disease: an assessment of the importance of socioeconomic position', *Ethnicity & Disease*, 11(3): 401–11.

Nazroo, J.Y. (2015) 'Ethnic inequalities in severe mental disorders: where is the harm?', *Social Psychiatry and Psychiatric Epidemiology*, 50(7): 1065–7, doi: 10.1007/s00127-015-1079-1

Nazroo, J.Y. (2017) *Introductory Comments on Ethnic Inequalities in Health*, UK: Workforce Race Equality Standard.

Nazroo, J.Y., Falaschetti, E., Pierce, M. and Primatesta, P. (2009) 'Ethnic inequalities in access to and outcomes of healthcare: analysis of the Health Survey for England', *Journal of Epidemiology and Community Health*, 63(12): 1022–7.

NHS (2013a) *A Refreshed Equality Delivery System for the NHS – EDS2 Making Sure that Everyone Counts*, UK: NHS England.

NHS (2013b) *Report of the Mid Staffordshire NHS Foundation Trust Public Inquiry*, UK: NHS England.

NHS (2014) *The Five Year Forward View*, UK: NHS England.

NHS (2016a) *The Workforce Race Equality Standard*, UK: NHS England.

NHS (2016b) *The Five Year Forward View for Mental Health*, UK: NHS.

NHS (2017) *Public Health Outcomes Framework Health Equity Report*, UK: NHS England.

NHS Digital (2017) *Mental Health Act Statistics, Annual Figures: 2016–17*, Experimental Statistics Publication, 10 October, Available from: www.digital.nhs.uk/catalogue/PUB30105 (accessed 12 November 2019).

NHS England Analytical Services & the Equality and Heath Inequalities Unit (2017) *England Analysis: NHS Outcome Framework Health Inequalities Indicators 2016/17*, UK: NHS England.

NHS England/Commissioning Strategy/Equality and Health Inequalities Unit (2015) *Guidance for NHS Commissioners on Equality and Health Inequalities: Legal Duties*, UK: NHS England.

NIdirect (2019) 'Introduction to the criminal justice system', Available from: www.nidirect.gov.uk/articles/introduction-justice-system (accessed 1 May 2019).

Norris, P. and Lovenduski, J. (1995) *Political Recruitment: Gender, Race and Class in the British Parliament*, Cambridge: Cambridge University Press.

Norris, P., Geddes, A. and Lovenduski, J. (1992) 'Race and parliamentary representation', *British Elections and Parties Yearbook*, 2(1): 92–110.

Nixon, S. and Crewe, B. (2004) 'Pleasure at work? Gender, consumption and work-based identities in the creative industries', *Consumption Markets and Culture*, 7(2): 129–47.

Oakley, K. and O'Brien, D. (2016) 'Learning to labour unequally: understanding the relationship between cultural production, cultural consumption and inequality', *Social Identities*, 22(5): 471–86.

Ofcom (2018) *Diversity and Equal Opportunities in Television: In-focus Report on the Main Five Broadcasters*, Available from: www.ofcom.org.uk/__data/assets/pdf_file/0019/121681/diversity-in-TV-2018-in-focus.pdf (accessed 4 May 2019).

Olusoga, A. (2018) 'The Windrush story was not a rosy one even before the ship arrived', *The Guardian*, 22 April, Available from: https://www.theguardian.com/commentisfree/2018/apr/22/windrush-story-not-a-rosy-one-even-before-ship-arrived (accessed 6 October 2019).

ONS (Office for National Statistics) (2013) *Immigration Patterns of Non-UK born Populations in England and Wales in 2011*, Newport: Office for National Statistics.

ONS (2015) 'People identifying as "Other White" has increased by over a million since 2001', 26 June, Available from: http://visual.ons.gov.uk/ethnicity-2011-census (accessed 30 October 2019).

ONS (2016a) *Public Sector Employment, UK: March 2016*, Available from: https://www.ons.gov.uk/employmentandlabourmarket/peopleinwork/publicsectorpersonnel/bulletins/publicsectoremployment/march2016 (accessed 19 November 2019).

ONS (2016b) Statistical bulletin: Public sector employment, UK: March 2016. The official measure of people employed in the UK public sector, including private sector estimates, based on the difference between total UK employment and public sector employment.

ONS (2017) Crime and Justice: Figures on Crime Levels and Trends for England and Wales Based Primarily on Two Sets of Statistics: The Crime Survey for England and Wales (CSEW) and Police Recorded Crime Data, Available from: https://www.ons.gov.uk/peoplepopulationandcommunity/crimeandjustice (accessed 31 March 2019).

ONS (2018) Crime Survey for England and Wales, year ending March 2018, Available from: www.ons.gov.uk/peoplepopulationandcommunity/crimeandjustice (accessed 20 September 2019).

ONS (2019) 'Female employment rate (aged 16 to 64, seasonally adjusted)', Available from: www.ons.gov.uk/employmentandlabourmarket/peopleinwork/employmentandemployeetypes/timeseries/lf25/lms (accessed 18 February 2019).

Pantazis, C. and Pemberton, S. (2009) 'From the "old" to the "new" suspect community: examining the impacts of recent UK counter-terrorist legislation', *British Journal of Criminology*, 49(5): 646–66.

Parekh, B. (2000) *The Future of Multi Ethnic Britain*, London: Runnymede Trust/Profile Books.

Parmar, A. (2011) 'Stop and search in London: counter-terrorist or counter-productive?', *Policing and Society*, 21(4): 369–82.

Parsons, C. (2018) 'The continuing school exclusion scandal in England', *FORUM: For Promoting 3-19 Comprehensive Education*, 60(2): 245–54.

Patel, N., Batista Ferrer, H., Tyrer, F., Wray, P., Farooqi, A., Davies, M J. et al (2016) 'Barriers and facilitators to healthy lifestyle changes in minority ethnic populations in the UK: a narrative review', *Journal of Racial and Ethnic Health Disparities*, 4(6): 1107–9.

Peace, T. and Akhtar, P. (2015) 'Biraderi, bloc votes and Bradford: investigating the Respect Party's campaign strategy', *British Journal of Politics and International Relations*, 17(2): 224–43.

Peach, C. (1998) 'South Asian and Caribbean ethnic minority housing choice in Britain', *Urban Studies*, 35(10): 1657–80.

Peach, C. (2006) 'South Asian migration and settlement in Great Britain, 1951–2001', *Contemporary South Asia*, 15(2): 133–46.

Peach, C. and Shah, S. (1980) 'The contribution of council house allocation to West Indian desegregation in London, 1961–71', *Urban Studies*, 17(3): 333–41.

Peacock, L. (2014) '"Black people don't become teachers": the racist careers advice Malorie Blackman ignored', *The Telegraph* [online], 4 April, Available from: https://www.telegraph.co.uk/women/womens-life/10744007/Black-people-dont-become-teachers-The-racist-careers-advice-author-Malorie-Blackman-ignored.html (accessed 28 November 2018).

Pemberton, S. (2009) 'Economic migration from the EU 'A8' accession countries and the impact on low-demand housing areas: opportunity or threat for Housing Market Renewal Pathfinder programmes in England?', *Urban Studies*, 46(7): 1363–84.

Perry, J. (2012) *UK Migrants and the Private Rented Sector: A Policy and Practice Report from the Housing and Migration network*, York: Joseph Rowntree Foundation.

Peters, S. (2015) 'Ethnic inequalities in low pay', in Manchester Policy Blogs: All posts, Available at: www.blog.policy.manchester.ac.uk/posts/2015/03/ethnic-inequality-in-low-pay/ (accessed 9 July 2018).

Phillips, C. (2010) 'Institutional racism and ethnic inequalities: an expanded multilevel framework', *Journal of Social Policy*, 40(1): 173–92.

Phillips, D. (2006) 'Parallel lives? Challenging discourses of British Muslim self-segregation', *Environment and Planning D: Society and Space*, 24(1): 25–40.

Phillips, D. and Karn, V. (1992) 'Race and housing in a property owning democracy', *Journal of Ethnic and Migration Studies*, 18(3): 355–69.

Phillips, D. and Robinson, D. (2015) 'Reflections on migration, community, and place', *Population, Space and Place*, 21(5): 409–20.

Phillips, D. and Unsworth, R. (2002) 'Widening locational choices for minority ethnic groups in the Social Rented Sector', in A. Steele and P. Somerville (eds) *'Race', Housing and Social Cohesion*, Oxford: Alden Press/Chartered Institute of Housing.

Pilkington, H. (2016) *Loud and Proud: Passion and Politics in the English Defence League*, Manchester: Manchester University Press.

Powell, A. (2019) *Apprenticeships and Skills Policy in England*, House of Commons Briefing, Number CBP 03052, 7 January, Available from: file://nask.man.ac.uk/home$/Downloads/SN03052.pdf (accessed 12 November 2019).

Poynting, S. and Mason, V. (2006) ' "Tolerance, freedom, justice and peace"? Britain, Australia and anti-Muslim racism since 11 September 2001', *Journal of Intercultural Studies*, 27(4): 365–91.

Prentoulis, M., Naidoo, R., Dorling, D., Ghadiali, A., Piacentini, T., Corbett, R. et al (2017) 'After Brexit', *Soundings*, 64(64): 41–82.

Press Association (2018) 'Arts should do more to embrace diversity', Available from: www.telegraph.co.uk/art/artists/arts-should-do-embrace-diversity-says-former-tate-chief/ (accessed 4 February 2019).

Pronczuk, M. (2018) 'Europeans caught up in Britain's homelessness crisis', Available from: www.ft.com/content/c59a288c-0451-11e9-99df-6183d3002ee1 (accessed 8 April 2019).

PAC (Public Accounts Committee) (2008) 'Increasing employment rates for ethnic minorities', Available from: https://publications.parliament.uk/pa/cm200708/cmselect/cmpubacc/472/472.pdf (accessed 12 November 2019).

Public Health England (2017) *Public Health Outcomes Framework: Health Equity Report – Focus on Ethnicity*, London: Public Health England.

Quarashi, F. (2018) 'The Prevent strategy and the UK 'war on terror': embedding infrastructures of surveillance in Muslim communities', *Palgrave Communications*, 4(17): 1–13.

Quinn, B. (2019) 'County lines drugs blamed for Kent's big rise in knife crime', *The Guardian*, 10 March, Available from: https://www.theguardian.com/uk-news/2019/mar/10/county-lines-drugs-kent-knife-crime-rise-cuts (accessed 07 April 2019).

Rallings, C. and Thrasher, M. (2013) *Local Elections in Britain*, Abingdon: Routledge.

Ram, M., Edwards, P., Meardi, G., Jones, T., Doldor, S., Kispeter, E. and Villares-Varela, M. (2017) *Non-Compliance and the National Living Wage: Case Study Evidence from Ethnic Minority and Migrant-Owned Businesses*, London: Low Pay Commission, Available from: https://assets.publishing.service.gov.uk/government/uploads/system/uploads/attachment_data/file/660578/RamEdwardsMeardiJonesDoldorKispeterVillares-Varela_FINAL_2017_Report.pdf (accessed 12 November 2019).

Rampton, A. (1981) *Interim Report of the Committee of Inquiry into the Education of Children from Ethnic Minority Groups: West Indian Children in our Schools*, London: The Stationery Office.

Ratcliffe, P. (1996) *'Race' and Housing in Bradford: Addressing the Needs of the South Asian, African and Caribbean Communities*, Bradford: Bradford Housing Forum, Bradford Metropolitan District Council.

Rattansi, A. (1992) 'Changing the subject: racism, culture and education', in J. Donald and A. Rattansi *Race, Culture and Difference*, London: Sage.

Reay, D. and Mirza, H.S. (1997) 'Uncovering genealogies of the margins: black supplementary schooling', *British Journal of Sociology of Education*, 18(4): 477–99.

Redclift, V. (2014) 'New racisms, new racial subjects? The neo-liberal moment and the racial landscape of contemporary Britain', *Ethnic and Racial Studies*, 37(4): 577–88.

Refugee Council (2018) 'Terms and definitions: glossary of terminology relating to asylum seekers and refugees in the UK', Available from: www.refugeecouncil.org.uk/glossary (accessed 10 May 2018).

Rehman, H. and Owen, D. (2013) *Mental Health Survey of Ethnic Minorities*, Ethnos Research and Consultancy, University of Warwick.

Rex, J. and Moore, R.S. (1969) *Race, Community and Conflict: A Study of Sparkbrook*, London: Institute of Race Relations.

Rhodes, J. and Brown, L. (2018) 'The rise and fall of the "inner city": race, space and urban policy in postwar England', *Journal of Ethnic and Migration Studies*: 1–17.

Richardson, R. (2015) 'Narrative, nation and classrooms: the latest twists and turns in a perennial debate', in C. Alexander, D. Weekes-Bernard and J. Arday (eds) *The Runnymede School Report: Race, Education and Inequality in Contemporary Britain*, London: Runnymede Trust.

Riley, C.L. (2018) 'Imperial history wars', *History Workshop*, 19 March, Available at: http://www.historyworkshop.org.uk/imperial-history-wars/ (accessed 7 August 2019).

Robinson, D. (2002) 'Missing the target? Discrimination and exclusion in the allocation of social housing', in A. Steele and P. Somerville (eds) *'Race', Housing and Social Exclusion*, London: Jessica Kingsley Publishers, pp 94–113.

Robinson, D. (2005) 'The search for community cohesion: key themes and dominant concepts of the public policy agenda', *Urban Studies*, 42(8): 1411–27.

Robinson, D. (2010) 'New immigrants and migrants in social housing in Britain: discursive themes and lived realities', *Policy & Politics*, 38(1): 57–77.

Robinson, V. (1986) *Transients, Settlers, and Refugees: Asians in Britain*, Oxford: Clarendon.

Robinson, V. and Andersson, R. (2003) *Spreading the 'Burden'?: A Review of Policies to Disperse Asylum Seekers and Refugees*, Bristol: Policy Press.

Rollock, N. (2019) *Staying Power: The Career Experiences of UK Black Female Professors*, report for the University and College Union, London.

Rose, J. (1969) *Colour and Citizenship: A Report on British Race Relations*, London: Institute of Race Relations/Oxford University Press.

Ross, A. and Rudgard, O. (2014) 'Al Jedda: the man mentioned 11 times by Home Office as it tried to change immigration bill', 17 June 2019, Available from: www.thebureauinvestigates.com/stories/2014-07-11/al-jedda-the-man-mentioned-11-times-by-home-office-as-it-tried-to-change-immigration-bill (accessed 12 November 2019.

Rudat, K. (1994) *Black and Minority Ethnic Groups in England: Health and Lifestyles*, London: Health Education Authority.

Runnymede Trust (1997) *Islamophobia: A Challenge for Us All*, London: Runnymede Trust.

Runnymede Trust (2007) *Discrimination Law Review: A Framework for Fairness – Green Paper Consultation Response*, London: Runnymede Trust.

Runnymede Trust (2017a) *Ethnic Minorities at the 2017 British General Election*, Available from: www.runnymedetrust.org/uploads/2017%20Election%20Briefing.pdf (accessed 4 June 2019).

Runnymede Trust (2017b) *Islamophobia: Still A Challenge for Us All*, London: Runnymede Trust.

Rzepnikowska, A. (2019) 'Racism and xenophobia experienced by Polish migrants in the UK before and after Brexit vote', *Journal of Ethnic and Migration Studies*, 45(1): 61–77.

Saalfeld, T. and Bischof, D. (2012) 'Minority-ethnic MPs and the substantive representation of minority interests in the House of Commons, 2005–2011', *Parliamentary Affairs*, 66(2): 305–28.

Sabater, A. and Simpson, L. (2009) 'Enhancing the population census: a time series for sub-national areas with age, sex, and ethnic group dimensions in England and Wales, 1991–2001', *Journal of Ethnic and Migration Studies*, 35(9): 1461–77.

Saggar, S. and Geddes, A. (2000) 'Negative and positive racialisation: re-examining ethnic minority political representation in the UK', *Journal of Ethnic and Migration studies*, 26(1): 25–44.

Sainsbury Centre for Mental Health (2002) *Breaking the Circles of Fear: A Review of the Relationships between Mental Health Services and African and African Caribbean Communities*, London: Sainsbury Centre for Mental Health.

Sallah, D., Sashidharan, S., Stone, R., Struthers, J. and Blofeld, J. (2003) *Independent Inquiry into the Death of David Bennett*, Cambridge: Norfolk, Suffolk and Cambridgeshire Strategic Health Authority.

Sanders, D., Heath, A., Fisher, S. and Sobolewska, M. (2014b) 'The calculus of ethnic minority voting in Britain', *Political Studies*, 62(2): 230–51.

Sandhu, K. (2016) *Universal Credit and Impact on Black and Minority Ethnic Communities*, Race Equality Foundation, Better Housing Briefing 27, Available from: https://raceequalityfoundation.org.uk/community/universal-credit-and-impact-on-black-and-minority-ethnic-communities/ (accessed 19 July 2018).

Scott, S. and Brindley, P. (2012) 'New geographies of migrant settlement in the UK', *Geography*, 97: 29–38.

Secret Teacher (2018) 'Secret teacher: the UK has a complex racial history. Why aren't we teaching it?', *The Guardian* [blog], 20 January, Available from: https://www.theguardian.com/teacher-network/2018/jan/20/secret-teacher-uk-history-of-race-bloody-racism (accessed 28 November 2018).

Sewell, H. and Waterhouse, S. (2012) *Making Progress on Race Equality in Mental Health*, UK: Mental Health Network NHS Confederation and the Afiya Trust.

Shaffi, S. (2016) 'Publishing seeks to address the industry's lack of diversity', *The Bookseller*, Available from: www.thebookseller.com/news/publishing-seeks-address-industry-s-lack-diversity-426031 (accessed 6 February 2019).

Shelter (2004) *The Black and Minority Ethnic Housing Crisis*, Available from: https://england.shelter.org.uk/__data/assets/pdf_file/0009/48555/The_Black_and_Ethnic_Minority_Housing_Crisis_Sep_2004.pdf (accessed 20 September 2018).

Shelter (2008) *Policy: Briefing – Eastern European Migrant Workers and Housing*,. Available from: https://england.shelter.org.uk/__data/assets/pdf_file/0005/88331/1519_PolicyBrief_MigrantWorkers_V6FIN_Lo.pdf (accessed 2 December 2019).

Shelter (2017) *BAME Homelessness Matters and is Disproportionately Rising – Time for the Government to Act*, Available from: blog.shelter.org.uk/2017/10/bame-homelessness-matters-and-is-disproportionateoy-rising-time-for-the-government-to-act/ (accessed 21 September 2018).

Shiner, M., Carre, Z., Delsol, R. and Eastwood, N. (2018) *The Colour of Injustice: 'Race', Drugs and Law Enforcement in England and Wales*, London: Stop Watch & Release.

Shukla, N. (2016) *The Good Immigrant*, London: Unbound.

Silverman, S.J. and Hajela, R. (2011) 'Immigration detention in the UK', Migration Observatory Briefing, COMPAS, University of Oxford, Available from: http://migrationobservatory. ox. ac. uk/sites/files/migobs/Immigration% 20Detention% 20Briefing. pdf.\ (accessed 1 November 2019).

Silverman, S.J. and Griffiths, M.E.B. (2019) 'Immigration detention in the UK', Oxford: Migration Observatory, COMPAS, University of Oxford, Available from: https://migrationobservatory.ox.ac.uk/resources/briefings/immigration-detention-in-the-uk/ (accessed 30 October 2019).

Simpson, J.M. (2018) Where are UK trained doctors? The migrant care law and its implications for the NHS', *British Medical Journal*, 361: k2336.

Simpson, L. and Jivraj, S. (2015) 'Why has ethnic diversity grown?', in S. Jivraj and L. Simpson (eds) *Ethnic Identity and Inequalities in Britain: The Dynamics of Diversity*, Bristol: Policy Press, pp 33–47.

Simpson, L., Jivraj, S. and Warren, J. (2016) 'The stability of ethnic identity in England and Wales 2001–2011', *Journal of the Royal Statistical Society. Series A (Statistics in Society)*, 179: 1025–49.

Singh, A. (2019) 'BBC appoints first white man – Britain's "only openly Tory comic" – to its diversity panel', Available from: www.telegraph.co.uk/news/2019/05/01/bbc-appoints-britains-openly-tory-comic-diversity-panel/ (accessed 4 May 2019).

Singh, S. and Khan, O. (2019) 'On National Windrush Day, this is the history of British immigration policy ...', *Independent*, 22 June, Available from: https://www.independent.co.uk/voices/national-windrush-day-2019-theresa-may-hostile-environment-race-migration-a8970421.html (accessed 30 October 2019).

Slater, T. (2018) 'The invention of the "sink estate": consequential categorisation and the UK housing crisis', *Sociological Review*, 66(4): 877–97.

Small, S. and Solomos, J. (2006) 'Race, immigration and politics in Britain: changing policy agendas and conceptual paradigms, 1940s–2000s', *International Journal of Comparative Sociology* 47(3–4): 235–57.

Snow, G. (2017) 'Exclusive: "Woeful" lack of diversity revealed among drama school teachers', Available from: www.thestage.co.uk/news/2017/woeful-lack-diversity-revealed-among-dramaschoolteachers/?login_to=https%3A%2F%2Fwww.thestage.co.uk%2Faccounts%2Fusers%2Fsign_up.popup (accessed 6 February 2019).

Snow, S. and Jones, E. (2011) *Immigration and the National Health Service: Putting History to the Forefront*, London: History and Policy.

Sobolewska, M. (2013) 'Party strategies and the descriptive representation of ethnic minorities: the 2010 British general election', *West European Politics*, 36(3): 615–33.

Sobolewska, M. (2015) 'The Conservatives' BME MPs may be game changers in the way we think about ethnic minority representation', Available from: www.democraticaudit.com/2015/04/07/the-conservatives-bme-mps-may-be-game-changers-in-the-way-we-think-about-ethnic-minority-representation (accessed 29 October 2018).

Sobolewska, M. (2017) 'Increased diversity in Parliament: the case for centralising candidate nominations', *British Politics Review*, Oslo: British Politics Society, pp 20–2.

Sobolewska, M. and Ford, R. (2019) 'British culture wars? Brexit and the future politics of immigration and ethnic diversity', *Political Quarterly* 90(S2): 142–54.

Sobolewska, M., Galandini, S. and Lessard-Phillips, L. (2017) 'The public view of immigrant integration: multidimensional and consensual – evidence from survey experiments in the UK and the Netherlands', *Journal of Ethnic and Migration Studies*, 43(1): 58–79.

Sobolewska, M., McKee, R. and Campbell, R. (2018) 'Explaining motivation to represent: how does descriptive representation lead to substantive representation of racial and ethnic minorities?', *West European Politics*, 41(6): 1237–61.

Solomon, J. (1988) *Black Youth, Racism and the State*, Cambridge: Cambridge University Press.

Solomos, J. (2003) *Race and Racism in Britain*, 3rd edn, Basingstoke: Palgrave Macmillan.

Solomos, J. (2013) 'Contemporary forms of racist movements and mobilization in Britain', in R. Wodak, M. Khosravinik and B. Mral (eds) *Right-wing Populism in Europe: Politics and Discourse*, London: Bloomsbury.

Stanchura, P.E. (ed) (2004) *The Poles in Britain 1940–2000: From Betrayal to Assimilation*, London: Frank Cass Publishers.

Stegmaier, M, Lewis-Beck, M.S. and Smets, K. (2012) 'Standing for Parliament: do Black, Asian and minority ethnic candidates pay extra?', *Parliamentary Affairs*, 66(2): 268–85.

Stevenson, J. (2017) *The Social Mobility Challenges Faced by Young Muslims*, London: Social Mobility Commission.

Storm, I., Sobolewska, M. and Ford, M. (2017) 'Is ethnic prejudice declining in Britain? Change in social distance attitudes among ethnic majority and minority Britons', *British Journal of Sociology*, 68(3): 410–34.

Streetly, A., Sisodia, R., Dick, M., Latinovic, R., Hounsell, K. and Dormandy, E. (2017) *Evaluation of Newborn Sickle Cell Screening Programme in England: 2010–2016*, London: BMJ Publishing Group Ltd (& RCPCH).

Sturge, G. (2019) 'Asylum statistics', Briefing paper SN01403, London: House of Commons Library.

Sumption, M. and Vargas-Silva, C. (2016) *The Minimum Income Requirement for Non-EEA Family Members in the UK Report*, Oxford: The Migration Observatory.

Sumption, M. and Vargas-Silva, C. (2019) *BRIEFING: Net Migration to the UK*, Oxford: University of Oxford.

Sveinsson, K. (2008) *A Tale of Two Englands: 'Race' and Violent Crime in the Press*, London: Runnymede Trust, Available from: www.runnymedetrust.org/uploads/publications/pdfs/TwoEnglands-2008.pdf (accessed 12 November 2019).

Swami, V., Barron, D., Weis, L. and Furnham, A. (2018) 'To Brexit or not to Brexit: the roles of Islamophobia, conspiracist beliefs, and integrated threat in voting intentions for the United Kingdom European Union membership referendum', *British Journal of Psychology*, 109(1): 156–79.

Szczepura, A. (2005) 'Access to health care for ethnic minority populations', *Postgraduate Medical Journal*, 81(953): 141–7.

Tatlow, P. (2015) 'Participation of BME students in UK higher education', in C. Alexander and J. Arday (eds) *Aiming Higher: Race, Inequality and Diversity in the Academy*, London: Runnymede Trust, pp 10–13.

Taylor, J.D. (2018) 'Suspect categories,' alienation and counterterrorism: critically assessing PREVENT in the UK', *Terrorism and Political Violence*: 1–23.

Tell Mama (2018a) *Gendered Anti-Muslim Hatred and Islamophobia*, London: Faith Matters.

Tell Mama (2018b) *Beyond the Incident: Outcomes for Victims of Anti-Muslim Prejudice*, London: Faith Matters.

The Stage (2017) 'BECTU and Writers' Guild boycott Project Diamond TV diversity scheme', Available from: www.thestage.co.uk/news/2017/bectu-writers-guild-boycott-project-diamond-tv-diversity-scheme/ (accessed 29 June 2018).

Thrasher, M., Borisyuk, G., Rallings, C. and Webber, R. (2017) 'Candidate ethnic origins and voter preferences: examining name discrimination in local elections in Britain', *British Journal of Political Science*, 47(2): 413–35.

Thurman, N. (2016) 'Methodology', in N. Thurman et al, *Journalists in the UK*, Oxford: Reuters Institute for the Study of Journalism.

Tomlinson, S. (2005) *Education in a Post-welfare Society*, Berkshire: Open University Press.

Tomlinson, S. (2014) The Politics of Race, Class and Special Education: The Selected Works of Sally Tomlinson, London: Routledge.

Tresadern, M. (2016) 'Ten Black British Artists to Celebrate', Available from: https://artuk.org/discover/stories/ten-black-british-artists-to-celebrate (accessed 6 February 2019).

TUC (Trade Union Congress) (2016) *Insecure Work and Ethnicity*, Available from: www.tuc.org.uk/sites/default/files/Insecure%20work%20and%20ethnicity_0.pdf (accessed 17 October 2018).

TUC (2019) 'TUC response to the ethnicity pay reporting consultation', Available from: www.tuc.org.uk/ResponsetoEthnicityPayReportingConsultation (accessed 1 November 2019).

UK Data Service (2017) *English Housing Survey, 2016: Housing Stock Data*, Special Licence Access, Available from: https://beta.ukdataservice.ac.uk/datacatalogue/studies/study?id=8387 (accessed 21 June 2019).

UN Refugee Agency (2015) *The Sea Route to Europe : The Mediterranean Passage in the Age of Refugees*, New York: UN Commissioner for Refugees.

Van Dijk, T. (2015) *Racism and the Press*, London: Routledge

Van Eijk, G. (2010) 'Does living in a poor neighbourhood result in network poverty? A study on local networks, locality-based relationships and neighbourhood settings', *Journal of Housing and the Built Environment*, 25(4): 467–80.

Van Ham, M., Tammaru, T., de Vuijst, E. and Zwiers, M. (2016) 'Spatial segregation and socio-economic mobility in European cities' IZA Discussion Paper No. 10277, IZA: Bonn,

Vargas-Silva, C. (2015) 'The fiscal impact of immigration in the UK', Migration Observatory briefing, COMPAS, University of Oxford, UK.

Varma-Joshi, M., Baker, C. and Tanaka, C. (2004) 'Names Will Never Hurt Me?', *Harvard Educational Review*, 74(2): 175–208.

Vertovec, S. (2007) 'Super-diversity and its implications', *Ethnic and Racial Studies*, 30(6): 1024–54.

Vieten, U.M. and Poynting, S. (2016) 'Contemporary far-right racist populism in Europe', *Journal of Intercultural Studies*, 37(6): 533–40.

Virdee, S. (2014) *Racism, Class and the Racialized Outsider*, Basingstoke: Palgrave Macmillan.

Virdee, S. and McGeever, B. (2018) 'Racism, crisis, Brexit', *Ethnic and Racial Studies*, 41(10): 1802–19.

Vote, O.B. (2008) *How to Achieve Better BME Political Representation*, London: Government Equalities Office.

Wallace, M. and Kulu, H. (2014) 'Low immigrant mortality in England and Wales: a data artefact?', *Social Science & Medicine*, 120: 100–9.

Wallace, M. and Kulu, H. (2015) 'Mortality among immigrants in England and Wales by major causes of death, 1971–2012: a longitudinal analysis of register-based data', *Social Science & Medicine*, 147: 209–21.

Wallace, S., Nazroo, J.Y. and Bécares, L. (2016) 'Cumulative exposure to racial discrimination across time and domains: exploring racism's long-term impact on the mental health of ethnic minority people in the UK', *American Journal of Public Health*, 106(7): 1294–300

Wardle, H. and Obermuller, L. (2018) 'The Windrush generation', *Anthropology Today*, 34(4): 3–4.

Warwick Commission (2015) *Enriching Britain: Culture, Creativity and Growth*, Available from: https://warwick.ac.uk/research/warwickcommission/futureculture/finalreport/warwick_commission_final_report.pdf (accessed 21 March 2019).

Weekes-Bernard, D. (2007) *School Choice and Ethnic Segregation: Educational Decision-making among Black and Minority Ethnic Parents*, London: Runnymede Trust.

Weekes-Bernard, D. (2017) *Poverty and Ethnicity in the Labour Market*, London: Joseph Rowntree Foundation.

Werbner, P. (1980) 'From rags to riches: Manchester Pakistanis in the textile trade', *New Community*, 8(1–2): 84–95.

West, M., Dawson, J. and Kaur, M. (2015) *Making the Difference: Diversity and Inclusion in the NHS*, London: King's Fund.

Whittaker, A. and Densley, J. (2019) 'London's gangs have changed, and its driving a surge in pitiless violence', Available from: www.theguardian.com/commentisfree/2019/jan/10/london-gangs-changed-violence-waltham-forest-drugs (accessed 12 March 2019).

Wilkins, C. and Lall, R. (2011) '"You've got to be tough and I'm trying": Black and minority ethnic student teachers' experiences of initial teacher education', *Race Ethnicity and Education*, 14(3): 365–86.

Williams, C. and Johnson, M.R.D. (2010) *Race and Ethnicity in a Welfare Society*, Maidenhead: Open University Press/McGraw Hill.

Williams, D.R., Neighbors, H.W. and Jackson, J.S. (2003) 'Racial/ethnic discrimination and health: findings from community studies', *American Journal of Public Health*, 93: 200–8.

Williams, P. and Clarke, B. (2016) *Dangerous Associations: Joint Enterprise, Gangs and Racism*, Centre for Crime and Justice Studies, Available from: www.crimeandjustice.org.uk/publications/dangerous-associations-joint-enterprise-gangs-and-racism (accessed 12 November 2019).

Williams, P. and Clarke, B. (2018) 'The black criminal Other as an object of social control', *Social Sciences*, 7(11): 234–48.

Wilson, M. (2010) *Delivering Race Equality Action Plan: A Five Year Review*, London: Mental Health Division – Equalities Department of Health.

Wood, J.D. (2017) 'The integrating role of private homeownership and mortgage credit in British neoliberalism', *Housing Studies*, 33(7): 1–21.

Wray, H. (2016) *Regulating Marriage Migration into the UK: A Stranger in the Home*, Abingdon: Routledge.

Wright, C., Maylor, U. and Watson, V. (2018) 'Black women academics and senior managers resisting gendered racism in British higher education institutions', in O. Perlow, D.I. Wheeler, S.L. Bethea and B.M. Scott (eds) *Black Women's Liberatory Pedagogies*, London: Palgrave Macmillan, pp 65–83.

Yeo, C. (2017) 'The immigration rules for adult dependant relatives: out with the old...', Available from: www.freemovement.org.uk/out-with-the-old/ (accessed 5 April 2019).

Young, M. (2018) 'We only have 26 black teachers out of 1,346 in Bristol and that's a problem', *Bristol Post*, 3 September, Available from: https://www.bristolpost.co.uk/news/bristol-news/black-teachers-bristol-schools-only-1958455 (accessed 28 November 2018).

Younge, G. (2018a) 'With Windrush, Theresa May mistook a national treasure for an easy target', *The Guardian*, 20 April 2018, Available from: www.theguardian.com/commentisfree/2018/apr/20/theresa-may-windrush-equality (accessed 12 November 2019).

Younge, G. (2018b) 'The NHS, Windrush and the debt we owe to immigration', *The Guardian*, 22 June, Available at: www.theguardian.com/commentisfree/2018/jun/22/honour-nhs-built-on-immigration-windrush (accessed 2 December 2019).

Youth Justice Board (2018) *Youth Justice Statistics, 2017/18*, Available from: https://assets.publishing.service.gov.uk/government/uploads/system/uploads/attachment_data/file/774866/youth_justice_statistics_bulletin_2017_2018.pdf (accessed 7 May 2019).

Zaiceva, A. and Zimmermann, K.F. (2016) 'Returning home at times of trouble? Return migration of EU enlargement migrants during the crisis', in M. Kahanec and K.F. Zimmermann *Labor Migration, EU Enlargement, and the Great Recession*, Berlin: Springer.

Index

Note: Page numbers in *italics* indicate figures, tables and boxes.

A

A levels 105–107
Aboah, Adwoa 181
Achiume, Tendayi 204–205, 211, 212, 215, 217
Aden, Halim 181
Africanisation policies 17, 37
Africans 10
  2011 Census, Scotland *23*
  educational attainment 95, 101
  electoral registration 199
  GP experience *85*
  health inequalities 78
  home ownership 160
  infant mortality rate *28*
  public sector employment 143
  slavery 230
  see also Black Africans
age profiles 25–26
Albania 46
anti-Black racism 213
anti-discrimination law and policy 230–231
anti-immigrant sentiment 217–221, 225
antisemitism 221–222
apprenticeship schemes 93, 105, 115–116, 240
Arabs 6, 10
  2011 Census, England and Wales *20*
  2011 Census, Northern Ireland *24*
  2011 Census, Scotland *23*
  age profile *26*
  employment *121*
  higher education *117*
  housing tenure 157, *158*, *159*, 160
  overcrowding *162*
  as victims of crime *59*
Armed Forces 145
arts consumption 176–177
Arts Council England 173, 184
arts teaching and studies 174–176
Asians 6, 10, 17
  2011 Census, England and Wales *20*
  2011 Census, Northern Ireland *24*
  2011 Census, Scotland *23*
  access to education 99, *100*, 145
  adults in custody *65*
  age profile *26*
  arts participation 176–177
  arts teaching 174
  children in custody *64*
  confidence in police 53
  conviction ratios *68*
  earnings 120
  educational attainment 101–102, 105, *108*
  employment *112*, 121, *122*, 129, 144
  experience of health services 83, *84*
  health inequalities 76, 79
  higher education 116, *118*, *119*
  homelessness 161
  housing tenure 157, *158*, *159*
  individual and interpersonal racism 208, 209, *210*
  journalism 172
  overcrowding *162*
  in police force 54, *55*
  political participation 198
  Prevent policies 93
  school exclusion *110*, 111
  school leavers *114*
  self-employment 138
  stop-and-search *58*, 61, 70
  terrorism-related policing *62*
  as victims of crime *60*
  welfare reforms 212, 230
  youth cautions *63*
  see also Bangladeshis; Chinese; Indians; Pakistanis
asylum accommodation 45
asylum seekers 38–39, 45, 46, 152, 217, 218, 238
Athena Swan award 123
austerity 68
austerity policies 212

B

Bangladeshis 6, 17, 233
  2011 Census, England and Wales 20
  2011 Census, Northern Ireland 24
  2011 Census, Scotland 23
  age profile 26
  apprenticeships 116
  custody 65
  deprivation 29
  earnings 120, 138, 139, 142
  economic activity 132, 133
  educational attainment 95, 101, 102,
    103, 104, 106, 108
  employment 94, 112, 121, 133,
    135, 143
  fertility rate 27
  health inequalities 76, 77, 85
  higher education 117, 119
  housing tenure 158, 159, 160
  immigration 44
  infant mortality rate 28
  labour market characteristics 132
  overcrowding 149, 161, 162
  racist victimisation 210
  residential segregation 32
  school exclusion 110
  school leavers 113, 114
  stop-and-search 57
  unemployment 136
  as victims of crime 58
BBC 171, 178–179, 181–182, 183,
  185, 241
  Equality Information Report
    2016-17 186–187
BBC Census 167
Begum, Shamima 48
Bennett, Rocky 85
Bennett inquiry 87
bias 203, 211–212
birthright citizenship 238
Black Africans 18, 20, 21–22
  2011 Census, England and Wales 20
  2011 Census, Northern Ireland 24
  2011 Census, Scotland 23
  age profile 26
  apprenticeships 116
  earnings 138, 139
  educational attainment 101, 102,
    103, 104, 106, 107, 108

  employment 94, 112, 121, 134, 135
  health inequalities 78
  higher education 113, 114, 116, 117,
    118, 119, 120
  housing tenure 158, 159
  labour market characteristics 132
  overcrowding 149, 161, 162
  racism towards 213
  racist victimisation 210
  residential segregation 32
  school exclusion 110
  self-employment 137
  stop-and-search rates 57
  unemployment 136
  as victims of crime 59
Black Caribbean 17, 22
  2011 Census, England and Wales 20
  2011 Census, Northern Ireland 24
  2011 Census, Scotland 23
  age profile 26
  apprenticeships 116
  confidence in police 53
  earnings 138
  educational attainment 93, 95, 101,
    102, 103, 104, 106, 107, 108
  employment 112, 120, 121, 134,
    135, 143
  fertility rate 27
  health inequalities 76, 77, 78, 85
  higher education 116, 117, 118, 119
  housing tenure 153, 157, 158,
    159, 165
  infant mortality rate 28
  labour market characteristics 132
  overcrowding 162
  racism towards 210, 213
  residential segregation 32
  school exclusion 110, 111
  school leavers 114
  stop-and-search 57
  unemployment 136
  as victims of crime 59
black histories 2
Black people
  access to education 145
  adult custody 65–66, 69
  austerity policies 212
  criminalisation 67
  educational attainment 102, 105
  employment 55, 121, 122, 144

health inequalities 82
homelessness 161
housing tenure 160
income 120
journalism 172–173
racial inequality 233
school exclusion 111
stop-and-search 53, 56–58
youth custody 64–65
youth justice system 63
Black Training and Enterprise
  Group 116
bordering practices 41–49
Bradley, Karen 182–183
Breaking the Circle of Fear (Sainsbury
  Centre for Mental Health, 2002) 87
Brexit 49, 165, 199–201, 201–202,
  203, 204–205, 224, 226–227; *see also*
  EU referendum
Britain First 223–224
British Future 197
British National Party (BNP) 225
British Nationality Act 1948 37
British Social Attitudes
  Survey 207, 219
British values 232
British Vogue 181
broadcasting 171–172, 178–179,
  181–183, 241
  diversity policy 184–188

C

Cameron, David 201
cancer services 83
Care Quality Commission 80–81, 86
Caribbean migrants 17, 37, 151;
  see also Black Caribbean
cautions 63
Census 2011 201
census categories 6–7, 19–20;
  see also specific ethnic groups, e.g. Black
  Africans, Black Caribbean etc
Centre for Literacy in Primary
  Education (CLPE) 180
Centre on the Dynamics of Ethnicity
  (CoDE) 196
Chakrabarti, Shami 221–222
Channel 4 185, 187–188
Channel 5 171
child poverty 240

childhood disability 78
children 95
  in custody 64–65
  history education 238
  immigration detention 45
  racial abuse towards 209
children's magazines 181
Chinese 17–18, 21, 22, 233
  2011 Census, England and
    Wales *20*
  2011 Census, Northern Ireland *24*
  2011 Census, Scotland *23*
  access to education 99, *100*
  age profile *26*
  conviction ratio *68*
  custody *65*, 66
  earnings 120, 138
  economic activity 132, 133
  educational attainment 93, 95, 102,
    103, 104, 105, *106*, 107, *108*
  employment 94, *112*, 121, *122*, 133,
    135, 144, 145
  health inequalities 77, *85*
  higher education 116, *117, 119*
  housing tenure *158, 159, 162*
  labour market characteristics *132*
  residential segregation 32
  school leavers 113, 114
  self-employment 127, 137
  stop-and-search *57, 58*
  unemployment 136
  as victims of crime *59*
  youth cautions *63*
citizen rights 238
citizenship 37–39, 47, 48–49, 238
civil service 144
class inequality 231
colonisation 2
Colour and Citizenship (Rose) 5
"coloured immigrants" 5, 6
commemoration 2–4
Commonwealth Immigrants Act
  1962 37
Commonwealth Immigrants Act
  1968 3, 37
Commonwealth immigration 129
Community Security Trust 221
compliant environment 43
comprehensive education 96
compulsory education 99, 105

Conservative party 189
  English Defence League (EDL) 223
  ethnic equality 200–201
  institutional racism 215
  Islamophobia 217
  political representation 191–192, 193,
    195, 197
  supporters 208
  xenophobia 218
conviction ratios 68–69
Counter-Terrorism and Security Act
  2015 214–215
counter-terrorism legislation 239
counter-terrorism policies 203
county lines 67–68
Cox, Jo 224
creative diversity 185
Creative Scotland 184
Criminal Justice and Public Order Act
  1994 56
criminal justice system (CJS) 51–71
  custody 65–66
  ethnic minority employees 54–55
  policing 53–54
  racialisation and
    criminalisation 66–69
  recommendations 238–239
  stop-and-search 56–58
  terrorism-related policing 60–62
  victims of crime 59–60
  youth justice system 62–65
criminalisation 66–69
cultural and creative industries
  (CCI) 167–188
  cultural consumption /
    participation 176–179
  cultural production 169–176
  arts teaching and studies 174–176
  film industry 167, 170–172, 172
  journalism 172–173
  leadership roles 173, 174
  publishing industry 173
  television 167, 171–172, 186–187
  cultural representation 179–183
  diversity policy in public
    broadcasting 184–188
  recommendations 241
cultural identity 7, 8
cultural policy 167, 184–188
custody 64–66, 69, 239

D

data 237, 241
deaths in custody 66, 239
deindustrialisation 129
"Delivering Race Equality (DRE) in
  Mental Health Care" 85–86
deportation 44, 45–46
deprivation 31–32, 215
design 167
detention 45
diabetes 76, 92
DIAMOND monitoring system 183
discrimination 10
  anti-discrimination law and
    policy 230–231
  criminal justice system (CJS) 53–55
  housing 149, 151, 154, 163
  immigration policy 43
  indicators of 79
  labour market 136–137, 138
  National Health Service (NHS) 75
dispersal 44–45, 46
diversity 6–7, 9–10, 18
diversity policy, broadcasting 184–188
Dorset 58
drama schools 174–175

E

earnings 120, *132*, 138–139; *see also*
    national minimum wage
East Africa 17
Eastern European migrants 219–221
economic activity 132–133
economic inequality 78–79
economic policy 231
education *see* drama schools; state
    education system
Education and Skills Act 2015 105
education policy 96–99
educational attainment 95
  GCSE 93, 101–105
  higher education 118–120
  and the labour market 130
  A levels 105–107, *108*
Electoral Commission 198, 199
electoral fraud 198
electoral participation 189–190
electoral registration 198–199
empire 2

employment *132*, 133–136
  after graduation 120
  criminal justice system
    (CJS) 54–55, 238
  cultural and creative industries
    (CCI) 167, 169–176, 241
  arts teaching and studies 174–176
  film industry 167, 170–171, 172
  journalism 172–173
  leadership roles 173, *174*
  publishing industry 173
  television 167, 171–172, 186–187
  education sector 94, 111–113
  higher education 120–123, 240
  and housing 152
  National Health Service (NHS) 74,
    89–91, 143–144, 239
  public sector employment 127,
    143–146
  recommendations 240–241
  targets 237
  see also labour market
employment rate gap 127, 140
English Defence League
  (EDL) 223, 224
English Housing Survey 155–156,
  157–158
Enninful, Edward 181
Equality, Diversity and the Creative Case
  (ACE, 2019) 184
Equality Act 2010 81–82, 98, 131, 240
Equality Information Report 2016-17,
  BBC 186–187
equality law 237
Essex 67
ethnic bloc vote 198
ethnic diversity 6–7, 9–10, 18
ethnic inequality 4–8, 10
ethnic minorities 11–12, 15, 19–25
  2011 Census
    England and Wales *20*
    Northern Ireland *24*
    Scotland *23*
  age profiles 25–26
  citizenship deprivation 48
  ethnic segregation 30–32
  fertility 26–28
  impact of immigration policy
    on 43–44, 46
  infant mortality *28*, 29

  residential settlement 29–30
Ethnic Minority British Election
  Study 199
Ethnic Minority Employment Task
  Force (EMETF) 139–140
ethnic segregation 10, 15, 30–32
EU referendum 49, 165, 190, 199,
  208, 209, 219, 224; *see also* Brexit
equality legislation 230–231
European Commission Against Racism
  and Intolerance (ECRI) 218–219
European Investment Bank (EIB) 165
European "migrant crisis" 218–219
European Union (EU) 18, 30, 35,
  40–41, 152
European Volunteer Workers
  Scheme 37
"Excellence in Schools" White Paper,
  1997 97

F

Facebook 224
far-right populist parties 205, 222–226
fertility 26–28
film industry 167, 170–171, 172
Five Year Forward View on Mental Health
  (NHS, 2016b) 86–87
forced migration 152; *see also* asylum
  seekers
free school meals (FSMs) 105
further education 93, 115–116
Future of Multi-Ethnic Britain, The
  (Parekh) 7–8

G

gangs 66–67, 239
GCSE 93, 101–105
gender 103–104, 182, 196–197; *see*
  also women
gendered Islamophobia 216
general election 2010 190–192, 193
general election 2015 193, 197
general election 2017 193
General Practice 73
generation rent 160
gentrification 154–155
glossy magazines 181
Golash-Boza, Tanya 206, 209
GP Experience Survey 83–84, *85*
GQ 181

Grenfell Tower 149, 150, 156, 165
Guardian 181
Gypsies and Irish Travellers 6
  2011 Census, England and Wales *20*
  2011 Census, Northern Ireland *24*
  2011 Census, Scotland *23*
  access to education 100
  age profile *26*
  educational attainment 93, 101,
    102–103, *104*, 105, *106*, 107
  higher education 113
  housing tenure *158*
  overcrowding *162*
  racism towards 203, 221, 233
  school exclusion 110–111
  school leavers 113, *114*

H

hate crime 107–108, 209, 215–216,
  217, 227
health inequalities 29, 73–74, 76–80
  access to and experience of health
    services 81–89
  policy initiatives 80–81, 91–92
  recommendations 239
healthy migrant hypothesis 25
heart disease 76
Help to Buy 149–150, 153
Hertfordshire 67
higher education 93–94, 113–114,
  116–123, 240
  access 116–118
  attainment 118–120
  cultural and creative industries
    (CCI) 174–175
  employment in 120–123, 240
  equality campaigning 123–124
history 229–230, 232, 238
Hollywood Diversity Report 172
Home Office 43, 45, 52, 154, 209
home ownership *see* owner-occupied
  housing
homelessness 149, 161–163
hostile environment 42–43, 95, 154,
  213, 234, 238
housing 149–166, 215
  ethnic inequalities 155–161
  homelessness 161–163
  housing debates 163–164
  recommendations 241

housing associations 156–157, 163–164
housing crisis 152–155
housing debates 163–164
housing market 43
housing policies 149–150, 153–155
housing tenure 153, 156–161, 241
hypertension 78

I

immigrants 213
  anti-immigrant
    sentiment 217–221, 225
immigration 35
  and Brexit 226–227
  from the Commonwealth 129
  emigration, immigration, asylum and
    net migration *39*
  from EU countries 35, 40–41, 152
Immigration Act 1971 37–38
Immigration Act 1993 38
Immigration Act 1996 38
Immigration Act 1999 38
Immigration Act 2002 38
Immigration Act 2014 42, 43, 48
Immigration Act 2016 43, 154, 166
Immigration Compliance and
  Enforcement (ICE) 43
immigration history 16–19, 36–37
immigration policy 35–36, 49–50
  and bordering practices (2010
    onwards) 41–49
  and citizenship 37–39
  recommendations 238
Immigration Removal Centres
  (IRCs) 45
income *see* earnings
index of dissimilarity 31, 32
India 46
Indians 6, 17, 21
  2011 Census, England and Wales *20*
  2011 Census, Northern Ireland *24*
  2011 Census, Scotland *23*
  age profile *26*
  apprenticeships 116
  custody 65
  earnings 120, 138, 139
  economic activity 132, 133
  educational attainment 93, 95, 101,
    102, *103*, *104*, *106*, 107, *108*

employment 37, 94, *112*, 120, 121, 133, 135
EU referendum 200
fertility rate *27*
health inequalities 76, 77, *85*
higher education *117*, *119*
housing tenure *158*, *159*, 160, 161
immigration 44
infant mortality rate *28*
labour market characteristics *132*
overcrowding *162*
racism towards *210*
residential segregation 32
school exclusion *110*
school leavers 113, *114*
stop-and-search *57*
as victims of crime *59*
voting behaviour 189, 197, 201
individual and interpersonal racism 207–209
individual electoral registration (IER) 199
infant mortality *28*, 29
institutional racism 52, 84–89, 203, 209–212, 215, 218
international students 42
interpreting services 87–88
intersectionality 196–197, 231
interview panels 241
Ireland 36
Irish *see* White Irish
Irish migrants 17, 22
Irish Travellers *see* Gypsies and Irish Travellers
Islamophobia 204, 213–217, 219, 223, 225, 226–227
ITV 171

J

Javid, Sajid 1
job applications 136–137
joint enterprise (JE) 69, 71, 239
journalism 172–173

K

Kent 67
knife crime 67–68

L

Labour Force Survey (LFS) 127
labour market 127–139

public policy 139–142
public sector employment 142–146
see also employment
labour market characteristics 132–139
labour market participation *see* economic activity
Labour party
all-women short lists 196
antisemitism 221–222
Islamophobia 217
political representation 191, 192, 194–195
supporters 197, 198
see also New Labour
Lammy review 2017 52, 62
Lawrence, Stephen 54, 70
leadership roles 173, 174
Leave.EU 226
Liberal Democrats 189, 191, 217
lived experience 234–235
living wage 240
local government 196
London
journalism 172
living wage 240
Olympic Village 155
residential mixing 32
schools 99
stop-and-search 58
unemployment 137

M

Macpherson report 54, 210–211
magazines 181
manufacturing industry 129–130
marginalisation 163–164
May, Theresa 42, 139, 201
McGregor-Smith review 139, 140–141
memorialisations 2–4
men 182
Men's Health 181
men's magazines 181
mental health 79
mental illness 82, 85–87
Metropolitan Police 54, 58, 61, 210
micro-aggressions 209
"migrant crisis" 218–219
migrant settlement 151–152
Migrants' Rights Network 227
migration 2, 9; *see also* immigration

Migration Observatory 44
minimum wage *see* national minimum wage
Ministry of Justice 52
mixed ethnic categories 10, 19, 21, 22
  2011 Census, England and Wales *20*
  2011 Census, Northern Ireland *24*
  2011 Census, Scotland *23*
  access to education 95, *100*, 145
  adults in custody *65*
  age profile 25, *26*
  apprenticeships 116, *117*, *118*, *119*
  arts participation 176, *177*
  children in custody *64*
  confidence in police 53
  conviction ratio *68*
  educational attainment 102, *103*, *104*, 105, *106*, *108*
  employment 54, *55*, 94, *112*, 113, 121, *122*, 144
  higher education 116
  homelessness 161
  housing tenure *158*, *159*
  overcrowding *162*
  residential segregation 32
  school exclusion *110*
  school leavers 113, *114*
  stop-and-search *57*, *58*
  as victims of crime *59*, *60*
multiculturalism 185
music 167
Muslim children 78
Muslim political candidates 194, 196
Muslim pupils 109
Muslim women 216
Muslims
  counter-terrorism legislation 203
  racial prejudice towards 208. *see also* Islamophobia

N

national (hi)stories 2–4
National Action 224
National Asylum Support Service (NASS) 38, 46
National Cancer Experience Patient Survey 2016 83
National Curriculum 97, 98
National Health Service (NHS) 2–3, 74, 75, 88–89, 89–91, 143–144, 239

national minimum wage 127, 142, 240
National Society for the Prevention of Cruelty to Children (NSPCC) 209
nationalism 222–226
Nationality Act 1948 2
Nationality Act 1981 38
Netflix 178
New Labour 7, 113, 152
New Universities 116, 117, 118–120
Northern Ireland
  criminal justice system (CJS) 45
  ethnic minorities 23–24, 100–101
  public broadcasting 185

O

Ofcom 171, 182–183
Ofsted 240
Olusoga, David 2
Olympic Village, London 155
Other White *see* White Other
othering 91, 206, 207
"Outcome Framework Equity Reports" (Public Health England, 2017) 80
outsourcing 45
overcrowding 149, 161, 163, 215, 241
owner-occupied housing 151, 153, 156, 157, 160

P

Pakistan 46
Pakistanis 6, 17, 21
  2011 Census, England and Wales *20*
  2011 Census, Northern Ireland *24*
  2011 Census, Scotland *23*
  access to education 100
  age profile *26*
  apprenticeships 116
  custody *65*
  deprivation 29
  earnings 120, 127, 138, 139, 142
  economic activity 132, 133
  educational attainment 93, 95, 101, 102, *103*, *104*, *106*, 107, *108*
  employment *112*, *121*, 133, *134*, 135, 136, 143
  fertility rate *27*
  health inequalities 76, 77, *85*
  higher education *117*, *119*
  housing tenure *158*, *159*, 160, 161
  immigration 31–32, 44

infant mortality rate *28*
labour market characteristics *132*
overcrowding 149, 161, *162*
racism towards *210*, 233
school exclusion *110*
school leavers *114*
self-employment 127, 137
stop-and-search *57*
unemployment 137
as victims of crime *59*
Parekh report 97
pay gap 144, 171, 240
Penguin Random House 173
performing arts 167
Poland 36
police force 54–55, 70, 145, 238
policing
 and discrimination 53–54
 stop-and-search 51, 53–54, 56–58,
  61, 69–70, 238
 terrorism-related 60–62, 70
Polish migrants 219–220
political participation 198–199; *see also*
 voting behaviour
political parties 189, 241;
 see also individual parties
political representation 189, 190–197,
 201, 241
populist parties 205, 222–226
post-millennial race and racism 9–11
poverty 68, 240
Powell, Enoch 75
Prevent agenda 214
Prevent Duty 98–99
primary health care 73, 82
private rented sector (PRS) 43, 149, 151,
 156, 157–159, 160–161, 166, 241
private sector 45
psychotic illness 78
Public Accounts Committee
 (PAC) 140
public funding 241
Public Health Outcomes Framework
 2010 80
public sector 237; *see also* National
 Health Service (NHS)
public sector employment 127,
 143–146
public services 230–231
publishing industry 173, 180–181

R

race, post-millennial 9–11
Race Disparity Audit (RDA) 139, 143,
 156, 204, 211
Race Equality Action Plan (DH,
 2005) 89
Race Equality Charter 240
Race Equality Mark 123–124
race equality strategy 237–238
Race Relations Act 1968 3
Race Relations (Amendment) Act
 2000 54, 94, 97, 109, 211
Racial and Religious Hatred Act
 2006 217
racial inequality 4–8, 10
racialisation 66–69, 82, 84–89
racism 203–228, 232–233
 anti-Black 213
 anti-immigrant
  sentiment 217–221, 225
 antisemitism 221–222
 definition 205–206
 and health 79
 health services 84–89
 housing 151, 163
 individual and interpersonal
  207–209
 institutional 52, 84–89, 203,
  209–212, 215, 218
 Islamophobia 204, 213–217, 219,
  223, 225, 226–227
 lived experience 234–235
 in the mainstream 226–227
 and political mobilisation 222–226
 political representation 195
 post-millennial 9–11
 recommendations 241
 schools 107–111
 societal 209–212
 training 237
 UN Special Rapporteur 203,
  204–205, 211, 212, 215, 217
racist victimisation by ethnic/religious
 group *210*
radicalisation 93
radio 167
refugees 152, 217
regeneration 155
religion 203

religious hate crime 215–216, 217;
  see also Islamophobia
Representative Audit of
  Britain 192, 195
resettlement 44–45, 46
residential clustering 30–31
residential settlement 29–30
Right to Rent 154
Rights to Buy 149, 153
right-wing populist parties 205,
  222–226
"rivers of blood" speech 75
Riz Test 179–180
Roma population 221, 233
Romania 46
Rudd, Amber 1
Runnymede Trust 4–5, 212, 214, 217,
  233, 234
Russell Group 116–117, 118–120

S

scarring effect 136
school exclusion 93, 109–111, 239
school leavers *114*
Scotland
  2011 Census 22–23
  access to education 112
  criminal justice system (CJS) 45
  public broadcasting 184
Scottish Credit and Qualification
  Framework (SCQF) 107
Seasonal Agricultural Workers Scheme
  (SAWS) 18
secondary health care 73
segregation 10, 15, 30–32
self-employment 127, *132*, 137–138
service-based economy 129, 130
severe mental illness 85–87
sexually transmitted illnesses 78
Shulman, Alexandra 181
sickle cell disease 88–89
sink housing estates 155
slavery 2, 230
social class 105
social inequality 29, 78, 79
social media 209, 224
Social Mobility Commission 215
social rented sector (SRS) 151, 152,
  153, 156, 157, 165, 241
social services 145

societal racism 209–212
Special Educational Needs
  (SEN) 96, 111
Staffordshire 67
state education system 93–125
  access 99–101, 116–118
  apprenticeship schemes 93, 105,
    115–116
  attainment 95
  GCSEs 93, 101–105
  higher education 118–120
  and the labour market 130
  A levels 105–107, *108*
  British history 238
  education policy 96–99
  ethnic minority employees 94,
    111–113, 145
  higher education 93–94, 113–114,
    116–123
  access 116–118
  attainment 118–120
  cultural and creative industries
    (CCI) 174–175
  employment in 120–123
  equality campaigning 123–124
  racism 107–111
  recommendations 239–240
  school leavers *114*
statutory homelessness 163
stereotypes 78
stereotyping 109, 188, 230
stop-and-search 51, 53–54, 56–58, 61,
  69–70, 238
stroke 78
students 42, 135
suicide 78
Swann report 97
Syrian refugees 46

T

teachers 145
technological change 129–130
television 167, 171–172, 178–179,
  181–182, 186–187
tenure 153, 156–161, 241
terrorism 98
Terrorism Act 2000 60–61
Terrorism Act 2006 214
terrorism-related policing 60–62, 70
thalassaemia disorder 88–89

Thatcher, Margaret 96
training 237
Travellers *see* Gypsies and Irish
    Travellers

U

UK
    emigration, immigration, asylum and
        net migration *39*
    ethnic and racial
        inequality 4–8, 11–13
    immigration history 16–19, 36–37
    national (hi)stories 2–4
    post-millennial race and racism 9–11
UK Household Longitudinal
    Study 156
UK Race Equality Mark 94
UKIP 218, 225–226
UN Special Rapporteur 203, 204–205,
    211, 212, 215, 217
unconscious bias 203, 211–212
Understanding Society
    survey 25–26, 198
unemployment *132*, 136–137
unionisation 131
United States 230
universal basic services 241
Universal Credit 127, 137, 141–142
universities *see* higher education

V

Viacom 171
victims of crime 59–60
video game sector 172
visual arts 167
visual effects sector 172
vocational training *see* apprenticeship
    schemes
Vote Leave 226
voting behaviour 189–190, 194,
    197–198
Vulnerable Persons Resettlement
    Scheme (VPRS) 46

W

Wales 19, *20*, 45, 100, 185
welfare reforms 212, 230
West Mercia 58
West Midlands 137
White, Sharon 182, 183

White British 19, 21, 22, 25
    2011 Census, England and Wales *20*
    access to education 99, *100*
    age profile *26*
    apprenticeships 93, 116
    confidence in police 53
    educational attainment *103, 104,
        106, 108*
    employment 54, *112*, 135, 145
    health inequalities 77
    higher education *117*
    housing tenure 157, *158, 159*,
        160, 161
    infant mortality rate *28*
    labour market characteristics *132*
    overcrowding 161, *162*
    party identity 198
    school exclusion *110*
    school leavers 113, *114*
    stop-and-search *57*
    as victims of crime *59*
    voting behaviour 194
white extremism 224
White Irish 6, 17
    2011 Census, England and Wales *20*
    age profile 25, *26*
    earnings 138
    educational attainment *103, 104,
        106, 108*
    employment *112*, 135
    housing tenure 157, *158, 159*
    labour market characteristics *132*
    overcrowding 161, *162*
    school exclusion *110*
    school leavers *114*
    stop-and-search *57*
    unemployment 136
    as victims of crime *59*
White Other 6, 10, 12, 18–19, 21
    2011 Census, England and Wales *20*
    2011 Census, Scotland *23*
    access to education 99, *100*
    age profile *26*
    educational attainment *103, 104,
        106, 108*
    employment 112, 133, *135*, 145
    health inequalities 77
    housing tenure 157, 158, *159*
    infant mortality rate *28*
    labour market characteristics *132*

overcrowding *162*
residential settlement 32
school exclusion *110*
school leavers *114*
self-employment 137
stop-and-search *57*
unemployment 136
as victims of crime *59*
White people
adults in custody 65
apprenticeships *115*
arts participation *177*
cautions 63
children in custody 64
conviction ratios *68*, 69
educational attainment 101
employment *55*, 90, *122*, *134*, 143,
    144, *171*
leadership roles *174*
health inequalities *84*
higher education *118*, *119*
homelessness 161
Islamophobia 216
journalism 172
serious violent offences 67
stop-and-search *58*
terrorism-related policing *62*

unemployment 137
as victims of crime *60*
welfare reforms 212
see also White British; White Other
Windrush scandal 1–3, 47, 154,
    213, 234
women
broadcasting 182
earnings 138, 139
economic activity 132–133
employment 129, 130, 133, *134*, 135
Islamophobia towards 216
as political candidates 196–197
political participation 198, 199
unemployment 136, 137
welfare reforms 212
women's magazines 181
worker protection 129
Workforce Race Equality Standard
    (WRES) 90–91, 239

X

xenophobia 217–221, 226–227
xeno-racism 218, 221

Y

youth justice system 51, 53, 62–65, 239
YouTube 224

www.ingramcontent.com/pod-product-compliance
Ingram Content Group UK Ltd.
Pitfield, Milton Keynes, MK11 3LW, UK
UKHW021821270225
455667UK00001B/1